KNOWING KINGS

THE SOCIETY OF BIBLICAL LITERATURE
SEMEIA STUDIES

Series Editor
Danna Nolan Fewell

Number 40
KNOWING KINGS
Knowledge, Power, and Narcissism
in the Hebrew Bible

Stuart Lasine

KNOWING KINGS
Knowledge, Power, and Narcissism
in the Hebrew Bible

Stuart Lasine

Society of Biblical Literature
Atlanta, Georgia

Knowing Kings
Knowledge, Power, and Narcissism in the Hebrew Bible

Stuart Lasine

Copyright © 2001 by The Society of Biblical Literature

Cover art: Fragment of a bust of Sesostris III (King Senwosret III). The Metropolitan Musem of Art, Purchase, Edward S. Harkness Gift, 1926. (26.7.1394) Photograph © 1983 The Metropolitan Musem of Art.

Library of Congress Cataloging-in-Publication Data
Knowing kings : knowledge, power, and narcissism in the Hebrew Bible / Stuart Lasine.
    p. cm. — (Semeia studies)
Includes bibliographical references and index.
ISBN 1-58983-004-0 (pbk. : alk. paper)
    1. Kings and rulers—Biblical Teaching. 2. Jews—kings and rulers
    3. Bible. O.T.—Criticism, interpretation, etc. I. Title. II. Series.

BS1199.K5 L37 2001
221.6—dc21   2001018399

09 08 07 06 05 04 03 02 01   5 4 3 2 1
Printed in the United States of America
on acid-free paper

To My Teachers

Fannie J. Lemoine

Richard Bjornson

and

Robert M. Rehder

TABLE OF CONTENTS

ABBREVIATIONS

Primary Sources

1QIsa^a	Dead Sea Scrolls, Isaiah^a

1QIsa^a — Dead Sea Scrolls, Isaiah^a

ABL — *Assyrian and Babylonian Letters Belonging to the Kouyunjik Collections of the British Museum.* Edited by R. F. Harper. 14 vols. Chicago: University of Chicago Press, 1892–1914.

ʾ*Abot R. Nat.* — ʾ*Abot de Rabbi Nathan*

Aeschines
    Ctes. — *In Ctesiphonem*
    Tim. — *In Timarchum*

Apoc. Mos. — *Apocalypse of Moses*

Apollonius of Rhodes
    Argon. — *Argonautica*

Aristophanes
    Eq. — *Equites*

Aristotle
    Eth. nic. — *Ethica nicomachea*
    Mag. mor. — *Magna moralia*
    [*Mund.*] — *De mundo (On the Cosmos)*
    Pol. — *Politica*

Arrian
    Epict. diss. — *Discourses of Epictetus*

b. — Babylonian Talmud

B. Bat. — *Baba Batra*

Ber. — *Berakot*

CTA — *Corpus des tablettes en cunéiformes alphabétiques découvertes à Ras Shamra-Ugarit de 1929 à 1939.* Edited by A. Herdner. Mission de Ras Shamra 10. Paris, 1963.

EA — El-Amarna tablets. According to the edition of J. A. Knudtzon. *Die el-Amarna-Tafeln.* Leipzig, 1908–1915. Repr., Aalen, 1965. Continued in A. F. Rainey, *El-Amarna Tablets, 359–379.* 2d rev. ed. Kevelaer, 1978.

Epictetus
    Ench. — *Enchiridion*
    Exod. Rab. — *Exodus Rabbah*

Herodotus
    Hist.   *Historiae*
Hesiod
    Op.   *Opera et dies*
Homer
    Il.   *Iliad*
    Od.   *Odyssey*
Isocrates
    Nic.   *Nicocles*
Josephus
    Ant.   *Jewish Antiquities*
Lev. Rab.   *Leviticus Rabbah*
Lucian
    Cal.   *Calumniae non temere credendum*
    Ver. hist.   *Vera historia*
Marcus Aurelius
    Med.   *Meditations*
Num. Rab.   *Numbers Rabbah*
Ovid
    Metam.   *Metamorphoses*
Pausanias
    Descr.   *Graeciae description*
Plato
    Alc. 1   *Alcibiades 1*
    Men.   *Meno*
    Phileb.   *Philebus*
    Prot.   *Protagoras*
    Rep.   *Republic*
    Symp.   *Symposium*
    Tim.   *Timaeus*
Plutarch
    Alc.   *Alcibiades*
    De lat. viv.   *De latenter vivendo*
    Mor.   *Moralia*
    Per.   *Pericles*
Pseudo-Aristotle
    Mund.   see Aristotle, [*Mund.*]
Sanh.   *Sanhedrin*
Sophocles
    Oed. tyr.   *Oedipus tyrannus*
Suetonius
    Aug.   *Divus Augustus*
VTE   Vassal treaties of Esarhaddon

Xenophon
> *Cyr.*   *Cyropaedia*
> *Mem.*   *Memorabilia*
> *Yebam.*   *Yebamot*

Secondary Sources

AB	Anchor Bible
ABD	*Anchor Bible Dictionary,* ed. D. N. Freedman. 6 vols. New York: Doubleday, 1992.
AfO	*Archiv für Orientforschung*
ANET	*Ancient Near Eastern Texts Relating to the Old Testament,* ed. J. B. Pritchard, 3d ed. Princeton, N.J.: Princeton University Press.
AOS	American Oriental Series
ARAB	*Ancient Records of Assyria and Babylonia.* Daniel David Luckenbill. 2 vols. Chicago: University of Chicago Press, 1926–1927. Reprint, New York: Greenwood, 1968.
ARE	*Ancient Records of Egypt.* Edited by James Henry Breasted. 5 vols. Chicago: University of Chicago Press, 1905–1907. Reprint, New York: Russell & Russell, 1962.
BEATAJ	Beiträge zur Erforschung des Alten Testaments und des antiken Judentum
Ber	*Berytus*
BibInt	*Biblical Interpretation*
Bijdr	*Bijdragen: Tijdschrift voor filosofie en theologie*
BLS	Bible and Literature Series
BN	*Biblische Notizen*
CBQ	*Catholic Biblical Quarterly*
CJ	*Classical Journal*
ConBOT	Coniectanea biblica: Old Testament Series
FOTL	Forms of the Old Testament Literature Series
HAR	*Hebrew Annual Review*
HS	*Hebrew Studies*
HSM	Harvard Semitic Monographs
HTR	*Harvard Theological Review*
HUCA	*Hebrew Union College Annual*
IBC	Interpretation: A Bible Commentary for Teaching and Preaching
ICC	International Critical Commentary
Int	*Interpretation*
JAAR	*Journal of the American Academy of Religion*
JANESCU	*Journal of the Ancient Near Eastern Society of*

	Columbia University
JAOS	*Journal of the American Oriental Society*
JBL	*Journal of Biblical Literature*
JEA	*Journal of Egyptian Archaeology*
JHS	*Journal of Hellenic Studies*
JNES	*Journal of Near Eastern Studies*
JSOT	*Journal for the Study of the Old Testament*
JSOTSup	Journal for the Study of the Old Testament Supplement Series
LCL	Loeb Classical Library
LSJ	Liddell, H. G., R. Scott, and H. S. Jones, *A Greek-English Lexicon*. 9th ed. with revised supplement. Oxford: Oxford University Press, 1996.
NCB	New Century Bible
NIB	*The New Interpreter's Bible*
OTL	Old Testament Library
OtSt	*Oudtestamentische Studiën*
SAAS	State Archives of Assyria Studies
SBT	Studies in Biblical Theology
ScrHier	Scripta hierosolymitana
SEÅ	*Svensk exegetisk årsbok*
SJOT	*Scandinavian Journal of the Old Testament*
U	Usener, Hermann. *Epicurea*. Leipzig, 1887. Reprint, Stuttgart: Teubner, 1966.
UF	*Ugarit-Forschungen*
VT	*Vetus Testamentum*
VTSup	Supplements to Vetus Testamentum
WBC	Word Biblical Commentary
ZAW	*Zeitschrift für die alttestamentliche Wissenschaft*

PREFACE

a man is spoken of as the same person [ὁ αὐτὸς λέγεται] from childhood until old age, yet ... he is continually becoming a new person, and there are things also which he loses—his hair, his flesh, his bones, his blood and his whole body.... and also ... in his soul ... no one's character, opinions, desires ... always remain the same.... And what is even stranger [ἀτοπώτερον], we do not retain our identity in regard to knowledge.
—Plato, *Symposium* 207d–208a

For one thousand years he [the great god Zurvan] offered sacrifice in order that he might perhaps have a son who would be called Ormazd.... Then he pondered in his heart and said: "... do I strive in vain?" And even while he reflected in this manner, Ormazd and Ahriman were conceived in the womb: Ormazd through the offered sacrifice, Ahriman through the doubt. When he became aware of this, Zurvan said, "Lo, two sons are in the womb. Whichever ... appears swiftly before me, him I shall make king." Ormazd, being aware of their father's purposes, revealed them to Ahriman ... [who] pierced the womb ... and presented himself to his father. Zurvan ... knew not who he might be, and asked "Who are you?" And he said: "I am your son." Zurvan answered him: "my son is fragrant and bright, and you, you are dark and stinking."
—Eznik of Kolb (Boyce 1984, 97–98)

Both of these epigraphs are concerned with identity and sameness over time. And for that reason, they mirror the history of this book. In one sense, I can speak of it as the same book Semeia Studies was ready to publish in 1991, under the title *Justice and Human Nature in the Hebrew Bible*. Yet, like its author's body, his soul, and his knowledge, the book has also gone through a process of continual replacement since 1991. In fact, nothing remains of the original book's content and style. Then why can I speak of it as "the same"? Because this version is what I wanted to write back then, but apparently could not. When I took a good hard look at the first version after the editors sent me their comments and suggestions, I felt like the mother in Solomon's judgment story, who says that she looked carefully at her baby in the morning light only to discover it was not alive, and it was not the child to whom she had given birth. No, it's even worse than that. I felt like Zurvan when the dark and stinking Ahriman came up and greeted him with "Hi, Dad!" Like Ahriman, the firstborn version of the book was a product of doubt. I'd gone and written it, but all the while I suspected that I, like Zurvan, was striving in vain. It took these intervening years of hair, flesh, and bone loss, changes in character and emotions, as well as the continual exchange of lost and found knowledge, for the book to take on the identity I had intended it to have from the start. I needed to undergo Platonic recollection of my past training as a comparatist and interdisciplinarian before that could happen, I had to more overtly link my choice of academic specializations with my nonacademic concerns, and I had to make use of a variety of styles in my writing.

Why was all this necessary? Because I had discovered that the problems I had been investigating kept directing my attention outside the traditional boundaries of such a study. I, and many others, had written about kings who were knowing, just, and powerful, but we had not fully traced the complex dynamic network of relationships linking royal power and *knowing* (in all senses of the word). I found that the exercise of royal power involved matters that at first glance might seem specifically modern and Western, for example, information management, gossip, and privacy. I discovered that the king's ability to define and maintain the boundary between private and public played a crucial role in his management of the flow of information, through which he is able to maintain power. It become increasingly clear that, while the king may seem to be totally independent and powerful, he is utterly dependent upon his courtiers to demonstrate their loyalty by sharing information with him. The paradoxical nature of the king's situation became more and more evident to me. He is simultaneously powerful and helpless, knowledgeable and ignorant, an idol and a potential scapegoat, an independent father figure and Freud's "His Majesty the Baby," the child whose welfare depends upon his parents' desire to recover their lost narcissism in him. These paradoxes also characterize the adult narcissistic personality, a type of individual who often becomes a leader. In fact, they might even characterize the personality of Yahweh himself, the divine king and narcissistic father.

All of these issues—information management, gossip, the private-public distinction, loyalty, scapegoating, narcissism, justice, and the possibility of divine parental abuse—call for interdisciplinary analysis. All of them are also best dealt with in a comparative manner. The specific nature of *biblical* knowledge, kingship, power, and narcissism becomes most perceptible, if not palpable, when viewed in comparison with the same dynamics in monarchies from different cultures and different periods. Moreover, to come to terms with the psychological dimension of the king (or queen) in each of us (as well as in the biblical characters and in Yahweh) requires not only a comparative interdisciplinary approach but the use of inventive styles that make it possible to communicate a kind of internal "kingship" that is ordinarily too close to us to be easily acknowledged.

Ed Greenstein was the editor of Semeia Studies when I submitted my original draft. I want to thank Ed, and Associate Editor Claudia Camp, for their continuing support of this book project through these long years. Also there from the start, giving incisive and detailed feedback to whatever manuscripts I foisted upon her, was my friend Diana Edelman. My friend and former colleague Stephen Moore is the person who implored me to find my "voice" as a writer and to add "sparkle" to my style; his feedback has also been extremely helpful. To Danna Nolan Fewell go my thanks for her continued encouragement over a number of years, beginning long before she took over as editor for Semeia Studies. For that—and for laughing at all the right places during my SBL presentations—I am deeply grateful. I also appreciate greatly the moral support offered me by Amy-Jill Levine. And during the months when the book was approaching completion, the sensitive observations of my friend Jane Diao have proved invaluable. For their help during the final phases of the publication process, I would like to thank Rex Matthews of the Society of Biblical Literature, Bob Buller, and my gifted student Vicki Jensen. Bob Buller also deserves the credit for creating the indexes for this book. A Fairmount College Summer Faculty Fellowship from Wichita State University gave me the opportunity to complete the project.

I would also like to thank those who encouraged me to gain the kind of background needed for a project like this, long before I began the writing. In the early 1980s, Michael V. Fox, Reuben Ahroni, and John Van Seters insisted that it was not utterly ridiculous for me to attempt a mid-career switch into biblical studies. I also want to thank the University of Michigan Society of Fellows for having given me the opportunity to undertake hubristically ambitious interdisciplinary projects early in my career. However, I have dedicated the book to the great teachers of my graduate school days in comparative literature, philosophy, and classics at the University of Wisconsin-Madison. I had the privilege of becoming the friend of all three, once we became colleagues at Wisconsin, as well as later, when I joined Dick Bjornson at the Center for Comparative Studies in the Humanities at Ohio State. Dick and Fannie Lemoine were brilliant, dedicated scholars with incredibly generous souls, who are missed by all who knew them. And I continue to treasure the friendship, wisdom, and intellectual integrity of Robert Rehder.

An earlier version of chapter 6 appeared in *The Age of Solomon: Scholarship at the Turn of the Millennium,* edited by Lowell K. Handy (Leiden: Brill, 1997). Portions of chapter 7 incorporate, in revised form, part of an article that appeared in *Semeia* 71 (1995) under the title, "The King of Desire: Indeterminacy, Audience, and the Solomon Narrative." An article based on parts of chapters 10 and 11 of the book will appear in a forthcoming issue of *Biblical Interpretation,* under the title "Divine Narcissism and Yahweh's Parenting Style." The story of Zurvan and his sons is discussed further in chapter 11, below.

1

INTRODUCTION

THE KING'S PARADOXICAL TRAITS

First Trait: Sleeping with Eyes Open

> The post which he held by this precarious tenure carried with it the title of king; but surely no crowned head ever lay uneasier, or was visited by more evil dreams, than his. For year in year out ... he had to keep his lonely watch, and whenever he snatched a troubled slumber it was at the peril of his life. The least relaxation of his vigilance, the smallest abatement of his strength of limb or skill of fence, put him in jeopardy; grey hairs might seal his death-warrant. His eyes probably acquired that restless, watchful look which, among the Esquimaux of Bering Strait, is said to betray infallibly the shedder of blood.
> —Frazer, *The Golden Bough* (1994, 11–12)

Frazer's restless king has a hard time sleeping, and for good reason. He's in danger. He's alone. He must remain vigilant and watchful at all times. He must avoid infirmity and old age at all costs. And he must shed blood—or at least look as if he had.

I doubt that most people would recognize this as the job description for a king. And, indeed, Frazer is describing a seemingly atypical monarch, the "king of the wood" at Nemi. This priest-king must constantly prowl around a special tree in the sacred grove, to protect against a contender for his position who might pluck a golden bough and then kill him. Not exactly how one usually imagines kings spending their time, whether we are talking about ancient Near Eastern, biblical, or Greek kings—or, for that matter, modern kings and leaders like James I, Louis XIV, or Bill Clinton.

Nevertheless, Frazer's depiction of the king of the wood is an accurate composite portrait of "*the* king" in a surprising number of ways. Take the element of restless wakefulness, which Frazer introduces by alluding to Shakespeare's *Henry IV, Pt. 2* ("uneasy lies the head that wears the crown" [3.1.31]). Other Shakespearean kings agree.[1] And Shakespeare's Richard II

---

[1] See, e. g., *Henry VI, Pt. 3* 2.5.49–54 and *Henry IV, Pt. 2* 4.5.23–31.

is well aware that kings may be assassinated if and when they do fall asleep (*Richard II* 3.2.159). Such insights are nothing new. The Twelfth Dynasty Egyptian pharaoh Amenemhet I warns his son of the need for constant vigilance, and of the possibility of assassination when asleep—he should know, for he himself was supposedly murdered in his sleep, before he gave these instructions to his son (Lichtheim 1973, 136–37; cf. Grimal 1992, 161–64)[2]. Being assassinated during sleep is also a distinct possibility in the Bible—just ask David's predecessor Saul and his rival Ishbosheth (1 Sam 26; 2 Sam 4).[3] Add to this the dangers of sleep for royal heroes like Gilgamesh and Odysseus (and for the antihero Jonah), and it's surprising that all monarchs don't have the tired, wrinkled, set-jawed look evident in statues of Twelfth Dynasty pharaohs who look like they haven't slept for a week (see ch. 3, below).

From another angle, "the sleeping king betrays his trust," as one Shakespeare scholar puts it (Fraser 1962, 75). Insomnia is a royal duty for the *people's* sake, as well as for their own safety. Thus, the Egyptian monarch's proof of his diligent commitment to his god's work is signaled by his own lack of sleep, a theme echoed by the words of the biblical "David" quoted in Ps 132:3–5.[4] And Shakespeare's vigilant King Henry V not only recognizes his duty but envies the sleeping subjects to whom he is actually subjected:

> No, not all these, thrice-gorgeous ceremony,
> Not all these, laid in bed majestical,
> Can sleep so soundly as the wretched slave....
> What watch the king keeps to maintain the peace,
> Whose hours the peasant best advantages. (4.1.283–85, 300–1)

---

[2] Compare Creon's question to his brother-in-law, King Oedipus: "do you think anyone prefers the anxieties of being ruler to sleeping without craven fear—if he has the same power?" (Sophocles, *Oed. tyr.* 584–586).

[3] For Saul, see below, ch. 2; for Ishbosheth, see ch. 4. Even the besotted Ahasuerus (Xerxes) of the book of Esther learns the prophylactic value of insomnia. When he has the royal annals read to him, he is reminded of an earlier assassination plot reported by Mordecai. When the king realizes that his loyal courtier Mordecai is threatened by Haman, he suspects Haman is a plotter, and even accuses Haman of trying to rape (לכבוש) the queen in the king's own palace, with the king there (Esth 7:8)! (Verses from the Hebrew Bible are cited according to MT numbering.)

[4] See, e.g., Ockinga 1980; cf. Seow 1989, 157–59. On other occasions, it is the king's courtiers who must prove both their diligence and their vigilance by staying awake. Thus, in his "autobiography," the vizier Rekhmire claims that he "knew not slumber night or day," and that he was "watchful"; indeed, he was "the ears and eyes of the Sovereign" (16–17; N. Davies 1973, 81), long before Persian monarchs appointed a "King's Eye."

The peasants who work during the day and sleep so well after dark seem much more "natural" than the night-walking king, as though they were enacting the natural human rhythms sketched in Ps 104.

In Henry's view, it is the king who is not a "natural" human being; his circadian rhythms are out of synch. He is an isolated outsider at the center of the kingdom. Aristotle says that a being who by nature chooses to live outside a *polis* must be either a beast or a god (ἢ θηρίον ἢ θεός; *Pol.* 1253a). Yet the king at the center of the state might also be a member of this little group, even when he does not enact his affinity with the beasts by engaging in a feral fugue, like Gilgamesh and Nebuchadnezzar. From the perspective of Aristotle and some Hellenistic thinkers (see Nussbaum 1994, 249–57), what beasts and gods have most in common is self-sufficiency. Yet even in this select group of "outsiders," the king is the odd man out. The king's self-sufficiency is merely an illusion, even though it is an illusion that may be needed equally by himself *and* the people from whom he is isolated.

Frazer's king is also utterly alone. So is Rekhmire's king, Thutmose III: "He is alone by himself, without an equal" (18; N. Davies 1973, 81). Doesn't that aloneness suggest self-sufficiency? Not when one considers that from another perspective kings never seem to be alone; they are constantly on view, whether to the public or to their courtiers and servants. Yet, like the American president Bill Clinton, the king is "confronted by the prisoner's paradox: an existence in which he is rarely by himself and yet always alone" (Maraniss 1998, A1). The king's dual status as totally public *and* totally private is but the first of many royal paradoxes we will encounter. In his study of "oriental despots," Wittfogel declared that both the seemingly all-powerful ruler and the people he controls are subject to the "total loneliness" and insecurity created by "polarized total power" (1957, 154–56). Liverani (1990, 116–17, 121–24) talks about the motif of the king's "loneliness" as a way of conveying his bravery in battle and the hunt, as well as his uniqueness (see further in ch. 11, below). But he also notes that when kinglets like Rib-Hadda express their isolation it means precisely the opposite. In general, a third possibility exists: that all kings are, in some areas of their lives, *both* the lonely war hero pharaoh *and* the craven kinglet.

The very fact of the leader's being surrounded by servants suggests that he could become totally dominated, even as he is lauded for being totally dominant. As Norbert Elias observes, "the more that is accumulated by an individual [who approaches the monopoly position], the less easily can it be supervised by this individual, and the more … he becomes dependent on his dependents" (1994, 348). Elias devotes many pages to describing the "interdependence" of the king and his courtiers in European monarchies after the Middle Ages. The courtier is "compelled to observe constant vigilance and to subject everything he says and does to minute scrutiny" (1994, 466). But the same is true, to a large extent, of the king as well. Both king and courtiers are "enmeshed" in the same network of interdependencies (1983, 136; cf. Bendix 1978, 7, 218–23). We're not just talking about Versailles here. As Liverani (1990, 287) puts it, "wherever a 'Palace' was located, it was a mesh in the network of interconnections."

In a way, Frazer's monarch is lucky. He is not interdependent. He has no bureaucracy or tax districts to set up and maintain, no standing army, no forced-labor projects to coordinate, no harem women and their sons plotting his overthrow—and no opinion polls. There's only one person out there whose opinion matters, and he already knows what his opinion is. Luckiest of all, he has no courtiers to betray his trust or to manipulate him by taking advantage of the fact that he isn't really omnipresent and omniscient. The servants who supply him with "legal ubiquity" (Kantorowicz 1957, 5) and total knowledge—the "King's Eyes and Ears"—are also uniquely suited to manipulate and topple their master. And, finally, although Frazer's king has to fear a rival in the shadows—the single serpent lurking in his garden—other kings and courtiers must fear all types of informers, including the *diabolos,* the *śāṭān,* and the *rābiṣu,* upon whom they must also depend (see further in chs. 3 and 8, below).

Frazer's *Rex Nemorensis* (1994, 13) does *not* have to face the threat of leaked information, seditious talk, and unlicensed gossip. The king's role as information manager in the ancient Near East may not be as familiar as his roles as judge and battle-leader, but it is just as essential for his survival. Frazer's king has only one sword to fear; other kings have to worry about the "sharp tongues" of many people, which cut like swords and razors (e.g., Pss 52:4; 57:5). Thus, the wakeful Henry V is well-aware that, in spite of his royal greatness, he can still be wounded by the words of every foolish gossiper in the kingdom: "Oh, hard condition, /Twin-born with greatness, subject to the breath/ Of every fool" (*Henry V* 4.1.250–52). Dealing with the "breath" of unlicensed speech is such an important royal duty, and so crucial for evaluating the nature of a king's knowledge and power, that we will have occasion to discuss it throughout the book.

Second Trait: The King As Microcosm and Micropolis

> … the state of man,
> Like to a little kingdom …
> —Shakespeare, *Julius Caesar,* 2.1.67–68

> … 'twixt his mental and his active parts
> Kingdomed Achilles in commotion rages
> and batters down himself.
> —Shakespeare, *Troilus and Cressida,* 2.3.183–85

The best man is the one who is the most kingly and a king over himself.
—Plato, *Republic* 580c

One question remains: Does Frazer's isolated king also illustrate monarchy[5] on the most profoundly microcosmic level, namely, you and me? *This* king is a lone individual forced to defend himself against an outside world that is seemingly paradisaical, but that is actually always hostile, thanks to the Other out to destroy the king—the Other who might see the king without the king seeing him.

You, my reader, may be saying: "That's not me, and that's not my world! When I was born my 'Others' were affectionate, attentive parents who treated me as 'His/Her Majesty the Baby,' exactly as described by Freud:

> [Affectionate parents] are under a compulsion to ascribe every perfection to the child.... [The child] shall not be subject to the necessities which they have recognized as paramount in life. Illness, death, renunciation of enjoyment, restrictions on his own will, shall not touch him; the laws of nature and of society shall be abrogated in his favour; he shall once more really be the centre and core of creation—"His Majesty the Baby", as we once fancied ourselves. (1914, 91)

"Now *that*," you might continue, "sounds like a typical king. His defining traits are nearly identical to those of the English kings' 'Body politic.' Frazer's king must urgently avoid infirmity, old age, and death. In the tradition of 'the king's two bodies' the urgency has vanished: the 'king, like the Crown, never died ... [was] never sick and never senile.' Nor is the king subject to 'restrictions of will' caused by folly—he not only can't *do* wrong; he can't even *think* wrong. And laws of nature are also 'abrogated' in *his* favor.[6] One big difference: the king's Body politic is 'devoid of infancy,' while Freud's *is* an infant—or, at least, an infantile adult."

"But," I reply, "Frazer's king—and you and I—have more in common with the English king's 'Body natural' than his Body politic. In fact, the Body politic can serve to obscure and deny the reality of the Body natural. Same

---

5 Although female monarchs such as Hatshepsut, Athaliah, Esther, Dido, and Elizabeth I will be brought into the discussion, the primary focus of this study is on male monarchs, both within and outside of the Hebrew Bible. For Sarah Kofman's argument that the royal trait of self-sufficiency is more characteristic of woman than of man, see below. On the "gendering" of knowledge, see n. 46, below.

6 Kantorowicz 1957, 4–5, 7, 378. For a study of "the king's two bodies" in relation to Shakespeare's *King Lear* and the Union controversy during the reign of James I, see Axton 1977, 131–47. On Elizabeth I and the theory of "the queen's two bodies," see Axton 1977, 11–25; and Monod 1999, 62–69.

for 'the myth of the infant's golden age'[7] that Freud's affectionate parents try to foist on their helpless baby-king in order to restore their own lost narcissism. We can't afford to overlook these psychological tricks we play on ourselves, especially because we're currently immersed in a 'culture of narcissism' (Lasch)."[8]

Of course, people may *experience* themselves as being royal tots and Bodies Politic. However, to be a "microcosm" means that the person is always both center *and* periphery, ruler *and* ruled, independent *and* dependent, both Achilles the "kingdomed" batterer *and* the Achilles he batters down. In reality, a number of varieties of monarchical micropoloi are "experienced." Probably the most powerful depiction of "the little kingdom of man" in Western culture is that given by Plato. The city (*polis*) is the soul (*psychē*) writ large (*Rep.* 368d–369b). In the *Timaeus,* Plato describes the various faculties of mind and their location in the body, as though the body were a city. The ruling and best part, the *logistikon,* is housed like a monarch in the *akropolis* of the head, with the palace guard in the lungs, and the mob in the stall, or manger, of the gut (70a–71a).[9] Plato emphasizes the effectiveness with which information and commands are transmitted from the *akropolis* and the speed with which data passes to and from the ruler (through the narrow channels of the blood stream; 70b). Nevertheless, this ideal self-government can be easily disrupted by a "civil war within the soul" (Plato, *Rep.* 440e; *Laws* 626e; cf. Prov 16:32).

The idea of the soul (and/or body) as a microcosm (and/or micropolis) has a long and varied history after Plato (see Altmann 1969, 19–28; Le Goff 1989). It survives in many forms, including Elias's "conception of

---

[7] The term is Bettelheim's (1967, 15). He thinks psychoanalysis created this myth.

[8] In addition to Lasch, see, e.g., Sennett 1977, 8–12, 323–36; and Lowen 1997, 196–228. For criticisms of Lasch's influential view, see A. M. Cooper 1986, 125–27; and Benjamin 1988, 137–41. Baudrillard (1993, 111–12) describes modern "neonarcissism" as "'synthetic'" and "planned"; it involves "the optimal management of the body on the market of signs."
Many students of narcissism would agree with Alice Miller that the word *narcissism* has "become part of everyday speech to such an extent … that it is difficult today to rescue it for scientific use" (1981, vi; cf. Benjamin 1988, 136). Miller points out that the noun "can be used … to project a variety of meanings: a condition, a stage of development, a character trait, an illness." Later in this chapter, and in chs. 10 and 11, we will have occasion to discuss "narcissism" in all of these senses. In most cases it will be possible to use the term in a precisely defined manner. For a history of the ways in which the word *narcissism* has been used within psychoanalysis and psychiatry, see, e. g., A. M. Cooper (1986). On the many meanings of the term within the body of Freud's work, see Baranger 1991, 109–11.

[9] Cf. *Rep.* 560b–c; on the *logistikon* as king, see Taylor 1928, 500.

the individual as *homo clausus,* a little world in himself," whose "true self appears ... as something divided within him by an invisible wall from everything outside" (1994, 204). This closed person is the result of a "civilizing process," for which royal court society was a crucial catalyst. Plato's notion of the *logistikon* as ruler also has a long after-history, from the Stoics (e.g., Arrian, *Epict. diss.* 4.1.86; 4.5.25–27; Marcus Aurelius, *Med.* 8.48) to Freud (see, e.g., B. Simon 1978, 200–12).

However, with Freud the idea comes full circle, because his ego-king (*das Ich*) is no longer "master [*Herr*] in his own house" (1917a, 11) let alone the dominant center of the universe. In fact, he is a king whose typicality resides in his vulnerability as information manager, in stark contrast to Plato's efficient *logistikon.* The "I" acts "like an absolute ruler [*wie ein absoluter Herrscher*] satisfied with the information given him by his court officials," who does not bother to "go down to the people in order to hear their voice" (1917a, 11). To *feel* sovereign, it has to believe that the highest of its courtiers and agencies have knowledge of everything happening and that the reports it receives are both complete and trustworthy—exactly what kings from Saul and Aristotle's tyrants to Louis XIV, and American presidents from Reagan to Clinton, want to believe. But it isn't so. Freud tells the ego, "you are *not* informed of all the important occurrences transpiring inside you.... the intelligence department [*Nachrichtendienst*] often fails, and *all* the reports received by your consciousness are incomplete and untrustworthy" (1917a, 10–11). And when the ego isn't truly sovereign, it becomes a sycophantic, disingenuous diplomat, the slave of internal and external tyrants (1925a, 219; 1933, 77–78; 1923, 56).

Neither are *historical* kings sovereign when it comes to information management. Evidence is everywhere, from 1 Samuel to the *topos* of the king's ignorance in European satire (Embree, 1985, 121–23). In fact, Freud's monarchical *psychai* sound just like Norbert Elias's court society, where the court acts as a filter mediating everything that reaches the king and everything that reaches the country *from* the king (1983, 42). The courtiers must all shell, armor, wall, and mask themselves against one another in order to survive (1983, 240–42, 253–55; 1994, 253). The king may try to do so as well, but his exposed position in the center makes it difficult. Berger and Luckmann even find such epistemological vulnerability among despots in the realm of the *oikos:*

> the reality of everyday life always appears as a zone of lucidity behind which there is a background of darkness.... Even if, for instance, I am a seemingly all-powerful despot in my family, and know this, I cannot know all the factors that go into the continuing success of my despotism.... There are always things that go on "behind my back." This ... explains, incidentally, why despots are endemically nervous. (1967, 44–45)

Perhaps the death blow to primary narcissism occurs when His Majesty the Baby learns that not even *he* can trust the information supplied by *his* courtiers—that is, his parents. This typically occurs when his royal position at the center of the family is threatened by the arrival of a sibling, and he wants to solve the great sphinx-riddle: Where do babies come from? This happened to Freud's five-year-old patient Little Hans (1909a). When the parents snuff out the child's curiosity with stories about storks and such, and dismiss his observations of the mother's changing body, kids like Hans receive this incomplete and unreliable information with "deep, though mostly silent, mistrust" (1905, 197). Sometimes they "never ... forgive [the adults] for having deceived them." Their "intellectual independence [dates] from this act of disbelief" (1910, 79).[10]

Even if we grant that individuals can experience themselves as having a "political" structure, why precisely should *monarchy* have priority in our personal micropolis, instead of, say, a parliamentary democracy, a military junta, or an amphictyony? There are many plausible reasons. The king has been said to be the "the only grownup in the society" (Sagan 1985, 327), and "the one person in whom character and role are indistinguishable" (Braudy 1997, 344). According to Weintraub, the "most common pattern" for political thought is to take "monarchy as its main point of reference," not just in various periods of Western history, but in other civilizations as well (1997, 12). Indeed, "royal authority has endured for the greater part of human history" (Bendix 1978, 21). In the ancient Near East, kingship is not only the most common form of government, it is "the very basis of civilization" (Frankfort 1978, 3). Bottero notes that the Mesopotamian ruler had "absolute primacy"; he was the country's "head, master, director, shepherd, and father" (1992, 144). Buccellati (1996, 132) goes even further: "[in urbanized Mesopotamia]

---

[10] The parental information management that, according to Freud, prompts such mistrust in children, is considered by Postman to be responsible for the continuing existence of the very notion of "childhood": "Childhood ... was an outgrowth of an environment in which a particular form of information, exclusively controlled by adults, was made available in stages to children.... The maintenance of childhood depended on the principles of managed information and sequential learning" (1994, 72). From this perspective, father Yahweh's response to the human building initiative at Babel (Gen 11:1–9) could be viewed as an attempt at information management designed to treat human beings as perpetual children, with Yahweh himself the only autonomous, fully informed, adult. As noted by Westermann (1994, 551), God's reflection in v. 6 is "colored ... by consideration of the possibilities that would now be open to people if all restrictions on information and understanding were set aside.... This must lead to the absolute autonomy of humankind." On Yahweh as a parent and his use of parental information management, see chs. 8, 10, and 11, below.

the king was not just a more powerful private individual, he embodied a distinct organism." In Egypt, "kingship was both the central institution and the main focus of power" (Baines 1991, 128; cf. Avruch 2000, 257 n. 19), and the king "was essential to world order" (Silverman 1991, 67). In addition, kingship "provided a *metaphor* for the way others were to conduct their lives" (Baines 1991, 128; emphasis added). And in spite of the fact that the Hebrew Bible includes antimonarchical voices, "one can hardly find any clear portrayal of a rival form of government" (Roberts 1987, 380). Finally, in ancient Greek tragedy and later Stoic drama, the king has been called "political man generalized and raised to his highest potential" (Rosenmeyer 1989, 89).

Or perhaps monarchy has priority in the experience of the self-state because those who feel this way are clinging to the notion of an integrated self, one single point at the tip of our imaginary self-pyramid—in spite of what we might sincerely say in print about the fictionality and social constructedness of the "self" when we put on our scholarly personae. Or is it because we tacitly agree with Plato that monarchy is the form of government from which the others derive—or devolve. Another possibility: that parents *do* tend to treat their infants as His Majesty the Baby, the center of creation. We will need to keep in mind all of these possibilities as we proceed, although we still have a number of royal traits to consider here.

Third Trait: Royal Dreams of Ocular Power

> [The function of kings consists of] keeping an eye on the whole earth, of constantly learning the news of all the provinces and of all the nations, the secrets of all the courts, ... of being informed of an infinite number of things that we are presumed to ignore, of seeing around us what is hidden from us with the greatest care, of discovering the most remote ideas and the most hidden interests of our courtiers.
> —Louis XIV, *Mémoires* (1970, 30)

> a king is he who has laid fear aside ... who, in safety established, sees all things beneath his feet [*qui tuto positus loco infra se videt omnia*].
> —Seneca, *Thyestes* 348, 365–367 (1953, 120–23)

The epigraph from the Sun King's *Mémoires* shows the flip side of Freud's information-hungry, Saul-like king. Frazer's king could only dream of exercising the kind of ocular control over his isolation that Louis recommends to the Dauphin in the epigraph. *In reality,* Louis's king is no less dependent upon information-gathering servants (the King's Eyes and Ears) than is Freud's ego-king. In Louis' ideal version, on the other hand, it is the king's *own eyes* and ears that exercise power by extending themselves automatically to great distances.[11] Because Louis sees what others think he does not see, he has been compared to Poe's Dupin (Lockwood 1987, 559 n. 10), whom Daniel dubs a "detective god" (1967, 103–5). Nowadays a detective can be a "private eye," an extension of the eyes of any private citizen who pays him or her, rather than a "King's Eye" or a police department controlled by the king or government.[12]

Yet, again, Louis claims to extend his own eyes, like an ancient sun god whose light penetrates into the darkest corners and depths. So it hardly seems a coincidence that Louis took the sun as his emblem, with the stars forming "*une espèce de cours*" around it (quoted in Hoffmann: 25). As Hoffmann puts it, "heliocentrism became the central myth of the new community" (1997, 27) at this royal court. This may be a "myth" or fantasy, but it is a *real* fantasy—that is, it has real effects on the king and his people. All one needs to create charisma is to create the illusion of omnipresence and omniscience. As Geertz remarks, "though a king could not, like God, quite be everywhere at once, he could try, at least, to give the impression that he was" (1983, 137). Liverani makes a similar point: "knowledge is more important than action.... It is not so important to truly control the world, as it is important to persuade the inner population that we control the world.... what matters is the king's prestige in the central kingdom" (1990, 47). Of course, such "knowledge" is quite paradoxical: the people must "know" something that isn't "truly" the case in order for the king to be able to rule *as though* it were truly the case. The king can promote such knowledge among the people through symbolic activities such as "royal reconnoitering tours" (Liverani 1990, 59).

---

[11] Taken literally, this would require more miraculous elasticity for the king's bodily organs than that displayed by the Egyptian princess who, according to one midrash, was able to extend the length of her arm (אמתה) and "send" it forth so far into the river (rather than sending her maid [אמתה], as in Exod 2:5) that she herself was able to retrieve Moses' baby ark (*Exod. Rab.* 1:23). According to some Egyptologists, the reason that Twelfth Dynasty monarchs like Sesostris III are depicted with such "huge ears" is to signify "the king's capacity to hear his subjects' petitions" (Parkinson 1999, 66; cf. 69 n. 40 and plate 9). However, given the fact that Twelfth Dynasty portrayals of the pharaoh are usually taken to emphasize the kings' sleepless and suspicious vigilance, the large ears could also convey the king's need to be ever-alert and to remain open to any information he might be offered by informers (see further in ch. 3, below).

[12] The French Lieutenant General of Police was also "the king's newsman," a modern version of the King's Eyes and Ears (Farge 1989, 595). Later, one of Balzac's narrators refers to "the famous Eye adopted as a fearsome police emblem during the Revolution" (Balzac 1972, 34). On the emergence of modern detective departments in relation to the situation of biblical "detectives," see Lasine 1987, 247–49 and n. 5.

In his fantastic description of the all-powerful king, Louis exercises ocular mastery over the entire world as much as an ancient Near Eastern king or god, including Yahweh. For humans, the distance sense of vision implies power and control. For Merleau-Ponty, "there is a fundamental narcissism of all vision" (1968, 139), but the "aerial view of the panorama" entails mastery as well: "the look dominates; it can dominate only things, and if it falls upon human beings it transforms them into puppets that move only by springs" (1968, 77). Divine kings have that kind of look, the kind that turns humans into toys, if not bugs, as Bildad and Shakespeare's Gloucester will attest (Job 25:6; *King Lear,* 4.1.36–37; see Lasine 1988, 32–35, 42–43). Is the same true of all "dominant" human beings?

Ocular mastery takes many forms. For example, Lucretius describes the pleasures of detached beholding in this way:

> Sweet it is, when on the great sea the winds are buffeting the waters, to gaze from the land on another's great struggles, ... because it is sweet to perceive from what misfortune you yourself are free.... But nothing is more gladdening than having sanctuaries, fortified and serene, built by the teaching of the wise, whence you can look down on others, and see them wandering ... going astray ... struggling night and day. (*De Rerum Natura* 2.1–12; 1947, 237, translation slightly modified)

From one of the *templa*[13] *serena,* Lucretius watches shipwrecks serenely, rather than being exposed by one, like the prototypical human infant he describes later (see below) or (in a bizarre variation) the biblical Jonah.

The kind of visual mastery described by Louis is *not* detached or disinterested in the way described by Lucretius, or by Seneca in the epigraph. Far from it. Louis's fantasy is shared by a number of ancient kings, as we shall see, but at this point it might be more helpful to cite Anton Fugger, a kingpin of sixteenth-century merchant capitalism, rather than another king. Fugger secretly consulted a crystal gazer named Anna Meglerer so that she could help him control his massive trading empire. With the aid of the knowing spirits trapped in the witch's crystal, he could instantly "see" what his subordinates were doing throughout his international realm, while he remained invisible. As Lyndal Roper puts it, "With this wonderful piece of early modern spy equipment, Fugger could see without being seen—a powerful fantasy of perfect visual mastery over a group of factors upon whose loyalty and devotion he was in real life utterly dependent" (1994, 129).

---

13 *Templa* here has been understood as "sanctuaries," "high places," "quarters," and "plateaus"; see Lasine 1977, 45–46, 124 n. 40. In all cases, however, the viewer is cut off from, and above, the seen world.

As Roper's statement acknowledges, ocular domination involves see-ing everything without been seen.[14] It is hardly a coincidence that the Lydian king Gyges was traditionally considered by the Greeks to be the first tyrant (see Drews 1972, 136–38) when one considers his involvement with peeping and invisibility. In Herodotus (*Hist.* 1.8–12), Gyges is a courtier who is forced by king Candaules to peep at the queen in her boudoir. However, the queen sees him peeping. Rather than putting him to death, the queen gives him the option of assassinating her husband and marrying her. No idiot, Gyges chooses this option, and, because he's no idiot, he carries out the regicide when the king is asleep. In Plato (*Rep.* 359d–360c; 612b), the name of Gyges is associated with a magical ring that grants the wearer the power to become *literally* invisible and therefore to commit the most characteristic acts of tyrannical injustice with impunity.

Nevertheless, ocular domination is often taken to be more typical of knowers and researchers—including detectives like Dupin—than of kings (although royal knowers *do* exist and will be examined closely later). Take the *flâneur* or the regal computer geek at the keyboard, who also craft imagined worlds of simulated power that others take seriously and enter.[15] According to Baudelaire, "the observer is a prince who enjoys his incog-nito everywhere" (1961, 1160). Invisibility of the viewer is also a royal trait. Kings who go in disguise to examine their subjects (like Shakespeare's Henry V [4.1.24.39–226]) are a well-known folktale motif (Burke 1978, 152). Gods do the same.[16] All such exalted *flâneurs* are primarily investi-gators, that is, researchers.

Baudelaire (1972, 244) calls the *flâneur* the public man and opposes him to the egoists locked in their box and the lazy man confined like a mollusc. For Plato, the mollusc is the lowest form of life (*Tim.* 91b). We will find that the king also inhabits a box, a box that serves an essential defensive function, similar to the function served by the images projected by the leaders in Plato's Cave from behind *their* puppeteer screens (*Rep.* 514b). Like the Wizard of Oz, if not David and Solomon, the most power-ful kings are the ones who master the arts of simulation and dissimulation.

Because sight allows one to gain knowledge from a distance, it offers the knower a kind of safety that must be surrendered if one wants to know

---

[14] In ch. 3 we will see that many ancient kings were not only aware of this fact but made fuller "disciplinary" use of it than Foucault's famous discussion in *Discipline and Punish* might have led one to expect.

[15] On the *flâneur,* see Tester (1994, 4–5); on the computer kings, see Roszak (1994, 186–87) and Bogard (1996, 139: "exercising absolute power over images").

[16] And so do angels, at least in Wim Wenders's film *Der Himmel über Berlin;* these angels should be viewed as classic examples of the "invisible" urban *flâneur.* In a literal sense, they are also King's Eyes and Ears, with the "King" being God.

through intimate experience, that is, know in the biblical sense. Nevertheless, on occasion kings may also resort to this investigative strategy. A good example is Augustus, who, in spite of sponsoring a harsh law against adultery, repeatedly engaged in it himself, ostensibly as a kind of "research method." According to Suetonius, the emperor's friends excused his apparently hypocritical and illicit behavior because it was motivated by calculation, not lust. Specifically, he committed adultery "so that he could the more easily acquire information about his rivals' plans from the women of their households" (*Aug.* 69; cf. Edwards 1993, 34–62).[17]

Mastery by "intercourse" involves penetrating others—in several possible senses—without being penetrated oneself; in this sense it is analogous to ocular mastery. Ocular domination takes place insofar as we inhabit a projective world, while relations between inside and outside take place in topological space.[18] To some extent, kings (and we all) can *choose* the ocular or topological mode as our primary defense. Ocular defenses obviously involve the King's Eyes. Topological ones involve the control of the flow of information and "leaks." These don't exist in a projective world, where everything, including information, is *hors d'atteinte*. I am referring here to Sartre's description of the imagination. Image-objects are present in absence; these *objets irreels* are "out of reach," "out of touch" (1940, 162).

When it comes to evaluating royal power, we must distinguish between the "irreality" of dissimulation and that of simulation. From Tiberius, James I took the motto, "he who does not know how to dissimulate, does not know how to rule" (see Goldberg 1983, 68). Dissimulation is key to the survival of all courtiers, as well as their king. Put roughly (for now), David's vaunted "impenetrability" is closer to dissimulation than simulation, while his son Solomon's elusiveness has much more to do with simulation. David is not impenetrable because all humans

---

17 This is a particularly cold-blooded example of what Peter Brooks (1993, 97) calls the "metaphysical Don Juan tradition," citing the *moraliste* Duclos's contention that sexual inconstancy is "a result of the desire to know Truth." Also compare Aristotle's advice to tyrants on the most effective ways of information gathering (*Pol.* 1313a–1314a), discussed in ch. 3, below.

18 Elsewhere (Lasine 1977) I draw a distinction between two fundamentally distinct modes of human experience and knowledge. One is based on the model of the body as a "kinesthetic amoeba" immersed in an enveloping fluid world in topological space. Topological experience is grounded in the biological processes of metabolic exchange, which govern all traffic (*Verkehr*) between outside and inside. The other mode of experience is based on the model of sight at a distance. Here the world is experienced as before and present to a disembodied ocular knower in projective space. Projective experience tends to defend against, and deny the fact of, bodily immersion in the fluid world.

are[19] but because David needs to be; like all those at court, he must be a master of impression management. His mystique—his charisma—may depend on it, and his narcissism may require it.

Courtly dissimulation is complex, because it *primarily* involves a topological task for those immersed in this very fluid social world: control of the *flow* of information. The projective task of remaining "deadpan," that is, of controlling visual appearance, is also necessary, but not so essential. This is not to say that those fascinated with David are in that condition because of his beauty. It's more than skin deep. Maybe *that* is what the Yahweh spirit granted him—his vaunted magnetism, his charisma. We are told that David is a man after God's own heart, a better man than his "neighbor" Saul (1 Sam 13:14; 15:28; 28:17). How can we possibly resist him, once we've heard *that,* even though we haven't seen him, as others in the text have?

Geertz connects charisma with the power of the center, and Yahweh makes wherever David is located into the new center. And because David is the center of Yahweh's attention, the little man in his eye, Saul is always marginal, no matter where he is. We know that Saul is often exposed, relative to David, whether he is defecating in a supposedly private place, sleeping, or lying naked in a prophetic fit. If David is *hors d'atteinte,* it is because people project their desires onto him (whether or not David knowingly orchestrates this), just as Samuel told Saul that all Israel had fixed all their desire on him (1 Sam 9:20). In spite of God's famous warning against evaluating others by their external appearance (1 Sam 16:7), people tend to evaluate David from outside and be drawn by his perceived "magnetism" toward the inside, as readers have tended to do for many centuries.

In contrast, Solomon is not only impermeable but the parade example of royal simulation. Even though he seems to be present and visible, he is uniquely out of reach of the reader of 1 Kings and Chronicles. Biblical kings do not use glass mirrors, but my later discussion (in ch. 6) may suggest that if Solomon ever played the role of Richard II and looked into a mirror, the glass would reflect an image as blank as a vampire's. All smoke and mirrors,[20] like the Great Oz. Why? Because the narratives that describe him merely simulate the reality of a potent imperial king, who degenerates into a simulation of a despotic one. This makes Solomon our contemporary, considering that we are now said to live in a postmodern cyberspace in which "privacy and publicity dissolve into one another," and the self-enclosed system "does not connect to an outside" (Bogard 1996, 140, 152). Everything is "present but absent" and *hors d'atteinte* in

---

[19] Whether ontologically (as Alter and others assume) or epistemologically; see Lasine 1986, 49–51.

[20] On the mirror scene from *Richard II,* see ch. 10, below.

hyper/cyber-space; everything is simulated. Theoretically, in the Hebrew Bible one can always be "reached," at least by Yahweh or his creation. Penetration and invasion from outside are always possible; just ask the loser Saul about the רוח רעה, the "evil spirit" (1 Sam 16:14). If David and Solomon are both out of reach, each in his own characteristic fashion, Saul is *too easily* reached, puppetized, and ultimately exposed to dismemberment.

Fourth Trait: Nightmares of His Majesty the Baby

> The human child, like a sailor tossed out from the fierce waves, lies naked on the ground, speechless, in need of every sort of aid to stay alive, when first Nature brings it forth by labor from its mother's womb into the shores of light. And it fills the place with a mournful crying, as is appropriate for one who has such troubles ahead in life. But the various sorts of cattle and wild beasts grow up and have no need of rattles, nor does anyone have to speak to them in the gentle broken speech of the fostering nurse, nor do they look for different clothing for the changes of season. Finally, they have no need of weapons, or of tall walls, to protect their own, since the earth itself supplies everything to all of them, and Nature the artful maker of things.
> —Lucretius, 5.222–234 (Nussbaum 1994, 254)

> And when I was born, I began to breathe the common air, and fell upon the kindred earth, and my first sound was a cry, like that of all. I was nursed with care in swaddling cloths. For no king has had a different beginning of existence; there is for all mankind one entrance into life, and a common departure.
> —Wisdom of Solomon 7:3–6 (RSV)

Lucretius and "Solomon" (and King Lear [4.6.174–79]) agree: all humans cry at birth. Lucretius says that we have good reason to do so. After all, didn't Eliphaz say that humans are born for trouble as the sparks fly upward (Job 5:7)? Assuming these authorities are correct, why is this a particularly *royal* trait? Do baby kings cry more than other babies? Are they *more* "shipwrecked" than the rest of us? The answer, sometimes, is *yes*. Consider all the exposure birth stories of future kings. Quite a distinguished group: Gilgamesh, Sargon, Oedipus, Cyrus, Cypelsus, Tenes, and others.[21] In the Hebrew Bible, on the other hand, the leaders who are exposed in this way are prophets, in other words, the very people often sent to oppose kings.[22] The parade example, of course, is Moses (although the

---

[21] For references, see especially Rank 1964, 14–64. On Cypelsus, see Herodotus, *Hist.* 5.92; McGlew 1993, 61–74; and Vernant 1990a, 216–26; on Ten[n]es, see Pausanias, *Descr.* 10.14.2–4; and McGlew 1993, 160–61.

[22] In another sense, of course, Israel itself is exposed as a child, in such passages as Deut 32 and Ezek 16. These texts will be looked at in detail in ch. 10, below.

rabbis sometimes refer to Moses as "king," usually on the basis of Deut 33:5[23]). The inverted-world example is Jonah the anti-Moses, who is first exposed in water when he is an infantile and narcissistic adult, only to be rebirthed from the fish, his *Ersatz* ark. Now, there aren't any exposure stories going around about *me,* so why are there so many about kings-to-be? Is it because they are indeed more exposed and vulnerable—and dangerous—than the rest of us? Once again, the answer is *yes.*

Yet if the apocryphal Solomon claims that he was "nursed with care in swaddling cloths," the same cannot be said of exposed baby-kings—unless they are either ensconced in a baby-sized ark (*tēbâ*) like Moses', which, in one modern retelling, is outfitted with goose feathers,[24] or conveyed by eagles or swans who still have their feathers attached.[25] In a way, the exposure stories could describe what kind of a childhood Frazer's king of the wood might have experienced. Frazer's king is often viewed as a scapegoat. Is being a scapegoat also a royal trait? René Girard (e.g., 1986, 18–19; 1987a, 84–93) is not the only one to think so. Just recall Shakespeare's Henry V and the wakeful pharaoh whom Liverani (1990, 125) describes as a king who suffers insomnia so that "everybody else can sleep in a paradise-like atmosphere of peace and security." In other words, by sacrificing himself he ushers in peace for the community.

At this point, someone might ask why I should spend so much time on a trait that in the Hebrew Bible is characteristic of prophets rather than their traditional adversaries, the kings. True, we learn about Josiah becoming king at eight years old, but we will never know if he had been consistently cuddled as a baby. However, we do know that the infant Joash was taken with his nurse from the bedchamber, and then hidden in the house of Yahweh, to prevent *him* from being murdered (2 Kgs 11:2–3), just as baby Cyrus was hidden in a jar (or beehive; Vernant 1990a, 470 n. 30), Cypelsus a chest, and Moses an ark. This time, one royal murder in a bedchamber was averted. Also, in this instance the would-be murderer is *not* a father-king. It is a woman, Athaliah, Joash's grandmother, who was in the

---

[23] See, e. g., *Exod. Rab.* 40:2; 48:4; 52:1; *Lev. Rab.* 31:4; *Num. Rab.* 15:13; 18:2; etc. On the unlikely possibility that the subject of "he became king in Jeshurun" in Deut 33:5 is Moses rather than God, see, e.g., Coats 1988, 19–21.

[24] In Hurston's *Moses: Man of the Mountain,* Jocheved lines the basket lovingly with one of her garments and then with goose feathers (38). However, the ark had already begun to be more capacious and cozy in Josephus (it is shaped in the form of a cradle, "spacious enough to give the infant ample room for repose" [*Ant.* 2.9.4 §220; Josephus 1930, 259]), and in one midrashic version a tiny canopy is put over the child to shade him (see Ginzberg 1969, 2:265).

[25] Eagle: Gilgamesh in Aelian (Rank 1964, 26–27); swan: Lohengrin (see Rank 1964, 60).

midst of establishing her reign in the same manner that Abimelech (Judg 9) and Solomon (1 Kgs 2) had established theirs. It is now obvious why potential baby-kings are especially exposed and vulnerable. On the other hand, the adult monarchs who seek their deaths could object that *they* are the ones who are truly exposed and vulnerable. These babies are threats to *their* regimes and, ultimately, to *their* lives. That's the point: infant kings, child kings, adult kings, queens, and queen mothers are all particularly exposed and vulnerable. Kings (*and* the prophets who threaten them) are threats from the moment they are washed up on the shore at birth or vomited out by a fish, if not earlier, when oracles announce their impending dangerous birth.

Of course, kings and prophets are not the only ones who are dumped into the drink. According to Genesis, we *all* were, in the sense that everybody's ancestors came over from the old country on Noah's *tēbâ*. Yahweh might have played the affectionate parent to the sea *Yam*, swaddling this big, wet baby in clouds (Job 38:9), but in this instance he chose to expose the humans made in his image in that same baby *Yam*. Those in the *tēbâ* dramatize in the "natural" realm the position of individuals surrounded by a hostile outside world. They are, most literally, the ultimate insiders. Only a very tiny fraction of humanity is enclosed and sheltered from this very hostile external fluid, boundary-collapsing, world. Only father's favorite Noah and his family are saved—and Ham, one of the saved, has a curse put on his descendants almost immediately after this. Why? Because Ham *exposed* Dad (or witnessed Dad's "exposed" state, whether wittingly or not). So, in effect, we are offered a choice: Do we want to identify with the ark passengers or the drowning victims, God's favorite Noah (and later David) or hard-luck Ham (and later Saul)? If we choose to side with the underdog and choose Ham, the sobering lesson is that we are only saved and enclosed provisionally, until or unless we expose "Dad," even if the exposure is accidental. Anticipating my later discussion (in ch. 10), I should add that narcissists, who are notorious for being their parents' special favorites, also tend to describe the outside world as hostile, dangerous, and devoid of love, much like the world that confronts Yahweh's "special" son Israel in the wilderness.

Concepts of what constitutes a safe vehicle for the self and the family change over time and in different cultures. Phillipe Ariès calls the home of the *modern* family a "turtle shell" (1979, 38) that protects its members from a hostile outside world. Small wonder that Ariès compares "the private fortress of the family car" (1979, 40) to Noah's ark: "as the ark permitted Noah to survive the flood, so the car permits its owners to pass through the hostile and dangerous world outside the front door" (1979, 39). The automobile is also the emblem of the modern individual, according to Baudrillard. It is "a technical

extension of [one's] own body" and serves as "a gigantic 'character armour'"
against death (1993, 178). The *tēbâ* has given way to the RV and the SUV. And
what about the safety features of the vehicles that transport kings and
prophets? Riding in a chariot certainly didn't save Jehoram and Ahaziah from
assassination (2 Kgs 9), and in 1 Kgs 13 the man of God's donkey did not have
an effective anti-lion airbag. So in the next section we will have to figure out
what *does* provide a king with turtle-shell or *tēbâ*-level security.

Fifth Trait: The Self-Sufficient Sovereign, or, the King as Hedgehog and Fox

> There's such divinity doth hedge a king
> That treason can but peep to what it would,
> Acts little of his will.
> —Shakespeare, *Hamlet,* 4.5.121–23

> The fox knows many things, but the hedgehog one big thing.
> —Archilochus (Edmonds 1961, 174)

> The hedgehog is a solitary animal that vigorously defends its territory.... It
> is intolerant.... There are many hedgehog legends because of their seem-
> ingly indifferent manner [and] aloof appearance.... [It moves] about in its
> territory constantly sniffing, investigating, and uncovering everything.
> —Grzimek, *Grzimek's Encyclopedia of Mammals* (1990, 462, 471, 460)

> Women, especially if they grow up with good looks, develop a certain
> self-contentment.... The charm of a child lies to a great extent in his nar-
> cissism, his self-contentment and inaccessibility, just as does the charm of
> certain animals which seem not to concern themselves about us, such as
> cats and the large beasts of prey. Indeed, even great criminals and hu-
> morists, as they are represented in literature, compel our interest by the
> narcissistic consistency with which they manage to keep away from their
> ego anything that would diminish it.
> —Freud, "On Narcissism: An Introduction" (1914, 88–89)

I ended the previous section with a question about the means used by
kings to protect themselves in a potentially hostile outside world from
which they must conceal their weakness and vulnerability. Hamlet's uncle,
King Claudius, thinks that he is sufficiently protected by the "divinity" that
"hedges" a king, the aura of inviolability that goes with having a body
politic or mystical body.[26] He assumes that he can keep potential assassins
at "peeping distance," looking through a hedge that they are unable to

---

[26] Similarly, Bennett (1999, 204) observes that Richard II attempted to create a
"carapace of regality."

penetrate. Here the king's mastery is not the result of his ability to see everything; it is the result of enemies being able to look but not touch.[27] Ironically, Claudius is in a perfect position to know that this fantasy is a bad joke. The only reason he is the king is because *he* was able to penetrate his predecessor's "hedge of divinity" in order to murder him, as old Hamlet slept in his orchard (1.5.59–79). If convincing your subjects of your invulnerability is one way of achieving security for a king, kings who believe their own press clippings can end up like old Hamlet and, eventually, Claudius. When the ghost of the old king tells Hamlet that he was murdered while sleeping "upon my secure hour" (1.5.61), he means "secure" in the sense of being unsuspecting, too sure of his own safety. A king who is overconfident of his security can never be secure—especially when he's asleep.

Among the ways in which kings seek to project an image of themselves as invulnerable is through being likened to strong, ferocious, and seemingly self-sufficient beasts like lions, bears, and eagles.[28] However, in terms of the king's *actual* defense mechanisms, the epigraph from Archilochus points us toward the right animals. Quilled hedgehogs turn their own hostile exterior surface out to the world. They live alone and self-protected. Foxes proverbially use their wits, the deceptiveness of appearances, and their mobility to deal with that outside world. Hedgehogs are often described as appearing aloof and indifferent, like the supposedly narcissistic and self-contained animals listed by Freud. But the hedgehog's quilled appearance and constant investigating suggest that he is sufficiently cognizant of external threats to present a prickly contact boundary to the world. This combination of defensive insularity and constant vigilance might seem paradoxical, but it is a paradox that is typical of most modes of defense. Are *kings* aloof in the sense that they belong on Freud's list of narcissistically indifferent beings, or are *they* (so to speak) rolled into a ball for defensive purposes?

When we think about a king like Homer's Odysseus, we think fox. Odysseus is *polytropon* (*Od.* 1.1), many-turning, not merely because of his many travels but because of his many-turning nature: his Jacob-like ability to change identities, to wrestle, to deceive. But the *polytropon* is actually *both* hedgehog and fox in the sense that he or she must *deal* with—that is, have "intercourse"[29] with—the "outside" in order to achieve

---

[27] In this fantasy, the "peepers" are in the position of Kafka's land surveyor K. in *Das Schloss,* when he looks at the supposedly majestic Klamm through a peephole. See further in ch. 6, below.

[28] The king may be likened to an "eagle" for *several* reasons; see ch. 11 n. 44, below.

[29] Images of intercourse are often used to describe flow across a topological boundary, in a number of languages (e.g., German *Verkehr;* see Lasine 1977, 537–638 and n. 18, above).

what he or she wants to achieve. *At the same time,* the *polytropon* is creating a Wizard of Oz–like screen—a functional equivalent of hedgehog
quills, even if this involves nothing more than pointed remarks and
barbed comments. Nietzsche goes so far as to claim that life itself is
always on the side of the "most unscrupulous πολύτροποι," precisely
because "life depends on appearance ... simulation, deception, self-
deception [*Blendung, Selbstblendung*]" (*Gay Science,* §344; Nietzsche
1973, 258). Life favors deception the way Athene favors Odysseus
(Homer, *Od.* 13.287–332) and Yahweh favors Jacob and David. But is
Odysseus different from the shelled type of personality, in terms of
functioning? When *he* is "shipwrecked" and exposed for the last time,
even his *tēbâ* fails him—that is, his raft, equipped with its half-decks
and its goddess-given gourmet food and wine (*Od.* 5.265–267). He even
has to shed the garments in which Calypso had clothed him (*Od.* 5.264,
343–344). Odysseus is a swimming fox, not a snug and dry baby Moses.

Can *hedgehogs* swim or, at least, go with the flow? Put differently, can
a hedgehog be a king, considering that the hedgehog is a hermit, has little or nothing to do with any others of his own "race," including *Verkehr*
in the biblical sense (Grzimek 1990, 462)? On the other hand, do foxes
want to be kings? Narcissists *do* "work" others, manipulate them in foxy
ways, but only in order to remain untouched at a deeper level, to be the
untouched toucher, the true center, a deity ruling a virtual reality. A king
might *want* to project a self-sufficient hedgehog *image,* but, *in fact,* he
must be foxy, because his defenses are always "really" permeable. A
hedgehog's quills say "keep out." A king who *really* kept all others out
would not last long on the throne, and he would be quite uncomfortable,
to boot. Shakespeare's Prince Henry expresses the paradoxical discom-
fort perfectly:

> O Majesty!
> When thou dost pinch thy bearer, thou dost sit
> Like a rich armour worn in heat of day
> That scalds with safety. (*Henry IV, Pt. 2,* 4.5.28–30)

Protective armor that scalds the wearer will not be worn for very long.[30]
Yet the king who merely *sees* from inside an air-conditioned fortress/shell
can't *really* rule either, unless, like the Wizard of Oz, people *think* that he
can, that is, that his palace is a Panopticon. Even then, he's only an unseen
movie director. Clearly, a king must master intercourse with the outside

---

[30] Our friend the hedgehog knows the problem well. The same quills that grant
him security against the jaws of large predators prevent him from scratching himself. Consequently, he is prey to all sorts of unpleasant (if not dreadful) skin
infestations from little critters. See Grzimek 1990, 469–70.

(especially in terms of managing information), not abstain from all relations with the outside.[31]

The Stoics would seem to have something akin to a hedgehog view of kingship, particularly those who claim that the person who has liberated himself from dependence on the sometimes hostile outside world has achieved "sovereignty" over himself. The metaphors used to convey this regal self-sufficiency and freedom also tend to be in hedgehog language rather than fox-speak. Thus, the defenses of this sovereign self-state include "fortresses," "walls," "roofs," "buffers," and "skin," all of which are capable of repelling whatever the outside hurls against it—whether "missiles," "siege engines," "blows of chance," or "hailstones."[32] Admittedly, Stoics like Marcus Aurelius (e.g., *Med.* 7.48; 9.30; 12.24) employ the language of *ocular* withdrawal. Far from being a Stoic, Baudelaire also addresses ocular withdrawal when he describes the stance of his poet-*flâneur*. This figure "is able ... to be at the very center of the world and yet to remain hidden from the world" (Baudelaire 1972, 400, translation modified). Epicurus would agree with the last phrase, which dovetails nicely with his advice: Λάθε βιώσας—live inconspicuously or invisibly (see Plutarch, *De lat. viv.* 1128–1129). If invisibility is a royal trait, so is being in the paradoxical situation of an individual who is simultaneously at the center of the world and hidden from it.

Also having more affinity with the Stoics than one might expect is one of Freud's self-sufficient, independent beings. This is the humorist. While all those listed by Freud "manage to keep away from their ego anything that would diminish it," Freud saw humor as "the triumph of narcissism, the victorious assertion of the ego's invulnerability. . . . It insists that it cannot be affected by the traumas of the external world" (1927, 162). Here the missiles aimed at the self are not so much deflected as transformed into material for stand-up routines. Nevertheless, I doubt that humor would be included in anyone's list of the king's defining traits.

Sixth Trait: The King As the Center of Paradox

> ... the center and core of creation—"His Majesty the Baby," as we once fancied ourselves.
> —Freud, "On Narcissism: An Introduction" (1914, 91)

---

[31] Nevertheless, kings may portray themselves as needing nothing from the outside, because they are self-sufficient and already possess everything worth having. For example, in the Amarna letters, King Burnaburiash II of Babylonia writes to the pharaoh: "as I am told, in my brother's country everything is available and my brother needs absolutely nothing. Furthermore, in my country everything too is available and I for my part nee[d] absolutely nothing" (EA 7:33–36; Moran 1992, 13).

[32] See Seneca, *Ep.* 45.9–10; 53.12; 65.21; 72.5–6; 82.4–5; Arrian, *Epict. diss.* 4.5.25–27.

Narcissism and the evil-eye superstition illuminate each other.... both iso-
late the individual at the center of the community.
—Siebers, *The Mirror of Medusa* (1983, 85–86)

add another marginal group to the poor and outsiders—the marginal insider.... The monarch and his court are often reminiscent of the eye of
the hurricane.... [In periods of crisis] crowds commonly turn on those
who originally held exceptional power over them.
—Girard, *The Scapegoat* (1986, 18–19)

There is no disputing the charisma that belongs to the king by virtue
of his position at the center of things. Geertz (1983, 146) speaks of "the
inherent sacredness of central authority" and notes the use of images,
myths, and other "symbolic forms" to guarantee that the charisma will be
experienced by those outside the center:

At the political center of any complexly organized society ... there is ...
a set of symbolic forms ...—crowns and coronations, limousines and conferences—that mark the center as center and give what goes on there its
aura of being not merely important but in some odd fashion connected
with the way the world is built. (1983, 124)

The idea that the power of the crown is linked to "the way the world is
built" is not new to biblical scholars. For example, Whitelam points out that
an essential function of royal ideology is to sell the idea of the king's central role in the *cosmic* order (1989, 128).[33] Meyers notes that "the symbolic
role of the capital as center" is to be "a microcosm [containing] all the elements of the world" (1983, 422). And it is well known that one function of
ancient Near Eastern royal palaces (including the biblical Solomon's) was
to serve as a world-omphalos theme park, featuring exotica of all kinds
(e.g., Solomon's apes and peacocks [or baboons; תכיים]) and drawing gift-
givers from the periphery with a magnetism strong enough to make
Disney's Michael Eisner green with envy (see, e.g., Meyers 1983, 420–22).

In spite of such apparent indications that the center is the supreme
comfort zone for a monarch, we have already had ample indication that
the center can also be a hot seat, if not a "scalding" one, at the very same
time. Even the notion that the king, as a representative human, is at the
center of the cosmos is not necessarily comforting or an indication of narcissistic grandiosity on the part of either king or his subjects. Earlier I
referred to Freud's account of the third blow to our narcissism: that the

---

[33] Elsewhere Whitelam asserts that "the development of the state with the king
as the central symbolic figure represents a major stage in the evolution of political
systems" (1992, 4:40).

royal ego is not master in its own house. The earlier blows were dealt by Copernicus and Darwin. In spite of all this, Freud would have to concede Elias's point that all the Copernican and Darwinian revolutions in the world cannot totally dislodge the human experience of inhabiting a geocentric, anthropocentric, and egocentric universe.

To complicate things further, Lovejoy points out that at one time "the geocentric cosmology served rather for man's humiliation than for his exaltation," because the medieval world was "diabolocentric" (1964, 102). In this period, "a certain racial *amour propre*" was justified by the notion that humans have "a unique share in the attention of Heaven" (1964, 102–3). Yet even this is a double-edged compliment. It conforms nicely to the sentiment of Ps 8, but the regal Job has other sentiments in mind when he asks the question "what is the human being [אֱנוֹשׁ]?" (Job 7:17). Job is not exactly thrilled to have a unique share of God's attention. Now, according to Nietzsche, the human "*will* to self-belittlement [has] progressed without stopping since Copernicus" (*Genealogy*, 3 §25; Nietzsche 1968, 422). Job is quite willing to "belittle" his ego, in the hope that it will make God recognize the absurdity of killing a fly with an ICBM, and back off long enough for him to swallow his spittle (7:12–19). Job is seemingly alone (except for his three deprogrammer-friends), yet he is under constant surveillance. He talks about having been like a king, while his friends tell him that he is a maggot, as they are (e.g., 25:6; see Lasine 1988, 32–33). Job is certainly experiencing the paradoxes of the king's position, even though he is not "officially" a monarch.

Earlier, I quoted Hoffmann's description of the central myth of the "heliocentric" king during Louis XIV's reign. I noted that this myth has real effects on both the people and the king. This marriage of the real and the unreal is closely related to the relationship between the king's two bodies. Speaking of the divinization of Greco-Roman emperors, Paul Veyne pins down this royal paradox:

> The faithful did not consider their all-powerful master to be an ordinary man, and the official hyperbole that made of this mortal a god was true in spirit. It corresponded to their filial devotion. Swept on by the linguistic tide, they experienced this feeling of dependence all the more strongly. However,... they *also* knew that their sublime master was *at the same time* a poor man, in the same way that at Versailles they made a cult of the Grand Monarch *and* gossiped about his slightest movements. (Veyne 1988, 89; emphasis added)

Veyne acknowledges that this "plurality of truths [is] an affront to logic," but, let's face it: logic has endured worse insults than this. Veyne also uses the metaphor of perspective to make his point even more tellingly: "when men depend on an all-powerful man they experience him as a man and see him from a valet's perspective as a mere mortal; but they also experience him as their master and therefore also see him as a god" (1988, 90). Veyne would not be surprised to note all the evidence we've collected on the king's simultaneous power and helplessness, his independence and dependence, his corporate and personal identities.[34]

Leader-follower and master-slave relations are admittedly very complex and subject to various interpretations;[35] nevertheless, their paradoxical nature is manifest. But where should one locate the *center* of the paradox? Opinions differ. Observers of historical kings and kings in literature locate the center of the paradox in different places. Thus, when tracing the idea of the king's ignorance in European satiric and didactic verse, Embree stresses that the *topos* is based on "this paradoxical proposition—that the most powerful person in the kingdom does not have the power to discover the extent of his people's plight or the extent of his officials' corruption" (1985, 121). Embree is focusing on the king's vulnerability as information manager. Commenting on Shakespeare's Richard II, Ure notes "the shocking paradox of the helpless king, the king who must" (see Shakespeare 1961, lxxxi). His focus is on the fact that a presumably powerful and free king can be so weak and subject to coercion by his subjects.

Scholars like Peter Schwartz (1989, 267) locate the "central paradox of royal authority" elsewhere. Rather than stressing the king's combination of omniscience and ignorance, or power and helplessness, Schwartz highlights the fact that the monarch conveys "an ideal of maturity while simultaneously expressing this ideal in grandiose, self-indulgent, and infantile terms" (P. Schwartz 1989, 267; cf. Sagan 1985, 327–28; Rank 1993, 91). The king is both mature father and immature infant. Kantorowicz would say that both aspects make sense from the point of view of the king's two bodies: "from the same corporational premises there could originate two diametrically opposed opinions: a king ever under age versus a king never

---

[34] Veyne might also have pointed to the "dual divine/human perspective on kings" in ancient Egypt (Silverman 1991, 62). Silverman believes that the "perceived fluidity of the human and divine components of the king's nature" is due in part to the interplay between the king's person (*ḥm*), and his role as king (*nswt*) when he acts "in the capacity of his office" (64, 67). And to his example of Louis being simultaneously a cult object and an object of gossip, Veyne could have noted the female Pharaoh Hatshepsut being both venerated and satirized in graffiti (Silverman 1991, 62). And in the modern world, Adorno (1951, 289) observes that the "Fascist leader type" must project a contradictory image: "While appearing as a superman, the leader must at the same time work the miracle of appearing as an average person, just as Hitler posed as a composite of King-Kong and the suburban barber." For other examples of leaders who project contradictory images, see chs. 6 and 11, below.

[35] See Lasine 1992, 143–45 and the references cited on 151 (in n. 16).

under age. In either case, the intention was to emphasize the exceptional position of the king and his rights" (1957, 378).

Schwartz, Sagan, and others like Girard would say that there's more to it than that. They all take some kind of "psychological" approach, returning (consciously or unconsciously) to Freud's notions of His Majesty the Baby and primary narcissism. Once you go in that direction, you have to acknowledge the paradoxes associated with infancy itself. For example, Winnicott (1958, 163) posits an initial stage of infancy that "could be described at one and the same time as of absolute independence and absolute dependence. There is no feeling of dependence, and therefore that dependence must be absolute." In chapters 10 and 11, I will ask whether this idea (and the related notion of an infantile "illusion of omnipotence") holds up under scrutiny. For now, it is sufficient to note that Winnicott, like Ure, discovers paradox along the continua of independence–dependence and power–helplessness. Other psychologists focus on the paradoxical nature of the adult narcissist's behavior. Thus, Kernberg seeks to explain "the paradox of [the narcissist's] relatively good ego functioning and surface adaptation in the presence of a predominance of ... primitive defenses, and the lack of integration of object representations" (1985, 266).

Clearly, *Freud's* narcissistic baby-king only has power because those around the baby give the infant power over them. Does Freud believe that adults with narcissistic personalities make effective kings? In a late essay on three "libidinal types," Freud does describe the narcissistic type as independent and not easily intimidated. They are "especially suited to act as a support for others, [and] to take on the role of leaders" (1931, 218). Freud had described child investigators like Little Hans as solitary, alienated, suspicious, and independent. The adult narcissistic type may be independent, but only in the sense of having little or no emotional investment in others. Slater (1968, 152) shrewdly observes that while leaders who reach the throne on their own tend to have narcissistic personalities anyway, those who had been born into hereditary monarchies are brought up in such a way as to keep them infantile, narcissistic, and ultimately dependent upon those who "baby" them even when they are adults. While biblical kings like the Saul of 1 Sam 22 illustrate the mistrust of "Little Hans" (or Freud's ego-king who has been made to realize that he is not master in his own house), it is kings like David and Ahab who (from the available textual data) best approximate the adult narcissistic type, His Majesty the *Big* Baby, so to speak. It is perhaps no accident that David and Ahab offer the two clearest examples of *pleonexia* and covetousness among biblical kings.

Sometimes, deciding who really holds the power in a monarchy (if power can be "held") seems like deciding under which walnut shell a prestidigitator's pea is hiding, or whether the chicken or the egg came first. Even if the courtiers and the royal family painstakingly rear the future king to be narcissistic and dependent, won't he still control them when he takes power, unless their control over the flow of information is very tight indeed? This puzzle of royal power is well illustrated in Aristophanes' *Knights* (1111–1150). The Chorus chides Demos ("the people"). Even though Demos has had the powers of a tyrant delegated to him, he is nevertheless led around by the nose by whatever false leaders flatter him the most. Demos replies that he acts like a baby on purpose. He is not being controlled by the leader he allows to steal from him. On the contrary, Demos brings up (supports, nurses; τρέφειν, 1128) the ruler-thief, but with the intention of squashing him flat when he is fully bloated. As the Chorus then puts it, Demos nourishes and brings up (τρέφεις, 1136) these politicians so that he can *eat* them when they are fat and ready. Demos concurs. While he has seemingly allowed the rulers to steal for their own benefit, he has kept his eye on them, so that when they have swallowed enough, Demos will make them disgorge it all and take it himself.

Aristophanes' version is unique in that both the ruler and the people who supposedly pamper him are described as infantile and manipulative, if not narcissistic. Nevertheless, the fundamental paradox of power is well-expressed. Freud himself noted this paradox in yet another context. In *Totem and Taboo* (1913, 43–48), Freud cites a number of kings whose lives are a "contradiction"; while they are exalted and enjoy freedoms and privileges forbidden to others, they are also isolated, endure special restrictions, and are even treated as though they were criminals. They are often kept under surveillance rather than conducting surveillance of the people (1913, 41–44, 48).[36] Freud is primarily talking about the traditional societies described by Frazer, but he also gives a few examples of modern European monarchs (1913, 42–43). Both the "primitive" and modern kings are made inaccessible by taboo, which, in the modern period, takes the form of court ceremonial and etiquette (1913, 43). Freud does not view the contradiction of the king's position as the inevitable result of the king's placement at the center, where he is supposedly best situated to see and control all but is actually dependent on others for information. Instead, he traces the contradiction of the monarch's position back to *emotional* ambivalence. The leader is treated with the same mixture of adoration and unacknowledged hostility as one's father. Freud believes that if we could hear the views of modern kings and rulers they would affirm the existence of this simultaneous adulation and hostility

---

[36] While Plato describes tyrants as ending up living like prisoners (*Rep.* 579b), this is not because of the people; it is the result of the ruler's own tyrannical *Eros*.

(1913, 51).[37] From this perspective, the paradox of royal power is nearly identical to the paradox of the royal scapegoat, who is simultaneously adored and reviled by the people (see, e.g., Girard 1987a, 3–13).

For Girard, the seeming contradictions surrounding the position of the king and other seemingly independent, self-sufficient beings are all expressions of "the paradoxes of mimetic desire" (1987b, 343). The mimetic process "implies that ... the more narcissistic you become—or the more 'egotistic,' as it used to be said—the more you become morbidly 'object-directed' or 'altruistic'." (1987b, 368). According to Girard, "the strategy of desire ... consists in setting up the dazzling illusion of a self-sufficiency that we shall believe in a little ourselves if we succeed in convincing the other person of it" (1987b, 371). To illustrate his theory, Girard points to supposedly "coquettish" women on Freud's puzzling list of self-sufficient beings, while paying little attention to Freud's other examples.[38]

Neither Freud nor Girard gets off scot-free for including women in this company. Sarah Kofman chides "men like Girard (or Freud himself in most of his other texts)" for conceiving of female self-sufficiency as "a pure stratagem." *Why* do they do so? "Because they find woman's self-sufficiency intolerable" (1985, 62). This issue is too complex to be adequately addressed here. However, at this point it *is* possible to conclude that the position of

---

[37] Interestingly, most of the aspects of the king's position described by Freud are reflected in his own life. Freud's disciple and biographer Ernest Jones came up with the idea of surrounding the master with a select group of "loyalists," a council that Freud insisted be "strictly secret." This group, which, with Freud, numbered seven, was dubbed "the Committee" (E. Jones 1955, 153). In a letter of 1912, Jones wrote that the Committee was to be "designed like the Paladins of Charlemagne, to guard the kingdom and policy of their master" (quoted in Gay [1989, 230]; cf. E. Jones 1955, 152). It was to be a "dependable palace guard" (Gay 1989, 229). One might say that its privileged members were distant relatives of the traditional seven Persian courtiers who saw the face of the king. Even prior to the formation of the Committee, Freud had referred to Jung as his "successor and Crown Prince" (Roazen 1976, 227). When Jung and other followers went their own way, Freud often experienced the defection as an act of disloyalty and betrayal. And when his courtiers withheld the information that the lesions in his mouth were cancerous (Gay 1989, 424–25; Kohut 1977, 65), Freud "found it hard to forgive the way the full truth had been kept from him" (E. Jones 1957, 96). This is precisely the way Freud himself described children's difficulty in forgiving their parents for not sharing the truth about where babies come from.

[38] Girard hardly mentions the literary great criminals and humorists (1987b, 382) and makes generalizations that totally ignore both them and the attractive women (e.g., "Freud can *only* describe this blessed awareness [of self-sufficiency] through recourse to beings that, though alive, are defective in self awareness—the wild beast and the small child" [1987b, 383; emphasis added]).

the king, if not that of all human beings—female or male, funny or morose—is riddled with paradox. We have now located the king's *ulti-mate* defining trait.

WAYS OF KNOWING KINGS: SLEEPING WITH EYES OPEN AS A RESEARCH METHOD

With Pharaoh sleepless and vigilant, the boundary is sure: the hostile forces will never prevail, the inner court will never be submerged by the frightful chaos. The king's watch is sure enough, everybody else can sleep in a paradise-like atmosphere of peace and security.
—Liverani, *Prestige and Interest* (1990, 125)

fieldwork is ... a strain.... you have to be up at daybreak, and then remain awake until the last native has gone to sleep, and even sometimes watch over him as he sleeps; you have to try to make yourself inconspicu-ous, while being constantly present; see everything, remember everything, note everything.... Above all, [the anthropologist] asks himself questions: Why has he come here? With what hopes or what objectives?
—Lévi-Strauss, *Tristes Tropiques* (1992, 375–76)

Sunk deep in the night.... All around people are asleep. A little bit of playacting, an innocent self-deception, that they are sleeping in houses, in solid beds, under a solid roof,... in reality they have encountered one an-other as they once did back then, and again later, in a desolate region, a camp in the open [*im Freien*], a countless number of people, an army, a nation [*Volk*], under cold sky on cold earth, thrown down where they had earlier stood.... And you are awake watching [*du wachst*], are one of the watchmen [*Wächter*], you find the next one by brandishing a piece of burning wood from the brushwood pile beside you. Why are you watch-ing? Someone must remain wakeful [*einer muss wachen*], it is said. Someone must be there.
—Kafka, "At Night" ("Nachts"; 1970, 309)

The knowers described in these epigraphs would make great panelists at an interdisciplinary conference on the nature of knowing and being a knower. They would have much to say to one another. But what would they say to their audience of "sleepers," in other words, us? If we add the sociologist Erving Goffman to the panel, I know what he would say, because he says it in the introduction to *Frame Analysis,* with typical frame-breaking candor: "I can only suggest that he who would combat false consciousness and awaken people to their true interests has much to do, because the sleep is very deep. And I do not intend here to provide a lull-aby but merely to sneak in and watch the way the people snore" (1974, 14). If we want sparks to fly, we could also invite Plato, a philosopher who has definite ideas about knowing and sleeping and waking people up. Plato is constitutionally unable to stand around like a *flâneur* watching people snore. His sound bite for the C-Span video would be the warning he puts in Socrates' mouth: anyone who clings to phantoms known by opinion and not by knowledge is "dreaming and dozing his present life away and won't wake up until he gets to Hades and falls asleep forever" (*Rep.* 534c).

So it is the sociologist and the anthropologist on the panel who would seemingly rest content with observing the people they want to know about. Plato (and his philosopher kings) would either lead them out of the Cave kicking and screaming, or, at least, project a better class of slide show on the walls of the Cave in which the "sleepers" are watching the shadow plays projected by their politicians, orators, and poets. The pharaoh would also control the spectacles watched by his subjects, using all the forms of royal propaganda, including the image of himself as he who knows everything to the ends of the earth.

But why would an anthropologist see *her* scholarly task as being so similar to that of pharaohs and philosopher-kings? One *could* say that Shakespeare's Henry V going in disguise among his sleeping soldiers is doing "fieldwork" of a sort. Lévi-Strauss's fieldworker must be invisible but omnipresent, seeing and remembering everything. As we have learned, these are among the defining traits of kings. And who is this wakeful, watching anthropologist guarding and from what? Is she or he a shepherd of the people? Isn't this a grandiose job description for an academic of any sort? Not for Lévi-Strauss, who elsewhere describes the "mission" of social anthropology in a utopian society[39] as a matter of "keeping watch" and "standing . . . vigilant guard," especially "in the most troubled times" (1983:30). He, like the kings, takes the process of knowing by surveillance to have a crucial social—and political—function. Perhaps this is the answer to his own questions: Why has he come here? With what hopes or what objectives?

In Lévi-Strauss's account, anthropology is a vocation that requires an ascetic, alienated way of life. It would be worthwhile to read *Triste Tropiques* in light of Nietzsche's description of science as the most devious expression of the ascetic ideal (*Genealogy*, 3 §25; Nietzsche 1968, 420–23). Is it also an "unnatural" life, in the sense in which I described the wakefulness of kings like Shakespeare's Henry V being unnatural? Nietzsche believes that asceticism, and the wholehearted devotion to truth, are against life and therefore against nature (*Genealogy*, 3 §11; Nietzsche 1968, 379–81).[40]

---

[39] In such a future, society would return to the "regular and quasi-crystalline structure" of so-called primitive societies, which he calls "cold" because "their internal environment borders on the zero of historical temperature" (1983, 29–30).

[40] Joseph Conrad (1983, xxxii) suggests that it is unnatural for humans to do research: "man may smile and smile but he is not an investigating animal."

However, the panelist whose position may be the most unnatural is the one whom I have not mentioned thus far, namely, the person addressed by Kafka's narrator. Except that here nature itself is illusory. That is, the part of the "natural" that includes sleeping in houses, in a secure bed, under a secure roof, things that humans make to protect and shelter themselves—the things that Lucretius said humans need that animals do not. All of that human-built security is "a little bit of playacting, an innocent self-deception." But the narrator is not deceived. He knows the truth, and so does the guard whom he is addressing. In "reality," the great mass of people who think that they are sleeping securely are actually sleeping out in the open in a desolate region, under a cold sky on cold earth. Who are these people? One Kafka scholar assumes that they are the biblical Israelites in the wilderness (Robertson 1985, 216). But Kafka is not thinking of any one distinct group of people in one particular desert. His sleepers are strange, like us. The security of their houses and beds is no more real than the Cave inhabited by Plato's prisoners, glued to the tube like troglodyte couch potatoes. Is Kafka's *Wächter* then a philosopher-king or Platonic guardian? The narrator asks the guard a similar question: Why are you awake guarding? The answer: it is said that someone must be awake and guard; someone must be there.

In this case, the guardian's job is not to rouse the people out of their dreams or even to watch them snore. Apparently, it is to protect their sleep—and their illusory security—from being disturbed. The guard is not only sacrificing sleep, he is sacrificing himself as one who bears knowledge of the unsettling truth in order that others are not burdened by it. He is not alone; he is merely "one of" the guards. But the guards are still isolated from one another. They merely signal each other with the burning pieces of wood they wave. Is *this* the best image of the scholar, awake to truths from which others must be protected? Talk about grandiose! As if waving burning wood could be replaced by waving processed-paper offprints of journal articles.

There is no doubt that Lévi-Strauss experienced his brief fieldwork in Brazil as a hero journey, a quest for discovery of the unknown.[41] Kafka was never so sanguine about the burden he bore as a knower. He hardly thought of himself as being kinglike.[42] Nevertheless, kings *can* be role models for researchers, as long as we recognize that different kings (including biblical kings) represent very different types of researchers. At this point, it is necessary to leave our epigraphs and consider the many types of researcher role models that have been offered in various narratives about

---

[41] For details, see Sontag (1966, 69–81), and Geertz (1973; 1988, 33–48).

[42] In fact, he described himself as the slave of his father, whom he likened to a tyrannical ruler; see ch. 11, below.

knowing, whether the narrative identifies itself as philosophy, literature, science, psychology, history, scripture, or anything else. Having done so, I will be able to situate myself among those types, and at the same time prepare for our later assessment of the various biblical kings as knowers.

The first type is the knower as a riddle solver or puzzle solver. The classic example is King Oedipus with the Sphinx's riddle, a scene of knowing that has been appropriated by knowers from Francis Bacon to Freud and depicted by painters from Ingres and Moreau to Tansey.[43] In the Bible, the knower Solomon is a riddle solver when he decides the case of the two harlots (see Lasine 1989a; 1993a[44]). In the modern academic world, Kuhn has been most influential in showing how "normal science" in general is a matter of puzzle solving. Most worrisome is his conclusion (1976, 37) that one function of the paradigm in normal science is to prevent questions from being asked that it cannot answer. The paradigm supplies a "relatively inflexible box into which normal science attempts to force nature." New phenomena that "will not fit in the box are often not seen at all" (1976, 24).[45] The growth of information theory has encouraged this notion of research as a matter of breaking puzzling codes. Whether we are talking about the "genetic code" hidden within DNA, "microhistory" (see, e.g., Burke 1993, 38–43), Sherlock Holmes–style detective work and psychoanalysis (e.g., Ginzburg 1989, 97–102), or even the recent pathetic attempts to "crack" the nonexistent "Bible code," all such work assumes the significance of detail, even seeming trivia. Anyone who spends a sizeable chunk of her or his life poring over the text of the Hebrew Bible knows the powerful attraction of this model.

---

[43] Bacon's Oedipus (1858a, 755–58) is undergoing an ordeal with the Sphinx-monster science. On Freud's identification with Oedipus the riddle solver, and his disciples celebrating that connection with a fiftieth birthday medallion, see Gay 1989, 154, 171, 442). Ingres painted two versions of Oedipus and the Sphinx, one fifty-six years after the other. The second was painted the same year as Gustave Moreau's version (1864). Mark Tansey's *Secret of the Sphinx (Homage to Elihu Vedder)* features a white male wearing a suit and equipped with a reel-to-reel tape recorder and earphones. Crouching, he holds a microphone up to the closed mouth of an Egyptian Sphinx; see Garber, Walkowitz, and Franklin 1996, 1–4.

[44] The discussion of all-seeing kings in ch. 3 will suggest an ideological function for the judgment story that did not receive much attention in these earlier studies. The story lets its audience know that even the most anonymous and marginal citizens would be unable to keep *any* secrets from a panoptic king, who is capable of unmasking the most deeply concealed private emotions and motives.

[45] We have already encountered a lot of "box"/enclosure imagery. Perhaps most significant in this context is J. R. Saul's account of current academic, bureaucratic, and economic "life in a box" (1992, 466–98).

Another time-honored model is knowing by appropriating or assimi-
lating forbidden or dangerous knowledge. Here the most famous example
is Eve in the garden. But other examples abound, from Odysseus's attempt
to learn the valuable knowledge possessed by the dangerous Sirens to
Faust's pact with Mephistopheles and the experiments of Dr. Frankenstein.
A third type is knowing by penetrating[46] and exploring hidden spaces,
both private, domestic spaces and those most foreign and distant. Ancient
knowers in this category include Gilgamesh, Odysseus, the Herodotus who
considered knowledge gained by autopsy to be the most reliable, Epicurus
"bursting through the narrow confines of the gates of nature" (Lucretius,
1.68–75), and Apuleius's Lucius penetrating into the most private areas
after he has been transformed into an ass.[47] In modern times, such knowers range from Descartes to Freud's five-year-old "Little Hans" with his
unquenchable *Wissbegierde,* computer hackers (see Roszak 1994, 149),
and hard-boiled detective heroes.

A fourth type has been discussed already. This is knowing through the
distance sense of sight, the role preferred by monarchs like Louis XIV and
all those who seek to adopt a pose of disinterested detachment when they
do their knowing.[48] A fifth category is knowing through the use of irony,

---

[46] Brenner associates knowing in the biblical sense with male penetration. Males
"are constructed largely as penetrators.... Men 'know' women: women might get
to the stage when they 'know a man' ... but most of them do not" (1997, 178). The
outcome of the events in the garden of Eden point, in part, to "his [Adam's] sexual
penetration (knowledge) of her" (1997, 180). Brenner does not pursue the relationship between knowledge, sexuality, and power beyond this point, in spite of
her book's suggestive title (*The Intercourse of Knowledge*).

[47] While Lucius is an ass in the stall, not a fly on the wall, he recognizes that being
an ass grants him the invisibility of a Gyges-style king and a perfect opportunity for
anthropological fieldwork: "[I indulged] my inborn curiosity, for everyone acted or
spoke as he pleased, without even noticing that I was there" (Apuleius 1962, 192).

[48] Francis Bacon describes a form of "collective research" model that incorporates elements of the researcher-explorer and royal unseen seeing, but with an
emphasis on the way knowledge brings power and profit when it is tightly controlled. In the "New Atlantis," Bacon describes the inhabitants of Bensalem, an
isolated and hidden island, whose society has been based on scientific knowledge
since it was set up centuries earlier by a king named Solamona. This king founded
a governing order of wise men called "Salomon's House," after the biblical king
Solomon (1857, 145). This order is "the very eye of this kingdom" (137, 145). The
fellows of Salomon's House allow none of their special knowledge to reach the
outside world, while they secretly leech out knowledge from the greater world in
order to enrich themselves. They also control what knowledge reaches their own
people: "[we] take all an oath of secrecy, for the concealing of those [discoveries]
which we think fit to keep secret" (165). In a way, Bensalem is the kind of exotic

play, pastiche, and other devices, in order to expose the ignorance of others, to unmask falsehoods, to reveal the social constructedness of "reality" and "the self," or to break down constricting disciplinary and conceptual fences. Writers who adopt such strategies range from Plato's Socrates to a wide variety of postmodern authors.

Someone who wants to analyze biblical kings would certainly seem to have a number of investigative options. In this era of interdisciplinarity, there is no lack of apparently compatible techniques just begging to be applied to any problem at all. And *this* problem? Some sort of psychoanalytic approach? Freud has already made his entree here, so he, and many other psychoanalysts, will be heard from when we discuss narcissism further. And scholars in various fields have claimed many disciplinary linkages to psychoanalysis. For example, psychoanalytic dream interpretation has been likened to both archaeology and detective work.[49] Detectives have been compared to literary critics, historians, riddle solvers, gossipers, and scientific researchers, as well as to archaeologists, kings, and gods.[50] For his part, the *flâneur* has not only been linked to detectives but to archaeologists, hunters, and kings. And gossipers, as well as researchers in general, have been called epistemophiliacs,[51] because they all have inquiring minds that want to know.

---

society that research heroes like Gilgamesh and Odysseus "discover" at the end of their worlds and from which they take back valuable knowledge. However, Bacon has set things up in such a way that this return with a "boon" of knowledge is impossible. Those who stumble upon the island almost always remain there, and the very few who have returned to their ordinary world are not believed when they recount their experiences. Bensalem actually reverses the heroic journey, by periodically sending out its own secret agents to acquire knowledge from the larger world (146; cf. Plato, *Laws* 951b–952d). In a sense, the "Merchants of Light" (Bacon 1857, 164) who conduct this unseen surveillance are the equivalent of King's Eyes and Ears. However, *their* mission involves industrial espionage as much as it does political spying.

[49] E.g., by Freud (see Gay 1989, 170–73; and Spence 1987, 113–19); also see D. Porter 1981, 239–44.

[50] See D. Porter 1981, 226; Winks 1968, xiii–xxiv; Cawelti 1976, 88–89; Lasine 1987; Daniel 1967.

[51] The *flâneur*-detective and *flâneur*-hunter analogies were first developed by Walter Benjamin; see Shields 1994; Ferguson 1994, 31; Frisby 1994, 95. On the *flâneur* as king, see Tester 1994, 4 (the *flâneur*/poet is the "self-proclaimed and self-believing monarch of the crowd"). On the gossiper as scientific researcher, see Ayim 1994, 86–89; Mellenkamp 1992, 156, 169. On affinities between the literary critic and the gossiper, see Ayim 1994, 90. On the knower in general as a hunter, see Ginzburg 1989, 102 and compare Sartre's "Actaeon complex" ("the scientist is the hunter who surprises a white nudity and who violates by looking at it"; 1943, 624).

Admittedly, not all scholars are in favor of an interdisciplinary (or even an eclectic) approach to complex problems. Some contend that *truly* interdisciplinary research is difficult, if not impossible, while others think we should "de-discipline" ourselves altogether.[52] And while there appear to be many methods to choose from, and many ways of combining methods, the fact remains that we usually end up employing the paradigms and methods that we're accustomed to use, perpetuating the biases of our academic fathers and mothers as we proceed. Even when we experiment with methodologies and jargons that are new to us, they soon accommodate themselves to patterns of thought that may date back in our personal histories as far as the crib, *tēbâ*, or exposure on the cold earth. In that sense, it seems inevitable that I will assimilate the biblical narratives to the regnant patterns of my thought, training, and experience,[53] no matter how much I might rummage around in my own bricoleur's tool kit.[54]

---

[52] Among the most prolific advocates of interdisciplinarity is Klein (1976). Among those who believe interdisciplinary research to be difficult or impossible are Fish (1994, 23–27, 231–42) and R. B. Schwartz (1988). The remark about "de-disciplining" ourselves was made by Foucault; see Goldstein 1994, 3. On the necessity of (*and* the problems inherent in) interdisciplinary work, see, among many others, Perloff 1995, 175–80. For two perspectives on the concept of academic "disciplines," see Perloff (1995, 176–77) and Goldstein (1984, 175–79).

[53] As well as the countertransference feelings that I (like everyone else) experience as a reader; see ch. 10 below.

[54] Recently, the terms "*bricolage*" and "*bricoleur*" have been appearing in a wide variety of books in literary theory, anthropology, and sociology, particularly in those devoted to cultural studies. The words have now been applied to a number of disparate phenomena (the *bricoleur's* workshop is even depicted in a witty painting by Mark Tansey [Freeman, Robbe-Grillet, and Tansey 1993, 27]). Here is part of Lévi-Strauss's own characterization of the bricoleur: "the *bricoleur* is … someone who works with his hands and uses circuitous means [*des moyens détournés*] compared to those of a craftsman.… The *bricoleur* is adept at performing a large number of diverse tasks; but, unlike the engineer, he does not subordinate each of them to the availability of raw materials and tools conceived and procured for the purpose of the project. His universe of instruments is closed and the rules of his game are always to make do with 'whatever is at hand' [*les 'moyens du bord'*], that is to say with a set of tools and materials which is … heterogeneous because what it contains bears no relation to the current project, or indeed to any particular project.… Without ever finishing his project, the *bricoleur* always puts something of himself into it" (1966, 17, 21; translation slightly modified). In a footnote, the translator says that while the word "has no precise equivalent in English," he is a "Jack of all trades" or "professional do-it-yourself man," with a "different standing from … the English … handyman." However, on the English-language version of the website for the French-owned chain of 340 "Mr. Bricolage" stores, *bricoleur* is rendered "handyman," and who would know better than Mr. Bricolage himself?

People who identify more with Little Hans than with His Majesty the Baby, and with Lucretius's shipwreck victim more than with Jonah, tend to become the kind of researcher who specializes in asking pesky questions such as "what *is* knowledge?" They do so only because they *have to*. More like Kafka's *Hungerkünstler* than Plato's Socrates, they fast only because they can't keep any food down. Some genetic defect seems to prevent them from swallowing whole many of the most popular academic assumptions, paradigms, and jargons of their time. Unable to emulate a scroll-eating prophet, they end up putting together their own methodological mélange, *bricoleur*-style, using the available academic tools and data that suit their immediate purpose and the problem at hand, leaving it to others to unmask the illusions implied by their idiosyncratic practices. At times, *that* will be my method here.[55]

Most of the chapters that follow deal in depth with a narrative about a biblical king, the divine "king" Yahweh, or quasi-royal figures such as Job and (according to some) Adam. Other sections take a broader approach, offering comparative studies of kings from the ancient Near East, Greece, and modern Europe. The style, presentation, and methodology vary from chapter to chapter, the style ranging from the soberly academic to more unusual styles designed to "defamiliarize" the texts, that is, to interrupt habitual ways of perceiving the narratives in order to promote the formation of new perspectives.[56] Throughout, we will often encounter our six royal traits (if not others) and learn how they express themselves in the specifically biblical context. My title, *Knowing Kings,* plays on several of the senses in which royal knowledge will be investigated. These include "knowing kings," that is, kings who are "knowing," or knowers. It also alludes to the need to consider monarchical knowers "in the biblical sense," that is, as they are described in the textual world of the Hebrew Bible, as opposed to nonbiblical portrayals of royal knowers. Finally, it points to the issue of biblical kings who "know in the biblical sense," that is, the role played by their intercourse with women in their acquisition of, and loss of, knowledge and power.

The textual analyses begin in chapter 2 with a study of Saul, the most vulnerable and exposed of biblical kings. The relationship between loyalty

---

[55] This does not mean that *I* consider my combination of methods and approaches to be arbitrarily chosen or ineffective. Quite the contrary, as one would expect. Nor would I agree with Nietzsche that the "essence" of interpreting *always* involves *all* of the following: "doing violence, pressing into orderly form, abridging, omitting, padding, fabricating, [and] falsifying" (*Genealogy,* 3 §24; Nietzsche, 1998, 109).

[56] On the Russian Formalist concept of defamiliarization (or "making strange"), see, e.g., Ehrlich 1981, 176, 180.

and royal information management is traced through 1 Sam 18–23, with
special emphasis on the roles played by Doeg the Edomite and David in
the fate of the priests at Nob. In this chapter, I directly address the four
main characters in this biblical drama in the second person. Chapter 3
widens the scope to make a detailed comparative analysis of royal information management and the threat of gossip throughout the ancient Near
East and Greece. The chapter concludes with a nonbiblical "case study" of
Sophocles' Oedipus, a king who is ultimately no more successful as an
information manager than was King Saul. In chapter 4, I trace the aspects
of the power-knowledge relationship in biblical narratives about kings.
The chapter begins by relating a bizarre dream populated by a number of
biblical kings. The dream serves to defamiliarize these monarchs, prior to
examining royal "bedroom behavior" in the Bible (e.g., the bedroom assassination of Ishbosheth and the bugged bedroom of the king of Aram in
2 Kgs 6) and suggesting a typology of knowing (and unknowing) biblical
kings. The chapter then proceeds to trace the themes of knowledge and
information management in the stories of David (2 Sam 15–16), Ahab (in
1 Kgs 18), and Zedekiah (in Jer 37–38).

In chapter 5, I begin with a discussion of the history of the terms *private* and *public* and then engage in a comparative study of the ways in
which ancient and modern kings have manipulated the private-public distinction in order to maintain power and avoid the dangers of unlicensed
speech and gossip. With that background, I turn to the court and bedroom
intrigues reported in the Court History of David (2 Sam 3; 11–12; and 1 Kgs
1). I then consider what this analysis implies about the historical value of
the so-called Succession Narrative. Chapters 6 and 7 concentrate on
Solomon. In chapter 6, I investigate the role played by royal "invisibility"
and simulation in monarchical power, comparing the Solomon of Kings
and Chronicles to figures as diverse as Herodotus's Deiokes, the Wizard of
Oz, and the mysterious Klamm in Kafka's *Das Schloss*. Chapter 7 explores
the presentation of Solomon as the "king of desire" in 1 Kgs 3–11, with
special attention to the role of "intertextual indeterminacy" and the portrayals of royal wealth and desire in the surrounding cultures. The issue of
divine testing is then raised for the first time, in relation to God granting
Solomon the wealth and prestige that he apparently did *not* desire. This
section broadens into an intertextual analysis, when I compare Solomon's
situation to that of the wealthy Hezekiah in 2 Chr 32, when he is abandoned and tested by Yahweh.

The last four chapters leave the kings of Israel and Judah in order to
examine the royal traits exhibited by Yahweh in the garden of Eden, the
book of Job, and other biblical texts. These chapters also continue to
address Yahweh's manner of testing his favorite humans and his "parenting style." Chapter 8 analyzes the performance of Yahweh and Adam as

information managers in relation to Eve and the role of the serpent as courtier and informer. The fact that Eve is castigated as a gossiper and made into a scapegoat in postbiblical tradition is taken very seriously, although the style of the chapter is anything but somber. Chapters 9 and 10 both deal with Yahweh's roles in the book of Job. Chapter 9 focuses on the frame narrative. It begins with a discussion of the royal "unaccountability" formula ("who can say to him, 'What are you doing?'"). I then turn to the issues of Yahweh's accountability for his treatment of Job in the prologue and his double role as victimizer and protector of victims. Special attention is given to Yahweh's claim that he had been "incited" by his divine agent and prosecutor, *haśśāṭān*, to move against his human courtier Job "for nothing" (Job 2:3). I conclude the chapter by discussing the relationship between Job's initial "patient" response to the divine testing and his subsequent "impatient" attitude.

The next chapter goes beyond chapter 1 in offering an extended treatment of narcissism in its various senses, all in relation to the behavior and traits of kings and royal parents. It does so by presenting the transcript of a biblical scholar's session with his psychotherapist. This device allows me to make a concise summary of the book's main themes, while defamiliarizing them at the same time. It also collapses the distance between the scholarly pose of detached investigator and my personal response as a reader of disturbing biblical texts. Both literary theorists and psychoanalysts have compared the interaction between therapist and patient to that which occurs when a reader is in the process of reading a text. In the first part of this chapter, I explore this analogy and show its importance for expressing the ways in which readers must (or at least should) come to grips with the ethical and personal issues that arise when they confront troubling biblical texts. The patient's account of his session begins with his report of a dream. He then uses the confidentiality of the therapeutic setting to share his view that the Yahweh of the Joban dialogues is not only a king but a narcissistic (if not abusive) father to Job. He also points to many other passages that display Yahweh's parenting techniques, both with individual creatures and with his "special" son Israel. By the end of the session, the patient has provided us with a number of provocative interpretations that are evaluated in the final chapter.

Chapter 11 takes up the challenge presented by the biblicist-patient by engaging in a multifaceted investigation of Yahweh as king and parent. In addition to asking whether the patient's characterization of Yahweh actually holds up under scrutiny, I view God's alleged abusiveness toward his human children from the perspective of the rapidly growing literature on current-day child abuse. This section of the chapter also considers the views of theologians such as Blumenthal, Chastain, and Brueggemann, who have already described Yahweh as either abusive or capricious. The next section looks at passages in which Yahweh is said to love or hate his human children and takes into account psychological studies of parental ambivalence, narcissism and emotional "splitting." I then turn to a New Testament example of parenting, in order to add another dimension to the analysis; this is the famous parable of the "prodigal son." The next sections take nonbiblical texts that were discussed at the beginning of the book and discuss them in this very different context, in order to shed added light on the biblical passages. The following section analyzes Third Isaiah's picture of Yahweh as father, king, *and* blood-splattered warrior, by contrasting Yahweh with two other divine (or semidivine) warriors, Ramesses II and Homer's Achilleus. Like Yahweh, they boast, in seemingly narcissistic fashion, of having won a victory all by themselves, with no one helping. The last sections of this final chapter make some tentative suggestions on an even thornier issue: whether monotheism itself is the most dramatic example of divine royal narcissism.

2

IN DEFENSE OF DOEG: LOYALTY AND INFORMA-
TION MANAGEMENT IN THE STORY OF SAUL

Secrecy lies at the very core of power. The act of lying in wait for prey is
essentially secret. Hiding,... the lurking creature disappears entirely....
[The despot of history] lies in wait ... the ruler is always currently informed.
—Canetti, *Crowds and Power* (1981, 290, 292)

You do not love me.... you have not told it to me.
—Judges 14:16

I will speak about you to my father; if I see anything I will tell you.... My
father does nothing either great or small without opening my ear about
it.... If I should at all know that it was decided by my father that evil
should come upon you, would I not tell it to you?
—1 Samuel 19:3; 20:2, 9

The slave [δοῦλος] does not know what the master is doing; but I have
called you intimate friends [φίλους],[1] because I have made known to you
everything that I heard from the father.
—John 15:15

THE PLOT

David comes to Nob and obtains holy bread, Goliath's sword, and any
information that might have been forthcoming if and when Ahimelech
inquired of God on David's behalf (1 Sam 21:2–10; 22:15). Among those
present at Nob that day "restrained before Yahweh" is Doeg the Edomite,
chief of Saul's herdsmen and apparently a courtier of special status (21:8;
22:9). Later, Saul accuses his courtiers of conspiracy because they had
failed to "open his ear" concerning his son going in league with the son of

---

[1] In the LXX of Exod 33:11, Yahweh speaks to Moses face to face, as a man does
speaks to his φίλον. On this verse, and the term *philos* (intimate friend or affectionate relative) in classical Greek, see further in ch. 11, below. According to
O'Day, given the way in which the word is used in the Fourth Gospel, "when Jesus
speaks of friends here, he is really saying 'those who are loved'" (1995, 9:758).

Jesse or open his ear about his son establishing his servant against him to lie in wait as an ambusher (לארב) as at that day (22:8). Doeg then informs the king that he had seen David coming to Ahimelech in Nob and that Ahimelech had inquired of Yahweh for him, given him provisions, and given him Goliath's sword (22:9–10). After questioning Ahimelech, Saul orders his runners to slay the priests because their hand was with the rebel David and because they knew that he fled and did not open the king's ear about it (22:17). After his servants refuse to follow Saul's command, the king orders Doeg to fall upon the priests. Doeg then slays eighty-five priests. In addition, he slays the citizens of Nob in the manner of the *ḥērem:* men, women, children and infants, oxen, asses, and sheep (22:18–19). Abiathar, one of Ahimelech's sons, escapes and informs David about the priests being killed. David replies that the deaths are his responsibility because he had known that Doeg would surely inform Saul (22:22).

SCENE I

You can't trust your own son; you can't trust those around you, even your supposedly loyal courtiers. You're supposed to be in the center of things, in the know, inside the Beltway, surrounded by a loving people who all train their desiring eyes on you (see 9:20). You're supposed to do whatever your hand will find (10:7). God's spirit is supposed to empower and inspire you.

But instead you feel alone and abandoned; those you need to trust still surround you, standing while you sit, but they have ceased sharing information with you, or, at least, they've managed and manipulated the information they *do* offer you. They're supposed to report everything to you, accurately, but instead their disinformation disses you, and their silence strips you of security.

You can't trust your son—or your daughter. Your God won't return your calls ("hi, I'm not in right now, well, actually, David's on the other line; we must do lunch—don't call me, I'll call you"). And to top it off, it's your son-in-law whom your people love most—that is, your son-in-law/military commander/music therapist. You are he who was asked for, but you didn't know what you were asking for when you accepted the job from that edgy prophet.

You're a victim of information disloyalty. You're out of the loop. In fact, the loop has become a noose, but not the Greek *noos*. In fact, being out of the loop helped you lose your *noos*—you're out of your mind. For a king, ignorance is not bliss. You get no fresh information, not even gossip, while David has cable and that ephod as a supermodem. David has Netscape and he escapes; you, on the other hand, have no TV, just a scary cable guy named Samuel, who made *one* house call at your request, but not at your house and not while he was alive—and he did *not* say what you wanted to hear.

If you'd been interviewed the way that Pharaoh interviewed old Jacob, you'd probably be asked, "What was the worst moment in your difficult, spirit-driven, life?" You'd answer, "That's easy. It's when I realized that I wasn't the hunter of my enemy but the prey of my trusted servants. There's no feeling of abandonment and despair to match *that* moment. Every bite of betrayed trust violates you and makes you vulnerable to a hostile world that surrounds you."

You felt like a Twelfth Dynasty pharaoh who's afraid to fall asleep at night. You were probably even afraid to go to the bathroom, lest you suffer the scatological fate of a fat Moabite king (Judg 3:20–22)—it's bad enough getting your skirt shortened when you're on the can in a cave (1 Sam 24:4–5). You felt like that Hittite king, Arnuwandas III, who imagined himself abandoned and alone with not a single palace official left, and his chamber-valet fleeing from the chamber (Liverani 1990, 191). You felt like that Aramean king in 2 Kgs 6, who suddenly suspects his courtiers of leaking his secret information to the enemy and not informing him of the leakage—making *him* feel, for the moment, alone and betrayed.

You're reconciled to fighting the Philistines one last time tomorrow, and you probably can't sleep. Ahaswerot used the chronicles detailing the events of his reign as a soporific (Esth 6:1–2). With your luck, you'd get the new revised version written by people with strange non-Israelite names like Polzin, Miscall, Exum, McCarter, Reis, Brueggemann, Gunn, Edelman, and Jobling. You'd read that at Nob you were "paranoid," "deluded," and "demented" (McCarter 1980, 364–65), "see-sawing between paranoid rage and maudlin self-pity" (Reis 1994, 69), "ranting and raving" against your servants like Captain Queeg and going "berserk" like the United States in Vietnam when you ordered the slaying of the priests (Brueggemann 1990, 158, 160). At the very least, you'd read that your accusations against your servants were "clearly somewhat wild" and your judgment against Ahimelech "reckless" (Gunn 1984, 87). Or that Doeg merely embodied your "obvious royal blunders" (Edelman 1991, 166). And, to top it off, you engaged in "epistemological rebellion"; you *weren't* kept in the dark—you simply *refused* to know your dynasty was rejected (Jobling 1986, 28).

So much for sleep and sweet dreams! You'd wish you had a chance to set the record straight, to explain to these strangers what loyalty, sharing information, and withholding information meant in your world. You'd lead them back to the past through Louis XIV's description of the king's function that I discussed in chapter 1. You'd rattle off a catalogue of ancient kings—and their advisors—who saw such panoptic knowledge as a basic requirement for rule and who claimed to have achieved it. You'd list other monarchs who acknowledged that they could extend their powers of perception only by extending their bodies to include their agents, as in the saying, "the king has many ears and many eyes." You'd cite the Neo-Assyrian kings who made every citizen a king's eye and ear by making them take an oath obligating them to open the king's ear about all that they saw and heard. Basically, you'd have them read chapter 3 of this book. Finally, you'd tell these *modern* scholars to review *their own* lives, to think about what it was like when *they* felt alone and abandoned, out of the loop, betrayed, and kept ignorant, like the proverbial husband who's always the last to know.

Everybody but you and Ahimelech knew everything. David fled to Adullam. That was no secret from David's family, *or* to the four hundred distressed, discontented, and indebted Michigan Militia men who gathered around their new commander (1 Sam 22:2). It was only after David heeded Gad and went to Judah proper that you, the king, with all your servants around you, *finally* "heard" that David and the men with him were discovered (נוֹדַע). You responded to this belated (and vague) intelligence report with outrage and hurt. You weren't outraged because information concerning David's whereabouts had been withheld from you—that would be one of your major grievances against the priests *later* (22:17). What concerned you *here* was the failure of your servants to inform you about David's pact with Jonathan: "no one uncovered my ear when my son went in league with the son of Jesse, and no one felt compassion [or pain] for me, or uncovered my ear that my son established (הֵקִים) my servant against me to lie in wait as an ambusher as at this day" (22:8; see Edelman 1991, 174).[2]

That accusation spoke volumes. Powerful kings commission agents to keep an eye on their subjects and their vassals, while the kings themselves remain invisible and inviolable—the kings certainly aren't supposed to be the ones "lurked upon" or ambushed! As Canetti observed, "secrecy lies at the very core of power.... Hiding,... the lurking creature disappears entirely.... [The despot of history] lies in wait ... the ruler is always currently informed" (1981, 290, 292). You, the hunted king, felt yourself surrounded by disloyal servants—the very people who should have been your eyes and ears. You felt that your servants had even severed their emotional bonds with you, so that they didn't have the compassion to feel your pain. This is in stark contrast to the loyal Ziphites later, who twice reported David's location to you, something you took as a sign of their compassion (23:21; 26:1). Your own courtiers didn't even measure up to the servants of *Achish,* who had earlier informed *their* ruler of David's identity (21:12). They even told Achish about that damned song, the one praising David for killing ten thousands in contrast to your thousands, a song that you seemed unable to keep off the airwaves (21:12; cf. 18:7; 29:5).

---

[2] On אָרַב, see Samson in Judg 16:9, 12, and cf. Josh 8:4 and Judg 20:33, 36–38.

Your feeling that *David* was the one lying in wait as an ambusher was actually something of a premonition. The fears you expressed in 22:8 were realized in chapters 24 and 26. In both chapters David accused you of lying in wait and hunting him down, as though he were a dead dog, flea, or partridge (24:12, 15; 26:20). Yet it was *he* who was in the position of the invisible lurker watching you at your most vulnerable, defecating and sleeping. When you covered your feet you did so in the presence of a man more tricky than Ehud. You slept like the royal victims Amenemhet I and Xerxes II, except that this *tardēmâ* was from *Yahweh,* so no one saw it, or knew it, or awoke when David snatched your spear and water jar (26:12). But *David* saw, *David* knew, *David* was awake. Here *David* was the one who sent out spies to obtain accurate information about *your* whereabouts. And in both these incidents one or more of David's men did want to ambush you (24:5, 8; 26:8). (At the same time, your vehement indictment of your courtiers did have one positive effect for you: you seemed to be somewhat better informed after your outburst.[3])

Did Doeg's report *really* cause you to go berserk? Hardly. You summoned all the other priests in Nob, and you interrogated Ahimelech before pronouncing judgment (22:11–18)—very much like the procedure outlined in Deut 13:13–16. And just as you didn't make your judgment on the basis of one uncorroborated report, so in Deut 13:13–15 hearsay concerning disloyalty to Yahweh must be corroborated by questioning before punishment begins. The procedures outlined in loyalty oaths are also quite similar, although the oaths don't always require procedures for investigating the truth of allegations.[4] In some oaths, both those

---

[3] In addition to Doeg's report, several other pieces of information are "reported [ויגד] to Saul," beginning with the fact that David went to Keilah with Abiathar and the ephod (23:7; cf. 23:13; 24:2; 27:4).

[4] While there exist no Israelite loyalty oaths of this type, scholars like Frankena and Weinfeld assume that they must have been in force, either because of the number of ancient Near Eastern oaths (Weinfeld 1972, 89–90) or because their existence would explain the wrath of Saul towards his courtiers in 1 Sam 22 (Frankena 1965, 143; cf. Weinfeld 1972, 99 n. 4). Frankena (1965, 143) notes that if Saul's officials did swear an oath of loyalty to their king, then it is *their* "negligence [that] caused the death of the priests of Nob and their families who had helped David during his flight." If so, the deaths cannot be blamed on a treacherous Doeg or a berserk Saul. The same conclusion can be drawn from Greenfield's citation of 1 Sam 22:19 in relation to Deut 13:13–16, a passage that describes the punishment of an Israelite city that had become disloyal to Yahweh. Apropos of Deut 13:16, Greenfield (1965, 5) notes that "an excellent example of a rebellious city which was treated this way was the priestly city of Nob." It is hardly surprising that scholars who cite ancient Near Eastern parallels and Deut 13 comprise most of the few who refrain from condemning Doeg and Saul in 1 Sam 22, because, from this perspective, Doeg appears

denounced as disloyal and those who fail to report what they have seen
or heard are to be brought to the king for questioning. And, like
Ahimelech, diviners are obligated to inform the king or risk punishment
(Parpola 1972, 31–32; see ch. 3, below).

SCENE II

You're there that day, restrained before Yahweh. Are you standing
there, just minding your own business? You notice David talking to the
priest Ahimelech. Are you even close enough to hear what they're saying
or to see that Ahimelech is trembling? You go back later to the king and
don't mention what you saw. Why? Didn't you think it was worth reporting? Did you forget? Were you being disloyal to your king? Didn't you
realize that David was now the king's enemy and that the best way to engineer a coup is to control the country's communications systems? Suddenly
you hear your king declare his desperate anger at being kept ignorant by
his courtiers. You respond by telling him about David speaking with
Ahimelech. Did you mention it then because you were sorry for Saul? Did
his impotent outrage remind you of your duty to fully and loyally inform
your sovereign?

Lots of questions, no possibility of definite answers. One can't make
a judgment without adequate data. Or *can* one? Let's say you had the
same unpleasant opportunity as Saul—the opportunity to hear how
future commentators would judge *your* fifteen minutes of fame. You'd
learn that you're an informer, a denouncer, a sycophant. And to top it
all off, you're an *E*-DO-MIIITE.... Nobody likes an informer, a snitch, a
stool pigeon, a fink, a *diabolos,*[5] a *śāṭān,* a whistle-blower. And you
weren't just standing there in Nob, you were *lurking and skulking.*
Those scholars with the strange names, and others called Alter and
Heller, declare that you're a "*skulking* Edomite" who was "*lurking* in the
temple" (McCarter 1980, 349, 365) or "*lurking* in the vicinity" (Edelman
1991, 166). You're an "eavesdropper" who was "*lurking* so that you
could witness the exchange between David and Ahimelech without, perhaps, being noticed by them" (R. Alter 1981, 70). Even David himself
describes you as "*skulking* about"—in a modern novel, anyway (Heller
1985, 182). In other words, you're kin to the wicked "skulkers"
and "lurkers" of Ps 10. Psalm 52 actually begins by referring to you,
not as a lurker, but as an informer. In so doing, it makes you into the

---

extremely loyal (especially in contrast to his fellow courtiers), and the seemingly
insane Saul exhibits the same concerns as the presumably sane monarchs discussed
in this book.

[5] Cf. Josephus, *Ant.* 6.12.7 §267 on Doeg's report to Saul.

prototypical treacherous defamer with a tongue like a sharp razor and a relative of the destructive slanderers in Psalms who have tongues like sharp swords (Ps 57:5; 64:4) or swords in their lips (Ps 59:8).[6]

Modern scholars echo these assessments. You are "treacherous" (Gunn 1984, 87)—or, "a treacherous piece of work" (Bartlett 1995, 18); you're "sinister" (McCarter 1980, 347), "ignoble" (Brueggemann 1990, 154), a "ruthless henchman" (Pyper 1996, 175), an "unscrupulous foreigner" (U. Simon 1990, 17), a "dubious adventurer" (Axskjöld 1998, 54). You are either "exceedingly eager" to inform and "excessively eager" to slay the priests (Brueggemann 1990, 159–60), or *slow* to reveal what you saw at Nob, either because you saw nothing amiss with David being at Nob (Miscall 1986, 135) or because your ad hoc report is intended to "cleverly deflect" the king's anger from his servants (Gunn 1984, 87) or "to advance yourself by this ill-advised intervention" (Brueggemann 1990, 159). And, leaving all that aside, your "Edomite associations make you an untrust-worthy entity" (Edelman 1991, 166, 175; cf. Hertzberg 1964, 181).[7]

---

6 These treacherous ones ask "for who does hear?" (59:8) and "who would see them?" (64:6), implying that they can get away with their slander because they act in secret, invisibly. It is because God is himself hiding, and therefore not watching, that they can watch and act in hiding: "He [God] hides his face; he will never see it" (Ps 10:11). According to Psalm 10, these evildoers sit in ambush in lurking places (במארב), stealthily watching or lurking (יצפנו) for vulnerable victims, lying in wait lurking (יארב; cf. 1 Sam 22:8, 13) in secret (Ps 10:8–9). Because the superscriptions to Pss 35, 52, 57, 59, and 64 relate their contents to David, and especially to events related in 1 Sam 19, 22, and 24, Renaissance commentators read them as composed by "David the slandered courtier," who was cruelly wronged by Saul's "followers, flatterers, and yes-men," including the "insidious murderer" Doeg (Prescott 1991, 167–72). In addition, Ps 52 says that Doeg "came to" Saul especially to inform on David, although this is not stated in 1 Sam 21–22.

7 Hertzberg: "the brief mention of the Edomite at this point would certainly have made the listener prick up his ears and think, 'This means no good'." This view overlooks the declarations of Edomite brotherhood in Deut 2 and 23 and reads Genesis in the conventional way, judging Esau/Edom negatively in order to salvage a saintly Jacob out of all that fraternal treachery. Moreover, I do not agree that Hadad the Edomite is a "bad guy" character in 1 Kgs 11:14–22 (Edelman 1995) or that he is even negatively portrayed. The analogies with the Moses and Joseph stories (and even the Jeroboam parallels) suggest a positive evaluation. Only if one assumes that David's and Joab's massacre is not heinous because David is David, and that the narrator assumes that it is acceptable to exterminate Edomites—only then would the parallels be antithetical.

Ironically, Doeg (LXX Doek) is not an Edomite in all versions. In LXX B, OL, and Josephus (*Ant.* 6.12.1 §244) he is an Aramean/Syrian (i.e., switching a *dalet* with a *resh*).

Scholars also find treachery in what you reported and how you reported it. Thus, you offered just enough information to make a damning case, omitting Ahimelech's cautious enquiries about the propriety of David's request (Gunn 1984, 87). Yes, I agree—you would have had to be close to Ahimelech in order to be an ear-witness to his inquiries. But there's no textual evidence that you were. To learn about the three actions you informed Saul about, you only needed to be an eye-witness at a greater distance. It doesn't even say that you were close enough to see that Ahimelech was trembling when he first approached David (1 Sam 21:2).

Nevertheless, Edelman agrees with Gunn that you intended to build "as damaging a case against Ahimelech as possible" (1991, 175), although her reasons differ. She (and Gunn) seem to assume that for the ancient audience and the narrator "the only truly questionable legal infraction" potentially committed by Ahimelech is "his bending of the cultic rules by giving David consecrated bread to eat," a charge that you then "converted ... into what you felt would be an even more incriminating charge for the king" (1991, 175–76). Edelman thinks that the reason that Ahimelech focuses exclusively on the charge that he inquired of God for David is because it's the "least damning" (178), not the most.

Given such universal condemnation, it might seem pointless to launch a defense for you. But how can one do otherwise? In 1 Sam 21–22 you demonstrated your loyalty by informing Saul, whether as an official informer or simply as one of the king's subjects. By the time David came to Nob he has become a major threat to Saul's kingship. David had made a covenant with the king's son that Saul rightly interpreted as signifying the end of his dynasty, for it would result in David replacing Saul's chosen successor Jonathan as the next king (1 Sam 18:3–4; 20:13–17, 30–31; cf. 23:17–18). Saul urgently needed to be informed about all this by his loyal servants.

Someone might object, "All that just means that he's a *loyal* lurker!" But *were* you lurking? The narrator reports that you were present because of sacral constraints that remain unexplained. That is all we know—there's little point in following those who suggest that your presence may have been connected with an act of penance (Hertzberg 1964, 181) or a bodily discharge (Reis 1994, 61). Only those already biased against you could conclude that your mere presence constituted "lurking." And even if it could be shown that you *were* lurking, that wouldn't necessarily have negative implications, from a monarch's point of view. As Canetti suggests in the epigraph, lurking secret agents give a ruler the power that comes from being "always currently informed." From the point of view of those being spied upon, of course, such surveillance could easily conjure up the negative associations surrounding terms like "lurking" and "skulking." In fact, Oppenheim suggests that Mesopotamian descriptions of "the lurking of demons," especially the crouching "ever-lurking *rābiṣu*," represent the "'demonization' of the informer, secret agent, spy or overseer of the king" generated by the "traumatic effect of the secret surveillance of the individual" (1968, 176–77, 179–80). Of course, traumatizing the people in this fashion is one way monarchs discipline and control their fearful subjects even when the kings are physically absent.

From this perspective, your report about the priest inquiring of Yahweh on David's behalf was hardly your least damning charge, as scholars have claimed. It was by far the *most* "damning" charge. Gunn (1984, 88) notes that the ephod Abiathar brings to David after the slayings at Nob gives David "the possibility of direct access to information belonging to the divine world of foreknowledge." The ephod is therefore a source for the kind of information kings require, a source far superior to that of any single King's Eye. This itself explains why you, the king's loyal servant, began with this charge and why both Saul and Ahimelech focused on this issue.

SCENE III

You're standing there, waiting for the king to find someone to execute you. You were trembling when you came to meet David—what are you feeling now? You told Saul that you provided David with information from Yahweh, but nobody seems to have informed *you* about what was really going on at court. You knew David's official titles and his legal relation to the royal family, and maybe you knew that ten-thousand-dead song. But you didn't know anything else, including the fact that the king's son-in-law was now an enemy of the state. Didn't any rumors, celebrity gossip, or tabloids reach you? In your trusting ignorance, little did you know that you were playing blind old Isaac to David's Jacob.

From Saul's perspective, you were doubly a traitor: you didn't share information concerning David's whereabouts with the king, at the same time that you did share information from God with the king's enemy David. You only dug your grave deeper with your three-part defense. You began by asking who among Saul's servants was as trustworthy as David, the king's son-in-law and honored captain of the bodyguard (22:14). Earlier, Jonathan had praised David for his loyalty and service to Saul and Israel, and it worked (19:4–5). But things had changed since then. Think about it. What do being the king's son-in-law, captain of the bodyguard, and honored in the king's house have in common? They are all situations that demand *extra* loyalty to the king, because they are all positions that give a disloyal subject the opportunity, the inside knowledge, and the power to oppose—if not assassinate and replace—the king.

Your second defense ("have I today begun to inquire for him?" [22:15]) only compounded the problem. Your final defense ("thy servant knows nothing of all this, small or great" [22:15]) is all too true. By deceiving you, David gave you what John Poindexter called "absolute deniability" (see ch. 3, below). In your case, however, deniability was a death warrant. Saul justified his capital verdict in two ways. The charge that the priests did not uncover his ear about David's flight (22:17) is true—but only because David had led you to assume that his arrival and departure were *for* Saul, not *from* Saul. Saul's other charge, that the priests had allied themselves with David (22:17), is also true—but only because David led you to assume that allying yourselves with his mission meant *demonstrating* your allegiance to Saul, not *breaking* it.[8]

SCENE IV

You saw the priest come trembling toward you, and all at once you knew how to get what you wanted. But you aren't about to tell a bunch of biblical scholars what you were really thinking and planning. Those scholars have spent years labeling you impenetrable, inscrutable, and elusive—you're not going to spoil their fun now. They'll have to remain as clueless as Ahimelech; you're holding on to your secrets.

You're the fox who knows many things *and* the hedgehog who knows one big one. Here the biggest thing to know is that one can tell who is loyal to whom—who trusts whom—and who loves whom—by noting who shares information with whom. Samson's wife told her bridegroom: "You don't love me.... you haven't told it to me" (Judg 14:16). Jonathan *did* love you, and he *did* tell you everything. Right after your Goliath performance, Jonathan demonstrated his love by making that covenant with you, and by stripping off his robe, clothing, sword, bow, and girdle and giving them to you (1 Sam 18:1, 3–4). But he *also* showed his loyalty and "delight in" (19:1) you by telling you of his father's intention to kill you. He told you to go to a secret place and promised to keep you informed. No wonder Saul accused Jonathan of establishing you against him as an ambusher! Of course, to be effective, Jonathan also had to withhold information from his father the king—not that this was anything new for Jonathan, considering his Rambo-like exploits against the Philistines earlier.

Admittedly, you had to educate Jonathan on the art of information management. Initially—and incredibly—he assumed that it would be easy to determine his father's intentions, because Saul uncovered his ears about everything he did—big or little—and had *no reason* [!] to hide this (20:2)! You quickly wised him up, pointing out that it was precisely *because* Saul knew how Jonathan felt about you (20:3) that he *wouldn't*

---

[8] In Josephus, "Abimelech" himself explicitly makes this point in his defense to Saul [*Ant.* 6.12.7 §§256–258].

let his son know his intentions. Once you clued Jonathan in, you used him to orchestrate a kind of "loyalty test" for Saul. You knew that kings tend to keep potential rivals at court, where they're subject to surveillance and out of contact with their families and supporters. Their children may even be educated with the king's kids, to make sure they learn to see things the king's way (see ch. 3, below). In your case, Saul initially let you go back to Jesse—in fact, he asked your father for permission to keep you at court (16:19, 22). But on the same day that Jonathan's soul became knit with yours, Saul took you and would no longer let you go home to your father's house (בית אביו; 18:2). Of course, Saul *did* send you away as captain of a thousand, and he *did* chase you out of town with assassination attempts. But you wanted to see how Saul would react to your absence when your presence was *expected* at the king's table during the new moon meal. If Saul missed you, Jonathan was to tell the king that you had returned home. Saul did *not* become angry when you were absent the first night or even ask Jonathan why you weren't there (20:24–26). Only when he asked on the second day and Jonathan answered as you directed did Saul become angry (20:27–29). What angered him was not merely the disloyalty implied by your absence and your visit with your family but that Jonathan's information loyalty to *you* constituted disloyalty to himself. *Saul* knew one big thing too, namely, that this was a zero-sum game. He knew that your loyalty pact with Jonathan would result in *your* succeeding to the throne and thereby end his hopes for a dynasty.

Clearly, by the time you showed up in Nob, you knew all about information management, loyalty, and power. When the trembling Ahimelech first approached you, he asked you a straight question: "Why are you alone, and no man [איש] with you?" (21:2). You *didn't* give him a straight answer: "The king has commanded me on a matter, and has said to me, 'Let no איש know anything about the matter on which I have sent you'" (21:3). Even your cover story was all about managing information. As a secret agent of the king, you *had* to be someone who was intensely loyal and close to Saul. By sharing this with the priest, you took him into your confidence, thereby making him part of your fictional mission. Of course, in reality you were conning him, taking him down the garden path.

Saul's fictional order to "let no איש know" is ironic for several reasons. While you were supposedly making Ahimelech an insider by letting him know, you were also letting another איש know—Doeg, "an איש of the servants of Saul." Of course, you weren't letting Ahimelech know anything. In contrast, by letting Doeg know of your interaction with Ahimelech, you were letting an איש who *did* do the king's real business know about your real business with Ahimelech, who had no idea what this real business really was! The fact that you did nothing to prevent or counter this information leak is what led directly to the deaths at Nob, as you (uncharacteristically) admitted in 22:22.

The extent of your guilt becomes *most* glaring when your actions are viewed in terms of the relationship between loyalty and information. At the same time, it is precisely because you were the best at managing the flow of information and truth for your own purposes that it is you and not Saul, Jonathan, or Ahimelech who is alive at the end of the book. And it is because you were a master of "impression management" (Goffman 1959, 208–37) that readers of the narrative are generally no more aware of your villainy than was Ahimelech, hailing you as the hero of the book as though they were Ahimelech or Jonathan praising you to a sceptical Saul—*unless,* of course, they recognize your guilt and *still* remain loyal and loving, echoing loyal O. J. Simpson supporters by declaring, "GUILTY OR NOT WE LOVE U[9] DAVID!!"

---

[9] Sign at a 1994 demonstration in support of O.J. Simpson (J. Alter 1994, 21).

3
ROYAL POWER AND INFORMATION MANAGEMENT IN THE ANCIENT NEAR EAST AND GREECE: A COMPARATIVE PERSPECTIVE

The last chapter was a biblical "case study" of royal information management. It suggested how the participants in such an information system might experience their various roles, from the masterful manager David and loyal informer Doeg, to the unknowing dupes Saul and Ahimelech. Nevertheless, that remains but one example. This chapter offers a comparative analysis of a variety of cases from different cultures and periods, all of which illustrate both the knowing monarch's dream of control and the nightmare of royal ignorance. The cumulative effect of such diverse evidence is to underscore the fact that information management is just as crucial for historical kings as it is for the royal ego described by Plato, Freud, and others (see ch. 1, above). To complete the picture, the chapter concludes with a nonbiblical "case study" of Sophocles' King Oedipus, whose success as information manager (and whose scapegoat function) parallels Saul's.

"A BIRD IS A WORD": MANAGING KNOWLEDGE IN MOTION

Even in your conscious thoughts [במדעך] do not curse the king, and do not curse a rich man even in your bed chamber [ובחדרי משכבך], for the birds of the sky will carry the voice, and a winged creature will report the matter.
—Qoheleth 10:20

Their e[yes] and their ears are near your mouth. Watch yourself.... watch your mouth and over what you h[eard] ... harden (your) heart. For a bird is a word and he who sends it forth is a person of no hea[rt].
—Aramaic Proverbs of Ahiqar, 6.3–4

as for the official in public view, the (very) winds and waters report all that he does; so, behold, his deeds ... cannot be unknown.... Behold, it is the official's place of refuge to act in conformance with the regulations.
—Rekhmire (ANET 213)

"The king has many ears and many eyes." … people are everywhere
afraid to say anything to the discredit of the king, just as if he himself
were listening; or to do anything to harm him, just as if he were present.
—Xenophon, *Cyropaedia* 8.2.12 (1953, 337)

The appeal to bird and wind metaphors in these texts highlights the
key factor of speed in the transmission of information. In addition, birds
(and of course wind) are impossible to grasp and control (hence the
prominence of avians in Yahweh's catalogue of creatures that evade
human control in Job 39). It's not surprising, then, that in one postbiblical
tradition King Solomon not only has a royal bird's-eye view of the world
but an actual hoopoe bird to act as the King's Eye![1] Of course, *gods* don't
need birds, wind, or King's Ears to make them aware of intimate goings on
among humans. Thus, the prayer for the coronation of King Assurbanipal
warns listeners that "he who thinks disrespectful thoughts of the king, a
whirlwind will crush him" (35; Foster 1993, 714). Rather than being a
means of conveying information to the king about the seditious talk, in this
instance the wind is a punishment threatened by gods who already know
that their royal protégé is being verbally attacked.[2]

With or without avian or Aeolian aid, the all-too-human king must
know how to control fast-flying information. Information has been defined
as "knowledge in motion between persons" (Paine 1970, 186; cf. Paine
1967, 282–83) and "a transfer of knowledge" (Machlup 1983, 642).
Information is knowledge on the move. It is appropriate that Rekhmire
speaks not only of wind but of the waters as a means of relaying information. Why? Because, in current English at least, information "flows," and
it can be "leaked." It moves as a liquid. All this moving and "transferring"
of knowledge has also been described with economic metaphors, as a kind
of exchange or *Verkehr*.[3] Information is "currency" that is traded, withheld,
and doled out (J. R. Saul 1992, 474; Spacks 1986, 68). It is not knowledge

---

[1] In these (mostly Islamic) legends, Solomon has a variety of animal assistants, one
of which is the hoopoe. The bird reports to Solomon the existence of a wealthy
queen in Sheba who does not acknowledge him or God (see, e.g., Qur'an 27:15–44).

[2] In sixteenth-century England, more prosaic punishments were decreed for such
offenses against the king. Legislation of 1555 "imposed heavy punishments of pillory
and fine for speaking 'false, sedicious and sclaunderous news, rumours, sayenges
and tales, ageynst our most dreadd sovereigne lorde and king,… of whome we ar
forbidden to thincke evill and muche more to speake evell'" (A. Fox 1997, 599).

[3] On the sexual and nonsexual meanings of *Verkehr*, see ch. 1. Seow (1997, 333)
suggests that מדע in Qoh 10:20, which is usually rendered "thoughts," may have
"sexual connotations, as the root *ydʿ* so often does." If so, מדע "would refer literally to a place of 'knowing' in the sexual sense" and be "a synonym for the
bedroom." Seow (328) translates במדעך with "in your intimacy."

itself that is power; the power comes from controlling the movement of knowledge. As J. R. Saul puts it, "[the power of the elites] depends *not* on the effect with which they use [their] knowledge but on the effectiveness with which they *control* its use" (1992, 8; emphasis added). This traffic in knowledge can even include "offering misleading information" (474), that is, counterfeit knowledge.

What Saul (1992, 8) goes on to say about modern authority applies to ancient monarchies as well: "uncontrolled words are consistently more dangerous to established authority than armed forces." These rulers must control the flow of information reaching the palace and prevent the "leaking" of state secrets. One reason that kings fear gossip—both gossip within the court and gossip among the populace in the public domain—is that it represents the flow of information outside the control of the monarch and his agents. Just as they want their subjects to be visible to them while they remain invisible, they want all information concerning what others say to flow exclusively to them, while their private speech remains inaudible to the public. In the monarch's dream of control, the flow of information is almost exclusively centripetal. And just as kings present a carefully crafted image of themselves to their subjects, they dream of managing and controlling whatever information they allow to flow centrifugally.

The fact that kings are aware of the importance of controlling the flow of information is evident from the emphasis given to the roles played by informers and spies in historical and bureaucratic writings composed at the court, as well as in loyalty oaths, royal correspondence, and divinatory texts. The destructive power assigned to gossip and rumor is equally evident. Accounts of succession struggles and harem conspiracies, letters sent to the king reporting cases of slander, and the advice given by (or to) monarchs in wisdom literature all testify to a pervasive fear of uncontrolled information, a fear that can turn the king's dream of control into a nightmare. In the nightmare, uncontrolled malicious and slanderous speech pollutes the stream of information flowing to and from the palace. The results can be catastrophic. As Sirach puts it, the "third tongue" can demolish great cities and turn the dynasties (οἰκίας) of the great upside down (28:14).[4]

Earlier we examined Louis XIV's fantasy of panoptic knowledge and control. That dream is not his alone; in fact, one could say that Louis is describing the collective dream of all kings, the royal wish-fulfillment dream par excellence. Similar depictions of royal knowledge and control can be found in a wide variety of ancient Near Eastern and Greek writings, as well as in texts written long after Louis's time. For example, Rekhmire proclaims that "his majesty knew that which occurred; there was nothing

---

[4] Cf. Herodotus *Hist.* 5.31; 6.9; Skehan and Di Lella 1987, 360, 365.

which he did not know" (*ARE* 2:267). Thutmose III himself attributes his success to his father Amon, who "knows heaven, and knows earth, he sees the whole earth hourly" (*ARE* 2:226). Anticipating Louis's claim of godlike insight into the secrets of his courtiers and subjects, Isocrates has King Nicocles of Cyprus tell his people, "let none of you imagine that even what he secretly thinks in his own heart will be hidden from me; nay, let him believe that, though I may be absent in body, yet my thoughts are present at what goes on; for, being of this opinion, you will be more restrained in your deliberations on all matters" (*Nic.* 51; 1961, 107).[5]

The king at the center of this dream of monarchical omniscience needs a dream home. Herodotus's Deiokes had his palace in Ecbatana constructed within seven concentric walls, outside of which the people were obliged to live (*Hist.* 1.99). He then inaugurated the practice of prohibiting anyone from having admittance to the king except through messengers, so that he might remain invisible, while the spies and eavesdroppers he put throughout his realm kept the people "visible" to him (1.100; see further in ch. 6, below). Pseudo-Aristotle improves this royal dream-house. He describes the king of Persia living "invisible to all" in a marvelous palace in Susa or Ecbatana. Among the leaders serving in various capacities at the surrounding wall and its many gate-towers and gateways were the "guardians of each outer wall, called Guards and Eavesdroppers [ὠτακουσταὶ], so that the King himself, who had the name of Master and God, might see everything and hear everything" (*Mund.* 398a14–20; 1955, 389 [trans. slightly modified]).

Pseudo-Aristotle's dream palace reveals how Louis, Rekhmire, and Nicocles can claim to know and see and hear everything in their realm, including the secret thoughts of their subjects. Here the king's body includes the eyes and ears of his agents, whether they are stationed at the palace wall or dispatched like the spies sent by Deiokes throughout his domain.[6] Both illustrate our epigraph from Xenophon: "The king has many ears and many eyes." Xenophon stresses that King Cyrus listened to anybody who may have heard or seen anything worthy of his attention and rewarded them liberally

---

[5] And if their thoughts cannot be hidden from the king, neither can their movements. In an Amarna letter from Tagi to the pharaoh, this vassal proclaims: "Should we go up into the sky, or should we go down into the netherworld, our head is in your hand" (EA 264:15–19; Moran 1992, 313). It is equally impossible to hide or escape from King Yahweh in the sky or in Sheol (Amos 9:2 and Ps 139:7–8), a fact that Jonah had to learn the hard way.

[6] Such spies may even be sent to the homes of the king's courtiers. Richard II of England possessed a treatise (*De quadripartita speculum regis specie libellum*) that recommends that "prior to appointing lords to his council, a king should first infiltrate their households to discover what they say in secret about him" (Bennett 1999, 43).

(*Cyr.* 8.2.10–11), although he also concedes that there was one official known as the King's Eye (8.6.16; cf. Herodotus, *Hist.* 1.114). And the epigraph echoes Nicocles in believing that informers cause all the people to be "afraid to say anything to the discredit of the king, just as if he himself were listening; or to do anything to harm him, just as if he were present."

Behind the claims of omniscience made by Louis, Rekhmire, and Nicocles is a similar dependence on spies and informers.[7] Louis's *intendants* "acted as the government's eyes and ears throughout France" and were themselves kept under close surveillance (D. L. Smith 1992, 22). According to Saint-Simon, Louis "had spies and reporters everywhere and of all descriptions" (1966, 255). Being "even more interested in gossip than people imagined," Louis ordered extra members of the Swiss Guard and had them secretly "prowl around morning, noon, and night on all the staircases and in the corridors, passages and privies," taking notes and making reports (Saint-Simon 1967, 277–78). An important official in the courts of Egyptian kings was the "chief of secrets," a position that could be divided into "chief of secrets of secret missions," "chief of things that only one man can see/hear," and "chief of the king everywhere" (Grimal 1992, 90). Thutmose's vizier Rekhmire himself bore the title "chief of secrets" (*ARE* 2:290). Even Isocrates' seemingly omniscient mind-reader Nicocles has to concede his dependence on informers when he tells his people "Do not keep silent if you see any who are disloyal to my rule, but expose them; and believe that those who aid in concealing crime deserve the same punishment as those who commit it" (*Nic.* 53; 1961, 107). For his part, Aristotle advises tyrants to "have spies like the women called 'talebearing *provocatrices*' [ποταγωγίδες] at Syracuse and the eavesdroppers [ὠτακουστὰς] that used to be sent out by Hiero … (for they speak less freely due to fear of such men and are less likely to escape notice if they do speak freely)" (*Pol.* 1313b11–17; 1959, 460). While Xenophon's Cyrus rewarded informers, Nicocles threatens punishment for failing to denounce disloyal subjects. Whether one uses the carrot or the stick, however, the fact remains that what prompts the self-discipline of the king's subjects is fear of spies and informers, the king's many ears and eyes.

Dreaming with a bird's-eye view, Louis XIV envisions a king who exercises control over his domain with seemingly godlike detachment and security. Seen from his subjects' worm's-eye view, however, this dream is based on the harsh realities of surveillance and denunciation by wakeful

---

[7] Writing during the Amarna period, about 150 years after Rekhmire, Rib-Hadda of Byblos writes to Pharaoh Amenhotep IV, saying, "I am your loyal servant, and whatever I hear I write to [my] lord" (EA 116:6–16; Moran 1992, 191; cf. xxxv–xxxvi). To R. Cohen (2000, 90), this "suggests that passing on intelligence was one of the understood duties of the vassal."

humans on whom the monarch is utterly dependent. The monarch who aspires to panoptic knowledge must depend on others to be his eyes and ears. Yet the informers upon whom he must place his trust have been made to live and to make their denunciations in a climate of total *dis*trust. This is hardly a comforting thought for any kind of leader. Referring to the French Revolution, one scholar recently remarked that "denunciation … was the democratization of surveillance" (Baker 1994, 200), but it is evident that pandemic denunciation also plays a key role in states led by a single ruler. Josef Stalin could have been following Aristotle's and Isocrates' examples when he made one of his central goals "the disintegration of family loyalty," isolated everyone, encouraged children and relatives to denounce their parents, and, like Assyrian loyalty oaths millennia in the past, required that a citizen "must report everything he sees and hears" (Conquest 1973, 378–79).

The instruction Pharaoh Amenemhet I wrote for his son and successor Sesostris (see ch. 1, above) contrasts dramatically with the instruction of Louis XIV for the Dauphin. The relationship between knowledge and trust stands out in this text. Amenemhet, who was attacked and probably killed by conspirators when he was asleep (see, e.g., Grimal 1992, 161–64; contrast Quirke 1992, 74), tells his son that when he lies down, he must guard his heart himself, for no man has adherents in the day of distress. Because others have betrayed his trust—including women and those he has aided and nurtured in the palace (Lichtheim 1973, 136–37; cf. *ANET* 419 n. 11)—he advises his son not to trust even his brother, friend, or intimates. Nor is he to trust "subjects who are nobodies," because of their "plotting one is not aware" (Lichtheim 1973, 136; cf. 138 n. 3). Sesostris must remember what has happened in the past, because "success will elude him who ignores what he should know" (137). What he most needs to know, it seems, is that he cannot count on the loyalty of even his courtiers and his family. A number of scholars have found a reflection of this ever-watchful, sleepless, suspicious, and bitter monarch in extant statues of Twelfth Dynasty kings, including Sesostris III and Amenemhet III. The faces of the kings typically feature hollows under heavy-lidded eyes, furrowed brows, and deep creases at the corners of the mouths (see the cover of this book; also Wilson 1958, 132–33; W. S. Smith 1981, 185–86; Hayes 1990, 175–76, 197–99). These are the faces of monarchs who cannot relax their vigilance long enough to fall asleep and have Louis's dream of royal omniscience and control.

Suspicions about the loyalty of family, friends, and courtiers also characterize Neo-Assyrian texts that direct the king's subjects to act as his eyes and ears. For the most part, these directives are embedded in loyalty oaths and treaties. In a letter to Assurbanipal, one of the king's servants notes that "in the oaths it is prescribed, 'All that you see, and hear write me'" ([*ina libbi*ᵇⁱ] *adie iššáṭir umma mala tammara ù tašimma' šuprani*; *ABL*

831, rev. 2–5; Pfeiffer 1935, 178–79). This formula is also cited in another letter, in which the writers denounce certain soldiers and let the king know that they are bringing the culprits and the witnesses to the king for questioning (*ABL* 472; Pfeiffer 1935, 59).

Examples of the oaths themselves are also in existence. In a loyalty oath to Assurbanipal imposed by his grandmother Zakutu, the royal family, courtiers, and the whole nation are told to "come and inform" Zakutu ([*uznī*] ... *latupattaniu;* lit. open the ear) if they should hear of any not-good word or plan of rebellion against Assurbanipal (*ABL* 1239, rev. 2–17; Parpola and Watanabe 1988, 63–64). Not only must they inform if the rebels are the king's brothers or the royal line; they must do so if the rebels are the *informer's* own brothers or friends (rev. 18–27). Assurbanipal's treaty with Babylonian allies (*ABL* 1105) has a different focus. Depending on how one reads the text, the allies either swear not to conceal or hide any message or messenger sent by the king's rebellious brother Šamaš-šumu-ukin (6–9, Parpola and Watanabe 1988, 65), or swear that they have concealed and will continue to conceal information from enemies of Assurbanipal (Grayson 1987, 141, 144). When they have heard or seen a conspirator who speaks not-good words against Assurbanipal, they will put him in irons and take him to the king (12–16; Grayson: 141, 144). The oaths also stipulate that those who have seen or heard something but do not tell the king will themselves be summoned and questioned (*ABL* 656; see Weisberg 1967, 36).

It is the so-called vassal treaties of Esarhaddon (VTE) that are most insistent about the people reporting and not concealing anything they might have heard that could endanger Esarhaddon's sons Assurbanipal and Šamaš-šumu-ukin. The existing composite text is primarily a loyalty pact rather than a vassal treaty, a pact that, like the later Zakutu treaty, was imposed on the entire nation (see Parpola and Watanabe 1988, xxx; McCarthy 1981, 116). The occasion is the irregular accession of the younger son Assurbanipal to the Assyrian throne, a situation that, like the irregular accession of his father Esarhaddon, invited rebellion by rival members of his family and the court. The treaty repeatedly stresses that if you hear of any such plot "you shall not conceal it but come and report it to Assurbanipal" (VTE 73–82, 108–122, 500–506; cf. 130–146 ["you shall open the ear"]; Parpola and Watanabe 1988, 31–50). The list of persons who might be plotting not only includes enemies, allies, courtiers, scholars, prophets, and ecstatics, but the members of the crown prince's family, including his brothers, uncles, and cousins. While his brothers might lead others to slander (*karṣu,* 323; cf. 332, 341) the crown prince, plotters might also slander his brothers in order to cause strife and division within the royal family (VTE 318–372). And as was the case with the Zakutu treaty, the informer must be prepared to denounce his own brothers as well as his own sons and daughters (VTE 115–116).

Only the extispicy texts that ask the god Šamaš whether certain individuals and classes will rebel against Esarhaddon and Assurbanipal have
more exhaustive lists of potentially disloyal people surrounding the king.
These include not only the relatives of the king and all officials, both
bearded and eunuch, but all military personnel, foreign nationals as well
as their brothers, friends and guests, all cooks, lackeys, craftsmen, tailors,
and so on (Starr 1990, 148–49, 152). Whatever the results of their inquiries,
Assyrian diviners were obliged to inform the king or risk punishment
(Parpola 1972, 31–32).

According to Paul Garelli (1973, 202), members of the Assyrian court
did not hesitate to denounce or even calumniate their rivals because they
had to compete for the attention of the king. The texts just cited lend support for Garelli's claim that the system "secreted" coteries and intrigues. He
also notes that the archives at Nineveh are "glutted" with denunciations
(202) and claims that an "atmosphere of delation" ruled in the court (206).
At times an individual might even write the king to denounce others for
their unfounded denunciations of the writer (e.g., *ABL* 716; Pfeiffer 1935,
145–46; Oppenheim 1967 179–81)! Given this climate of distrust, suspected
disloyalty, and intrigue—a climate one might have thought more characteristic of the court of Louis XIV than the court of Esarhaddon or
Assurbanipal—it should not be surprising that Assyrians in responsible
positions had to "submit to a triple, nay, quadruple surveillance": in addition to the surveillance that accompanied the *adê* agreements, they had to
render an account of their activities to their superiors at every level of the
administrative pyramid (Garelli 1973, 206).

Clearly, the ways in which Assyrian, Egyptian, and Greek texts envision the monarch's dream—and the devices needed to make that dream a
practical reality—are remarkably similar.[8] However, they are also remarkably similar to a recent dream of social and political control that is not only
said to be fundamentally different from the power exercised by monarchy
but to have replaced it. This is Foucault's now-familiar notion of panopticism, the architectural symbol of which is Bentham's Panopticon. The
Panopticon is a circular structure consisting of cells along the periphery,
from which all inmates can be watched by a supervisor in a central tower
(Foucault 1979, 200). Because of the arrangement of windows and light,
"in the peripheric ring, one is totally seen, without ever seeing; in the central tower, one sees everything without ever being seen" (1979, 202). While
Foucault considers such unseen surveillance to be an innovation opposed
to the monarchical use of spectacle, it is profoundly characteristic of

---

[8] Two new studies of ancient "information gathering" and "intelligence" have just
appeared, one on Amarna Age Egypt and Palestine (R. Cohen 2000) and one on
classical Greece (Russell 1999).

monarchical power. The walls of the Panopticon could just as well be the walls surrounding the palace of the unseen Deiokes or the palace gates along which the people are to remain "always visible," as Aristotle puts it in his advice to tyrants. In fact, one could say that the monarchical state is the Panopticon writ large.

As far as the invisible observer is concerned, Foucault notes that in the central tower the director may spy on all his subordinates, while inspectors can in turn observe the director (1979, 204). Again, this is little different from the three or four levels of surveillance to which Assyrian officials had to submit or the close surveillance of Louis XIV's *intendants*. Foucault even finds that the eighteenth-century police, who were admittedly "in the hands of the king," actually added a new disciplinary function to monarchical power by linking it "to the lowest levels of power disseminated in society" (214). Yet when Foucault describes the dissemination of power with the police, his account is identical to the ancient accounts of the capillaries of monarchical power discussed earlier: "this power had to be given the instrument of ... omnipresent surveillance, capable of making all visible, as long as it could itself remain invisible.... thousands of eyes posted everywhere" (214). These "eyes" included observers, secret agents, informers, and other spies (214).

Foucault's advocates might object that what is truly new about panopticism is "disciplinary power, a system of surveillance that is interiorized to the point that each person is his or her own overseer" (Sarup 1989, 74). Yet, how different is this phenomenon from the self-discipline of the subjects described by Xenophon, Isocrates, and Aristotle, who restrain their thoughts, words, and actions just as if the absent king were present, and who end up having little spirit of their own? It seems that the monarchical dream of control is still being dreamt, no matter whether there is an invisible king sleeping behind palace walls or an anonymous observer in the central tower of the Panopticon.

THE NIGHTMARE BIRD *FAMA*: UNCONTROLLED SPEECH AND HAREM CONSPIRACY

A Thousand busy Tongues the Goddess bears,
And Thousand open Eyes, and Thousand list'ning Ears.
—Pope, *Temple of Fame,* 268–69 (1942, 259)

Gossip [*Fama*], an evil which nothing outstrips in speed; she grows from her swiftness, she acquires strength by moving; ... a monster to be dreaded, huge; and, as many as are the feathers on the body, so many, amazing to tell, are the eyes ... which watch below her, so many the tongues, so many the mouths that tattle, so many the ears she causes to prick up ... and [she] does not close her eyes in sleep.... she sits at

watch high on a roof or lofty tower, and terrifies great cities, as much a
messenger of what is false and distorted as of the truth.
—Virgil, *Aeneid* 4.174–175, 181–183, 185 (Dyer 1989, 31); 186–187 (Virgil
   1965, 75); 188 (Virgil 1972, 348, modified)

Foucault's version of the monarch's dream featured "thousands of eyes
posted everywhere" in the service of omnipresent surveillance. Virgil's
goddess Fama (Gossip or Rumor), as Pope describes it, also features "a
thousand open eyes." However, these eyes and the thousand listening ears
are not the *king's* eyes and ears, directing the flow of information exclusively to the monarch in his palace. On the contrary, Fama reverses the
direction of the flow from the palace to the periphery, making public the
private secrets of the ruler. The "dreaded monster" Fama is the king's worst
nightmare, an avian Goodyear blimp from hell.

In this case it is Queen Dido's nightmare, for Gossip is spreading
abroad word of her love affair with the hero Aeneas. With the publicity
comes shame. This is not because Dido's indulgence of her private desires
has led the queen to neglect her royal duties, as is commonly—but incor-
rectly—assumed (see 4.260, 265–267; cf. Rudd 1990, 149–51). This
assumption is promoted by Fama herself. Gossip, says Virgil, "acquires
strength" by moving; that is, the news being disseminated grows, but only
in a specific direction. Gossip tendentiously interprets the actions of public figures in terms of personalities rather than issues, magnifying the role
of lust and deception even as it deplores lust and deception. Hence, gossip is the messenger of what is false and distorted as well as of what is
true. This is particularly true concerning intrigue and conspiracy in the
royal court. In this instance, the shame brought on Dido comes from the
fact that in "marrying" Aeneas she has violated the oath of loyalty she had
made to her deceased first husband Synchaeus, the victim of Dido's devious and disloyal brother Pygmalion the ruler of Tyre, who murdered
Synchaeus to acquire his vast wealth (1.340–364; 4.15–29, 552). Because
Dido had vowed never to marry again, and now considers herself married
to Aeneas, she joins her brother in being disloyal to Synchaeus. In the
king's dream of control, loyalty oaths ensure that news of disloyalty
throughout the kingdom will be sent to the ruler in the palace. In contrast,
Queen Dido's violation of her own loyalty oath leads to gossip spreading
throughout the kingdom from the palace.

Yet the news that is actually disseminated through the kingdom does
not focus on the queen's oath. Rather, the lurid account broadcast by Fama
alleges that Dido and Aeneas are warming the winter with their sensual
lovemaking, forgetful of their kingdoms (4.193–194). It is this distorted
account that infuriates the African king Iarbas, a rejected suitor who sees
himself as Dido's benefactor and ally. Iarbas now feels himself wronged by

a woman who rejected him in favor of a perfumed Paris with a half-male crew. This is just one of the elements that he adds to his augmented and distorted version of the gossip when he indignantly prays to Jupiter (4.206–218). As a result, when Jupiter turns *his* divine eye to the palace walls and sends *his* swift messenger Mercury to Aeneas with orders to abandon Dido, he does so not as a divine king who has been an eye-witness to the events, or even as a king who has been correctly informed by one of his human agents. On the contrary, he "sees" the two lovers with the eyes of Gossip—and Iarbas—and sees them as forgetting their better fame (4.221).

The role played by Fama in the story of Dido and Aeneas shows how easily the monarch's dream of control can be turned upside down. Most of the elements of the dream are still present, but they serve inverted functions. Instead of the King's Eyes and Ears directing the flow of information centripetally to the palace, the eyes and ears of gossipers spread information centrifugally from the palace walls, transforming the information as they proceed. While the information flows in opposite directions and with opposite effect, in both cases it moves with amazing speed. Soldiers who took a loyalty oath to Eumenes I promise that, if someone should hear of a person plotting rebellion, "he will inform as fast as possible" (Weinfeld 1976, 388). Pseudo-Aristotle claims that thanks to the Persian kings' Eavesdroppers, couriers, scouts, and messengers, "the King knew the same day all that was news in Asia" (6.398a34–35; 1955, 389). Oppenheim is even more hyperbolic when he asserts that the King's Eyes and Ears described in Greek and Mesopotamian texts keep the king "constantly informed and aware of every ... disloyal act the very moment it is committed" (1968, 175; cf. 180). Virgil's Gossip displays equally astounding speed. In fact, "nothing outstrips [her] in speed"—she even "grows from her swiftness."

This fact is well known to Memucan, the high official of King Ahasuerus (Xerxes) in the book of Esther. Memucan advises the king that an act just committed by Queen Vashti poses an immediate and serious threat to the entire empire: "Not only has Queen Vashti done wrong to the king, but also to *all* the officials and *all* the peoples who are in *all* the provinces.... For this deed ... will go out to *all* women.... they will say, 'King Ahasuerus commanded Queen Vashti to be brought before him, and she did not come.' *This very day* the princesses ... who have heard of the queen's deed will say this to *all* the king's princes" (1:16–18; NRSV modified, emphasis added). Memucan raises the frightening specter (for his male audience) of gossip about the queen's refusal spreading swiftly through the empire out of the king's control, from one female to the next. This, he imagines, will cause the gossipers to feel contempt for their husbands (1:17–18), precisely the kind of self-righteous moral judgment that is characteristic of gossip.

Royal fear of uncontrolled and uncontrollable speech is also evident in a variety of other ancient Near Eastern texts, albeit without the baroque touches of Virgil's Fama and the panicky tones of Memucan's vision. Even divinatory texts exhibit deep concern about uncontrolled speech and information flow. One prediction says that a *šatammu* (palace steward or *intendant*) will not cease to divulge (secret) matters (Bottero 1973, 141). This text knows that information is liquid, and can therefore be leaked. Similarly, Bottero (142) interprets references to the *namzaqu*, the "woman who delivers the key," as denoting a gossip or busybody (*commère*) who will have improperly handed over the key to the palace or main gate to an enemy, for whatever reward. In general, Bottero finds that the dossier of spies in the oracular literature is rather hefty, whether it is a matter of "people of the tongue" (*ša lišânim*), those who listen (*ša uzni;* lit., people of the ears), or those who observe (*ša daqilti*). Finally, these texts are also aware of uncontrolled speech in the nation at large. When it takes the form of public conversation and palaver, or rumor and hearsay (*on-dit*), it is called "mouth of the country" (*pî mâtim;* 145–46).

However, it is in the treaties and loyalty oaths that the dangers of gossip, rumor, and calumny are most urgently expressed. For example, in their zeal to prevent any kind of plotting against Assurbanipal and Šamaš-šumu-ukin, the vassal treaties of Esarhaddon focus primarily on the problem of uncontrolled speech. Any "improper, unsuitable or unseemly word" hostile to Assurbanipal must be reported by the hearer (VTE 73–82; cf. 108–122, 147–152, 502, and above). The same is true of "malicious whispers" or those who "spread rumors" (VTE 500; Parpola and Watanabe 1988, 50; Weinfeld 1972, 93 n. 8). Those accepting the treaty must not engage in slander or say any evil word about the royal family (VTE 270, 360–372). Esarhaddon's accession treaty indicates that loyal subjects must not only report those who speak not-good words about the king; they themselves must "(only) speak good of [the king]" (rev. 8; Parpola and Watanabe 1988, 22).

Because the treaties consistently target gossip, rumor, and slander as the secret weapons that are consistently employed by conspirators, they are in effect "arms control treaties." The need for such control is underscored in Esarhaddon's own account of his irregular succession to the throne. By choosing the youngest son among his elder brothers (A.I.8–11; Borger 1956, 40), Sennacherib prompted the very sort of family rivalry and strife that the later loyalty oaths and vassal treaties of his chosen son Esarhaddon are so desperate to prevent. Esarhaddon reports that his brothers used evil gossip (*lišân lemuttim;* lit. evil tongue), slander (*karṣi*), and lies (*tašqirti*) behind his back to alienate his father from him (A.I.25–29; Borger 1956, 41). He is quick to add that "secretly" his father still intended to make Esarhaddon his successor (A.I.30–31; Borger 1956, 42). After fleeing and hiding in a secret location, his brothers fought one another in

Nineveh like butting goats, as the gods looked on. Because the Assyrians had taken a loyalty oath (*adê;* A.I.50; Borger 1956, 43) to protect his kingship, they did not aid his brothers (just as those addressed by the later vassal treaties are admonished not to join any plots against Assurbanipal [e.g., VTE 173–179, 214–225]). Fortunately for Esarhaddon, the news of his brothers' evil deeds reached him immediately (*urrubiš;* A.I.55; Borger 1956, 43)—that is, with the speed of a rumor—so that he could pray to the gods and follow their advice to attack his enemies without delay.

A similar concern over the threat posed by uncontrolled speech is expressed in Egyptian texts, including accounts of succession struggles and harem conspiracies. I have already alluded to the conspiracy directed against the Twelfth Dynasty pharaoh Amenemhet, who was not so lucky as Esarhaddon. Is it merely a coincidence that the curses in the Egyptian execration texts, which date from the middle of the Twelfth Dynasty, lay great emphasis on the danger presented by "every evil word, every evil speech, every evil slander," uttered by every male, female, official, or eunuch who "may talk of fighting, or who may talk of rebelling" (*ANET* 329)?

Records of the later conspiracy against Ramesses III show that it is indeed no coincidence. Like the account of the harem conspiracy against Amenemhet I, the plot against Ramesses III is also reported by the king himself in a text that was probably composed after his death, during the reign of his successor. However, in this case the text (as well as the evidence provided by the king's mummy) suggests that the conspiracy failed (see Gardiner 1961, 291–92; Grimal 1992, 276). The most complete report of the event is the description of the conspirators' trial (*ANET* 214–16; cf. de Buck 1937). The number of conspirators is extraordinary. The instigator of the plot is Tiy, a second wife of Ramesses, who is attempting to secure the succession for her son Pentaweret. The twenty-eight defendants, who either participated or failed to report their knowledge of the conspiracy, include a number of high-ranking harem officials and "the women of the harem," as well as the wives of the doorkeepers and a troup commander suborned by his sister who had sent him a message from within the harem (de Buck 1937, 154–55; *ANET* 214–15). For the plot to succeed, the conspirators had to be able to pass information between the ultraprivate zone of the harem and the world outside. To do so they had to disable whatever mechanisms the king had put in place to prevent unwanted access to whatever he wanted to keep secret. Two fragmentary papyri describing the harem conspiracy claim that the rebels attempted to use magic scrolls and wax figurines to disable the harem guards so that they could not detect or resist the passage of short messages in and out of the harem (*ARE* 4:221; see Wilson 1958, 269 and contrast Goedicke 1963). For reasons left unstated, the plot failed and the pharaoh gained full knowledge of the conspiracy before it was too late. With this knowledge ended the threat to royal control over the flow of information—and thereby the threat against the life of the king himself.

While the monarch's dream of control typically stresses the people's visibility and the king's invisibility, the plot against Ramesses III implies that the monarch must also control oral communication by his visible subjects, especially across the boundary that separates the king's invisible private realm from the world outside. The Panopticon suggests a radical way for kings to meet this royal need. According to Foucault (1979, 200), the side walls that separate the inmates in their individual cells along the periphery prevent each from coming in contact with "his companions." As a result, "he is seen, but he does not see; he is the object of information, never a subject in communication." A king who could put his people into such individual cages could prevent them from ever becoming "subjects in communication." Communicating information is the prerogative of subjects, not the subjected. The ruler of such a Panopticon-like kingdom would not have to fear seditious gossip among his visible, caged subjects. He would not need spies to mingle among the people listening for seditious talk or loyalty oaths to force the people to report everything they might hear to the king, because the people would not be able to hear anything new about which they might inform him. However, considering that the zealous agents of the Russian Tsars and Josef Stalin could not prevent isolated prisoners from communicating with one another by means of a complicated system of tapping on the plumbing and walls (Conquest 1973, 398), this method of preventing uncontrolled speech would seem to be just another unrealizable royal fantasy.

Taken together, the many texts already cited imply that the king can best avoid a nightmarish loss of control by using the King's Ears and Eyes to know his subjects (while remaining invisible and unknowable to them) and by directing the flow of information to himself (while interrupting attempts by the people to reverse that flow). Amenemhet I and Ktesias's Xerxes II (König 1972, 18), who were asleep and therefore unaware of their subjects' plotting, fall prey to a conspiracy, while kings like Ramesses III and Artaxerxes II are informed in time and survive to punish the plotters. These events show the value of the advice given to King Merikare by his father: "Those who know that he knows will not attack him" (Lichtheim 1973, 99). Moreover, kings like Thutmose III not only "know that which occurred" but control the knowledge acquired by their vassals, educating them to see with the pharaoh's ideological eyes. Thutmose III did so by initiating the policy of taking the children and brothers of conquered chiefs as hostages to be brought up in the royal court (*ANET* 239, 242; cf. Redford 1992, 198–99, 224). In some cases they may have been housed and educated along with the children of the king and the high nobility (Schulman 1986, 128; cf. 1 Kgs 11:20), a practice that may have antedated Thutmose's reign (Kitchen 1973, 274 n. 185). Later Assyrian kings did much the same thing (see Parpola 1972, 33–34). For example, Sennacherib installed on the throne of Babylon a Babylonian native "who had grown up in my palace like a puppy" (Parpola and Watanabe 1988, xxi).

DENIAL AIN'T JUST A RIVER IN EGYPT

But is it always in the king's best interest to "know that which occurred"? Are there situations in which the king is better off *not* knowing—or, at least, *denying* that he knows? In general, when servants of monarchs like Assurbanipal write to the king and say "the king does not know it" (*ABL* 415, obv. 10; Pfeiffer 1935, 127; *ABL* 716), or describe events occurring "without the king knowing about it" (*ABL* 716; Oppenheim 1967, 180), they assume that these are situations about which the king *should* know. Yet the same Ramesses III who knew of the plot against him in time to save himself stresses the fact that he did *not* know about the trial of the conspirators: "As for the matters which the people—I do not know who— have plotted, go and examine them … and they caused to die by their own hands those whom they caused to die, though [I] do not know [wh]o, [and they] also punished [the] others, though I do not know who" (de Buck 1937, 154, 157; Breasted [in *ARE* 4:213]: "without my knowing it"). Gardiner (1961, 291) remarks that the passage reads "like an apologia on Ramesses III's part." If it is indeed an example of court apology, it is an apology that defines innocence in terms of ignorance, not the king's initial ignorance of the plot but his ignorance of the punishment (whether one understands his ignorance as referring to the identity of the punished or the fact that the punishment occurred).

In effect, Ramesses disclaims any responsibility for the punishment of the conspirators by invoking the notion of deniability: he is not responsible because he did not know. The concept of deniability has recently become familiar due to the Iran Contra hearings held during the administration of the American president Ronald Reagan. The term "plausible deniability" used by Reagan's representatives goes back to a 1955 National Security Council directive on the CIA (Draper 1992, 6–7). Its purpose was to allow the government to plausibly disclaim any responsibility for covert operations that had been uncovered. The CIA itself was established by President Harry Truman to be the equivalent of the Eyes and Ears of the king. According to Truman, it was "set up … for the sole purpose of getting all the available information to the President." If it was not the President's Eyes or Ears, it was his arm, his "intelligence arm" (Draper 1992, 7). The original CIA policy on plausible deniability did not include denying knowledge or responsibility within the United States government, although that is how it was used during

Reagan's term in office. However, Reagan's main apologist, John Poindexter, had to admit under questioning that he did not give the president plausible deniability, but what Senator Nunn dubbed "absolute deniability" (Draper 1992, 562). That is, the president could honestly deny knowledge of significant actions taken by his own agents because the president's Eyes and Ears never made him aware of them. In other words, Poindexter is like Jezebel, who did not inform Ahab of the means by which she obtained for him Naboth's vineyard (1 Kgs 21:15–16). (Of course Ahab did not ask her how she had done it, thereby establishing a precedent for later governmental "don't ask, don't tell" policies.) If Poindexter's testimony was truthful (which cannot be taken for granted; see Hertsgaard 1988, 335–36), he managed to reverse the original purpose of both the King's Eyes and Ears and the CIA; instead of making sure that all essential information will flow to the king, he took it upon himself to stop that flow. As a result, Reagan merely committed "the sin of inattention" (John Chancellor quoted in Hertsgaard 1988, 327).

In general, deniability *is* an "ability." The ability to deny requires effective royal control over the private-public boundary and the ruler's visibility. Thus, even deniability testifies to royal power, *if* the king actually does possess the information hidden in his private realm, and if he is able to plausibly deny having this (guilty) knowledge. If his invisibility is truly effective, he need *not* know—any more than an observer need actually be watching the inmates every second in the central tower of the Panopticon, as long as the king's subjects must assume the king does know—or at least are unable to determine whether the inscrutable monarch does or does not know. As long as his knowledge is hidden, the king need not share Deiokes's fear that anyone who could see him up close might find that he knows nothing more than anyone else.

Absolute deniability is a different matter. Leaders who deny all knowledge of crucial affairs in their own government—that is, leaders like Ramesses III, Reagan, and the David of 2 Sam 3 and 1 Kgs 1—jeopardize a four-thousand-year-old dream of monarchical power and risk being viewed as the kind of king who is kept unknowing by his manipulative courtiers and family, like the older Louis XIV and, perhaps, like the David of 1 Kgs 1 (see ch. 5 below). Repeated and emphatic admissions of royal ignorance like those made by Ronald Reagan are truly remarkable, not merely for the reasons just given, but because leaders still have at their disposal the old idea that "the king can do no wrong." This maxim assumes, in Blackstone's formulation, that "the king cannot misuse his power without evil counsellors" (quoted in Kutler 1990, 473). From this perspective it is the advisors who are responsible, like Rehoboam's young advisors in 2 Chr 13:7 (cf. Josephus, *Ant.* 8.11.2, §277). While Reagan did blame his underlings, it was not because they had given him bad advice.

That would have required that Reagan admit that he did know what they were up to, and it is that admission that seems to have been this leader's greatest fear.

A NONBIBLICAL CASE STUDY: SOPHOCLES' KING OEDIPUS

While Oedipus has the same fate as information manager as does Saul, his life has a surprising number of features in common with the life of Saul's *bête noire* David. Here are eight areas of similarity, some closer than others: (1) Both kill a "monster," getting a woman of the royal family and eventually the throne as prizes. (2) Saul also tries to kill David, as Laius does with Oedipus. In a sense, David has two families (as does Oedipus), because David's parents play no active role at all, while Saul (who calls him "son") and Jonathan do. In fact, Jonathan plays a much more essential role than do David's biological brothers. David doesn't kill his father, but his men threaten to kill his "foster-father" (and father-in-law) Saul twice. (3) David, like Oedipus, hurls a legal curse that ultimately comes back to him as the criminal. David obviously knows what he has done but acts as though he hadn't done anything, while Oedipus really doesn't know. Instead of the Sphinx's riddle and the oracle, we have Nathan's parable and God's oracle. Both crimes involve tabooed sex and murder, and in both cases the murdered man is husband of the woman who had (or will have) intercourse with the killer-king. (4) Both have cases of incest in the family. (5) In both cases there is fratricide in next generation and fratricidal "civil war." (6) In both cases daughters must die barren and unmarried (Antigone and Ismene [*Oed. tyr.* 1502]; Tamar [2 Sam 13:20]). (7) David is cited as the cause of a plague and as its cure, after he, like Oedipus, accepts the scapegoat role. In 2 Sam 24 David is more like Oedipus than ever, because he is subjectively innocent, and he is acting as a public servant who will sacrifice all to save his people.

The eighth similarity concerns David and Oedipus being manipulated by information givers; to that extent, they both resemble Saul in this case. Both old David and middle-aged Oedipus are manipulated through information transmission by a prophet and a wife. In a sense, Oedipus is in the position of both King David and Louis XIV when they were old and infirm (see ch. 5). If the prophet Nathan controls the information David receives, so does the prophet Teiresias. And if the royal wives Bathsheba and Maintenant attempt to manage the information that reaches King David and King Louis, the same is true of Oedipus's wife/mother Jocasta, once she realizes who Oedipus really is.

By fifth-century Athenian standards, Sophocles' Oedipus would seem to be a perfect candidate for master knower and information manager. He is the quintessential scientific investigator, a point reinforced by the terminology applied to him (and used by him) in the play (see esp. Knox 1971, 116–38). Of course, he's also a legal investigator and detective, for he is investigating a murder committed decades earlier, namely, the slaying of his predecessor as king. His drive to uncover the truth is total: "I shall go to any length in the search" (*Oed. tyr.* 266). He seeks clues and relentlessly questions anyone who might shed light on the case. He will resort to any method in order to extract information from them. When interrogating the professional seer Teiresias, Oedipus shows his pride in the fact that he is neither an expert nor professionally trained. Oedipus earned his reputation for intelligence and problem solving by answering the riddle of the Sphinx, something that he accomplished "with no instruction," as an old priest points out near the beginning of the drama (*Oed. tyr.* 38). In his bitter argument with Teiresias (*Oed. tyr.* 391–399), he points out that the old prophet could not solve the Sphinx's riddle, while he, "Mr. Know-nothing Oedipus" did so using "thought" (or, "the ability to figure things out"). He's dripping with sarcasm here. "Mr. Know-nothing Oedipus" is so assonant in Greek that it sounds almost like a jingle (*ho mēden eidōs Oidipous; Oed. tyr.* 397); his point is that he, the supposedly ignorant one, ended the crisis using only his intelligence. Yet the joke is on Oedipus. This ostensively objective investigator, who will sacrifice anything to discover the truth, doesn't have a clue that he is the murderer he seeks. He can't even see that his own name, which means both "swollen foot" and "knows-a-foot," points to his true identity and, ultimately, to his culpability. He is blind to the relationship between his personal life, including his marriage, and the reality of his situation. He has no trace of personal jealousy. His lack of interest in even the basic facts about his wife's former husband, the murder victim, keeps him from recognizing that Jocasta's first husband was his own father. He hasn't even bothered to tell Jocasta that doubt had been cast on the identity of his parents or that the oracle had declared that he would commit incest and patricide (*Oed. tyr.* 769–800).

In a sense, Sophocles' play both glorifies the ideal of disinterested scientific investigation and total commitment to one's research at any cost and debunks that ideal at the same time. By being so detached, impersonal, and cerebral, the great knower doesn't even know who he is, to whom he's married, who his parents are, whom he killed, the meaning of his own name, why Teiresias didn't unriddle the Sphinx, and so on. Even his assumption that it was his thinking that solved the riddle is mistaken. It was actually his unique *personal* qualifications. The riddle asks what creature walks on four legs in morning, two legs at noon, and on three legs in the evening. The answer is the human being. Oedipus has reason to be more aware of this than anyone. When he was an infant his ankles were pierced together and he was to be abandoned on a mountainside, crawling until the gods killed him. As an adult, he stood on his own two feet more than any-one, precisely because of his independence and his reliance on his own powers of thought. And by the end of his play, he will need a third leg more than anyone who can see, for he blinds himself and is in need of a stick or cane.

While the successful tyrant manages to keep well informed thanks to loyal agents, and to keep the people from knowing what he does not want them to know, Oedipus is committed to sharing all information with the people and it is he, the tyrant, who is ill-informed. He is out of the loop—out of all loops. When Oedipus refers to himself as "I, know-nothing Oedipus," he is speaking ironically, but he is being accurate. He has been kept ignorant by his Corinthian foster parents, the Corinthian shepherd who accepted him as an infant, the Theban shepherd who handed him over, and by Teiresias.

From the perspective of a Greek monarch, Teiresias's refusal to share the information he possesses is a sign of treasonous disloyalty, especially because the prophet lets Oedipus know that he does possess crucial information. Oedipus concludes that Teiresias must be part of a conspiracy; he can imagine no other reason for his silence.[9] Oedipus's suspicion of conspiracy is not a sign that Oedipus suffers from the kinds of paranoid fears and distrustfulness described by Herodotus's and Plato's tyrants. There is no sign that Oedipus had ever viewed Creon as a rival or tried to destroy him. Nor is there any indication that he had ever challenged the prophet's authority. Given the history of tyrants in Greece (as recorded by Herodotus and others), Oedipus's conclusion was reasonable, even if his refusal to listen to Creon's defenses is not.

However, while David and the Louis XIV described by Saint-Simon seem to accept much of the information they are fed by these "significant others," Oedipus starts being suspicious of all information givers once he takes on the role of investigator. Is Oedipus's investigative zeal and curios-ity sparked by the fact that others have consistently withheld information from him or lied to him? The first time there is any evidence that he has been deceived (when the drunk at the feast relays the truth, and it seems to generate gossip) Oedipus is nagged by the idea and goes to investigate. Was he a curious person before this? The play doesn't say. In a sense Oedipus comes into existence as a person at this moment (Teiresias implies as much when he says, "Today will give you birth, and ruin as well"; *Oed. tyr.* 438) There's no evidence that Oedipus ever wondered why he didn't

---

9 Oedipus uses the verb σύνοιδα to refer to what Teiresias knows (*Oed. tyr.* 330); this verb is often used of knowledge about a person that can be used as a witness against him and that is shared with someone else. Oedipus cannot believe that Teiresias would not share such knowledge, especially at this critical moment, but Teiresias merely replies, "I'll tell you nothing."

look more like his "parents." We know he hasn't been curious about his wife's first husband/his predecessor in office.[10] But didn't anyone ever ask him, "Say, did you know that you look a lot like King Laius?" Jocasta *seems* to notice this for the first time when Oedipus finally asks her about Laius's appearance during his investigation.[11]

All this implies that everyone around Oedipus has been great at keeping secrets, especially his adoptive parents and the two shepherds. *Yet how did the drunk come to know the truth?* Why did it take so long for this fact to get back to Oedipus, if an unnamed courtier knew it? When Oedipus is nagged by the words of the drunk, did he ask himself, "How many *other* people have known this all along?!" According to the saying, "the husband is the last to know." In this case, the last to know is the husband/son/ adopted child/father/brother/nephew/brother-in-law! No wonder Oedipus zealously wants to get at the truth once he realizes he's been duped by those he trusted, and no wonder he is suspicious of information givers from this point on. Yet he is not sufficiently careful about the first information he gathers after hearing the drunk's gossip. He is gratified by his adoptive parents' angry response but nevertheless seeks information from a divine source at Delphi. In spite of the fact that the priestess (the Pythia) at Delphi can give oracles that are ambiguous or even "counterfeit" (κίβ-δηλος),[12] Oedipus does not recognize the ambiguity of the response he receives from Apollo.

Finally, while Oedipus commits incest and parricide, crimes that are said to be typical of tyrants, he does so in a very atypical way. Unlike the tyrants described by Herodotus and Plato, Oedipus is not motivated by a personal desire to commit these deeds (i.e., he has no inkling of an Oedipus complex). Nor does he commit them because he feels he can do anything at all with impunity, like a god. In fact, when these events occur

---

[10] Whether or not this is because Oedipus is so totally a "public servant" that he doesn't pay attention to his personal situation or feel emotions like jealousy; see ch. 4, below.

[11] *Had* she suspected, or is it true that "believing is seeing" (Gombrich 1969, 210)? That is, she believes her child is dead, so Oedipus couldn't possibly be her son, so he couldn't possibly look like her former husband.

[12] Herodotus, *Hist.* 1.66; 1.75; 5.91. Real oracles, as opposed to those in tragedy and in Herodotus, were asked questions that prompted a yes or no answer and were therefore less ambiguous (Vidal-Naquet 1990, 317). This reflects the procedure used when consulting the ephod, Urim, and Thummim, as envisioned by McCarter (1980, 250, 371) in relation to 1 Sam 14:41; 23:9–12. Just as "historicizing" interpreters of 2 Kgs 6 like Gray assume that Elisha's *real* source was "an efficient intelligence service" (see ch. 4, below), so have some classical scholars concluded that the reputation of the Pythia and the oracles "must have rested partly on an excellent intelligence service" (Dodds 1951, 74).

in Oedipus's case, he does not even know that he is committing parricide and incest.

The process by which Oedipus discovers the incest can be traced by noting references to the bed on which it occurred. At the beginning of his investigation, Oedipus does not hesitate to point out that he now has his predecessor's power, the bed (λέκτρα), and the wife who shares their seed (*Oed. tyr.* 260; cf. 460). Later, when he realizes that he may be the one who assassinated the former king and that the curses he has pronounced may fall upon himself, Oedipus shudders to think that he stains the dead man's bed (λέχη) with his hands (821). When he learns that his Corinthian "father" has died, Oedipus takes heart, scoffing at the prophecies, although he feels that he still must avoid his mother's bed (λέκτρον; 976). In response, Jocasta, his unknown mother, recommends that he ignore fate and incest, noting that men have often slept with their own mothers in their dreams (981–982). When the whole truth finally comes to light, Jocasta rushes to the marriage bed (λέχη; 1243), mourns the bed (εὐνάς; 1249) on which she had "bred double," and hangs herself, after the fashion of the Sphinx who, in one tradition, disposed of males by throttling them in a sexual embrace.

Whatever else *Oedipus tyrannus* might tell us about kingship and knowledge, it certainly exhibits the full range of dangers that can attend "knowing" someone in bed, that most private of spaces in most royal palaces. In the next chapter, we will encounter a number of dangers that confront *biblical* kings (and biblicists!) in bed. In chapter 5, we will return to Oedipus and David, and view their bedroom behavior in terms of the private-public distinction. We will find that the dangers I have been discussing are especially great in two situations that are mirror images of each other: first, when the king, like Oedipus, is so totally public-minded that he ignores his own private life, and second, when the king, like David, becomes so guided by his private emotions and personal survival that his public duties are ignored and he nearly loses his kingdom.

4

ROYAL POWER AND KNOWING
IN THE *BIBLICAL* SENSE

Having outlined royal traits and tracked instances of royal information management (and mismanagement) throughout the ancient Near East and Greece, it is time for me to ask how these themes manifest themselves in the Hebrew Bible, not merely in the case of Saul and the priests at Nob, but in general. This chapter is devoted to the relationship between royal knowing and power in its specifically *biblical* form. However, when I sat down to write it, I fell asleep and had a dream. It was kind of an incubation dream, in the sense that it helped to hatch this chapter.

I dreamt that I was sitting in a waiting room. I looked up at the people around me because none of the magazines was new; the most recent were *Esther* and *Daniel*. What a motley group! Every stratum and style of humanity from high-court officials to prostitutes, all waiting on, or waiting for, the king. One minute a phalanx of FedEx guys comes flying out of the king's private chamber carrying letters ordering the annihilation and plundering of "a certain people" within the kingdom, and everybody—not just here but all over the capital—scratches their bewildered heads. Meanwhile, the king and whoever's advising him are sitting down to have a drink together. Who *is* in there advising him, anyway?

Then there are those four guys in the cool chamber above the waiting room, with that teenager craning his neck to hear what's being said. One of the four isn't only scratching his head; he's scratching his whole body—he's full of sores and looks terrible. I can't hear everything they're saying, but the sick, impoverished one can't make head or tail of a different command invisibly given and surreptitiously carried out by the king and his agents. Apparently the king had a courtier kill the man's whole family and almost all his servants, give him those diseases, and confiscate his property so that he could no longer rescue the poor and homeless people he used to help when he was richer than the guys he's talking to. From the way they act, the other guys are loyal advisors of the king. They talk as if they know exactly what the usually invisible and inscrutable king is thinking, although they keep saying that *nobody* knows the king's thoughts. You would think they were as at home in the king's private chamber as that bed-warmer woman who was brought to the king a minute ago. They act as though they too are privileged flies on the king's bedroom wall, although the only bugs they talk about are human maggots and worms. They keep telling the sick guy that what happened was all his fault, and if the king did order it, the guy had it coming. They are even quoting from their English law dictionary, chanting "the king can do no wrong."

Leaving the men's room and returning to the main waiting area, I spot a flock of cosmeticians filing through the room and being ushered inside. Some of them carry enough perfume and oil to take care of the entire populace of Paris for a year, but apparently it's all for the contestants in the king's "Be the next Ms. Persia" pageant. Others are mumbling something in Babylonian about needing to give the king an emergency haircut and pedicure before he climbs over the palace walls toward the forest. One is even rushing in a bottle of salad dressing.

They aren't the only ones to get immediate access. Those two call girls are going in next. Good! I was afraid that baby'd get yanked apart like the two branches of a wishbone. It seems like women get preferential treatment here. There goes a smart-looking old woman, after being dropped off by some tough-looking military muck-a-muck who promptly vanished. Now she's coming back out, smiling, Mona Lisa–like. Even that famished woman is getting in, the one exuding the moral outrage of a plaintiff on the "People's Court" show, furious that her dry-cleaner friend ruined her new suede coat. Only here it's not about a coat—she's demanding that the king make her friend cough up her son, so the two women can do lunch. Now she's coming back out, and she's *not* smiling.

Maybe women aren't so privileged after all. It seems the queen "just said no," and soon another exodus of FedEx men comes pouring out, parting the seas of waiting humanity as they sweep along—this time carrying an order that women must obey their husbands and speak to them only in the language of football. The hum of head scratching is audible again, inside and outside the waiting room.

And then over there, by the *ficus benjamina,* that naked man and woman are scratching their heads about some fruit tree. Apparently they received an order from the king not to touch it or at least not to eat it. They hardly seem like courtiers, and their nakedness isn't at all like the guy with the skin sores. But there is a very tall, sinewy, too-smart-for-his-own-good-looking courtier giving them advice about the king—just like the three deprogrammers brainwashing the guy with the sores. I wonder if this slick, tall courtier is the one who advised the king to turn the sore guy's world upside down. Actually, if he weren't so shriveled up and sick, the man with the sores could pass for a king himself.

The king's certainly getting some interesting advice. It's never boring here. Now some loud frat boys are barging through with their music thumping, on their way to counsel the king. Later they come out laughing among themselves, carrying freshly painted signs that look like the ones candidates put their political slogans on. My little thing is thicker than my father's *what?!* Whip *whom* with scorpions?! Maybe it's time to rethink that maxim about the king doing no wrong. That's interesting. No more advisors have gone in or out for a long time, neither the loud kind nor the whispering ones. Here come two FedEx men with packages ordered by the king without the help of counselors. Two golden *what?!* Put them *where?!* Sabbath services on Monday night? Instead of football? That'll cause some helmet scratching.

Just when things are calming down again, a rather mangled man comes limping in. He looks like he could use a pedicure too—and a shave. He's obviously here to testify to the king on a judicial matter, just like those prostitutes and that hungry woman. I just hope he doesn't want to slice or eat anybody. He was only in the inner chamber for a minute or less, and he wasn't exactly smiling when he came out; it was more like the beatific obsequious smile he carried in with him had frozen into stunned puzzlement.

Everything seems quiet now, and I'm guessing that the king might have gone to bed; he's certainly been working overtime. But some tiptoeing lackeys emerging from the inner chamber are whispering something about needing a cure for the king's insomnia. The next thing I know they're carting in loads of the king's own royal annals to read to him. And I'd thought that knowing in another biblical sense was the best soporific!

All of a sudden, I look out one of the windows and see a rabbinical student racing like a meshugga through the waiting room of an adjacent building and pouring Puritan oil on the head of some heavy dude who's obviously packing. Now he's zipping out just as fast—shades of guru Ji being crowned with a cream pie by some nut in Detroit. The dude's buddies in the waiting room ask him who that nutcase was and what he said, and before you know it, the room's exploding with "Long live the king!" The newly creamed king is extricating himself from the circle of well-wishers, and now he's zooming out to the parking lot. He jumps in his car, and peels rubber like a meshugga out for a Sunday drive of royal road rage.

The dream-images are starting to break up, but I can still see a man in the corner of my waiting room, a foreign-looking guy with a southeastern accent. His hat has a Bozrah University logo on it, a reddish figure in the belligerent stance of Wisconsin's Bucky Badger, but this mascot is human, a ruddy outdoorsy man with a built-in hair coat. The waiting man looks like a royal courtier, but right now he seems to be waiting for the king's priest rather than for the king himself. As I wake up I can here a loud chorus of academic voices chanting in unison: "He's lurking; he's lurking."

My first thoughts after I awoke were identical to those of Plato's Glaucon when he had listened to Socrates' description of the Cave. He said, "a strange image ... and the prisoners are strange." Socrates replied, "like us" (*Rep.* 515a). The behavior of the people in the dream was certainly strange enough to qualify as real, at least in terms of my own reality concept. And it was obviously all about biblical kings. But at the same time, the monarchs were distorted and superimposed on top of one another—both the human kings *and* the divine one—forming a bizarre composite portrait of "*The King*," an amusement-park "mirror for princes" or monarchical Marx Brothers movie. An oneiric example of "defamiliarization," to be sure.

Although the stories of many biblical kings were folded into the dream, a number of royal traits showed through repeatedly. There was the continual distinction between those who have access to the king and the outsiders who can only guess at what motivates the often weird-sounding decisions emanating from inside the Beltway. There was the continual emphasis on the flow of traffic between inside and outside, with the vaunted speed of FedEx overnight. There were repeated occurrences of the king playing a judicial role, with mixed reviews by the litigants. There was a fleeting glimpse of the British legal principle of the king being unable to do wrong, which we'd earlier traced back to the notion of the king's two bodies. There was a reference to a king who behaved tyrannically, using forced labor and overtaxation, and an allusion to a king who initiated cult reforms that seemed puzzling to some outsiders. There was one king who leaves the throne—not in disguise in order to examine his subjects—but to remain far from humans on a kind of vegetarian feral excursion. Royal insomnia made one appearance, while the king's complex relationship with advisors and secret agents made several. There were also allusions to informers and spies. That lone man at the end of the dream, from Bozrah U., must have been Doeg the Edomite, the scapegoat-villain of our chapter 2.[1]

---

[1] In order of appearance, then, the kings were Ahasuerus (Xerxes) in Esth 3; the regal Job; David (with Abishag; 1 Kgs 1); Esther preparing for the king (Esth 2); Nebuchadnezzar (Dan 4); Solomon (1 Kgs 3); David (with the wise woman and Joab; 2 Sam 14); Jehoram of Israel (with the cannibal mother; 2 Kgs 6); Ahasuerus again (Esth 1); King Yahweh with courtiers Adam, Eve, and the serpent (Gen 3); Rehoboam (1 Kgs 12); Jeroboam (1 Kgs 12); David (with Mephibosheth; 2 Sam 19); Ahasuerus (Esth 6); Jehu (2 Kgs 9); and David (with Doeg; 1 Sam 21–22).

The dream also refers to an incident involving a certain guru Ji. In order to check my memory of this event, and thereby establish the "historicity" of this dream element, I contacted David Crumm, a religion writer for the *Detroit Free Press*. After some investigation, Mr. Crumm found a long-time *Free Press* reporter (Bill McGraw) who recalled the incident vividly, so vividly, in fact, that I cannot resist quoting Mr. Crumm's report to me at some length: "Apparently the incident took place back in 1970 or 1971. It did involve a Guru named Ji and a high-profile visit he paid to

The dream didn't just defamiliarize these biblical narratives; it also highlighted their built-in potential for absurd satire. I have a hard time imagining an Assyriologist having an analogous experience after spending the evening poring over Neo-Assyrian royal inscriptions. On the other hand, Herodotus must have had recurring dreams about the antics of his Candaules (*Hist.* 1.8–12), Amasis (2.172), and Amestris (7.114, 9.109–112), if not his many other risible and raging royals. Nevertheless, it was high time I got out of bed and got down to business, cataloging the experiences of biblical kings when *they* were in bed—and in all the other private areas to which my dreaming observer-self was apparently not given access.

KINGS IN BED AND ON THE THRONE: TYPES OF ROYAL KNOWING IN THE HEBREW BIBLE

They came into the house, and he [Ishbosheth] lay in his bedchamber [בחדר משכבו], and they struck him and killed him and beheaded him.... [David said] "wicked men have murdered a righteous man in his house, upon his bed."
—2 Samuel 4:7, 11

Pharaoh said ... "I do not know Yahweh." ... Yahweh spoke to Moses ... "say to [Pharaoh], '... frogs ... shall come into your house, and into your bedchamber [ובחדר משכבך], and into your bed....'" ... Moses said ... "that you may know that there is no one like Yahweh, the frogs will leave you and your houses...."
—Exodus 5:2; 7:26, 28; 8:5–7

Detroit. Apparently the city officials here were enough in awe of this guy that they invited him over to the City Council chambers and there was going to be some kind of welcoming proclamation given to him. In any case, a young would-be anarchist named Pat Riley (I think that was his name) showed up with a cream pie and hit Ji square in the face.... But that's not the end of the story. Riley apparently, some years later, traveled out West (I think that's what Bill said) and once again encountered some followers of Ji. He got to talking with them and they actually lured him into some kind of meditation technique they wanted him to try. While he was doing it and his eyes were closed, they attacked him with hammers and nearly killed him. They damaged his skull so severely that he had to have a steel plate put into his head. Today, he's a cab driver in Detroit—still alive and actually you could talk with him, if you want. I think my friend here has a number for him. Apparently he remains a good-humored, countercultural kind of guy. At one point, some reporter re-interviewed him about the whole pie incident and the nearly fatal aftermath of it—and he actually joked about it. He said something like: 'Hey, it's not all bad having a steel plate in your head. I don't need a radio anymore to tune in my favorite station!'" (e-mail communication, May 25, 1999).

Elisha ... tells the king of Israel the words that you [king of Aram] speak
in your bedchamber [בַּחֲדַר מִשְׁכָּבְךָ].
—2 Kings 6:12

These epigraphs, together with Qoh 10:20 (cited above in ch. 3), constitute the only four examples of the expression חֲדַר מִשְׁכָּב ("bedchamber")
in the Hebrew Bible. Together they illustrate several of the roles played by
royal knowledge and information management in the Hebrew Bible.
Significantly, though they refer to the king's bedroom, none of the passages describes the king in the act of knowing a woman in the biblical
sense. In three of the four passages, the bedroom marks a king's vulnerability: the unsuspecting Ishbosheth unable to prevent being assassinated in
bed, a fate experienced by a number of ancient Near Eastern kings and
feared by many others; the Pharaoh unable to prevent Yahweh's invading
his most private room with frogs; and, as we have seen, the king of Aram
unable to prevent secret information from being acquired by his enemies,
including information restricted to the privacy of his own bedchamber. In
all three passages, the vulnerable, uninformed king is the loser in a con-
test with a more powerful and knowing king. In 2 Sam 3–4, David is the
"winner"; as we will discuss in chapter 5, his repeated claim to ignorance
is at least open to question. The loser pharaoh's proud ignorance of the
divine sovereign Yahweh ("I don't know any Yahweh"; see Exod 5:2)
ensures his loss and death. In 2 Kgs 6, King Jehoram of Israel is a winner
only because of the powerful and all-knowing prophet-informer Elisha.
Together, these three very different cases show that the king with superior
knowledge and information possesses the power to win a zero-sum game
when two monarchs are in competition.

In contrast, the fourth text presents a king (Qoheleth) who is addressing subjects on behalf of all monarchs. He describes a king who is
invulnerable because he is able to acquire private knowledge about his
vulnerable subjects, not merely knowledge of curses made in their bedrooms (he assumes any rich man can do that), but even curses against the
king made in the privacy of their thoughts. This is precisely the claim made
by Isocrates' King Nicocles of Cyprus and our other would-be omniscient
kings. Qoheleth stresses the speed at which this dangerous information
will be transmitted to the king, with birds as the swift informers. This image
of birds carrying information to the king recurs in Solomonic folklore and
is often used to convey the speed at which gossip and rumor are transmitted (see above on Virgil's *Fama*).

These texts show that monarchs need to be informed in order to stay
in power, whether they need to know in advance of assassination plots, of
the leakage of secret military plans, or of the power of a hitherto unknown
deity. While kings have a great need for knowledge, their very position

makes it difficult for them to acquire what Herodotus would call the best kind of information: *autopsy,* that is, seeing with their own eyes. To the extent to which they remain on the throne in the capital of their kingdom, they are pretty much restricted to what Herodotus considers the second- and third-best means of acquiring knowledge and information: reports from eyewitnesses and hearsay (see Herodotus, *Hist.* 2.29, 99; 3.115). To the extent that they remain in their private space in the center, it is impossible for kings to become the kind of investigative knower or researcher typified by kings like Gilgamesh. It is even difficult for kings to acquire any reliable information, if they take at face value all the reports given them by their informants, including courtiers and the King's Eyes and Ears. As mentioned earlier, Freud believes that it is equally dangerous for the ego to act like a complacent absolute ruler who trusts the information given to him by his courtiers and therefore doesn't bother to do his own research by going down among his people to hear their voice.

Biblical texts furnish examples of at least six types of royal knower, or, at least, six ways in which knowledge (and the lack of it) plays a key role in their careers:

The king as "panoptic," or all-knowing. The two biblical kings who come closest to approximating this type, the type idealized by Isocrates, Louis XIV, and the other monarchs already discussed, are David and Solomon. Of course, David at times must rely on God's reports, either directly or through the medium of Abiathar and the ephod, or on information supplied by human beings. In 2 Sam 3 and 1 Kgs 1, David actually wields power by acting as though he were ignorant of key events. Most strikingly, David is surprisingly uninformed when Absalom is preparing his rebellion (see below). For his part, Solomon comes closest to demonstrating Yahweh's ability to see into the hearts of every human being (the ability that Qoheleth predicates of all kings) when he adjudicates the dispute between the two prostitutes. However, he does not see into their hearts or hear their private thoughts; rather, he "extracts" information about their true natures with a ruse, just as Samson's wife and Delilah extract Samson's secrets through *their* techniques. Even later, when Solomon has his worldwide reputation for wisdom, that wisdom is not shown to be panoptic in nature (see ch. 6, below).

As I will discuss later, the biblical personage who comes closest to demonstrating panoptic knowledge is Elisha. This prophet is not only able to convey God's wishes and judgments, but secret military intelligence about enemy troop movements. The fact that Elisha helps his marvelous deeds to become known outside Israel (see, e.g., Cogan and Tadmor 1988, 75) suggests that the tales of his deeds are functioning in the manner of royal ideology. In the end, however, the sovereign Yahweh co-opts all human kings who would profess to be panoptic, even though kings who seek information from him by means of dreams, Urim, or prophets are attempting to make God into their King's Eye. In addition, it is Yahweh who best demonstrates royal unaccountability, inaccessibility, and inscrutability.

Kings who do not know what they need to know and are therefore helpless (including kings who are unable to keep their secret information private). There are many examples of this type of king in the Hebrew Bible. We have already witnessed Saul's painful inability to discover what he needs to know, and the predicament of the king of Aram (in 2 Kgs 6) will be discussed later in this chapter.

Kings who think they know and/or control more than they do. Whether this is called conceit of wisdom or, with Plato, *doxosophia* (e.g., *Phileb.* 49a, d; cf. *Symp.* 204a), this type of royal *hubris* (ὕβρις) is illustrated by the two pharaohs of Exodus, as well as by Rehoboam, when he follows the idiotic advice of his young counselors (1 Kgs 12:6–14).

Kings who employ counselors in order to make decisions from known data. This type is relatively rare in the Hebrew Bible, the prime examples being David in 2 Sam 15–16 and Rehoboam in 1 Kgs 12 (on this see Polzin [1993, 169–75], whose approach to 2 Sam 15–16 differs from the one I give below), although Ahasuerus's emergency meeting in Esth 1 certainly qualifies, as does his consultation with Haman in Esth 6:1–10.

Kings who get off the throne in order to acquire knowledge or experience first-hand. As I mentioned in chapter 1, there is a well-documented type of folk story that the motif index dubs "king in disguise to learn secrets of subjects," although the purpose is usually to ensure that justice is being done or to share the life of ordinary people, not to "snoop" (Burke 1978, 152). When one thinks of a biblical king who leaves the throne, gains experience, and hears the people's voice, the David of 2 Sam 15–17 comes to mind, although David certainly does not flee Jerusalem for these reasons (see below). Nor can it be said that the Nebuchadnezzar in Dan 4 left the throne in order to acquire knowledge, although knowledge of Yahweh's sovereignty is the outcome. Nebuchadnezzar's wildness does not signal that he is being initiated into a counterreality, as is the case with the "wild" Gilgamesh when he identifies with his deceased double Enkidu. Nebuchadnezzar does not have experiences with people or "the Other"; he doesn't even have the faculty of reason that would allow him to learn from experience.

Kings in bed; kings who know in the biblical sense. In the Hebrew Bible, there are at least twelve examples of kings (or heirs apparent) who are

described as being in bed. However, these passages often involve types of
activity other than knowing someone in the biblical sense. These are the passages, with the addition of Sophocles' *Oedipus* for comparative purposes:

1. 1 Sam 19:13, 15–16
2. 1 Sam 26:7
3. 1 Sam 28:23
4. 2 Sam 4:7, 11
5. 2 Sam 11:2, 4 (contrast Uriah in v. 13)
6. 2 Sam 13:5
7. 2 Sam 16:22
8. 1 Kgs 1:1–4, 15–48 (note מׁשכב in v. 47)
9. 1 Kgs 21:4
10. 2 Kgs 1:4
11. 2 Kgs 8:7–15
12. 2 Kgs 20:1–7
13. *Oed. tyr.* 260, 821, 976 [cf. 981–982], 1243, 1249

Six of these passages deal with the transmitting or withholding of information (nos. 1, 3, 8, 9, 11, 13), four with assassination (nos. 1, 2, 4, 11),
four with illness or infirmity (nos. 8, 10, 11, 12), two with feigned illness
(nos. 1, 6), and three with the king being "mothered" (nos. 3, 8, 9). Only
four involve actual sexual intercourse (nos. 5, 6, 7, 13). As noted earlier in
regard to the passages in which the phrase חדר מׁשכב appears, most of
these situations (assassination, illness, the king having information withheld, the king being mothered) involve vulnerability, weakness, and
passivity, if not death. And, as was the case in the earlier texts, a number
of these passages involve two kings (or princes) who are in competition
(nos. 1, 2, 4, 7, 8, 11).

The relatively few examples of biblical kings and princes "knowing
someone in the biblical sense" all involve David or his sons. All of them
have inappropriate or tabooed women as the sexual partner, and all are
punished with death (in every case a son of David dies, rather than the
king himself). Even the two examples in which intercourse is noticeably
absent involve either David (no. 8) or the man whose wife David has
recently impregnated (no. 5; v. 13). In the case of Oedipus, the king has
no more knowledge of whom he was knowing in the biblical sense than
does the "newlywed" Jacob in Gen 29:21–25. When Oedipus finally discovers the identity of his partner, the marriage bed quickly becomes the
scene of a suicide.

Women play significant roles in at least five of the biblical passages
(nos. 1, 3, 6, 8, 9), even though intercourse occurs only in number 6,
Amnon's rape of Tamar. In the other four cases, the males are passive and
the women (three of whom are wives) are active. In biblical texts involving

men other than kings in bed, women tend to play an even larger and more powerful role. This is true in five of these six cases: Gen 27; 29; Judg 4; 16; Ruth 3; and Jdt 12–13. Almost all of these situations involve elements of deception (a type of information management), and, in all but Gen 29, it is the woman who controls the information and therefore the male. While assassination and illness are also present as themes in some of these passages, the red thread that runs through all nineteen of the texts listed in this section is control of knowledge and information.

Only in the case of Samson and Delilah (and Samson's wife earlier) is there an obvious link between knowing a powerful male in the biblical sense and getting secret knowledge from him in the process. There are no biblical examples of such "sexually transmitted information" in relation to kings, although scholars like Gray surmise that Israelite women who were taken as prisoner by the Arameans and made concubines might have become the source of "a leakage of secrets from the bedchamber," a leakage that helped to sustain Elisha's "efficient intelligence service" (J. Gray 1970, 515, 513). Rather than leaking knowledge exclusive to themselves, biblical kings more commonly have information withheld from them or have disinformation given to them (nos. 1, 3, 8, 9, 11).[2] The very fact that the monarchs must depend so heavily on information being reported to them by others makes it difficult for a situation analogous to Samson's to arise. The fundamental point is that kings do not *need* to possess secret knowledge in reality; they merely need others to *think* that they do.

EXAMPLES OF ROYAL KNOWLEDGE AND INFORMATION MANAGEMENT IN BIBLICAL TEXTS

2 Samuel 15–17

While different aspects of David's career were cited to illustrate most of the types of royal knowing listed above, the cases in which he displays mastery of information management (with or without divine help) include the most famous events of his reign, as depicted in Samuel and Kings (see ch. 5, below). Yet David is hardly panoptic. He is not generally depicted as a king to whom all report everything that they see and hear or as a king concerned with "keeping an eye on" the people as a whole. In fact, the story of Absalom's rebellion presents a David who is often the opposite of

---

[2] In no. 1 it is Saul, the king to whom the bed is brought, who is tricked and lied to; David, his recently anointed replacement, is not even present. In no. 9, the wife Jezebel does not report to her husband, "bedded" king Ahab, information on how the vineyard was obtained, but that may be no more than catering to his preference or continuing to grant him deniability.

a panoptic king. Admittedly, David is informed about Absalom's actions once the rebellion has begun, and Joab does inform the king about the condition of the people after the rebellion has been quashed. Nevertheless, in 2 Sam 15:1–12 David is astoundingly *un*informed about Absalom's seditious behavior, even though it is precisely the kind of activity that ancient Near Eastern kings most want to be informed about—the same kind of activity in which Saul had thought David had been engaged and about which Saul believed himself to be uninformed.

Verses 1–12 of chapter 15 report a long series of frequent activities by Absalom that highlight his efforts at communication with the people (he apparently took Freud's advice about listening to the voice of his people, even if his father did not). Absalom here displays mastery of "impression management" (see Goffman 1959, 208–37) in relation to the people (vv. 1–6) and information management in his manipulation of David (vv. 7–12; cf. 13:24–27). These activities had to take place over a long period of time, yet no one apparently informs David about *any* of them. Absalom's initial act of acquiring the chariot, horses, and fifty runners is by its very nature public; it's the very same act that is urgently and quickly reported to David in 1 Kgs 1, when it is done by Adonijah! Brueggemann (1990, 301) notes that "one has an image of constant street parades in Jerusalem, calling attention to this prince and heir." While this "image" seems a bit exaggerated to me, it does underscore the publicity of the act and the puzzling fact that David is either unaware of it or does not grasp its political significance. Similarly, Hertzberg observes that reports of Absalom's gladhanding of citizens in his campaign for judge "will have run like wildfire through the villages" (1964, 337)—yet again, apparently not through the halls of the palace to the throne room. Oddly, these commentators and others do not remark on David's ignorance of such long-term seditious behavior; instead, they note David's quick response of taking flight after he receives the "news" of the conspiracy. This is not even yesterday's news; it's news from the previous four years, if not longer (15:7 LXX Luc; 14:28)! It's the first time David hears about it, and it's already time to flee the capital. David needs to fire all the members of his CIA and FBI.

In the courtiers' defense, 2 Sam 12 and 14 may indicate that giving bad news to David may be a delicate matter, but that is still no excuse. In a sense, all of David's courtiers, including Joab, seem to have been disloyal as regards this crucial matter, for loyalty and reporting information are synonymous. The fact that David doesn't learn about all this on his own shows how insulated and isolated he has become. If he had gotten off the throne and gone to the gate, he could have heard Absalom's *Spiel* for himself. Of course, if he had done that, Absalom would have had no grounds on which to appeal to the people in the first place. David's total ignorance of Absalom's information-management activities is shown by

Absalom fooling David about his true reason for going to Hebron. The king apparently did not learn any lesson from Absalom's previous success at manipulating him with false information, in the matter of the sheepshearing feast that became the scene of Amnon's assassination. Fittingly, Absalom succeeded in that instance because David did not want to get off his throne to go to the feast himself, a fact that Absalom had anticipated and used to manipulate his father.

Ironically, the long series of information-management blunders by David's Eyes and Ears forces David to relearn his information-management skills after he is forced out of Jerusalem. It almost seems that he had to lose his information-handling power in order to regain it. And regain it he does. He immediately begins to improve his impression-management technique with Ittai and then lays the foundation for an underground news source in Jerusalem with Zadok (15:27–28). A few verses later we are told that this net-work will be put to use by David's newly recruited double agent Hushai, who will relay secret information he has heard in the private space of the palace (15:35–36). Here, at last, David is telling trusted citizens to report to him everything they see and hear, in quintessential ancient Near Eastern form.

If one grades monarchs according to their information-management abilities, the David of 2 Sam 13:6–15:12 deserves an F. Once he is off the throne, David shoots up to an A+, for in addition to creating a secret infor-mation network, and enlisting a double agent/spy, he also instructs that spy to disseminate disinformation (thereby anticipating John Poindexter by mil-lennia) and, at the same time, communicates with Yahweh, so that the Lord might achieve the same result using his own devices.

The narrative that describes the effective passage of private information from Hushai to David in 2 Sam 17 puts great emphasis on all the human links in the chain of secret communication. It's all here: the double agent passing on false advice at Absalom's "court," priests [secretly?] loyal to David and their messenger-sons, the unnamed servant woman who carries reports[3] and is loyal to the messengers. This woman's actions even recall another spy story, that of Rahab, who also hides spies and gives a false report to a king, as well as the story of Michal lying to King Saul in 1 Sam 19. In addition, we have the נער who shows loyalty to Absalom when he sees the priests' sons and informs Absalom (v. 18). All these scenes call attention to the elements of loyalty and risk, and the need for speed, in the process of reporting secret information by human channels—all in stark contrast to the long preceding period when David was monumentally unin-formed about the events that led directly to this crisis.

At the same time, the process initiated by Hushai, Abiathar, and Zadok *functions* in the same way as the process by which Yahweh had informed

---

[3] Assuming that it is the same woman in vv. 19–20 as in v. 17.

David earlier, either directly or through Abiathar's ephod. The fact that Abiathar plays a role in both cases highlights their functional equivalence. David's immediate flight in response to Hushai's warning not to spend the night in his present location (17:16, 21)[4] recalls his earlier response to Yahweh's warning through Abiathar's ephod, when David was being pursued by his father-in-law and not his son (1 Sam 23:11–13). While 2 Sam 15–17 showcases both "dual causality" (with David simultaneously using human cunning and appealing for direct divine action) *and* the role of human beings who function in the same way that God does elsewhere, the primary emphasis is definitely on the human element in controlling and transmitting information.

1 Kings 18

The story of Obadiah in 1 Kgs 18:1–16 illustrates both the crucial role played by information management in royal courts and the misreadings that can be produced by commentators who do not take this historically attested factor into account when they interpret Samuel–Kings. At the beginning of the chapter, Yahweh tells Elijah to present himself to Ahab, and Elijah sets out to do so (vv. 1–2). Elijah is not ordered to present himself to Obadiah. Nor is he told to make Obadiah his go-between with Ahab. In terms of Yahweh's command, the narrative could move from verse 2 to verse 17 (when Elijah presents himself to Ahab) without any disruption. This means that verses 3–16 can be viewed as an integral unit, one that focuses exclusively on the issues of information control and loyalty in relation to Obadiah.

The Obadiah narrative begins with Ahab calling for Obadiah, ordering him to go in search of water and grass to keep the horses and mules alive. They then divide the land between them and go off separately, each by himself (vv. 3, 5–6). The narrator interrupts this scene (in which Obadiah remains silent) by telling us that Obadiah feared Yahweh greatly and demonstrated that fear by hiding and feeding a hundred prophets in caves, so that Jezebel could not "cut them off" (vv. 3–4). In verse 7, Elijah encounters Obadiah, and the latter falls on his face, calling Elijah "my lord." The prophet then orders Obadiah to go and inform "your lord" that Elijah is here (v. 8). Obadiah asks how he might have sinned, considering that Elijah intends to deliver him into the hand of Ahab, to put him to death (v. 9). Swearing by Yahweh, Obadiah informs Elijah that Ahab has sent to

---

[4] These verses are not without problems. The message delivered to David in v. 21 sounds as though Ahithophel's advice had been accepted after all. Also, the communication setup with Jonathan and Ahimaaz and the woman servant is given with frequentative verbs (v. 17), even though this is a new situation (if this is still the first day of David's flight), and the setup must end immediately after the first message.

every nation and kingdom in search of him, and when each reported that
Elijah was not there, Ahab had made them swear an oath that they had not
found him (v. 10). With that background, Obadiah explains that if he were
to go to Ahab and announce that Elijah is here, the spirit of Yahweh might
carry the prophet to some unknown place, and when Ahab could not find
him, he would put Obadiah to death (vv. 11–12). Obadiah protests that he
has been loyal to Yahweh from his youth and asks Elijah if the prophet has
not been informed of Obadiah's loyal deed of saving the hundred prophets
(v. 13). After Obadiah reiterates that Ahab would put him to death, Elijah
swears that he will indeed show himself to the king that day (v. 15).
Obadiah then informs Ahab, and Elijah appears as promised (v. 16).

It is clear from this summary that Ahab trusts his courtier to go off
alone on the mission that the king finds most urgent. However, it is
Obadiah's loyalty to Yahweh that is stressed by the narrator and by
Obadiah himself. Nevertheless, many commentators assert that Obadiah
is "ambivalent" (Walsh 1996, 239, 242, 260), that he displays a "conflict of
loyalties" (Nelson 1987, 118), or that "the tension between [his] desire to
serve Yahweh and his desire to serve Ahab" illustrates his "torn loyalties"
(Hauser and Gregory 1990, 25). Some contend that Obadiah's reason for
fearing that Ahab will kill him in verse 12 is "an excuse to cover up the
real reason," namely, the fact that he is a "closet Yahwist" (Hauser and
Gregory 1990, 27), in spite of the fact that the text gives no indication
that Obadiah attempted to conceal (or needed to conceal) his faith in
Yahweh. Others suggest that it is unclear whether Obadiah is sincere or
merely giving an excuse in verse 12 (e.g., G. Jones 1984, 313). Finally,
Obadiah's use of the phrase "my lord" in reference to Ahab has also been
taken as a sign of his split loyalties (e.g., Nelson 1987, 118).

All of these interpretations fail to take into account the relationship
between information control and loyalty in the ancient Near East, as well
as the special requirements of Obadiah's position. Scholars who think that
Obadiah's reason in verse 12 is an excuse or a cover-up tend to view him
as a "fainthearted" man with "flustered fears" (Hauser and Gregory 1990,
27; Nelson 1987, 118). Yet, given extensive evidence from ancient loyalty
oaths, as well as other ancient Near Eastern data we have reviewed,
Obadiah's fears are entirely reasonable and well-founded. Courtiers, if not
all citizens, are bound by oath to inform the king of whatever they see or
hear. Failure to do so is usually punishable by death. If Elijah were to van-
ish after Obadiah had reported his presence, Obadiah could easily be
judged to have given the king a false report and be subject to execution.[5]

---

[5] G. Jones (1984, 313) assumes that Obadiah fears the king's lethal rage, just
as scholars assume that the Saul who orders the execution of the priests at Nob
has gone "berserk" (see ch. 2, above). Yet in both cases the king acted (or would

To show that this is the appropriate context in which to evaluate verse 12, one need only refer to the background with which Obadiah provided Elijah in verse 10. Ahab had asked foreign nations and monarchies to report to him, and when they told him that they had not found Elijah, Ahab made them swear what amounts to a loyalty oath in order to verify their statement. Concerning Obadiah's worry that the spirit of Yahweh might whisk Elijah away somewhere, there is enough evidence of Elijah's mysterious movements in 1–2 Kings to suggest that it is not far-fetched for Obadiah to view him as an ancestor of the spy-hero, the Scarlet Pimpernel: "they seek him here, they seek him there, that damned elusive Pimpernel" (*The Scarlet Pimpernel,* film, 1935).

Clearly, Obadiah is afraid of being viewed as disloyal by the king he supposedly serves. Ironically, his fear concerns an act that would actually be a *loyal* one but that would *appear* disloyal if Elijah were to disappear. That is, Obadiah is afraid that Elijah might be disloyal to *him*. It is to allay these fears that Elijah *swears* he will show himself that day (v. 15). Even more ironic is that there is no mention of Obadiah having been afraid when he was *actually* disloyal. If Elijah can hide himself from Ahab, Obadiah successfully hid a hundred prophets from Jezebel and presumably her husband—an act of *gross* disloyalty to the king. Far from being afraid that this act of disloyalty might be exposed, Obadiah expects that someone has already told Elijah about it (v. 13).[6] A final irony is that if Obadiah *were* put to death for allegedly giving a false report about Elijah, he would no longer be able to engage in secret acts of loyalty to Yahweh, such as rescuing his prophets.

Even if one leaves all this evidence of Obadiah's total loyalty to Yahweh aside, there is absolutely *no* evidence for the view that Obadiah's loyalties are nevertheless divided or "torn." Ahab's trust in Obadiah is simply misplaced. Nowhere is it said or implied that Obadiah "desires" to serve Ahab. We see Obadiah going in search of water and grass, as Ahab commanded. Does that prove his loyalty to Ahab? Hardly. If Obadiah is to retain his key position at the center of power, he must at least give the appearance of serving the king, precisely so that he might be in a position to aid others loyal to Yahweh (cf. the value for David of his court "spy" [and disloyal son and courtier] Jonathan). Besides, searching for fodder and water is, in itself, a relatively neutral and innocuous act. What about Obadiah's use of "my lord" in relation to Ahab (v. 10)? For one thing, Obadiah is here echoing *Elijah's* reference to Ahab as Obadiah's "lord" in verse

---

. be acting) in accordance with ancient Near Eastern practice; it is not necessary to add the motive of irrational anger.

[6] Is Obadiah implying that Elijah's informant was God, and not a human being? Nothing in v. 13 suggests this.

8. For another, it is likely that a courtier would refer to the king in this manner whether he were loyal to the king or not.

2 Kings 6

If Obadiah fears that Ahab would take an unsubstantiated report of Elijah's presence as a sign of his disloyalty, the king of Aram fears that the leakage of secrets from his counsel meetings is a sign that one of his courtiers has been disloyal to him. Kings like Saul fear that their courtiers *are keeping information from them;* the king of Aram fears that his courtiers are *not keeping his information secret.* More than once or twice, the king of Aram plans to move troops to a specific place, and Elisha informs the king of Israel, who takes appropriate countermeasures (vv. 8–10). The heart of the king of Aram is agitated; he calls his courtiers and asks, "Will you tell me which of us is for the king of Israel?" (v. 11). This might seem like a rather naive question, asking a traitor to reveal himself in public. It may also be naive to expect another courtier to denounce the traitor, because he who does so shows that he too has been disloyal, because he had this crucial knowledge and did not report it earlier to the king. The question also illustrates the feelings of desperation and isolation experienced by a king who feels that he has not been fully informed by his trusted servants. One of "us" is not for us, but for my enemy. All of "you" need to inform "me." The uninformed king is alone and vulnerable. "You" are together and know what is going on; I am alone and in the dark.

The courtier who answers actually *supports the king's accusation of disloyalty in the very act of denying it.* He says that it is not they who have given the secret information to the enemy; it is Elisha, who even tells the king of Israel the words the Aramean king utters in his bedchamber (v. 12). If the courtier already knows this, why hasn't he told his king, the same way that Elisha tells the king of Israel what he knows? As we have seen, Doeg has been accused of being too slow (*and too fast!*) in reporting to Saul David's presence at Nob. That case is complex and somewhat ambiguous. Here, however, the courtier's dilatory behavior seems clearly disloyal. This is not acknowledged by the Aramean king, however.[7] The king merely orders his men to go and see where Elisha is, so that he may send and take him. Locating Elisha seems to be no problem; the king is told that the prophet is in Dothan (v. 13; the narrator does not say whether this information was difficult to obtain or ready at hand).

---

[7] This may be due to the fact that the story is designed to direct our attention to the wonder-working prophet from this point on, and not on the king's problems with his courtiers. The king's predicament merely sets the stage for Elisha's dramatic confrontation with the Aramean soldiers.

If the king of Aram is in an analogous position to Saul and Ahab,[8] Elisha is in an analogous position to Abiathar's ephod *and* David's secret communications network in 2 Sam 17. In all three cases, top secret information about the movements of one king (or would-be king) are reported to another. Elisha's prophetic insight, the priestly device of the ephod (and presumably the Urim), and the human spy network all function equivalently.

This fact may have influenced the way in which the history/narrative relationship in 2 Kgs 6 has been understood by commentators. In the case of 1 Kgs 18, commentators who did not take into account the historical link between sharing information and loyalty tended to misconstrue the narrative. Here the functional equivalence of the three methods of transmitting information may have contributed both to historical explanations of Elisha's feats and to dismissals of such explanations as "historicizing." As mentioned earlier in relation to Samson, John Gray believes that Elisha's amazing knowledge about the enemy really means that he had organized "an efficient intelligence service" (1970, 513). Gray surmises that Elisha had access to information through his mobility, through his "local contacts," and through secrets leaked by Israelite women prisoners who had become maids and concubines (513, 515). In regard to this last source he alludes to evidence from "recent wars" (515–16). In other words, Elisha's knowledge *stands for* or *represents* the acquisition of knowledge by human means, including information acquired through knowing in the biblical sense in the palace bedrooms. Montgomery and Gehman do not go as far as Gray, but they also draw an analogy between Elisha's famous deeds and recent wars, specifically, "the fame of underground reports" in World War I and World War II (1951, 381).

Cogan and Tadmor, on the other hand, find Gray's "kind of historicizing" to be "wide of the mark," adding that this deprives Elisha of his "prophetic qualities" (1988, 75 n. 1). For his part, Gwilym Jones merely notes that the text does not need to be "justified" by using Gray's approach, because the "parapsychological knowledge" predicated of Elisha "obviously contains an exaggeration" (1984, 425–26). In other words, Jones prefers a psychologizing interpretation to a historicizing one. He does not add that hyperbole and exaggeration characterize ancient and modern royal propaganda about the *king's* ability to gain information from bedrooms and even the minds of the occupants (see the discussion of Qoh 10:20 in ch. 3, above).

Neither the pro- or antihistoricizing scholars cited here consider whether the *ancient audiences* of 2 Kgs 6 would view Elisha's knowledge

---

[8] Although Ahab differs from the others in the sense that he is never said to suspect that his courtier (Obadiah) has been disloyal or that Obadiah has hidden the prophets.

as standing for human spy networks or as prophetic second-sight. As far as the ideal narrative audience[9] is concerned, it is doubtful whether that audience would take Elisha (or the ephod in 1 Sam 23 and 30) as merely standing for the kind of human spy network described in 2 Sam 17. The same would be true for the authorial audience, as long as they accepted the reality of God as being able to know everything and as working miracles, the mode of reality promoted by many biblical texts. In 2 Kgs, Elisha's "reality" is based on his own miraculous powers, including his power in matters of knowledge acquisition and political information management. One need only think of 2 Kgs 8:7–15, where Elisha's transmission of his special knowledge to Hazael leads directly to the assassination of the king of Aram. The king is replaced by his assassin, the very man to whom Elisha had confided this dangerous information. Hazael transformed the knowledge he received from Elisha into power in the most human, and the most direct, way possible.

Jeremiah 37–38

The interaction between King Zedekiah and the prophet Jeremiah demonstrates the life-and-death importance of knowing when to share information, when to withhold it, and when to disseminate *dis*information. The king asks Jeremiah for information (דבר) and tells him not to hide anything from him. If Jeremiah complies, the king will not put him to death, as Jeremiah fears, regardless of what the prophet might say (38:14–16). Later, Zedekiah predicts that his courtiers will do the same thing: ask Jeremiah for information (about Jeremiah's conversation with the king), tell the prophet not to hide anything, and add that they will not put him to death if he complies (38:25). The king then reverses roles with the advisor Jeremiah, advising him to answer the courtiers with disinformation rather than refusing to talk (38:26). The courtiers do approach Jeremiah and ask him, and the prophet replies as the king directed. The strategy works: "and they were silent with him because the דבר had not been heard" (38:27).

This scene is instructive for several reasons. With both king and courtiers, sharing secret information is presented as a way for the informer to avoid being killed. *All* information must be shared ("don't hide anything" [38:14, 25; cf. 1 Sam 3:17; 2 Sam 14:18]). However, the courtiers add the implicit threat that if Jeremiah does not comply they will kill him, while

---

[9] One of the roles played by any reader. This role is that of a member of an audience that accepts uncritically what the narrator has to say, as opposed to the authorial audience, the hypothetical audience for whom the author rhetorically designs the work; see Rabinowitz 1977, 134; cf. 126–27).

the king makes no such threat.

At the same time, Jeremiah fears he will be killed if he *does* comply. Zedekiah allays this fear by swearing a secret oath not to kill Jeremiah if the prophet shares his information with him (38:16). This is a variation of the normal loyalty oath, in which subjects swear to report all information to the king (often with implicit or explicit threat of death for noncompliance). In other words, instead of the usual "if you don't tell, you will die," we have "if you tell, you won't die." An even greater deviation from the norm is that in this instance the one who swears is the king, not a subject of the king.

The element of secrecy is stressed both here and in the king's earlier request for information in chapter 37. Matters are to be conducted in secret (בסתר; 37:17; 38:16). The king also tells Jeremiah that he should "let no man know" about their communication; if he obeys, he will not die (38:24). In this case, withholding secret information, rather than sharing it, is the key to staying alive. The key in all these cases is to retain *control* over the flow of information. By telling Jeremiah to give the courtiers false information about their *tête-à-tête,* Zedekiah keeps Jeremiah alive, at least as long as the courtiers remain unaware that they have been lied to. In fact, Jeremiah's answer effectively ends their oral communication with him ("they were silent with him"). Zedekiah's strategy also serves his own interests. Having Jeremiah withhold the truth by sharing a falsehood, he ensures that his courtiers remain uninformed and presumably off-balance. While in most cases courtiers attempt to control the king by withholding information from him, or "leak" secret information about the king to others, here the king attempts to control his courtiers by keeping *them* "out of the loop."

The narratives surveyed (and dreamt about) in this chapter give some indication of the pervasiveness and subtlety of royal information management in the Hebrew Bible. However, if we want to assess the role played by the king's manipulation of the private-public distinction, we must examine the history and operation of that distinction in various settings, before zeroing in on the crucial role played by privacy in the David narrative. This will be our task in the next chapter.

5

INVADING DAVID'S PRIVACY: POWER, GOSSIP, AND THE PRIVATE-PUBLIC DISTINCTION

PRIVATE LIFE AND A LEADER'S PUBLIC PERFORMANCE

If we are going to discuss the private lives of *any* kings, biblical or nonbiblical, our first duty is to admit that the terms *private* and *public* are extremely complex and that the concept of privacy has changed considerably over the centuries. It might therefore be helpful to begin by listing the most common understandings of the terms.[1] The *private* has been described as that which is hidden, inaccessible, invisible, unaccountable, home- (*oikos*) and family-related, secluded, personal, protected from the public, independent, individual, and as that which is one's own (*idion*). Over time, the meanings have tended to shift from privacy in the sense of being "deprived" (e.g., of participation in public communal life) to being "privileged," that is, able to enjoy rights, benefits, and intimacy to the exclusion of others (or *by* excluding others) in the community (see Williams 1983, 203–4). In contrast, the *public* is that which is open, accessible, visible, accountable, state (*polis*)-related, collective, and that which is common to all (*koinon*). The concept of the public has also shifted over time. In fact, Ariès (1989, 9) offers a "dual definition of the public." The first definition centers on changes in "sociability" over the centuries, and the second focuses on the state (making the private whatever falls outside the state's purview).

Where does the king fit in to all this? He is the quintessential public figure, but most kings also jealously guard their privacy and invisibility. And if the king is the only true individual (see ch. 1), only he can be totally private. Privacy can also imply being secluded and alone, and we have already talked about the unparalleled aloneness of the king. Kings also attempt to sustain a cognitive societal boundary between private and public that will allow them to maintain their power and security. The Roman imperial concept of "sovereignty," as characterized by Weintraub (1997, 11), is a

---

[1] See especially Arendt 1958, 22–78; Williams 1983, 242–43; Sennett 1977, 17–18; and the essays in Weintraub and Kumar 1997. Other scholars are cited in the discussion itself.

clear-cut example: "a centralized, unified, and omnipotent apparatus of rule which stands above the society and governs it through the enactment and administration of laws. The 'public' power of the sovereign rules over, and in principle on behalf of, a society of 'private' and politically passive individuals who are bearers of rights granted to them and guaranteed by the sovereign." Weintraub believes that this notion of *sovereign* accords with the common tendency for political thought to make monarchy its "main point of reference" in this and other civilizations (1997, 12).

At the same time, we must not lose sight of the fact that monarchy is a complex and Protean phenomenon that feeds on paradox. For example, the king creates a private realm as "not-me," yet his location at the center of the public realm is the most private and exclusive position of all. In one sense, he is alone on the point of the pyramid of power, while in another his "body politic" is coextensive with the state as a whole. This is what Buccellati means when he says that "the king was not just a more powerful private individual, he embodied a distinct organism" (1996, 132). He also remarks that "the Assyrian Empire was an extended palace of the king" (151). Does this mean that the palace represents all public space or merely that these kings attempt to keep the people under surveillance as Louis XIV spied on his corralled courtiers at Versailles? Perhaps it implies that Assyrian kings ran the country the way an Assyrian father would run his household. For someone like Arendt, this notion of "nation-wide 'housekeeping'" is quite modern and a way of looking at the public realm that is antithetical to ancient Greek practice (60; cf. 28–49). In either case, paradox remains. The very fact that the Assyrian kings administered royal (and therefore public) property at their own discretion has itself been cited as evidence that it should be "considered to be the first truly *private* property" (Hudson 1996, 10).

Of the opposed private and public traits listed above, we have already become very familiar with the distinctions between the hidden and the open, the visible and invisible, the accessible and the inaccessible. Or to use the animal emblems employed in the introduction, the opposition between the hedgehog and the fox. There we concluded that a successful king must be both, at least to some extent. When it comes to the king's private life and its effect on the ruler's public performance, we will find once again that the opposition between the visible and the invisible—the hidden and the open—are most crucial for the analysis.

In his 1984 book *Privacy,* Barrington Moore notes a "recent" tendency among "an educated but very influential elite" in "Western circles" to "bracket sexual preference and the use of alcohol as purely private matters which have nothing to do with a person's performance of a public role ... in politics." Indeed, "newspaper reporters have been inclined to be very discreet about the ... sexual behavior of high government officials"

(Moore 1984, 153–54). Suddenly, 1984 C.E. seems eons ago. Actually, one could argue that the attitude Moore is describing was not always in evidence even when he published his work. In 1977, Richard Sennett had argued that a culture of personality has developed since the mid-nineteenth century that focuses "on what the person felt, rather than on what he did" (1977, 269). Sennett emphasizes the way modern leaders use their "secular charisma" to divert the people's attention from their public deeds to their personal motives and authenticity (265–75). He believes that "the electronic media play a crucial role in this deflection, by simultaneously overexposing the leader's personal life and obscuring his work in office" (265). Journalist Michael Janeway lends support to Sennett's view of the media's role when he traces the current interest in leaders' personalities to the fact that "government doesn't work." This leads top government officials to "act out roles," and "the more the job description has to do with image, ... the more the press is of a mind to treat office-holders ... as 'personalities'" (Janeway 1993, 115).

At the same time it is clear that many people currently exhibit great interest in their leaders' personal motives and private lives without being manipulated to do so by those leaders or the media. Ancient and early modern texts show that this form of curiosity is nothing new. In his "Precepts of Statecraft," Plutarch remarks that "men in public life [are not only] held responsible for their public words and actions, but people busy themselves with all their concerns: dinner, love affair, marriage, amusement, and every serious interest" (*Mor.* 800d–e; 1960, 171). If the people discover "small faults" in the lives of leaders they will "appear great" because the majority regard governing and public office "as a great thing which ought to be clean of all eccentricities and errors." (1960, 171). Writing in the late sixteenth century, Montaigne notes the same interest in observation and severe judgment: "the great are watched even to their expressions and thoughts, since all the people think they have a right and an interest to judge them; moreover, blemishes are magnified according to the eminence and brightness of the place where they are located" (Montaigne 1958, 194). Clearly, these observers of "the great" assume that private behavior is so intimately linked with a leader's public performance that it must be judged far more rigorously than would be the case with ordinary people.

It seems likely that these observers would also agree with Aeschines's contention that "the man who is wicked in his private relations (ὁ ἰδίᾳ) would never be found trustworthy in public affairs" (Aeschines, *Ctes.* 78; 1948, 371; cf. *Tim.* 30; 1948, 29). Nevertheless, both ancient and modern observers acknowledge that in some cases personal peccadilloes are tolerated, ignored, or even admired, if there is general satisfaction with the leader's public behavior. Thus, Isocrates' Nicocles notes "that those kings also are highly thought of by the multitude who are just in their dealing with their citizens, even though they provide themselves with pleasures from outside their households" (*Nic.* 37; 1961, 99).[2]

Examples ancient and modern suggest that the public can react in a variety of ways to reports of a leader's private failings and sexual transgressions. While they sometimes renounce or do away with leaders who commit such offenses, in other cases they continue to support them in spite of—or even because of—these private transgressions. The career of one extraordinary leader can furnish us with excellent examples of *all* these seemingly contradictory attitudes. This is Alcibiades, the charismatic fifth-century Athenian aristocrat whose leadership and generalship played such a key role in the conduct of the Peloponnesian War. All sources agree that Alcibiades' private life was characterized by extravagant behavior that violated social and moral norms. Orators and comic poets attacked his sexual conduct, including his adultery and wife-stealing (see Ostwald 1986, 116–18, 298). Thucydides reports that he indulged desires even though their satisfaction cost more than he could afford (6.15.3). Plutarch (*Alc.* 16.1.4) singles out his hubristic indulgence in drunkenness and lewdness as well as his lavish expenditures and domineering conduct.

If ever a private life were to affect a leader's public performance—or at least the public perception of that performance—this would be it. Yet the popular response to Alcibiades' personal life was just as complex and contradictory as the man himself. According to Thucydides, his political rival Nicias attacked his policies by claiming that they were motivated solely by self-interest. Nicias charges that Alcibiades' desire to live a brilliant personal life could endanger the state, for such people do harm to public affairs (τὰ δημόσια) while they waste what is their own (τὰ ἴδια; 6.12.2). Thucydides himself seems to agree. He repeatedly claims to know that Alcibiades' motives for public actions were actually selfish and personal. And after describing Alcibiades' personal excesses, he declares that it was this sort of thing that later brought about the downfall of the Athenian *polis* (6.15.3–4).[3] Yet Thucydides does not attribute this disastrous outcome to the effect Alcibiades' private behavior had on his ability to lead. On the contrary,

---

[2] At this point in the earlier versions of the chapter that were presented at the 1994 CBA meeting and the 1995 SBL, I briefly discussed public reaction to revelations of adultery among former United States presidents (and similar allegations against the then-current president). After all the bizarrerie surrounding the Monica Lewinsky fiasco, I do not have the heart (or stomach) to update and revise that material. Too much has already been said and written.

[3] Seager (1967, 8) observes that "Thucydides is not elsewhere concerned with men's private lives; that he is so here testifies to the importance of Alcibiades's private affairs in determining his public fortunes."

"publicly he managed the conduct of the war most excellently" (6.15.4); even much later Alcibiades benefitted the state more than anyone else could have done, because of his unique abilities as a leader (8.86.4).

Ironically, Alcibiades' private conduct had disastrous public effects because it frightened the people enough to remove him and entrust their affairs to inferior public servants who soon brought about the ruin of the state:

> For the masses, afraid of the magnitude of his personal lawlessness [τὸ ἑαυτοῦ σῶμα παρανομίας] in his manner of living ... became hostile to him on the ground that he was aiming at a tyranny; ... in his private life [τὰ ἰδίᾳ] every man had been offended at his practices. (6.15.4; 1966, 209, 211 [trans. modified])

While the ultimate outcome of Alcibiades' private behavior might have been his removal and his near-scapegoating, this does not occur until after his political foes use his private life to substantiate the trumped-up charge that Alcibiades was involved in a religious transgression, the desecration of the herms (6.28). In fact, Plutarch claims that prior to his removal the people were actually quite tolerant of Alcibiades' private excesses, describing them with euphemisms and writing them off with a "boys will be boys" rationalization (*Alc.* 16.3). What leads to such apologetics is the Athenians' appreciation of Alcibiades' financial support for public enterprises, together with his exalted pedigree, oratorical skill, personal attractiveness, and military ability (16.3). In this instance, popular approval of a leader's public actions and enviable personal traits lead to tolerance of his private peccadilloes, rather than the objectionable private behavior leading to disapproval of his public performance.

Kings As Totally Public

If many of these thinkers disagree about the ways in which wealth, power, satiety, and personal desire will affect a leader's public performance, they all seem to assume that the ideal leader will be totally devoted to his or her public role, totally detached from private desires and goals. Studies of powerful kings like Louis XIV and James I often do describe these leaders as being so totally enveloped in their public role that they no longer have any trace of a private life. Speaking of Louis XIV, Castan observes that "the king devoured the man, dispossessing him of privacy even in death"; he enjoyed little intimacy and still less family life (1989, 403, 419). Referring to James I, Goldberg notes that "the king, so fully a public person, scarcely even had ... a moment to himself; his most intimate bodily functions, his dressing, undressing, and going to bed, were attended, public events" (Goldberg: 150 1983, cf. Castan [1989, 420] on Louis XIV's *levers*). In a prefatory letter to the *Basilikon Doron,* James I

describes the king's public exposure in terms that are the exact reverse of
Louis XIV's panoptic dream: "Kings ... are as it were set (as it was said
of old) upon a publike stage, in the sight of all the people; where all the
beholders eyes are attentively bent to looke and pry in the least circum-
stance of their secretest drifts" (quoted in Goldberg 1983, 113–14).
Similarly, Montaigne (1958, 194) attributes to King Alfonso XI of Castile
the comment that in one respect "asses were better off than kings: their
masters let them eat in peace, whereas kings cannot obtain that favor of
their servants." Montaigne (1958, 702) sums up the problem nicely in his
essay "Of the Disadvantage of Greatness": "Their royal status stifles and
consumes their other real and essential qualities; these are sunk in royalty.... It takes so much to be a king that he exists only as such."

The fact that kings may be "sunk in royalty" so much that the "king
devours the man" does not guarantee that they will prove successful in their
public performance, even when their devotion to their public role annihi-
lates all remnants of personal desire and private life. The best example is the
consummate public servant, Sophocles' King Oedipus, who has already
been discussed as a king manipulated by the information managers who surround him. According to Benardete (1964, 3), "Oedipus is the completely
public man. He has an openness and transparency that leave no room for
the private and secret." His "utter publicity" stems from "his being only what
he is as ruler of Thebes" (4). Oedipus continually stresses that he wants all
new information concerning the unknown regicide who has caused the
plague to be broadcast for all to hear (e.g., *Oed. tyr.* 93). He points out that
he himself, and not some messenger, came to speak with the supplicants
who want him to save the city as he earlier saved it from the Sphinx (*Oed.
tyr.* 7–9). He calls this assemblage of old men and youths his "children"
(*Oed. tyr.* 1) and tells them that he is more sick than any of them, because
"your grief comes to each alone, ... but my soul laments for the city, for
myself, and for you, all at once [πόλιν τε κἀμὲ καὶ σ' ὁμοῦ]" (*Oed. tyr.* 59–64).

Here is a king who is not only "sunk in royalty" but experiences the
state as his *oikia* and himself as the *paterfamilias*. This should come as no
surprise in light of our earlier discussion of Oedipus's abysmal ignorance
about intimate matters involving his actual household, that is, his wife and
children, and his private self. In one sense, Oedipus's detachment from
personal emotions and his total absorption in his role as king do seem to
contribute to his success as a public servant—at least until the arrival of the
plague that turns out to be caused by his private and political crimes.
Benardete (1964, 7) asserts that Oedipus's "crimes have their origin in the
privacy of the body..., and they are detected through his body; but his
own lack of privacy, which perfectly accords with the absence of all desires
in Oedipus, leads him to look away from the body." Oedipus's obliviousness
to everything private, including private emotions, keeps him from recogniz-

ing that the swollen ankles that gave him his name are the *symbolon* (*Oed. tyr.* 221)—the knuckle-bone clue—he needs to lead him to the criminal.

Perhaps one moral of this story is that a leader who lacks privacy and desire may not succeed as a public servant, because every leader has a private history, a body, and a personal life, which, if ignored, may come back to rewrite public history, undermine the body politic, and threaten the life of the city. Even if one follows Girard (1987a, 68–88) and views Oedipus as a scapegoat who is willing to accept all responsibility for the plague by pleading guilty to what Girard believes are false charges of incest and patricide, the fact that he is so oblivious to his own personal life makes it easier to attach these particular crimes to him. Along with adultery and cannibalism, incest and patricide destroy the distinctions that define and support the private realm, including the concepts of family and the body. And because these acts undermine the stability of the private sphere, they also destroy the boundary separating the private and the public, thereby threatening the public realm as well (see Lasine 1991a, 29–35; 1993, 178). When the alleged perpetrator of these actions is the king, the resulting crisis is as fully political as it is personal.

Kings As Managers of the Private-Public Distinction

If Oedipus's kingship is characterized by openness and visibility, the typical tyrant acquires and maintains power through invisibility and secrecy. The parade example is Gyges, the Lydian king who "was widely regarded as the first tyrant" in antiquity (Drews 1972, 138; see ch. 1, above). In both Herodotus and Plato, the power of Gyges (or his ancestor) is based on his ability to remain invisible while invading others' privacy and seeing what should not be seen. And in both cases the result is the murder of a king, marriage to the murdered king's wife, and appropriation of the kingdom— in other words, the same series of acts committed unwittingly by Oedipus. Plato's Glaucon believes that even a just man who was given Gyges's power of invisibility would violate the privacy of others in ways characteristic of a tyrant, including taking "what he wanted from the market without fear" and going "into houses and [having] intercourse with whomever he wanted" (*Rep.* 360b; 1968, 38). Later in *Republic* Socrates asserts that the man ruled by *Eros tyrannos* may commit incest or a blood-polluting murder as well (*Rep.* 571c–d; 574e–575a). The actions of the invisible tyrant illustrate what the Greeks call *pleonexia,* the desire for "more," when acquiring more comes at the expense of another (*Rep.* 359c; see Vlastos 1971, 71, 75). Of course, not all tyrants become invisible thanks to a magic ring (*Rep.* 359d–360b) or by peeping at a queen from behind a door in her private chamber at the insistence of her husband (Herodotus, *Hist.* 1.9–10). We will discuss several more mundane methods in the next chapter.

However, even visible kings are not necessarily knowable. As noted by Castan (1989, 419), the fact that Louis XIV lived on view amid public places and had little intimacy and still less family life resulted in his becoming the "inscrutable master of himself and his realm." Admittedly, James I likens his breast to a "Christall window" (Goldberg 1983, 114) and describes the king as being viewed by prying beholders. Yet James also fears that the people may misinterpret the king's inward intention because they "seeth but the outward part" (114). Goldberg shows that James I actually used the rhetoric of the *arcana imperii* to conceal his "inward part": "the king's retired mysteries clothe royal pleasures; beneath his assertions of the inscrutability of the royal will are secret desires and delights," such as his frequent absences from court, pleasure jaunts, and disinclination to take seriously the business of state (82–83). When the king does appear in public it is "his own unobservability" that is on display, for public figures "create the private as that which is displayed but cannot be seen" (150, 153).

The managed inscrutability of kings and other public figures creates problems for a public that is intensely interested in their leaders' private lives and sexual sins. According to Mellencamp (1992, 156), gossip also "searches for the authentic behind the representation," only to discover "the impossibility of knowing: we are intimate with the public persona, the familiar tics, habits, and performed behavior, yet can never know the 'real' person." This itself promotes "epistemophilia" (169). However, the unknowability of public persons is not the only factor that triggers the drive for knowledge. In his description of individualism and privacy in late nineteenth-century Europe, Corbin notes that "fears of violation of self and its secrets produced a tremendous desire to unmask others and penetrate their secrets" (1990, 473). Such explanations of epistemophilia are consistent with the biblical accounts of what one critic of detective fiction (Brand 1985, 43; see Lasine 1987, 248) calls "epistemological anxiety," that is, anxiety over the inability to decipher the private motives and thoughts of one's fellows, a cognitive failing that makes one vulnerable to others' duplicity and maliciousness. In other words, *know others before they can know you*. And who is in a better position to violate an ordinary person's privacy than inscrutable leaders who employ spies and informers to make others visible to themselves—a practice characteristic not only of Deiokes but of later kings like Louix XIV (and queens like Elizabeth I; see Archer 1993, 45–49).

As mentioned earlier, Aristotle is among those who advise tyrants to make full use of spies and eavesdroppers (*Pol.* 1313b11–14).[4] He also recommends that the ruler should arrange "for the people in the city to be always visible and to hang about the palace-gates," where they have the

---

[4] Aristotle cites the tyrant Periander of Corinth and Persian monarchs as his sources for many of these practices (*Pol.* 1313a38–39).

least opportunity to conceal what they are doing (*Pol.* 1313b7–8; 1959, 459–61). In addition, the ruler should prohibit all sorts of social and political gatherings among his people and, in general, make them unknown (ἀγνῶτες) to one another as much as possible, for such knowledge increases mutual confidence (1313b1–6). In fact, the ruler should actively undermine confidence between friends and family members and encourage mutual distrust (1314a18). He should set his people "to accusing [διαβάλλειν] one another, ... cause conflict between friend and friend" and encourage the power of women in the home, so that they will inform against the men (1313b17–18, 34–35). The tyrant must also distrust *his* friends more than anyone (1313b31–32; cf. Plato, *Rep.* 567d–568a; 576a). If a tyrant keeps the people under constant surveillance, prohibits free social intercourse, sows distrust, discourages open expression of one's thoughts, and encourages informers, the people will become used to having little mind of their own because they will always be acting in a servile way (Aristotle, *Pol.* 1313b8–9). In so doing, the tyrant can effectively destroy any feeling of community among the people, and eliminate the public realm as a space for productive interchange.[5]

Aristotle goes on to counsel the tyrant that he should not parade his vices to the world (1314b31). In addition, he should be viewed collecting taxes and requiring public services only for state purposes, as if these funds "belong to the public and not himself" (1314b14–18). This advice implies that the tyrant actually does the opposite of what this display implies; that is, he treats public funds as if they were his private possessions. So when Aristotle interprets Jason of Pherae's statement that "he felt hungry when he could not rule tyrannically" to mean "that he did not know how to live as a private citizen" (*Pol.* 1277a24–25), he is saying that Jason does not know how to live without treating the public's funds as his own private possession. Aristotle's emphasis on the tyrant being viewed as if he were a true public servant implies that a leader may seek invisibility not only to hide his private vices but to be in a position to display to his people a convincing image of public virtue.

PRIVACY, GOSSIP AND ROYAL INFORMATION MANAGEMENT IN THE COURT HISTORY

One does not have to be a professional reader of the Bible to note that the Court History of David is "largely a chronicle of throne and bed," as Rosenberg (1986, 124) puts it. Actually, it is often more bed than throne, for,

---

5 Some of the writers who have traced the history of the public-private distinction (e.g., Arendt and Sennett) have concluded that it is the *modern* Western world that has experienced the end of "the public realm."

as Whybray (1968, 16) points out, "the author lets us into many secrets about private motives, [while] the public and political aspects of David's reign are extremely meagerly dealt with." This emphasis on the private and personal raises a number of complex issues involving the relationship between leaders' personal desires and their political duties. How relevant is a king's private behavior to his public performance? Do kings and other public figures have any right to privacy, or must they accept Teresa of Avila's conclusion that "nothing is private in the life of the great" (quoted in Castan 1989, 403)? Why has there been so much popular interest in learning the details of leaders' private lives, from ancient Israel and Greece to the present day?

Such questions are especially urgent at a time when morbid, obsessive curiosity about the private lives and sexual sins of leaders has become the norm. The very fact that this international obsession has become an accepted part of our social machinery helps to explain why some present-day nonprofessional readers of the Court History view the story of King David as surprisingly modern and why they might describe it as having a "soap-opera" or "tabloid" quality. Such labels are not as outlandish as they might seem at first glance. Elite journalists like A. M. Rosenthal of *The New York Times* distance themselves from tabloid journalism by lamenting that they "did not become a newspaperman to hide outside a politician's house to find out whether he was in bed with somebody" (quoted in Janeway 1993, 119). Yet this is precisely where the narrator of 2 Sam 11 and 13 places his readers! Is the author of the Court History addressing an audience of "inquiring minds [who] want to know"? Whybray actually goes a step further when he asserts that the narrative takes "the reader ... into corners and private rooms *to spy upon* secret meetings and to listen to intimate and secret conversations" (1968, 15; emphasis mine). Here the reader actually works for the *National Enquirer*. It is *the reader* who ultimately invades David's privacy and witnesses the exposure of his shameful deeds.

Elite biblical scholars often envision the author, rather than the reader, to be little different from a tabloid journalist or a professional gossiper. Whybray (1968, 16) and many others suggest that the origin of all the private information we receive in 2 Samuel is "common court gossip" (Weingreen 1969, 265). M. H. Segal speculates that "the writer was one of David's closest servants, always in attendance..., with a personal and inside knowledge of ... both public and private affairs" (quoted in M. Sternberg 1985, 62). The fact that the reader is informed about David's unethical and criminal acts is thought to ensure a tenth-century date and an origin in court gossip, "because the things [David] did were publicly known and could not be baldly denied" (McCarter 1984, 15). Leaving aside the fact that political leaders *do* "baldly" (and "plausibly") deny things that are publicly known or believed, it is clear that these commentators have tremendous respect for the power of gossip and do not put much faith in a monarch's efforts to control the flow of information. They assume that the most the apologetic narrative can achieve is spin control. As Whitelam (1984, 62, 64) puts it, the Court History is an exercise in "image-projection" and propaganda. Whether or not one accepts the notion of a tenth-century date, conjectures about eye- and earwitnesses supplying the historian with court gossip do call attention to the fact that the reader is presented with data that in "real life" could only be gathered from a self-effacing Watergate-style "Deep Throat" inside the house of David or from the self-renewing spring of popular gossip.

The control of gossip and the maintenance of a firm boundary between the private and public realms play a much larger role in the success of kings than one might expect. If one is to appreciate this fact, one must go beyond the superficial use of the concepts of privacy and gossip found in existing studies of the Court History. Only then can one appreciate why kings like the biblical David focus on problems of information management and are presented as personally impenetrable.

According to Spacks (1986, 262), gossip occupies "a liminal position" between public and private: "blurring the boundaries between the personal and the widely known, it implicitly challenges the separation of realms." As Bergmann puts it (1993, 118), gossipers are "border-runners." Spacks also notes that gossip "interprets public facts in private terms" (1986, 262). This is precisely the purpose assigned to the private data in the Court History by Whybray (1968, 16), who notes that "it is almost entirely by means of ... private scenes that [the author] gives his interpretation of ... the principal personages."

Finally, gossipers typically seek personal knowledge about people in order to make judgments about them. Gossip has been described as "a prime vehicle for moral evaluation" (Bok 1984, 92). It is characteristically self-righteous or moralistic (e.g., Bergmann 1993, 99–100, 122, 129; Spacks 1986, 136). As noted by Bergmann (1993, 128; 134), gossip "relentlessly and remorselessly penetrates" the facade of reputation in order to seek out "private mistakes and flaws" and turn them into "publicly relevant" flaws. Apparently, most gossipers would agree with Aeschines' contention that "the man who is wicked in his private relations would never be found trustworthy in public affairs" (Aeschines, *Ctes.* 78; 1948, 371; see above).

If gossip tends to invade privacy in order to discover and judge a person's character, kings seek to maintain their power by creating a private zone in which they and their family members can remain invisible to their subjects, by publicly displaying themselves to their people while remaining personally impenetrable, and by controlling the flow of information going to and from their court—including information that evaluates their actions and character. In so doing they illustrate most of the senses given to the term *private* since the ancient period, namely, the invisible, the inaccessible or privileged, the personal, and that which is related to family. Kings control the flow of information and inhibit gossip by stationing loyal agents—the King's Ears and Eyes—throughout their realm, who not only keep them informed but lead the people to control their speech so that they say or do nothing to harm the kings or their dynasties. Put another way, the ideal monarchical state is Bentham's Panopticon writ large.

The managed inscrutability of kings and other public figures creates problems for a public that is intensely interested in their leaders' private lives and sexual sins. Even the modern charismatic leader discussed by Sennett burdens his followers with "making sense of him as a person in order to understand what he is doing once in power," although "the very terms of personality are such that they can never succeed in that act" (Sennett 1977, 265). Sennett contends that "suicide in modern politics lies in insisting that 'you need know nothing about my private life; all you need to know is what I believe and the programs I'll enact'" (270). This focus on the personal can even take priority over the gossiper's penchant for moral judgment; thus, popular reaction to the private failings of leaders from David and Alcibiades to JFK and Bill Clinton has ranged from moral condemnation to indifference to *increased* adulation (with the exception of the last-named leader).

Our survey of nonbiblical perspectives on leadership and private life indicates that the private desires and sexual misconduct of leaders can be interpreted as having a variety of effects on their public performance. Moreover, the people who are so intently interested in their leaders' private lives respond to such behavior in a number of different ways. The narrator of the Court History is just as interested in David's love affairs and marriages—and just as likely to watch and judge even his expressions and thoughts—as are the observers of the great described by Plutarch, Montaigne, and students of modern tabloid journalism. But do David's people and the narrator of 2 Samuel agree with Aeschines that the man who is wicked in his private life cannot be trustworthy in public affairs? We cannot know whether the people or members of the court were as tolerant of David's sins against Bathsheba and Uriah as were the followers of Plutarch's Alcibiades, because their response (if any) is not reported. We do not even know who—in the textual world of 2 Samuel—was aware of these actions, other than Joab and David's anonymous agents. Nevertheless, the narrator provides sufficient information for readers to gauge the impact of David's private actions as a husband and father on his public conduct as king.

The Court History also furnishes much data on David's visibility and invisibility as king. His leadership style rarely approaches the openness and publicity of Oedipus, who, like David, attained power by defeating a monstrous, seemingly invincible foe and married a tabooed woman after killing her former husband (see ch. 3, above). On the other hand, David occasionally approaches James I's king who is displayed but not seen— either by the people in the story or by the readers of that story. After examining the texts that focus on these aspects of David's private life, I will conclude by grappling with these key questions: How *are* we expected to respond to all the data given—and withheld—about David's private life and personal emotions? Are we to view his private conduct as shameful, so that we might condemn the king in a way that was not possible for his followers in the text?

Tyranny, Secrecy, and Sin in the Story of David and Bathsheba

This was a war we had today, not a family quarrel.
—Joab to David, in Heller, *God Knows* (1985, 372)

As we have seen, the typical Greek tyrant acquires and maintains power—and then abuses that power in order to indulge his illicit desires—by means of invisibility and secrecy. From this perspective, David's actions toward Bathsheba and Uriah are a parade example of tyrannical behavior. Like the tyrants described by Aristotle (*Pol.* 1277a24–25), David "does not know how to live as a private person," because he uses his public power to treat what rightfully belongs to private citizens as if it were his own. Like Gyges and his ancestor, David commits his crimes in secret, presumably invisible to all but those who act as his agents. The same is true of other biblical sinners. Deuteronomy 27:24 curses the man who slays his neighbor "in secret." According to Ps 10, the wicked one slays the innocent and seizes the poor in "secret places" (vv. 8, 9). This evildoer arrogantly assumes that God will never see or punish him (vv. 6, 11; cf. Ps 94:7). Like David, he acts as though he has forgotten the reality of constant divine surveillance. As Goldberg said of James I, "even the opaque king has an audience, God" (1983, 149).

Several biblical texts insist that other humans will also see their sins, in the sense that the crimes committed in secret will be exposed or punished in public. Proverbs 26:26 states that a deceiver's "wickedness will be uncovered before the assembly" (McKane [1970, 253]: "in public"). According to Elihu, God smites the wicked "in a place of spectacle" (Job 34:26). Proverbs 6:32–34 is particularly relevant for a discussion of 2 Sam 11–12: "He who commits adultery ... will get wounds and dishonor [קלון]

and his disgrace [חרפה]⁶ will not be wiped away," thanks to the jealous husband's fury.

The David who is on view prior to 2 Sam 11 is a public figure who inspires universal desire and approval. He is introduced as a figure whom *everyone* desires and "loves," in every sense of the word (1 Sam 16:21; 18:1, 3, 16, 20, 22; 20:17; 2 Sam 1:26; 19:7; see Thompson 1974). When all the people take notice of David's very public lament for Abner, "it was good in their eyes, as *everything* the king did was good in the eyes of the people" (2 Sam 3:36; emphasis mine). On the other hand, very little reference is made to David's *private* desires and loves. While Abner had told David that he would gather all Israel for him so that "you may reign over all that your soul desires" (2 Sam 3:21), this ultimately occurs because of Yahweh's many gifts to the desirable David, the "man after his own heart" (see 1 Sam 13:14).

Yet it is precisely when David has received Yahweh's gifts of power, security, and women that he becomes insatiable and criminal. When Yahweh condemns David for his actions against Bathsheba and Uriah, he does not consider the possibility that it was his gifts to the king that led David to violate his commandments against coveting, adultery, and murder: "I anointed you king.... I delivered you out of the hand of Saul.... I gave you the house of your master, and the wives of your master into your bosom, and I gave you the house of Israel and Judah; and if that were too little, then I would add to you more and more such as these" (2 Sam 12:8). Given the statements on satiety in Deuteronomy and other biblical texts (see ch. 6), it should hardly have come as a surprise that a man who had been given his master's wives would go on to "take" more women who belonged to another (2 Sam 12:9–10; cf. 1 Sam 8:11–19). Like the ancestor of Gyges described by Plato's Glaucon, David is driven by *pleonexia*. David does not desire what he lacks; he has many wives. Nor is it that he simply desires more. Rather, he desires what belongs to another.

Yahweh's punishment of David underscores the element of secrecy in David's sins, partly by highlighting the fact that the punishment will be public and shameful, visible not only to God but to the people from whom he had hidden his sinful acts: "I will take your wives before your eyes, and give them to your neighbor [or "another" (רע); see Weinfeld 1972, 131], and he will lie with your wives in the sight of this sun. For you did it secretly [בסתר], but I will do this thing before all Israel and before the sun" (2 Sam 12:11–12). The punishment will occur "before the eyes of [לעיני]" the sun and of all Israel, while the adultery occurred after sunset (2 Sam 11:1–4), hidden from the eyes of all Israel. This prediction is fulfilled when

---

⁶ On the various biblical terms that describe shame and disgrace, see Bechtel 1991, 54–55. On חרפה, see ch. 11 n. 36, below.

Absalom publicly goes into his father's concubines "in the sight of all Israel" on the top of the house (2 Sam 16:22). In effect, Yahweh's punishment emphasizes David's transgression of the private-public boundary by reenacting it in reverse, with David in the role of the person whose privacy is invaded and whose property (i. e., the concubines) is violated.

Ahithophel had advised Absalom to commit this act in order that "all Israel will *hear* that you made yourself stink [נבאשת] with your father" (2 Sam 16:21; emphasis mine). The fact that both Yahweh and the narrator of chapter 16 stress the people's *seeing* David's disgrace (2 Sam 12:11–12; 16:22) suggests that part of the purpose of this public punishment is to shame David, for sight is an essential element in the experience of shame. This emphasis is shared by the Septuagint's version of Ahithophel's statement in 16:21: "all Israel hearing that you put to shame [κατήσχυνα] your father." Like the MT, this reading stresses that Absalom's breach with his father is beyond repair. Unlike the MT, however, it shifts the emphasis from public knowledge of the odium Absalom's action will engender in David to the fact that Absalom will be publicly humiliating David, the king who cannot keep his own women safe in his private dwelling, and that this disgrace will become public knowledge.[7]

In the Hebrew Bible, adultery is "an affront to the deity" (Milgrom 1990, 348), which God will punish if the clandestine adulterers are not exposed by other human beings. Milgrom (1990, 349) notes that this "great sin" is one of the sexual offenses for which God banishes the Israelites from their land and sentences them to death (see Lev 18:20, 25, 28). It is therefore related to other abominable acts[8] that lead to exile, including incest and the shedding of innocent blood (see Lasine 1993, 178–79). Because these crimes all threaten fundamental cultural categories, they are often attributed to leaders during periods of social crisis, so that the social chaos can be blamed on one scapegoat whose elimination promises to restore the society's system of differences. However, David's adultery with Bathsheba and his shedding the blood of Uriah with the sword of the Ammonites do not occur during a period of social crisis; on the contrary, they occur during a period of relative

---

[7] While it is בוש that usually expresses feeling ashamed and acting shamefully, Stansell (1994, 69, 72–73) notes that באש (to stink) is also associated with acting shamefully in verses such as 2 Sam 10:6 and 16:21.

[8] Perhaps surprisingly, it is also grouped with gossip and curiosity in some traditions. For example, Plutarch cites the legislator of Thurii and comments that "adultery does seem to be a sort of curiosity [πολυπραγμοσύνη] about another's pleasure and a searching out and examination of matters which are closely guarded and escape general observation, while πολυπραγμοσύνη is an encroaching, a debauching and denuding of secret things … a necessary concomitant of inquisitiveness is to speak evil" (*Mor.* 519b–c; 1957, 494–95; cf. 516f–517a).

security for king and kingdom. By taking Bathsheba and killing her husband David has undermined the very cultural categories a king is to stabilize and maintain (see, e.g., Prov 29:4). He has also transgressed the boundary separating the private and the public, as that boundary is drawn in biblical texts. Like the tyrants described by Aristotle, he "does not know how to live as a private person," because he uses his public power to treat what rightfully belongs to private citizens as if it were his own.

Gros Louis (1977, 28) also stresses the appropriateness of the punishment announced in 2 Sam 12:11–12. In fact, he believes that "it is almost as if the narrative is emphasizing to us the private nature of David's sin, having the Lord make it public because David is a public figure." As I noted earlier, one could *also* say that the punishment emphasizes David's transgression of the private-public boundary by reenacting it in reverse. However, one *cannot* say that "disturbing sex scenes" like the story of David taking Bathsheba show that "politics *are* sexual, and sexuality is political" and that 2 Sam 12:11–12 itself "claims their synonymity" (R. M. Schwartz 1989, 201). For Schwartz, to say "that the private acts of David have public consequences" is to engage in a "misguided quest" for such causality (201). In a revised version of her paper, she adds that "it is anachronistic to even understand [politics and sexuality] as two different spheres of life" (1991, 46). However, all of the ancient and modern texts we have been discussing recognize *some* distinction between public and private, although they might define them in different ways, and have different ideas about the ways in which the boundary separating them can be obscured or transgressed. And just as the meanings of "public" and "private" have changed over time, so have the meanings of "sex" and "sexuality" (see Foucault 1978; Posner 1992, 37–69). Therefore, to claim that politics and sexuality are simply "synonymous" is to leave *oneself* open to the charge of being ahistorical and anachronistic.

David's Inscrutability and the Reader: David's Role in the Assassination of Abner

> Would anyone observing me that day have guessed that these lofty tributes were for the death of a human who, alive, had meant as much to me, precisely, as a stone in my shoe, or a frog in my throat?
> —David, in Heller, *God Knows* (1985, 264)

Earlier I discussed gossip as a way to negotiate the boundary between public and private and as a means of demystifying the inscrutability of leaders. Spacks (1986, 262) contends that gossip "implicitly challenges the separation of realms ('home' as opposed to what lies outside it) assumed in modern times." However, challenging the separation is not the same thing as making public and private, or *polis* and *oikia,* synonymous. Spacks is closer to the mark when she says that "gossip interprets public facts in private terms" (262). Gossipers are epistemophiliacs for the same reason that biblical speakers express "epistemological anxiety." Biblical texts provide ample evidence that the citizens of urban monarchical Israel also experienced grave concern over their inability to decipher the private motives and thoughts of their fellows, a cognitive failing that made them vulnerable to others' duplicity (see Lasine 1989a, 72–74). The story of Solomon's judgment responds to such anxiety by illustrating how a human being with "godlike" wisdom about human nature might be able to overcome human cognitive limitations and expose hidden evils like the deadly envy and spite that drove the bereaved mother. In this story the royal judge conceals his thoughts and devices from the anonymous prostitutes, apparently only for the public good. He is the agent of openness and publicity (meaning that his subjects' minds are potentially open to him too), whose own inscrutability and private emotions are not a problem—as yet.

But what of Solomon's father David? Referring to the private-public distinction in the Jacobean period, Goldberg (1983, 149) remarks that "even the opaque king ... stands beneath [God's] searching and observing eye." David stands beneath the observing eye, not only of God, but of a narrator who may or may not share his much-discussed omniscience with us, his interested and anxious public. Scholars like Exum and Ackerman stress David's impenetrability and, in some cases, the "opaque quality" of a text "woven by an artful narrator" who "leaves many possibilities for us to ponder" (Ackerman 1990, 47). That is, David *does* retain his privacy with readers in the sense of invisibility or inscrutability. In a way, the reader is placed in the position of the typical courtier described by writers like Saint-Simon and La Bruyère, who must discern what the king and the other courtiers feel and know by interpreting their staged performances and looking for ways to penetrate their facades. Readers must make determinate judgments about David even when the reports of his thoughts and behavior are indeterminate. David's response to Nathan's parable and his actions (or lack of action) in relation to Amnon, Tamar, and Absalom all testify to his vacillating personal emotions and his failure in his public role (see Lasine 1984a). And while some commentators find the dispute between Mephibosheth and Ziba to be too ambiguous for either David or the reader to solve, the narrative does allow one to conclude that David mishandles the case, in stark contrast to Solomon's successful resolution of the harlot dispute (see Lasine 1989b).

Even when definite motives and feelings are attributed to David, readers may conclude that David remains inscrutable and the "truth" a mystery. Take Abner's assassination. The story begins with Ishbosheth demanding to know why Abner has been sleeping with his father's concubine. Far from implying that he did so as a political maneuver (or even admitting that he did so at all), Abner's response points to the political benefit he has brought to Saul's house and expresses outrage over Ishbosheth's charge "concerning this woman," that is, a merely personal matter (2 Sam 3:7–8). The narrator then describes Abner's apparent shift of political allegiance from Ishbosheth to David (3:12–21). He makes a "personal deal" (VanderKam 1980, 532) with David (vv. 12–13) and later "speaks personally" (McCarter 1984, 116) with the Benjaminites and with David (v. 19). Joab only learns of Abner's visit after Abner has been sent away in peace (v. 23). Joab immediately confronts David, telling him that he knows Abner has come to seduce him and to know David's comings and goings and to know all David is doing (v. 25). David is not said to respond to these charges; instead, the narrator notes that Joab sent messengers after Abner, and "David did not know it" (v. 26). After Abner returns, Joab takes him aside to speak to him "privately" (בשלי) and assassinates him, ostensibly because Abner had slain Joab's brother (v. 27). This basically private (i.e., family) motive is the only reason given for the slaying, both in verse 27 and in verse 30. When David hears of this, he lets it be known that he and his kingdom had nothing to do with this act and makes a "harsh and apparently public denunciation of Joab" (McCarter 1984, 117), consisting of a dreadful curse against Joab and his בית אב (vv. 28–29). David then makes "all the people" (vv. 31, 32, 34, 35) the audience as he displays his "highly visible grief" (VanderKam 1980, 533) in his lament for Abner. "All the people" take notice of David's fasting for Abner; it is good in their eyes, as "all the king did was good in the eyes of all the people" (v. 36). All the people and all Israel then "know" that it was not David's will to slay Abner (v. 37).

The narrator's account seems unambiguous when it comes to the feelings and motivations of the characters at key points in the story. Thus, it is *definitely* Abner's great anger at Ishbosheth (v. 8) that prompts his offer to David. It is *definitely* Joab's desire for blood-vengeance that leads him to slay Abner, even though Joab tells David that Abner is a treacherous spy. David *definitely* does not know of Joab's plot to slay Abner and weeps at Abner's grave (vv. 26, 32). To take the narrator's report at face value, however, means that we must ignore many questions raised by his account. Would David be so eager to make a covenant with a man who has already betrayed one royal figure, especially when David once told that very man that he deserved death for his failure to guard Yahweh's anointed (1 Sam 26:16)? Would David really grieve so strongly at the death of such a person? Isn't it more likely that David would "know" that Abner might possibly be a spy, especially considering the fact that David himself once engaged in similar activity with Achish king of Gath (1 Sam 27) and the Ammonites still think David capable of the same hidden agenda long after the death of Abner (2 Sam 10:3)? Could David have been oblivious to the fact that the simultaneous presence of Abner and Joab would generate a crisis in David's inner circle, not just because they would be rivals for the same post, but because of the blood feud that began with Abner's slaying of Joab's brother? Wouldn't David realize that the death of Abner would strengthen his position? And, finally, wouldn't David realize that making a public display of his grief would conveniently serve to allay any popular suspicion of his complicity in Abner's death (see Hertzberg 1964, 261 on v. 37)?

Questions like these have prevented many commentators from playing their readerly role as members of what Rabinowitz (1977, 134) calls "the ideal narrative audience," the audience that accepts "uncritically" what the narrator has to say. Many scholars assume that the author is writing "court apologetic" (McCarter 1984, 11, 121) or propaganda (Whitelam 1984, 76). For propaganda to succeed, readers must not be aware that they are reading propaganda; that is, they must adopt the role of the ideal narrative audience. In this case, they must remain unaware of what the scholars suspect, namely, that the assertions of David's ignorance and innocence cover up a totally different reality. Scholars who believe that they have uncovered the tendentiousness of the narrative, however, can then turn the narrator's definite statements about David's and Joab's knowledge and intentions upside down. The stress on Joab's private motive for killing Abner and the insistence on David's innocence become evidence that Joab *did* have a political motive for slaying Abner and that David was a co-conspirator in Abner's death. As VanderKam (1980, 533), Gunn (1978, 96), Exum (1992, 105), and Ahlström (1993, 465) all put it, the narrator "protests too much."

Of course, one can argue that the author *expected* his hypothetical audience to recognize this excessive protestation and to conclude that they should take the narrator's protests as ironic (*David didn't know—yeah, right!*). Or one can simply ignore the narrator's assertions and the question of *Tendenz*, like the rabbis[9] who declared that all of David's curses against Joab "were upheld against the seed of David, for he did not curse justly, for it was in his intention to order him killed, and so he did" (quoted in Rosenberg 1986, 246 n. 65). In the end, however, we have no way of determining whether or not the author is addressing an audience that was expected to take the narrator's word at face value—as all the people are said to have taken David's public display of grief at face value—or an audience that would assume a private truth that was the opposite of this public image.

Ultimately, debates about the authorial audience and propaganda must return to the private-public distinction. If this narrative were being recounted by the press secretary of a post-Watergate American president to

---

9 Cited by Radaq [from *b. Sanh.* 37b] in connection with 2 Sam 3:29.

an audience of network reporters and gossip columnists, that episte-
mophiliac audience would immediately echo Senator Baker's question
concerning Richard Nixon: "what did the President know and when did he
know it?" (see Kutler 1990, 361, 370, 535). They would assume a private
agenda behind the public facade. The press secretary of 2 Samuel repeatedly says that David did not know of Joab's plot; the scholarly and
rabbinical press assume he did know. When one of Freud's patients insists
that the person in his dream was not his mother, Freud (1925b, 11)
"emends this to: 'So it is his mother.' In our interpretation, we take the liberty of disregarding the negation." Interpreters who read 2 Sam 3 as
propaganda take the liberty of disregarding the narrator's negations and
emend the historical record accordingly. If the press secretary presented
the same report at a convention held by the president's *own* party, rather
than at a press conference—or a meeting of the psychoanalytical associa-
tion—everything the secretary said about David would again be good in
the eyes of all the assembled people.

When David displays himself to all the people, he directs their attention away from whatever political machinations resulted in Abner's death
and toward the mystery of his own personality and feelings, in precisely
the same way as the politicians analyzed by Sennett. David's "live" audience in the textual world of 2 Sam 3:32–37 see David and "know" that
David did not intend Abner's murder.[10] But what about the *reading* audience of 2 Sam 3, who are privy to the narrator's account of behind-the-
scenes activity? The commentators discussed earlier scrutinize the David
who is put on display by the narrator and "know" that David *was* complicit
in Abner's death. In addition, they assume that the historical David failed
to prevent "the court or urban elite" from suspecting his complicity,
because it is their rumors and suspicions that made the apology necessary
(Whitelam 1984, 71).

Scholars like Rosenberg go so far as to place the David of 2 Sam 11 "at
the center of a vast network of anonymous gossips, informers, and emissaries." This court society "renders David all the more vulnerable to public
scandal, and thus necessitates the ... coverup" that leads to the deaths of

---

[10] Considering the way in which the next chapter begins, we might ask whether
all the members of this "textual audience" ("all the people and all Israel"; 3:37) really
believe that David had nothing to do with the assassination. The narrator reports in
2 Sam 4:1 that when Ishbosheth heard about Abner's death, his hands dropped, and
all Israel became terrified. Why should Ishbosheth be so unstrung by Abner's death,
considering that Abner had become his enemy? Is it because Ishbosheth takes it for
granted that David *was* behind the assassination and might now do the same to him?
Is Israel terrified for a similar reason? If Abner's death really was the result of a *private* feud and his death really was regretted and sincerely mourned by David, why
should the Israelite *public* and their king be so frightened?

Uriah and the soldiers with him (1987, 134; cf. M. Sternberg 1985, 202). Here it is David, and not the narrator, who is responding to gossip and rumor.

David's alleged fear of "public scandal" could also be understood as a fear of being shamed. Goodfriend (1992, 1:85) points in this direction when she suggests that the fear of disclosure that led David to kill Uriah "was prompted certainly by the expected popular censure of his deed (Prov 6:33)." I have already noted that Prov 6:32–34, Prov 26:26, and other texts express the belief that adulterers and other clandestine criminals and deceivers will be exposed in public. Such exposure would not only shame the sinner but assuage the "epistemological anxiety" experienced by people who are unable to see through the sinner's public facade. For the people within the story world of the Hebrew Bible, the unmasking and shaming of secret sins usually remains an unfulfilled desire. David, for one, is not publicly exposed as a murderer and adulterer in 2 Sam 11–12. Nor is he explicitly said to feel shame when Absalom violates his concubines. But readers of 2 Samuel are not within the story world. We see the tyrannical David who commits shameful and criminal acts in private. And if Goodfriend is correct, we, the reading public, are also the realization of his worst fear: being shamed by public scandal.

Penetrating David's Facade: Information, Intrigue, and Deniability in 1 Kings 1

> Power is impenetrable.
> —Canetti, *Crowds and Power* (1981, 292)

> A perfect courtier [is] impenetrable.... [A good ruler] must be secret, close, and impenetrable in his motives and plans.
> —La Bruyère, *Characters* (1963, 116, 171)

> David's personality is complex, elusive, and impenetrable.
> —Exum, *Tragedy and Biblical Narrative* (1992, 142)

> Gossip ... is not deceived by the ... facade with which the subject surrounds himself. Relentlessly and remorselessly it penetrates its subject's private mistakes and flaws.
> —Bergmann, *Discreet Indiscretions* (1993, 128)

The story of Joab's assassination of Abner is not the only part of the Court History in which claims are made about the inscrutable David's ignorance, claims that readers may have difficulty taking at face value. Another such text is 1 Kgs 1–2. Here too the events about which David is apparently uninformed involve conflict between rivals when David is physically or mentally absent, ending with one rival causing the death of his double. The story begins with David not "knowing" the beautiful Abishag (1:4). According to Nathan, and then Bathsheba, David also does not know that Adonijah is reigning (1:11, 18). And later, after Solomon has ordered the death of his rival brother Adonijah, he evokes David's earlier case of ignorance, reminding Benaiah that David had not known about Joab's slaying of Abner and Amasa (2:32). Put another way, the narrator of 1 Kgs 1–2 is describing an aged and bed-ridden King David who has not been informed about the intrigues and conspiracies being planned by his own courtiers and family members. In this sense, David is now in the role of the uninformed Saul whom he had earlier outfoxed, thanks to his mastery as an information manager and Saul's disloyal courtiers and family members (see ch. 2, above).

If one takes the statements concerning the elderly David's ignorance of Adonijah's activities at face value, the King's Eyes and Ears have not been doing their job, to put it mildly. Is it possible that Bathsheba and Nathan were the first and only ones to belatedly inform David of acts that, from their perspective, were tantamount to a coup? Could David have been totally ignorant of the fact that Adonijah had exalted himself, declaring "I will be king," that he had procured chariots and runners, and that he was hosting a feast to which Nathan, Benaiah, and Solomon had not been invited (1:5, 9–10)? David himself cannot answer these questions for us, because the narrator does not record how the king responded to Bathsheba's and Nathan's remarks concerning Adonijah. Bathsheba actually makes several strong statements to which David does not respond. Her claim that David does not know of Adonijah's reigning follows a question concerning David's alleged vow to make her son Solomon his successor and precedes a reminder that "the eyes of all Israel" are on David because he has not let them know who will be his successor (1:17–20). The narrator tells us that Nathan entered while Bathsheba was still talking to the king, but he does not tell us what David might have been saying when Nathan entered (1:21). After Nathan speaks, David calls for Bathsheba, but he merely tells her that he will keep his vow concerning Solomon that very day, then calls Zadok, Nathan, and Benaiah to begin the process (1:31–35). Not one word about Adonijah is recorded.

A number of commentators have noted that Adonijah's behavior might be quite innocent. The heir apparent Adonijah may have simply been establishing himself as coregent, while his feast may have been nothing more than a celebration intended to consolidate his party (G. Jones 1990, 47–48). If so, Nathan and Bathsheba may be engaging in their own "court cabal" (Montgomery and Gehman 1951, 74) or "counterconspiracy" (Long 1984, 36), putting Adonijah's actions in the worst possible light and fabricating deeds that are not confirmed by the narrator (e.g., Nathan's allegation that Adonijah's followers had declared "Long live King

Adonijah" [1:19]). Their motive would be to manipulate the confused David into accepting their unconfirmed claim that he had sworn to make Solomon his successor, thereby assuring their personal safety with the new king (see 1:21).

A good example of such manipulation is Nathan's pretense of ignorance. According to his own words, Nathan is the only personage in chapter 1 besides David who has not been informed of actions that allegedly involve Adonijah's accession to the throne. When he breaks in on Bathsheba's audience with the king, Nathan does not act as an informer making his king aware of a political danger. On the contrary, he speaks as though David knows everything and he, Nathan, knows nothing, because David has not informed *him*. Nathan pretends to believe that Adonijah would not have acted as he did if David had not secretly made him the next king, leaving his courtiers in the dark ("Is this thing done by my lord the king, and you have not made known [הודעת] to your servant who should sit on the throne … after [you]?"; 1:27). On the surface, this flatters the king in typical courtly fashion by assuming that David is in control, that he knows all, that he has the royal prerogative of informing or not informing his servants, and that his son would only act in this fashion if he had his father's permission. However, readers of this speech are aware that from Nathan's point of view David could not have permitted Adonijah to reign, because he did not even *know* Adonijah was reigning (v. 11). The thrust of Nathan's feigned ignorance, therefore, is not to flatter the king but to confuse him further and to show him how out of control he really is.

If the elderly David really is as uninformed as Nathan and Bathsheba assume, and thus ripe for manipulation, he is very like the aged Louis XIV. Many commentators actually do describe the David of 1 Kgs 1 as being in the same situation, and in the same state of mind, as the pathetic Louis. Like David, Louis went from being a supposed master of information management to being manipulated, deceived, and kept ignorant by his ministers, and especially by his "Solomon" and "Bathsheba." These are the Duc du Maine, Louis's favorite son from his relationship with an already married woman, and Mme de Maintenon, Louis's privately wed morganatic second wife whom du Maine viewed as a mother. Together they induced Louis to change his will, making the now-legitimized Duc du Maine capable of succession if the legitimate collateral branches of the family were to die out. To achieve this end, the son and his "mother" controlled what the king heard and knew, manipulated his moods, and defamed with false rumor and gossip the Duc d'Orleans, Louis's nephew and regent by birthright (see Hatton 1977, 235–38; Saint-Simon 1968, 241–48, 350–57). In addition, Mme de Maintenon would confuse the king by controlling what he was told by his ministers, while she "played the simpleton" (as Bathsheba may be doing in 1 Kgs 2:13–22). Thanks to such manipulations, the unknowing king would believe that he had avoided being influenced by his ministers, while in fact "he was entirely ruled by them" (Saint-Simon 1966, 281–82).

Few (if any) of the scholars who recognize the tendentiousness of Nathan's and Bathsheba's reports concerning Adonijah and Solomon go on to challenge the pair when they claim that David "does not know" what is going on in his own realm. Yet the narrator provides no more confirmation of David's ignorance than he does of Adonijah's alleged conspiracy. It is therefore possible that the David of 1 Kgs 1 *does* know about his son's chariots, horsemen, and feast but finds nothing unsettling about it. It may be that the only thing that David doesn't know is how to see and interpret Adonijah's actions in the same way as do Nathan and Bathsheba. If this is the case, one can dispense with the dubious notion that no one in David's court, family, or military (including the serviceable Benaiah) had thought to inform their king of such significant events.

If the David of 1 Kgs 1 is not ignorant and confused, why would he keep his awareness of events so secret, and why had he not declared a successor or coregent earlier? The violent deaths of such ancient Near Eastern kings as Amenemhet I and Sennacherib in harem conspiracies suggest an answer. Both Amenemhet and Sennacherib had declared a younger son to be their successor, either as heir apparent or coregent; Amenemhet had actually inaugurated the practice of coregency in Egypt (see Grimal 1992, 60; B. Porter 1993, 16–26). In both cases the declaration prompted rival parties in the royal family to engage in disloyal and devious actions that led to the assassination of the reigning king. When one takes these cases into account, one can understand why David might have wanted to exercise caution and patience before choosing any son as his successor, particularly a younger son like Solomon who had as a rival claimant an elder brother backed by a large and established party within the court and the army. A premature or precipitous declaration could easily cause the deaths of both the king and his chosen son.

Bathsheba herself hints at another reason when she tells the king that "the eyes of all Israel are upon you" (1:20). By holding back his thoughts on the succession and his opinions on events that were taking place, David keeps attention on himself and he keeps others guessing. As one character in Stefan Heym's novel *The King David Report* puts it, David "saw quite well how they were watching him, waiting for a word from him that they might use in the struggle for his succession: that word was all that was left him of the sway he had held over Israel" (Heym 1973, 24). Heym's David already knows what modern leaders are thought to have discovered: the value of keeping the people focused on their personalities rather than on their actions and the issues raised by those actions. This does not mean that leaders must surrender their invisibility and impenetrability in order to expose their "true" personalities (if any). On the contrary, it is the impenetrability that keeps the people guessing.

David's impenetrability and ostensible ignorance are indistinguishable from the "deniability" that saved Ronald Reagan from the threat of impeachment. Because Poindexter and Reagan's other aides allegedly did not inform him of what they were doing in the palace basement, the president could honestly and absolutely deny knowledge of significant actions taken by his own agents. Just as Reagan was given deniability in the Iran Contra scandal, 2 Sam 3 and 1 Kgs 1 give David either plausible or absolute deniability, depending on whether one believes that David actually did know what Joab, Adonijah, and Nathan and Bathsheba were up to.

Clearly, the fact that readers have been granted an insider's access to the private zones of David's palace does not provide them with definite information about the king's thoughts, motives, or degree of knowledge. But why would the narrator put readers in the position of a courtier who is "out of the loop"? The narrator's strategy bears some resemblance to the device Goffman (1974, 474) calls "insider's folly." This technique can be employed whenever one wants to grant someone "a glimpse behind the scenes [in order to induce] the belief that you are seeing the backstage of *something*." A relevant example for the present discussion is the secret agent's "reserve story," a "cover tale an [intelligence] agent can provide the moment his initial cover story is broken and he seems beyond any further fabrication" (478). In other words, the cover tale grants the agent plausible deniability, which it enhances by giving the person who has broken the cover story the impression that she or he has penetrated to the backstage area where the behavior of the exposed agent must be genuine, unscripted, and unstaged. Thus, in 2 Sam 3 and 1 Kgs 1 the narrator may be giving the audience a "glimpse behind the scenes" in order to win their trust and incline them to believe that whatever David and his courtiers say in this private backstage setting must be the true inside scoop. The fact that the narrator seems to expose David's profound ignorance may actually *increase* the impression of genuineness. The revelation that David, like Ronald Reagan, had committed "the sin of inattention" is itself so compromising that there must surely be nothing left to hide. Yet this inside scoop may be nothing more than *the narrator's* cover story, designed to satisfy the reader's epistemophilia, preempting any *further* attempts to penetrate David's—and the narrator's—facade. If this is the case, the narrator is *arousing and then co-opting* the gossiper's instinct for inquiry and moral evaluation, in order to keep David invisible and impenetrable.

THE HISTORIAN AS INFORMER AND THE READER AS KING

The Historian As Gossiper and the Narrator of the David Story

> Issues don't exist anymore, but personalities do.
> —Robert Darnton (Lapham 1986, 48)

> History is merely gossip.
> —Character in Wilde, *Lady Windermere's Fan* (1930, 125)

> He lies like an eyewitness.
> —Russian proverb (Conquest 1973, 177)

The focus on impenetrable personalities in 1 Kgs 1 and other political texts characterizes not only the world of kings and courtiers but also the private realm where information can flow as gossip. If kings attempt to create an impenetrable facade, gossip penetrates facades. As already discussed, gossip seeks out private flaws that it makes publicly relevant. If there is one thing about which students of gossip agree, it is that gossip "supplies a weapon for outsiders—directed at the facade of reputation people construct around themselves" (Spacks 1986, 45). People who gossip know "the importance of not taking everything at face value"; this creates a desire "to go beneath the surface of what is said and shown" (Bok 1984, 90) and to speculate about "the subject's motives" (Bergmann 1993, 100). According to Mellencamp, it is "our lack of personal knowledge [that] paradoxically triggers an epistemophilia and a scopophilia ... a desire for intimacy which points to our lack of knowledge" (1992, 169).

Most analysts of gossip find that an interest in moral evaluation, if not a self-righteous or moralistic attitude, also fuels the desire to penetrate facades (e.g., Bergmann 1993, 99–100, 122, 129; Spacks 1986, 136; Bok 1984, 92). Collins (1994, 110) puts it this way: "when the individual herself determines by which aspects of her life she is to be judged, hypocrisy and self-deception flourish. Precisely because gossip may refuse to take the individual on her own terms, to respect her definition of the split between public and private, it is particularly good at uncovering these vices." In the case of journalistic gossip, such violation of other people's privacy is itself hypocritical, for such gossip "[makes] public what *it* insists is private" (Spacks 1986, 67). This is typical of gossip's "equivocal character": "gossipers are border-runners who in their exciting excursions into the zones of the improper do not simply ignore the boundaries of the domains of virtue and vice, but recognize and disdain them at the same time" (Bergmann 1993, 118).

Reports of political court intrigue and harem conspiracy typically reflect, not only the gossiper's interest in making private moral flaws publicly relevant and "interpreting public facts in private terms" (Spacks 1986, 262), but the gossiper's ambivalence concerning the violation of the private-public boundary. A good example is Ktesias, the Greek doctor who lived at the court of the Persian king Artaxerxes II and who is the sole source for many of the events he describes. Ktesias presents himself as an eyewitness (αὐτόπτης) to most of what he reports and an earwitness (αὐτήκοος) to Persian informants for the rest (no. 1; König 1972, 1). As noted by Sancisi-Weerdenburg (1983, 31), Ktesias is "predominantly interested in personalities and then mainly in their plotting and intriguing against each other and against the king." In fact, Ktesias's "interest in Persian affairs [is] apparently limited to events on a personalistic level.... his Persian empire is the court" (Sancisi-Weerdenburg 1987, 35). Thus, Ktesias focuses on events such as the assassination of the drunken and sleeping Xerxes II, the machinations of the eunuchs at the court of Darius II and those of his cunning and ruthless wife Parysatis, and the plot to take over the throne by the eunuch Artoxares, who was informed on by his wife after he ordered her to make him a false beard and moustache so that he could impersonate a male (nos. 45, 48, 49, 53; König 1972, 18–21).

Sancisi-Weerdenburg believes that Ktesias highlighted events occurring in the harem and court because he "was struck by the intermingling of official and private affairs" (1987, 38). Having come from Greece, where the division between family affairs and the state had recently become clearly delineated, he naturally viewed "the intrusion of family affairs on the official level of the state [as] morally wrong" (1987, 38). In other words, Ktesias is just as fascinated by what he condemns as the typical gossiper. Considering that Ktesias's source is often considered to be "kitchen gossip" (Drews 1973, 107), this should come as no surprise. To some, Ktesias's presumed dependence on gossip undermines the doctor's claim to have been an eye- and earwitness to events. Referring to Ktesias's writings on India, Lucian parodies Ktesias's self-presentation, asserting that Ktesias wrote on matters "that he had never seen himself nor heard from anyone else with a reputation for truthfulness" (*Ver. hist.* 1.3; 1953, 251). To others, however, Ktesias remains a valuable source with access to real inside information (e.g., the scholars cited by Sancisi-Weerdenburg 1987, 36–37). Sancisi-Weerdenburg asks the key question: "can an informant be trusted just because he has been on the spot?" (1987, 37). While she does not cite the Russian proverb "He lies like an eyewitness," Sancisi-Weerdenburg rightly notes that Ktesias "was seeing what he was taught to see as, later on, he was to tell what he was expected to tell. In a certain sense, no *autoptes* ever escapes such a verdict" (1987, 37).

Textual evidence from ancient Greece indicates that bias in a writer of contemporary history was expected. Plutarch criticizes those whose research (ἱστορία) into the deeds and lives of their contemporaries is biased, defiling and distorting the truth "partly through envious hatred and partly through fawning flattery" (*Per.* 13.12; 1958, 47). Luce (1989, 25) notes that contemporary historians were in a no-win situation: "If they published a favorable picture of an autocrat during his lifetime they laid themselves open to charges of flattery and self-promotion; if the account was critical, they risked punishment."

These comments reveal the similarity between the historian and the informer. Like the King's Eyes and Ears, the court historian may claim to have been an eye- and earwitness to contemporary events. And just as informers (and gossipers) make judgments and accusations, so do historians who are "expected to make suitable pronouncements on the goodness and badness" of those on whom they report (Luce 1989, 21). And in each case the accusation may be true or false; the informer (*diabolos*) can also be the slanderer. Plutarch had listed envy and flattery as causes of bias in history writing. In his essay on slander (διαβολή), Lucian cites envy, rivalry, and flattery as motivations for slander, especially in the courts of kings (*Cal.* 2–5, 10; 1953, 362–67, 372–73). Plutarch himself is well aware of the connection between slandering historians and informers. His comments on historians are prompted by his account of the way Pericles and Pheidias were sacrificed "to the evil deity of popular envy" when Pericles was accused of committing wanton adultery with the aid of Pheidias (*Per.* 9–11). Therefore, just as the king must assess the reliability of the reports he receives from his informers, readers must evaluate the reliability of the accounts they receive from their *diabolos,* their historian-informer. Is their informer an honest insider, a gossiper, or one who "lies like an eyewitness"?

The same issues that arise when attempting to evaluate the writing of a contemporary historian like Ktesias must also be dealt with when assessing 1 Kgs 1 and the Davidic Court History as a whole. This is particularly true if one shares the common assumption that the author was an insider at David's court who begins 1 Kings 1 with "an apparently gossipy detail of harem history" (Montgomery and Gehman 1951, 68), and who often depended on "common court gossip." The author does have many of the same interests as Ktesias and other gossipers. Like gossip, the narrative serves as "a prime vehicle for moral evaluation" (Bok 1984, 92). Much emphasis is given to the personalities, desires, and motives of the characters, because it is their personal and private flaws that are shown to determine the course of public and political events. An exception is David, whose personality and motives cannot be fathomed because the narrator often allows the king to remain impenetrable. The gossiper's interest in crossing the boundary separating public and private is actually thematized in the narrative, especially when David transgresses that boundary to appropriate Bathsheba. As discussed earlier, Yahweh gives full emphasis to this transgression in his announcement of David's punishment (2 Sam 12:11–12; 16:22).

If David transgresses the private-public boundary, the narrator who informs readers of this fact himself engages in the kind of "border-running" between public and private that characterizes the gossiper. It is this boundary violation that most attracts the attention of scholars who believe that the narrative has its source in court gossip. At times the reader is like the fly on the wall, a silent witness to private conversations and actions—not unlike Abishag, who is present but totally ignored when Bathsheba and Nathan make their appeals to David (see 1 Kgs 1:15). However, because David's thoughts and motives remain so elusive, being granted an insider's access to the private zones of the palace does not mean that the reader will gain definite information about the king's thoughts, motives, or degree of knowledge. Once again, it appears that the reader is placed in the position of the typical courtier, who must discern what others feel and know by interpreting their staged performances and looking for ways to penetrate their facades.

History, Gossip, and the Date of the Court History

> I [told the king that] I had listed the various possibilities of dealing with undesirable matter: (a) tell it all, (b) tell it with discretion, (c) don't tell it. To tell it all ... was obviously unwise; people were quick to draw the wrong conclusions from facts and to form wrong opinions of persons whom we wished to be highly regarded. Not to tell it ... was equally unwise; things had a way of being noised about and people always picked up what they were not supposed to know. This left us with possibility (b): tell it with discretion. Discretion, I said, was not the same as lying; surely the Wisest of Kings, Solomon, would never condone lying in a history of his father King David. Discretion was truth controlled by wisdom.
>
> —Ethan the historian to Solomon, in Heym, *The King David Report* (1973, 84; cf. 42, 244–45)

Narratives like 1 Sam 18–23, 2 Sam 3, and 1 Kgs 1 do not furnish any unequivocal clues as to their date of composition, authorship, or purpose. Nor are there any extrabiblical data concerning David and his regime that might help one to fix a date or to determine the *Tendenz* of the story. All speculation as to date and authorship must ultimately be based on a scholar's interpretation of the story itself. Randall Bailey is therefore correct when he concludes from his survey of proposed dates for the Court

History that "all of these positions about dating and authorship are predicated upon particular views about the genre and function of the materials" (1990, 30). However, the present study suggests that we can be quite a bit more specific about the importance of genre and function for a discussion of dating. In fact, we can say with some confidence that a scholar's views on genre, function, dating, and authorship are, to a large extent, all based on her or his assumptions concerning information management, gossip, and the presentation of David's personality—whether this is acknowledged by the scholar or not. A brief review of the arguments for proposed dates will demonstrate this fact.

Many scholars believe that the Court History originated in David's reign. As "evidence" they point to all the private and personal information given by the narrator and to the fact that much of this information puts David in a negative light. The intimate details are viewed as realistic and taken as evidence that the author must have been "a master historian informed by an eyewitness" (Lods, quoted in Montgomery and Gehman 1951, 69), if not "one of David's closest servants, always in attendance" (M. H. Segal, quoted in M. Sternberg 1985, 62; see above). The fact that the reader is informed about David's unethical and criminal acts ensures a tenth-century date, for "it can hardly be assumed that somebody would later have dared to expose David in this way without sound evidence" (Rost 1982, 104). However, the negative information is included not because the narrator is hostile to David but "because the things he did were publicly known and could not be baldly denied" (McCarter 1984, 15).

Leaving aside the fact that political leaders *do* "baldly deny" (and "plausibly deny") things that are publicly known or believed, one must ask how these scholars can assume that David's adultery with Bathsheba, his murder of Uriah, and the intrigues that ensured Solomon's succession were "publicly known" when the narrator describes them as private, notes David's efforts to keep the Bathsheba-Uriah matter secret, and gives no hint that any of David's "cover stories" were exposed. The answer is that these commentators argue as though they have tremendous respect for the power of gossip and do not put much faith in a monarch's efforts to control the flow of information. It is respect for uncontrollable gossip that leads Heym's historian Ethan to advise against withholding "undesirable matter" from the King David Report: "things had a way of being noised about and people always picked up what they were not supposed to know." Scholars like Weingreen and Whitelam share this assumption. Weingreen (1969, 265) contends that David's crime against Bathsheba and Uriah "was not a well-guarded secret, but must have been common court gossip." Whitelam (1984, 62, 70) suggests that "the various political machinations involved in the power struggle" leading to David's seizure of the Saulide throne and "many of the incidents such as the damaging circumstances surrounding the death of Uriah" might have been widely and well known, at least "within court circles or among the élite in the main urban centres of power."

Some commentators specify the harem as the source for such secret political news, and a few go so far as to target women as the reader's Eyes and Ears, if not the author's. For example, the Chadwicks claim that most or all of the Court History is "of feminine provenance"; it has been "composed either by women or for the entertainment of women" (1936, 649; cf. 650). Thus, 1 Kgs 1 comes from Bathsheba and "a large part ... of the story of David is derived from saga inspired by Bathsheba in Solomon's court" (762). Gunn (1978, 62) finds that the Chadwicks's "interesting suggestion of a link with the harem ... remains well within the bounds of possibility." Carlson (1964, 136 and n. 2) agrees. He believes that the Chadwicks's notion of a source based on orally transmitted "court sagas" composed for the entertainment of harem women "draws attention to points of view that are worth exploring," even if the Zadokite priesthood was more likely to have transmitted such material. Even Burke Long thinks that "it is perhaps not too farfetched" to connect the author-editor of 1–2 Kings with "those highly placed courtesans of Judah's last few kings who seemed to have had a vested interest in transmitting the traditions of Jeremiah with a pro-Yahweh and pro-Babylonian slant" (1984, 32).[11]

It is quite possible that such readiness to cite women as the transmitters, if not the authors, of the information related in the text is based on the age-old male assumption that it is only women who gossip. Evidence of this attitude can be found in many cultures from the ancient period to the present (see, e.g., Bergmann 1993, 59–67; Emler 1994, 118–20). Rysman (1977, 179) suggests that the reason female gossiping came to have negative associations is that these associations constituted "a way of controlling female solidarity." The fact that this solidarity can help to create a centrifugal flow of information out of "urban power centres," and out of the

---

11 On the question of whether Long's view here is compatible with his general attitude about the "historical truth" of the narratives, see J. M. Miller 1987, 54–55. Long's qualification ("it is perhaps not too farfetched") puts me in mind of one of Freud's habitual disclaimers: "What follows is speculation, often far-fetched [*weitausholende*] speculation.... It may be asked whether and how far I am myself convinced by the hypotheses that have been set out here. My answer would be that I am not convinced myself and that I do not seek to recruit others to believe in them. More precisely: I don't know how far I believe in them" (1920, 24, 59; translation modified). I sometimes wonder if biblical scholars writing on the historical truth of the David and Solomon stories haven't thought something similar, but without following Freud in boldly committing it to writing. Unfortunately, the way the academic enterprise currently operates almost forces one to "recruit others" to believe our hypotheses, even when we don't know how much we believe them ourselves.

control of the males who exercise power in those centers, is what panics Memucan in Esth 1:16–18. It may also be the reason why male biblical scholars are so uncharacteristically prepared to grant the possibility of female authorship for this part of the Deuteronomistic History.

The Chadwicks's suggestion that the Court History might have been composed for the entertainment of women is one example of an assumption shared by a number of those who argue for a date of composition during David's (or Solomon's) reign. These commentators assume that the history not only has its source in court or harem gossip but was aimed at this same audience. For example, Whitelam argues that David and his successors had to "present an interpretation of the general situation which held the assent of ... *those parts of the population which were a threat or potential threat to his ambitions*" (1984, 62). The Court History is an exercise in "image-projection" and propaganda aimed at the elite minority in the center of power (62, 64). Whitelam does not discuss exactly how the ideological message would have been delivered to this audience. However, when Barbara Nevling Porter (1993, 106–10) imagines how such an apologetic document (in this case Esarhaddon's account of the struggles surrounding his accession) might be communicated to this elite target audience, she envisions a process that resembles the informal communication of gossip more than it does the official presentation of a written piece of propaganda. Porter suggests that members of the court might have become the first audience for the official royal interpretation encapsulated in the text by means of "oral transmission and informal discussion." During this process "the official version ... would have percolated through the king's court, reaching the bureaucrats, military officers, professional advisors, ... royal relatives and others present at the court" (1993, 110 n. 236). The metaphor of "percolation" captures very well the subtle process through which informal modes of communication such as gossip disseminate information and again suggests the difficulty experienced by official sources when they seek to prevent the flow of uncontrolled information and the leaking of secrets.

Scholars who argue for a tenth-century date of composition are not the only ones to take seriously the issue of information management. This factor may be granted equal importance by those who argue for a late date. For example, Ahlström (1993, 491) contends that the Court History was "most probably not written by a person contemporary with the events because there is an anti-Davidic tendency in it." Ahlström asks where such literature would have been preserved in an autocratic state and "how would it have been distributed and circulated so that the king would not have known about it and executed the narrator [*sic*]?" (491; cf. 51 on the reason for the lack of criticism of Akkadian kings in royal inscriptions). In this case it is not the impossibility of the king keeping his secrets that is envisioned, but the impossibility of keeping the king from being informed about his critics, whom Ahlström seems to assume would have been treated by the king as disloyal subjects and punished accordingly. This is precisely the problem that, according to Luce, faced Greek contemporary historians critical of their leader: "if they published a [critical account] of an autocrat during his lifetime, ... they risked punishment" (Luce 1989, 25). The way this problem was solved supports Ahlström's argument: "a common solution was to withhold publication until after the autocrat had died" (Luce 1989, 25).

These examples are sufficient to indicate that the issue of information management must be taken into account whenever *any* date is being proposed for 1 Sam 18–23, 2 Sam 3, 1 Kgs 1, or the Court History as a whole. But precisely because phenomena associated with the king's dream of control and his nightmare of uncontrolled gossip must play a role in any proposed date and setting for these narratives, even a detailed analysis of these phenomena cannot in itself lead to any definite conclusions concerning one particular date or author. We cannot even determine the extent to which the Court History illustrates any of the three strategies Ethan outlines to Solomon in the epigraph to this section. In the quoted passage, Ethan opts for "telling it with discretion" and defines discretion as "truth controlled by wisdom." Perhaps the biblical Court History is "wisdom literature" in *this* sense. Or perhaps it is more akin to gossip, which Bergmann (1993, 151) defines as "the social form of discreet indiscretion." If so, it has incorporated those things that Ethan says have "a way of being noised about," so that penetrating readers with inquiring minds may ultimately be able to pick up "what we are not supposed to know."

6

SOLOMON AND THE WIZARD OF OZ:
POWER AND INVISIBILITY IN A VERBAL PALACE

It is the glory of God to conceal things;
and the glory of kings is to penetrate [חקר] things.

. . .

And the heart of kings is impenetrable [אין חקר].
—Proverbs 25:2; 3b

He who does not know how to dissimulate,
does not know how to rule.
—Motto of James I, alluding to Tiberius (Goldberg 1983, 68)

Power is impenetrable
—Canetti, *Crowds and Power* (1981, 292)

INVISIBILITY AND POWER: DEIOKES, THE WIZARD OF OZ, AND KING SOLOMON

Once there was a Median judge named Deiokes who was in love with royal power (Herodotus, *Hist*. 1.96). When a gathering of Medes responds to an outbreak of lawlessness and injustice by declaring "Come, let us set up a king for ourselves"[1] and choosing Deiokes, Deiokes immediately has the people build seven concentric ring walls around his royal palace, with the people dwelling outside (1.98–99). He then establishes a new rule, "that no one should come into the presence of the king, but all should be dealt with by ... messengers," so that "the king should be seen by no man" (1.99; 1981, 131). Deiokes's motive is to prevent any nobles of his own age and similar background from seeing him and plotting against him because they discovered they were his equal (1.99). By remaining invisible, he hopes that they would assume that he had become different (i.e., superior) to them.[2]

---

[1] Herodotus, *Hist*. 1.97; 1981, 129. Note the uncanny resemblance to the situation in 1 Sam 8, especially v. 5.

[2] Compare the strategy adopted by Shakespeare's King Henry IV: "By being seldom seen, I could not stir but like a comet I was wondered at.... Thus did I keep

Once there was a Wizard in Oz who was viewed by his people as both wise and powerful (Baum 1958, 9, 61, 64). However, the people's knowledge of Oz's power and knowledge is hardly direct, for no one outside the palace has seen him. Like King Solomon's "descendant" Haile Sellassie I, the Wizard sits behind a screen when inside the palace, so that "even those who wait upon him do not see him face to face."[3] The Wizard's motive is identical to that of Deiokes. After his balloon accidentally lands in this country, his descent from the clouds leads the people to take him for a great wizard. To maintain this illusion, he has the people build Emerald City and his palace, so that he can "shut [himself] up and ... not see any of [the people]" (Baum 1958, 113). Invisibility is power: "I will not see even my subjects, *and so* they believe I am something terrible" (110; emphasis added). The people fill in the gaps created by his invisibility with the assumption that he possesses great power and wisdom.[4]

Traditionally, royal ideology forbids citizens from penetrating the *arcana imperii*, the secrets of political power (see Ginzburg 1989, 63; Goldberg 1983, 68). With invisible leaders like Deiokes and Oz, the *arcana imperii* become identified with the person of the leader himself. Deiokes and Oz have learned the power inherent in invisibility or, at least, in managed inscrutability.[5] Even when such leaders *are* visible, they remain inscrutable. Everyone who views them may see a different being. For example, Dorothy and her friends are told by the farmer that Oz is a great wizard who "can take on any form he wishes," appearing differently

---

my person fresh and new, my presence, like a robe pontifical, ne'er seen but wondered at" (*Henry IV, Pt. 1,* 3.2.46–47, 55–58).

[3] Baum 1958, 60–61; cf. 11, 67, 69. According to the revised Ethiopian constitution of 1955, the ancestry of emperor Haile Sellassie I traces directly back to Menelik I, son of Solomon and the Queen of Sheba. The person of the emperor has a quasi-sacred separateness. He is shielded by a screen from the gaze of the populace and does not eat in public. At times, his face was even veiled, and he spoke through an intermediary called "mouth of the king" (Ullendorff 1974, 105–6).

[4] The power of invisibility sought by Deiokes and Oz resembles the force exerted by Big Brother in Orwell's fantasy world of *1984*. Here too the people trace "all knowledge, all wisdom, ... all virtue" back to their leader, even though "nobody has ever seen Big Brother." While pictures of Big Brother saturate the landscape, with captions reading "Big Brother is watching you," this ostensibly panoptic leader does not even exist as a person (Orwell 1983, 5, 214). Instead, the idea and image of this invisible ruler act as a "focusing point for love, fear, and reverence" (171).

[5] As we discussed in ch. 3, in order to remain powerful, invisible leaders must at the same time make their followers visible to themselves. Thus, Oz claims to be like a panoptic, omnipresent king or deity (Baum 1958, 108), and Deiokes has spies and eavesdroppers everywhere (Herodotus, *Hist.* 1.100).

to everyone (Baum 1958, 60–61). When they are granted separate individual audiences with Oz, they do not converse with him through the screen. Instead, each sees a different, visually entrancing, manifestation, none of which is the true Oz. This elusive Wizard is analogous not only to the European stereotype of shape-shifting witches and wizards but to such famous and powerful leaders as Alcibiades and Napoleon. According to Plutarch, Alcibiades possessed one special gift that, more than any other, attracted followers to him. He could "submit himself to more transformations than a chameleon" (*Alc.* 23.4; Scott-Kilvert 1960, 267). Thus, in Sparta he was an austere athlete, in Ionia a hedonist, in Thrace a heavy drinker, and so on. In other words, he "assumed whatever manner or exterior was appropriate to the situation" (*Alc.* 23.5–6).[6]

Just as the Wizard of Oz and Alcibiades appear in a variety of different forms, scholars describe Solomon and his reign in so many varying ways that one could almost conclude that the king himself was a shape-shifter. Solomon may appear to be wise—or "decadent" (Noth 1960, 216), a "philosopher king" (Parker 1992, 76, 89)—or a "typical oriental despot" (Clements 1974, 403; cf. Crenshaw 1981, 53), a sultan (Kittel, in Donner 1982, 205) or a pharaoh (Heaton 1974, 28). To some, the account of his accession in 1 Kgs 1–2 appears to be pro-Solomonic, while others see this tale of court intrigue as a "searing indictment" (Hoppe 1992, 3:561) of the monarchy. The fact that Yahweh grants Solomon the riches and honor he did not request may be perceived as an example of "the blessings of free, unsolicited grace" (DeVries 1985, 53) or as a divine "trap" to "unbalance Solomon with temptation that the latter had avoided" (Eslinger: 137). Solomon's use of thirty thousand Israelites in the corvée may be viewed as an example of the tyrannical rule forecast by Samuel, or as an example of "the justice of Solomon's rule" (Parker: 80–81). Some see negative reports about Solomon in 1 Kgs 9 (Noth, 1991:97; Brettler 1989, 95–97) or as early as chapters 3–5 (Eslinger 1989, 129–43; Walsh 1996, 69–101). In others' eyes, the narrator appears to be offering an "unambiguous" portrait of Solomon's reign as a "golden age" or "utopia" as late as 1 Kgs 10 (Knoppers 1993, 77, 111, 126, 134; cf. Jobling 1991, 60, 67).

Solomon's motives for building his palace do not seem to parallel those of Deiokes and the Wizard. Nor does Solomon express a need to hide from his people. Yet an analogy does exist, once one realizes that Solomon is being kept hidden from readers of 1 Kings, not from the people in the story.

---

6 Similarly, Napoleon allegedly told the Council of State that "it was by becoming a Catholic that I terminated the Vendeen war, by becoming a Mussulman that I obtained a footing in Egypt, by becoming an Ultramontane that I won over the Italian priests, and had I to govern a nation of Jews I would rebuild Solomon's temple" (quoted in Le Bon 1977, 69).

In what follows I will argue that readers of Kings and Chronicles are locked out of Solomon's psyche in the same way that citizens are locked out of a palace where a king or tyrant remains invisible, and perhaps for similar reasons. *The text functions as a verbal palace,* with the king mysteriously and provocatively concealed inside. Readers are therefore prevented from knowing Solomon, the ultimate knower. While we have found ample evidence that our "inquiring minds want to know" about the personal lives of leaders, this text, and therefore Solomon, remain impenetrable. We are interested in his personality but are forced to give him one, just as God gave him wisdom, wealth, and honor. Speculations about Solomon's personality and knowledge reflect readers' assumptions of what a magnificent and wise king must be like, whether they take their cues from Deut 17 and 1 Sam 8, from traditional descriptions of invisible, all-knowing leaders from the ancient Near East, from the France of Louis XIV, or from modern fantasies about the Wizard of Oz and Kafka's protean official, Klamm (see below).

Solomon's Invisibility in 1 Kings 3–11: the Screening Effect of Indeterminacy

This is what the sovereign displays in public, his own unobservability, observed in his spectacles.
—Goldberg, *James I and the Politics of Literature* (1983, 150)

In the Solomon narratives, it is the narrator who is the wizard. The way the narrator describes Solomon and his reign is what allows the king to appear so differently to different readers. In *The Wizard of Oz* the dog Toto upsets the screen, exposing the mechanism that produced the Wizard's protean appearance. If Solomon is "screened" by the narrator, we must investigate the nature of this screen and see whether it too can be upset and made to reveal the source and function of Solomon's protean appearance.

One way to gauge the extent to which the character of Solomon is hidden from readers of 1 Kings is by contrasting this account of his life with those of his two royal predecessors. For example, Solomon is the first king of Israel whose physical appearance does not play a role in his early career. In fact, his appearance is not even described, let alone praised as extraordinarily attractive, as is the case for Saul and David. In spite of his thousand wives and concubines, readers do not witness any illuminating exchanges between the king and his famous loves, as one is allowed to follow David's interactions with Michal, Abigail, and Bathsheba. None of Solomon's many wives is said to love him as David was loved by Michal. None pursues and flatters Solomon, as did David's wife-to-be Abigail.

In fact, of Solomon's one thousand wives and concubines only Pharaoh's daughter receives any attention at all in 1 Kgs 3–11, and remarkably little is said about her or about Solomon loving her. This is most evident when one compares the narrative with other accounts of diplomatic marriages. When the Egyptian king Ramesses II first saw the Hittite princess who was to be his diplomatic bride he perceived her god-like beauty, and "he loved her more than anything" (*ANET* 258). Similarly, when Amenhotep III requested the Mitannian king Tušratta's daughter as a bride, Tušratta enthusiastically agreed to send her, telling the pharaoh that "he will find that she is exactly what his heart desired" (EA 20:29; Schulman 1979, 184 n. 35[7]). In contrast, the arrival of Pharaoh's daughter is not even reported in 1 Kings, let alone Solomon's reaction to her (see further in ch. 7, below). In view of the fact that a marriage between a daughter of an Egyptian king and a foreign monarch is almost unprecedented (Schulman 1979, 179–80), this silence is particularly striking. While 1 Kings does describe the arrival of one royal woman from another land, that report concerns the only woman in 1 Kgs 3–11 whom Solomon is *not* said to love: the Queen of Sheba.

While Solomon's many marriages might lead one to imagine that the halls of his palace would echo continuously with the pitter-patter of little feet, we hear nothing about any sons of Solomon in all of 1 Kgs 3–11, let alone overhear conversations between father and sons such as occurred between Saul and Jonathan and between David and his sons Amnon and Absalom. Those conversations give readers valuable information regarding the character of the kings, even if all readers do not draw the same conclusions from the reports. In the same way, we are unable to learn about Solomon by listening to his confrontations with strong, named, prophets like Samuel and Nathan. There are no such prophets in 1 Kgs 3–11.

Nor are readers granted access to Solomon's private thoughts or feelings in 1 Kgs 4–11, in spite of the fact that these eight chapters focus on Solomon's administration of his empire, his building projects, his international relations, and, ultimately, his harem. While readers hear Solomon speak at length when he is on public display at the dedication of the temple (1 Kgs 8:12–61), they never hear the words spoken by Solomon to any *individual* in face-to-face conversation. Nor does he address any "long-distance" quoted speeches (i.e., messages or letters) to an individual Israelite or to his foreign wives. In fact, the only individual to whom Solomon's quoted words are addressed in these chapters is Hiram of Tyre, to whom Solomon "sends word" from Jerusalem (5:16 MT). Even in the report of Solomon's verbal and economic exchange with the Queen of

---

[7] Moran (1992, 47) renders the line "[She] has been fashioned according to my brother's desire." In Moran's translation (1992, 44, 46–47), Tušratta declares "May Šauška and Aman make her the image of my brother's desire" (*adi šunū-ma*) in EA 19:24 (cf. 20:27).

Sheba, it is only *her* words that are quoted directly, and then at some length (10:6–9). Only once does the narrator even report that Solomon responded to her with speech (10:3). No mention is made of Solomon responding to either Hiram's complaint after 9:15 or to the queen's praise after 10:9. Solomon does not even reply to *Yahweh's* warnings at 9:9 or to his condemnation speech at 11:13. This absence of royal direct speech in dialogue is almost unique in 1–2 Kings. All the other kings whose reigns are described at length *are* quoted in such situations, with the exception of the one-dimensional villain Manasseh.[8] The blank spots in the narrator's portrait of Solomon invite the audience to engage in ventriloquism and mind-reading. Those who accept this invitation can then project their biblical Solomon onto the blank screen of history, for Solomon is not mentioned in any contemporary extrabiblical document or artifact (Garbini 1988, 17, 30–32; Ishida 1992, 6:105).[9]

While Solomon's personal character remains hidden from readers, at least we can still point to the king's reputation for knowledge and wisdom as his distinguishing trait. Or can we? Gilgamesh and Odysseus, the most famous knowers in ancient Near Eastern and Greek epic, penetrate to the far reaches of the earth, crossing boundaries behind which the secrets of life and death, and past and future, had remained invisible. They see the cities of many men and know their thought, discover the hidden and bring back knowledge from before the flood. They learn through experience, hard experience. Even the swollen-footed Oedipus, who "learned the hard way" more than anyone else, had traveled many wandering roads of thought (Sophocles, *Oed. tyr.* 67). Can we say the same of Solomon? Only the "Solomon" of Qoheleth, he who "has been king over Israel in Jerusalem" (1:12). Qoheleth applies his heart and wisdom to investigate and search out everything done under heaven (1:13). This includes investigating the effects of wealth, pleasure, luxury, and women (2:1–10), all things that the Solomon of Kings has at his disposal but with which we do not see him interacting in a way that might grant him "learning by experience." The Solomon of Kings *has* knowledge; he doesn't achieve it. He is *given* wisdom; he is not given an education. Solomon *receives* knowledge; he doesn't earn it. He is given the knowledge that Eve and Adam take. He undergoes

---

[8] They include Jeroboam, Rehoboam, Ahab, Jehoshaphat, Jehoram of Israel, Hezekiah, and Josiah. On the function of direct quotation in the Jeroboam narrative, see Lasine 1992, 139–45. On the significance of Manasseh's "silence," see Lasine 1993b, 164–67, 173–75.

[9] In the next chapter, we will see that the narrator also keeps Solomon's personal character hidden from readers by describing the king's activities in terms that are so typical of ancient Near Eastern royal ideology that the description is almost an extended cliché.

no youthful learning by experience, no *Bildung*. He is acquisitive, not inquisitive. With the possible exception of the judgment story, he is not driven to discover what had lain invisible; instead, *he* remains invisible.

The absence of information regarding young Solomon's experiences and education is just as unusual as the other gaps in his biography. To cite just a few contrasting examples, we hear no tales of Solomon's formative years analogous to the wise Joseph's experiences with his brothers or the Egyptians. Nothing like Moses' early career as killer, fugitive, or shepherd. Nothing similar to David's "education" as shepherd and animal-fighter. And nothing analogous to the early years of his future enemy Jeroboam, the self-made, industrious leader. For all we know, Solomon might have been sent away to a boarding school for children of the very rich in Switzerland. His absence from all of 2 Samuel after the report of his birth is total and mysterious. In a sense, Qoheleth's "adult education" retroactively grants Solomon the learning by experience he does not receive as the "young lad" king of 1 Kgs 3:7.[10]

Here one might object that we can learn much of Solomon's character from the fact that he asks God only for judicial wisdom in his dream at Gibeon. Considering that one of the king's main responsibilities is to establish and maintain justice, Solomon is asking for "work-related" knowledge. He does not even ask for the kind of panoptic knowledge of his people's actions and words that ancient monarchs sought so strenuously to acquire. As far as intelligence concerning foreign monarchs is concerned, the leaders about whom Solomon might want to be informed come to him of their own accord! Nor has he any need to journey to remote exotic locales, such as Gilgamesh, because everything exotic and remote is brought to him as a gift, without any effort on his part. Even in the story of the two harlots, where Solomon does display the working equivalent of panoptic knowledge of his subjects' hearts, he does not do so by "exploring" or investigating the women—he significantly chooses not to do so. And unlike Nicocles and the other kings we discussed earlier, he does not simply tell us (or them) that he can read his subjects' minds. Instead, he employs a ruse that leads to their true natures being

---

[10] Readers of Samuel–Kings are not even granted enough information about the future king to determine whether his case supports the Athenian in Plato's *Laws*. Plato has the Athenian contrast the bad Persian kings Cambyses and Xerxes to their fathers Cyrus and Darius. The difference is that the fathers were not brought up in an environment of incredible wealth and luxury. No child of excessively rich monarchs who is raised amid royal pampering will ever excel in *aretē;* usually they will live an evil life (696a). While the career of Rehoboam might seem to fit this scenario (and perhaps that of Adonijah as well), we simply cannot be sure about Solomon. See further in ch. 10, below.

"brought to him" from deep inside, as though their unguarded words in verses 26–27 were gifts brought from remote Sheba. However, the emphasis on the king's judicial sagacity in 1 Kgs 3 is a bit of misdirection, a red herring, because the king's wisdom is not juridical in nature anywhere else in 1 Kgs 1–11.[11]

In fact, the nature of Solomon's "wisdom" becomes increasingly indeterminate as the narrative proceeds. By 1 Kgs 10 it has become empty of content; it is no longer judicial, proverbial, or economic. It is simply that indeterminate element of Solomon's "character" that makes him desirable, attracting gift-bearing admirers like a magnet. Back in 1 Kgs 5 the giving of tribute by the kingdoms was not said to be spurred by Solomon's wisdom (5:1 MT), and the visits by foreign dignitaries who came to hear his wisdom are not said to include the giving of tribute or gifts (5:14 MT). In 1 Kgs 10, on the other hand, when "all the earth" comes to hear the wisdom of the king who exceeds all others in riches and in wisdom, every visitor brings a lavish gift. The report of the visit by the Queen of Sheba reinforces the idea that Solomon's wisdom simply represents his wealth-enhancing desirability. The queen serves as a focalizer, through whose eyes the narrator invites readers to view and evaluate Solomon's wealth-wisdom.

Solomon possesses wisdom in the same sense as he possesses gold, silver, and wives: in huge quantities. His wisdom is quantified and marketed in the form of proverbs and lectures on botany and zoology (1 Kgs 5:12–13). He "speaks" these pieces of wisdom, but readers do not hear them, just as readers do not hear what he says to his many (politically valuable) foreign wives. Again, the contents are empty. The desirable wisdom and wealth described in 1 Kgs 4–10 could be found in a travel brochure for a golden age paradise. In a sense, the wealth becomes an icon for the wisdom. As such, it is no less vacuous than the images used in marketing consumer products like perfume, beer, and catsup; the products bear no real relationship to the icons used to advertise them.[12] Solomon himself remains empty of personality, although (or *because?*) he is the object of the entire world's desire.[13] We will address that "because" in the next chapter.

---

[11] On the judgment story as a "folktale sound bite," see especially Lasine 1993a, 42–47.

[12] According to Ernest Sternberg (1995, 84–85), in a "postmodern iconic" economy consumer desires are triggered by images that carry no information. Images—simulacra—do the selling. The desirable images convey no information; they have no real content.

[13] In this respect, Solomon reminds me of Roger Moore as the movie character James Bond. When Moore replaced Sean Connery as Bond, one critic (whose name I've long since forgotten) referred to him as "a hole in the middle of the screen."

Solomon's Invisibility and Power in 1 Chronicles 22– 2 Chronicles 9

When I was a child, there was school.... I am a smart scribe whom nothing escapes.
—The Sumerian king Šulgi (Civil 1990, 2:304–5)

Scholarly perceptions of the Chronicler's elusive Solomon do not differ as widely, or as profoundly, as is the case with 1 Kings. On the other
hand, the unique status of Chronicles generates a cause for indeterminacy
absent from Kings. This is because all readers must choose whether to read
Chronicles in the light of Samuel–Kings (e.g., Willi 1972, 66; Ackroyd 1991,
339, 341; Childs 1979, 646–47) or as what has recently been called "independent" literature (Sugimoto 1992, 63, 74; cf. Fishbane 1985, 382). Was the
Chronicler *expecting* his audience to have some version of Kings in mind
when reading his Solomon story? If so, did he expect those readers to har-
monize the two accounts as they proceeded (Greenstein 1988, 352–53) or
to replace the Kings version with his own? Most commentators tend to discuss passages in Chronicles in terms of the extent to which they agree with
or deviate from Kings, although others do attempt to describe the contents
of Chronicles as though Samuel–Kings did not exist (e. g., Wright 1993,
87–88). I will do a little bit of both.

The Chronicler provides even less insight into Solomon's character
and inner life than was the case in Kings. There is no direct quotation of
Solomon's words anywhere in 1 Chr 22–29, in spite of the fact that three
of these chapters (22, 28, and 29) focus on Yahweh's choice of Solomon
to build the temple as David's successor and the affirmation of this choice
by David and the people. This silence is even more striking when one
notes that David repeatedly exhorts Solomon to "arise and act," "arise
and build," or "be strong and act" (22:16, 19; 28:10, 20). Instead, David,
the mentor and "fundraiser" (Tarr 1987, 500), does *all* the talking to young
Solomon in private, and *all* the talking about Solomon in increasingly
public forums.

As was the case in Kings, young Solomon is not said to receive an
education, even though he no longer seems to possess the political "wisdom" (1 Kgs 2:6; cf. 2:9) that allowed the Solomon of Kings to establish his
kingdom and remain in power without much guidance from his father. In
Chronicles David justifies his exhaustive preparations for the building of
the temple by stressing his son's lack of education, twice describing
Solomon as young and inexperienced (or "tender"; נער ורך; 1 Chr 22:5;

Bond is found to be irresistibly desirable to every woman (and most men) in the
film. Yet if viewers bracket out *their* desire, Moore's Bond is exposed as a cipher.

29:1; cf. 2 Chr 13:7). Rather than eliminate his son's lack of experience by arranging for him to get the kind of formal schooling obtained by ancient kings like the Sumerian Ur-Nammu's son Šulgi,[14] David commands the princes of Israel to help his son (1 Chr 22:17)[15] and hands Solomon the "blueprints" for the temple (28:11).

Nor does David attempt to increase his son's understanding by composing instructions for his son/successor, in the manner of so many other ancient Near Eastern kings. Instead, he merely tells Solomon that he hopes Yahweh will give him "discretion and understanding" (שכל ובינה) so that he might know God, keep his laws, and prosper (22:12; 28:9; cf. 29:19). While David does not target judicial understanding, readers of Chronicles may come away with the impression that it is David who inspired Solomon's later request for judicial wisdom and knowledge. When God finally asks Solomon what he wants after David's death, the new king requests wisdom and knowledge to go out and come in before the people and to judge them (2 Chr 1:10). While God tells Solomon that he has granted him his request (1:12), readers are not given the opportunity to witness Solomon acting with judicial wisdom.[16] For these reasons, readers would be hard pressed to specify the precise nature of Solomon's special wisdom, let alone determine the senses in which it might be unique or incomparable.[17]

Scholarly disagreement about the characterization of Solomon in 1 Chr 22, 28–29 usually centers on the issue of whether David is being elevated at the expense of Solomon or vice versa. Some note that David is the one who actively prepares everything for the temple, including funds, while Solomon apparently just listens to his father expatiate on his extensive preparations and his great generosity. All that's left for Solomon to "arise and do" is to keep fundraising and follow his father's game plan (see, e.g., Curtis and Madsen 1910, 259). Others argue that it is Solomon who is glorified at David's expense.[18] They point out that Solomon is now

---

[14] This difference goes unnoticed in S. N. Kramer's "comparative portrait" of Solomon and Šulgi (1991, 193–95).

[15] Apparently they are not to help him personally, for Solomon is not mentioned in David's quoted exhortation to the princes (22:18–19)

[16] The Chronicler does expand one reference to Solomon's wisdom, however, when he has Huram bless Yahweh for giving David a son who possesses wisdom, knowledge, discretion, and understanding (חכם יודע שכל ובינה; 2 Chr 2:11). Yet Huram goes on to use the same language when praising Huram the craftsman as one who also possesses wisdom, knowledge, and understanding (חכם יודע ובינה; 2:12).

[17] While God says that he is giving Solomon incomparable wisdom in 1 Kgs 3:12, this is not said in the parallel passage in Chronicles (2 Chr 1:12).

[18] E.g., Braun 1973, 512; McConville 1984, 109; cf. Dillard 1987, 3. On Braun's view, see DeVries 1989, 228.

Yahweh's chosen temple builder, while David is disqualified due to the fact that he shed so much blood (22:8; 28:3). In other words, the "man of wars" (28:3) is eclipsed by the "man of rest" and peace (22:9), even if David's wars prepared for that peace. And while David is the active party in chapters 28–29, his activity is focused on grooming the people to view Solomon—if not himself—in an adoring fashion. David's other sons join in as well. Like Esarhaddon's brothers, who all witness Sennacherib's designation of their younger brother as his successor and take a solemn oath to support him (Borger 1956, 40 [1.8–11]), all of young Solomon's brothers give a hand in support (29:24). Finally, in 29:25 the narrator declares that Yahweh magnified Solomon greatly, giving him royal majesty the likes of which had not been bestowed on any king before him [in Israel, MT]; cf. 2 Chr 1:12).

The theme of magnification recalls Yahweh's public-relations work on the image of Moses' successor Joshua, as do the repeated admonitions to Solomon and Joshua that they be strong and courageous and not be afraid. However, likening David and the magnified Solomon to Moses and the magnified Joshua strengthens the case of those who view 1 Chronicles as elevating David more than Solomon. Joshua is no Moses, even though Yahweh grooms him to appear Moses-like to his people. As the rabbis put it, Moses is the sun and Joshua the moon (e.g., *b. B. Bat.* 75a); any light reflected by Joshua has its source in Moses' charisma.

In 2 Chronicles Solomon is no longer silent, although his words are not directly quoted until he responds to Yahweh's gift offer. After that he is quoted on only three occasions: in writing to Huram, in his temple speeches, and in offering a cultic rationale for moving his otherwise unknown Egyptian wife (2 Chr 8:11). On the other hand, Solomon's abbreviated response to Yahweh's offer and his letter to Huram are both more assertive and business-like than their counterparts in 1 Kings. Solomon no longer claims help from Yahweh because he is a little child. Perhaps this is because David has already provided help when he still viewed his son as an inexperienced child—a child who was seen but not heard. Similarly, the Solomon who takes the initiative to contact Huram and set the terms of their building-materials contract does not feel any need to assure Huram that his borders are secure and that he has no enemies. Nor does he explain to Huram why David was unable to build the temple. On the contrary, Solomon is the more powerful party both here and later, when it is Huram who extends the borders of Israel by giving twenty cities to Solomon, not the other way around (2 Chr 8:2; cf. 1 Kgs 9:11).

The Solomon of 1–2 Chronicles is all business, that is, temple business. He has no private life *or* private desires. Gone are the thousand loves of his life. Here he has only two wives—and we learn of them only incidentally. We learn of Pharaoh's daughter only because of Solomon's concern not to defile the area in which the ark resides and of the second wife thanks only to his son Rehoboam's later regnal resume, which includes both his mother's name (Naamah) and her ethnic identity as an Ammonite (2 Chr 12:13).

The fact that this obedient Solomon has only two wives and one named child is significant. In Chronicles a large number of wives and children is a reliable indicator of success and divine approval. Thus, Solomon's father David had many wives and concubines and nineteen sons (1 Chr 3:1–9; 14:3–7). Solomon's son Rehoboam is even more prolific; he has eighteen wives and sixty concubines, including his wife Maacah, whom he loved most of all. These women give birth to twenty-eight sons and sixty daughters (2 Chr 11:18–21). In this key sense, Solomon's own peaceful, obedient kingdom is sterile and unproductive, even more than was the case in Kings.

The Chronicler's Solomon is not only magnified but blameless. Considering that we are told so little about Solomon's personality and personal life, it is hardly surprising that no personal sin is attributed to him. The good news for this blameless and sterile Solomon is that he has no external enemies at the end of this career, precisely because he has no multitude of wives to incite him to idolatry. Nevertheless, rebellion breaks out in the northern half of Solomon's peaceful united kingdom immediately after his death, when his "young and tender-hearted" (i.e., faint-hearted or irresolute) son takes the throne (נער ורך־לבב; 2 Chr 13:7; cf. 12:13). When it comes to the cause for the rebellion, the narrator is neither ambiguous nor vague: the blame is laid squarely on the shoulders of a Jeroboam who has been stripped of his divine mandate and on the people who here have no good reason to complain of excessive taxation. Because of the narrator's silences—he never says that Solomon used his own people for the corvée, never says that he formed administrative tax districts to support his extravagant court and his building projects, and never says that he had to sell off part of the Holy Land—it is the sheer perversity of Jeroboam and the Israelites that is—by default—totally responsible for the disastrous schism following the death of this idealized "man of rest."

Conclusion: Solomon and Kafka's Klamm

Some individuals have seen him, everybody has heard of him, and out of glimpses and rumors and through various distorting factors an image of Klamm has been constructed which is certainly true in fundamentals. But only in fundamentals. Otherwise it fluctuates, and yet perhaps it does not fluctuate so much as Klamm's real appearance.
—Kafka, *Das Schloss* (1946, 257)

Once there was a castle official named Klamm. In the village below the castle the people say that Klamm is enormously powerful. A man named K. seeks an audience with Klamm as urgently as Dorothy sought an audience with the Wizard. Yet Klamm is as elusive and protean as any panoptic king.

While no one can hide from him, he is rarely seen and never speaks to any-one in the village. The two letters that K. receives, apparently from Klamm, are so ambiguous that K. and others engage in intense literary analysis trying to tease out their meaning and intention. When Klamm is seen, it is only for a moment. Even in those moments they are never capable of "really seeing" him (1946, 74). According to a character named Olga, "a man like Klamm, who is so much sought after and so rarely accessible, easily takes on differ-ent shapes in people's imagination" (265). Indeed, he is reported to have one appearance when he comes into the village and another on leaving it, one when he is alone and another with people, and so on.

Given Klamm's inscrutable and protean nature, how can one construct an image of him that is even "true in fundamentals"? According to Olga, the differences in Klamm's appearance "aren't the result of magic"—in other words, Klamm is no more a wizard than is Oz. She believes that they are the result of the momentary mood of the observer—the viewer's "countless gradations" of hope, despair, or excitement—and by the fact that Klamm is usually seen only for a moment (257–58). This, she concludes, would be a sufficient explanation for anyone not personally interested in the matter. For her and K., however, it is a life-and-death matter.

In a sense, readers of the Solomon narratives share the predicament of K. and Olga, whether they are seemingly disinterested scholars or observers for whom the question of Solomon's personality is as urgent and vital as Klamm's is for K. and Olga. Solomon appears one way in Kings and another in Chronicles, not to mention the variety of different ways he appears to different commentators. Are these varying images of Solomon also a function of the observer's "momentary mood" (or ideology, or hermeneutical habits)? Scholars would not like to say so. Yet if the texts describe the king in such a way that the "real" Solomon (both the literary Solomon and the historical personage) remains invisible, it is unlikely that any academic attempt to bracket out subjective factors will produce an "objective" portrait of the king. The lack of extrabiblical information on Solomon and the lack of certainty concerning the date and social context of the narratives[19] only decrease the likelihood of constructing an unam-biguous image of the king that is "true in fundamentals."

While the elusiveness of the biblical Solomon might be distressing to readers who want to penetrate the king's public facade, the narratives themselves seem designed to keep Solomon hidden, thereby *encouraging* a variety of subjective responses to the texts. This is hardly surprising, con-sidering the function served by invisibility and protean appearance for leaders like Deiokes, the Wizard, and many others. Whether they are called "court apologetic" or propaganda, the narratives create an indeterminate

---

[19] On this, see ch. 7, below.

image of the king that bypasses the dilemma faced by court historians who must otherwise affirm or deny unflattering facts about their monarchs. The solution represented by these narratives is not unlike the strategy called "telling it with discretion" in Stefan Heym's novel *The King David Report*, which we discussed in the last chapter. Rather than telling all the "undesirable matter" about Solomon's father or denying it (when the audience might learn about it anyway through unofficial channels), Ethan chooses to tell it with discretion. Discretion is "truth controlled by wisdom" (Heym 1973, 84). In this case, to be discreet and wise means to show a king who is neither invisible nor totally visible. Instead, the king is presented as being discreetly inscrutable, capable of being viewed in many different ways. This means that scholars cannot even determine whether the reconstructions they produce from these textual "glimpses" and age-old "rumors" are even "fundamentally" true. What *can* be determined, however, is that the narratives constitute one of the most unique and complex examples of political rhetoric in ancient literature. And best of all, this rhetoric—Solomon's verbal palace—*is* visible and therefore available for analysis, if only from the outside.

7

THE KING OF DESIRE: INTERTEXTUALITY AND CHARACTER IN THE SOLOMON NARRATIVE

In the last chapter, I emphasized the ways in which the narrators of the Solomon narratives grant the king "invisibility" by withholding information concerning his thoughts and "private" life. In this chapter, I will ask whether Solomon is also made inaccessible through the *opposite* narrative strategy: giving *too much* information to the reader. I am not talking about the text exhibiting indeterminacy caused by "ambiguity" (contradictory or ill-fitting information), in addition to the indeterminacy caused by "vagueness" (too little information), although both types are indeed present.[1] Instead, I am talking about the "glut" of statements that describe Solomon and his rule in terms that would be very familiar to an elite audience from royal inscriptions and other textual genres produced by the surrounding cultures. Nowadays, social critics and historians use the term "data glut" to refer to a "new variety of politics" in which "governments do not restrict the flow of information but flood the public with it" (Roszak 1994, 162–63). Why? So that "a statistical blizzard numbs the attention" and the citizen "shuts off his value-weighing perceptions the moment he hears a number" (Roszak 1994, 163; J. R. Saul 1992, 141–42). I am not suggesting that the ancient writers "flooded" the Solomon narratives with literary clichés and quantitative data in order to "numb our attention" to Solomon's faults and to "shut off" our evaluative urges. However, I *will* ask whether Solomon is described with so much stereotypical abundance that we learn nothing at all about "him," in the sense that we are able to learn something about the personalities and thoughts of other biblical kings. If this turns out to be the case, we would be talking about what might be called "intertextual indeterminacy." This would remain true whether or not these intertextual allusions and quantitative lists also served to grant the narratives verisimilitude or an aura of historicity (see, e.g., Long 1987, 12–14; Walsh 1996, 90–91).[2]

---

[1] For the distinction between vagueness and ambiguity, see Lasine 1986, 70 n. 1.

[2] Of course, one can go a step further and take the administrative lists, names, and numbers as indicative of *actual* historicity, requiring the author to be a member of Solomon's court with "firsthand knowledge." For a recent example, see Lemaire 1995, 116 and n. 73.

In order to investigate this possibility, I will concentrate on one major theme in 1 Kgs 3–11: Solomon's desires. This theme is crucial not only for evaluating the king's personality and private life but for determining the ethical implications of Yahweh's fostering of Solomon's desire and granting Solomon gifts he did *not* desire. I will begin by asking what readers familiar with Deut 8, Deut 17:14–20, 1 Sam 8:11–17, and the Court History would *expect* to be the result of God granting unprecedented wealth and prestige to Solomon. What would the statements on wealth and desire in later texts attributed to Solomon (i.e., Qoheleth, Psalms, Wisdom of Solomon) prepare one to expect? In particular, what would other ancient Near Eastern texts on the subject suggest as the outcome—or, for that matter, descriptions of the golden age from "classical mythology" such as those to which Jobling (1991, 58–60) refers when investigating the Solomon narrative? And what about the many statements on desire, wealth, satiety made by other classical writers (including Plato, whose philosopher king Parker [1992, 75–76] compares and contrasts with Solomon) and later thinkers? Would the narrator's "data-glutted" account of Israel's happy prosperity in 1 Kgs 4–10 seem so extreme that postmonarchic (and even monarchic) audiences would have viewed it as unbelievable and therefore blatantly tendentious?

This chapter will conclude with an assessment of Yahweh's influence on Solomon's career. Should readers of 1 Kgs 3–11 conclude that Yahweh served as Solomon's "enabler," encouraging the young obedient king to develop and satisfy a desire for incalculable wealth and opulence, in spite of the fact that Moses and Samuel had warned against the misuse of wealth and power by monarchs and described the danger of satiety for all the people? Is Yahweh testing Solomon with success, as he does later with Hezekiah? Or is he tempting Solomon with dangerous gifts that he knows are certain to make the king insatiable?

"INTERTEXTUAL INDETERMINACY" IN THE SOLOMON NARRATIVE

Readers of the Solomon narrative may have to look no further than its first verse to find an example of intertextual indeterminacy, especially if they are reading the present text of Genesis–Kings as one narrative complex. According to 1 Kgs 3:1 Solomon becomes Pharaoh's son-in-law, taking Pharaoh's daughter and bringing her into the city of David. While some texts in Exodus and Deuteronomy seem to guarantee that this marriage would be condemnable, others suggest that the alliance may not be an egregious sin, and analogous ancient Near Eastern texts describe such diplomatic alliances as laudable. Even if one assumes that ambivalence toward Pharaoh's daughter in 1 Kgs 3–11 is the result of a series of redactional stages through which the marriage "evolved" from praiseworthy to condemnable (S. Cohen 1984–1985, 26), the fact remains that the resulting portrayal is ambivalent and therefore indeterminate.

The fact that the issues raised by the marriage are crucial (especially in light of 1 Kgs 11:1–8) suggests that one *must* choose among these competing intertexts. For if we find that Solomon *is* violating the laws governing exogamy and those prohibiting royal intercourse with things Egyptian (Deut 17:16), this means that Yahweh blesses Solomon with wisdom, wealth, and honor even *after* Solomon has violated Yahweh's own laws. If so, Yahweh's motives become problematic at best. On the other hand, the relative leniency toward Egyptians in the laws governing the presence of foreigners in the קהל via intermarriage (Deut 23:8; see Milgrom 1982, 173) suggests that the marriage to Pharaoh's daughter may not constitute a direct violation of the law of Deut 7:1–3, which also refrains from mentioning marriages with Egyptians. And while the pharaohs of Exodus are tyrannical and villainous, this does not mean that readers of 1 Kgs 3:1 will necessarily identify this new pharaoh as "the archvillain," as Eslinger assumes (1989, 129). One cannot simply reduce *all* Egyptian kings in the Bible to one "anathematic opponent" of Yahweh (129). This caricature does not jibe with the portrayal of the pharaoh in Gen 41–50, a narrative whose wise hero Joseph bears a number of similarities to Solomon, or with the presentation of another pharaoh's daughter in Exod 2:5–10. Finally, readers who interpret Solomon's marriage solely in terms of extrabiblical data concerning the rarity of diplomatic marriages between the Egyptian king's daughter and alien monarchs[3] (and assume that ancient readers did the same) will also tend to judge the marriage positively. However, they too must ask why such a momentous international event is described in such a cursory and cryptic manner.

Consciously or unconsciously, readers make choices concerning the genre of the text they are reading. In so doing, they expand the intertextual matrix of their reading by linking the text with biblical and extrabiblical literature that is perceived as belonging to the same genre. However, it is often difficult or impossible to reach a consensus about the genre (or genres) of a text, or if the text is an example of any genre at all. Readers who note the affinities between 1 Kgs 3–10 and ancient Near Eastern royal inscriptions, incubation reports, and building inscriptions may conclude that they should read the biblical text in terms of the genre conventions that govern such

---

[3] Meier (2000, 171) believes that the other "Great Kings" were willing to give their daughters to the Egyptian monarch because the Egyptian view of diplomatic marriages was "peculiar": "where Egypt regularly receives princesses in marriage as a sign of sovereignty, the other players regularly give princesses in marriage as an expression of sovereignty." As a result, "both sides walk away claiming (under their breath) that they had a better deal."

texts. However, in the immediate context of the Deuteronomistic History these features could also be interpreted as examples of parody, irony, or hyperbole.[4] For example, does the portrait of Solomon conform to the typical image of the ancient Near Eastern imperial ruler to such an extent that it can be read as a caricature of that image, like the reductive portrait of Manasseh as the limiting case of villainy in 2 Kgs 21 (see Lasine 1993b)? Does the fact that these international textual affinities show Solomon to be a king "like all the nations" around Israel ensure that this ostensibly positive depiction is ironic, given the warnings of Deut 17:14–20 and 1 Sam 8:5–20? Or is it only modern historical scepticism, a modern unwillingness to suspend disbelief when reading imperial propaganda, and modern uneasiness with social stratification and national service programs that make the Solomon of 1 Kgs 4–10 seem unbelievable or condemnable and his depiction ironic? Once again, to "read" the text interpreters must make determinate judgments about the significance of the undeniable affinities between 1 Kgs 3–10 and other ancient texts. In particular, what would readers familiar with these other texts expect to be the result of God giving Solomon so much wealth and power? Does 1 Kgs 3–11 fulfill these expectations?

Expectable Positive Effects of Royal Wealth and Honor

For the German philosopher Schopenhauer, enormous wealth and power are absolutely necessary if a king is to rule justly. In fact, this is the "fundamental idea" of monarchy:

> because men remain men, one must be placed so high, and be given so much power, wealth, security, and absolute inviolability, that *for himself* there is nothing left to desire, to hope, or to fear. In this way, the egoism that dwells in him, as in everyone, is annihilated, as it were, by neutralization; and, just as if he were not a human being, he is now enabled to practice justice, and to have in view no longer his own welfare, but only that of the public. (Schopenhauer 1966, 595)

While Schopenhauer makes what is perhaps the most extensive argument on behalf of monarchical wealth and power, he is not the first to stress the link between personal wealth and disinterested rule. In *De Monarchia,* Dante argues that the extreme opposite of justice is greed, and "where there is nothing left to desire, greed is impossible.... a universal ruler has nothing left that he still desires, for his jurisdiction is bounded only by the ocean" (1.11; 1957, 14). Dante uses the idealized "Solomon" of Ps 72:1 to support his argument (1.13) and refers to the "Solomon" of Qoheleth when

---

[4] On indeterminacy and parody, see Lasine 1993a, 47–51.

warning against the insatiable nature of the desire for wealth (*Banquet* 4.12.8). Nevertheless, it is the Solomon of 1 Kings to whom Dante assigns a privileged place in his *Paradiso,* precisely because he responded to God's invitation by asking for kingly wisdom (*Paradiso* 10.112–14; 13.92–108).

The idea that wealth and power create just, public-minded kings by eliminating their personal desires actually goes back to the man whom Dante calls "the Philosopher."[5] In the *Ethics* Aristotle argues that kingship is a better form of constitution than aristocracy or republic, but that "a man is not a king if he ... is not better supplied with goods of every kind than his subjects." Because "a man so situated lacks nothing," he "will not study his own interests but those of his subjects." (*Eth. nic.* 1160a35–1160b5; 1934, 491). Readers who share the view of royal wealth and power expressed by Aristotle, Dante, and Schopenhauer will certainly expect Solomon to remain a successful and just king when he receives the wealth and honor that God has promised him.

Expectable Positive Effects according to the Hebrew Bible and Ancient Near Eastern Texts

After Solomon goes to sacrifice at Gibeon Yahweh appears to him in a dream and says, "Ask what I shall give you" (1 Kgs 3:5). Readers of the royal psalms will not find this divine invitation to be unusual or be surprised to hear that it resulted in good things for king and kingdom. In Ps 2:8 Yahweh tells his son the king, "ask of me, and I will give the nations for your inheritance and the ends of the earth for your possession." The speaker in Ps 21 describes a king who has already made such a request of the Lord and who has already been given his "heart's desire" (תאות לבו): "He asked life of you, you gave it to him.... honor and majesty you lay upon him" (21:3, 5–6). And in Ps 72, a psalm "of Solomon," the king to whom God gives his justice will rule in peace and prosperity, having dominion "from sea to sea, and from the River to the ends of the earth" (vv. 1, 7–8). Kings will render tribute (מנחה), and the kings of Sheba and Seba will offer gifts (v. 10). In the same vein, readers of Prov 3:16 will not be surprised that Yahweh's gift of wisdom also helped Solomon to acquire riches and honor, for Wisdom has riches and honor in her left hand (cf. 1 Kgs 3:13) and long life in her right hand (cf. 1 Kgs 3:11).

Similar divine invitations and divine gifts are reported in many ancient Near Eastern texts. For example, the Canaanite goddess Anat tells Aqhat,

---

[5] If not millennia earlier; note this observation from the "Instruction for Merikare," an Egyptian king who ruled in the twenty-second century B.C.E.: "He who has wealth in his home will not cause trouble, for the rich man cannot want for anything" (Grimal 1992, 145; cf. Lichtheim 1973, 100).

"Ask for silver and I will give to you, [gold, and I w]ill deliver it to you.... Ask life and I will give (it) you" (*CTA* 17.6.17–18, 27; Seow 1984, 149–50; Gibson 1978, 108–9). When the Canaanite god El visits Kirta in his dream and asks him whether he desires the kingship of the bull his father, the king also gets what he desires. Although his desire is for sons and not for wisdom, Kirta is similar to Solomon in not asking for silver, yellow metal, slaves, horses, or chariots (*CTA* 14.1.38–58; 14.3.138–55; Gibson 1978, 83–86).

In general, ancient Near Eastern kings who claim to have received the blessings of life and wisdom from the gods describe their regimes as blissful, just, and prosperous. According to his son Barrakkab, Panammu possessed silver and gold because of his wisdom and his righteousness (line 11; Gibson 1975, 81). Because grain was plentiful and inexpensive, "then did (the land) eat and drink" (9–10; Gibson 1975, 79). Azitiwada claims that he extended the boundaries of his land, used his righteousness and wisdom to bring about peace, and made the land so prosperous that all the people "had plenty (of grain), and fine food, and a gracious life, and peace of mind" (A.2.8; cf. A.1.1–2.6; Gibson 1982, 49). During the early years of Naram-Sin's reign the city of Agade was filled with wealth and joy, "all lands lived in security," and "their people witnessed (nothing but) happiness" (38–39; *ANET* 647–48). The pharaoh Hatshepsut claims to have no enemy in any land (Lichtheim 1976, 28–29). And in Egypt during the reigns of Amenhotep III and Amenhotep IV "gold is as dust," according to the Mitannian king Tušratta and the Assyrian king Aššur-uballiṭ (EA 16:14; 19:59-61; 27:106, Knudtzon, Weber, and Ebeling 1964, 129, 141, 239).[6] Tušratta goes so far as to claim that Egypt contains whatever is desirable in greater quantities than dust (Knudtzon, Weber, and Ebeling 1964, 149). Similarly, the Assyrian Sargon II brags that he heaped up goods without number in his city Dur-Šarrukin, so that people in Assyria valued the price of silver equal to that of copper (233–34; Lie 1929, 39).

God-given wisdom, righteousness, and longevity are not the sole means by which these kings achieve their great prosperity; human-given tribute and gifts are said to play a role as well. Such contributions can be freely offered presents as well as compulsory tribute or taxation. Ishme-Dagan of Isin declares "Of themselves they [foreigners] bring … their gifts" (265; Römer 1965, 53). Esarhaddon says of one donor, "year by year, without cease, he came to Nineveh with his heavy gifts [*tâmartu*] and kissed my feet" (Postgate 1974, 126). Temples and palaces also attract gifts, especially when they are being constructed or dedicated. The Gudea cylinders describe how trees, gold

---

[6] According to Zaccagnini (2000, 147), in the Amarna letters this is a "standard metaphor" used by kings writing to Pharaoh in order to request gold. It suggests that the desired quantity "should be of little concern" to Pharaoh, since gold is so abundant in his country.

dust, silver, and copper were brought from distant lands for the construction of the Eninnu temple for Ningirsu (Jacobsen 1987, 406–8). The Sumerian Hymn to Enlil praises the temple Ekur, claiming that "all the lords and princes bring there their pure gifts" (*ANET* 573). And Pharaoh Amenhotep III relates how the great temple he erected in the viewing place for his father Amun received gifts of silver, gold, and costly stones in enormous quantities from all foreign countries (Lichtheim 1976, 45). In addition, a number of these kings engage in trade with one another, granting each other's wishes and satisfying one another's wants and desires (see Hurowitz: 186–87).

One more index of kingly prosperity and power deserves mention: the royal harem. When Amenhotep III commissioned scarabs to announce the arrival of a new Mitannian royal wife, one of the "wonders" he mentions along with the princess are the 317 harem women who accompany her (Schulman 1979, 192). In addition to arranging diplomatic marriages for himself, the pharaoh has the power to *demand* that vassals send him their daughters (EA 99; 187; Moran 1992, 171; 269). His prosperity also allows him to "special order" women, such as the forty "extremely beautiful female cupbearers in whom there is no defect" he acquires from his vassal Milkilu of Gazru (EA 369; Moran 1992, 366).

Actual Positive Effects in 1 Kings 4–10

On the surface, the report of Solomon's prosperous reign seems to meet all the expectations raised by these biblical and extrabiblical texts. Like Azitiwada and the king of Ps 72:8, Solomon greatly extends the boundaries of his rule (1 Kgs 5:1, 4 MT). Like Hatshepsut he has no enemies (1 Kgs 5:18 MT). And like Naram-Sin and Azitiwada he brings peace of mind, security, and happiness to the land (1 Kgs 5:4–5 MT) so that the people of Judah and Israel can eat, drink, and make merry (1 Kgs 4:20) as did Panammu's people. As was the case with Panammu, Solomon is wealthy because of his wisdom; he displays the "wide understanding" sought by Sargon and his successors (1 Kgs 5:9 MT; *ARAB* 2:127, 670). Like many of these kings, Solomon receives tribute from all lands (1 Kgs 5:1 MT) and engages in trade with another monarch who satisfies his desires (1 Kgs 5:22–23 MT). As was the case with Gudea, to whom a god also appeared in dreams (Jacobsen 1987, 389–403), trees and precious metals are brought to Solomon from foreign lands for the erection of a temple (1 Kgs 5–6 MT; cf. 10:14–25). In addition, a steady stream of freely offered gifts arrives from "all the earth," because all want to witness Solomon's God-given wisdom (1 Kgs 10:24–25). If Ps 72:10 predicted gifts from the king of Sheba, Solomon receives the gift of spices, gold, and precious stones from the Queen of Sheba (1 Kgs 10:2). Finally, just as silver was so common as to be equal in price with copper in Sargon's city and gold was like dust in Amenhotep's Egypt, silver was like stones in Solomon's Jerusalem (1 Kgs 10:27) because of the overabundance of gold acquired by the king (1 Kgs 10:21; cf. 10:14).

Only in the case of Solomon's enormous royal harem does an expectable positive result turn out to be negative. Deuteronomy 17:17 prohibits the king from multiplying wives for himself, "lest his heart turn away." The alien origin of the wives (including Sidonian and Hittite) only multiplies the problem (cf. 1 Kgs 11:1–2 with Exod 34:11–16; Deut 7:1–4; 23:4; Judg 3:3–6). In this context, the size of the royal harem signals corruption rather than prosperity or splendor. While the acquisition of foreign princesses and concubines by monarchs like Amenhotep III illustrates the king's power over other nations, in 1 Kgs 11 foreign wives represent the power of foreigners over the king of Israel, as they turn his heart away to their gods.

Expectable Negative according to Greek Texts

Earlier, I traced Schopenhauer's sanguine view of royal wealth and power back through Dante to the fourth-century Greek philosopher Aristotle. Their king who needs nothing is remarkably similar to His Majesty the Baby, the infant king we discussed in chapter 1. In the psychoanalytical fantasy of the *infant's* "golden age," the child is also without needs. In fact, it is in "a state in which one does not even need to need" and is, in that sense, omnipotent (Glatzer and Evans 1977, 89). However, in chapter 10 we will investigate the behavior of *adults* who are labeled narcissistic. When we do, we will discover that the so-called "narcissistic libidinal type" of person does often become a leader, but *not* a leader who has no needs to fulfill. Far from it. Such people are neither self-sufficient nor free from envious desire. Thus, this modern psychological model suggests that we should lower our expectations for a king who has no need to need. But what do *ancient* psychological models suggest?

The vast majority of ancient Greek authors also tend to be much less optimistic than Schopenhauer and company. As Aristotle himself puts it in the *Politics,* "he who urges that man should rule [as opposed to law, God (τὸν θεόν), or intellect] adds also an element of the brute [θηρίον]; for desire [ἐπιθυμία] partakes of such element, and temper [θυμός] distorts rulers and even the best of men" (1287a29–34; 1986, 101). The idea that desire leads to insatiability, *hubris* (ὕβρις), envy and injustice in even the best rulers had already been expressed by Herodotus and Plato. In Herodotus's famous constitutional debate, Otanes asserts that even when the power to act with impunity is given "to the best man of all" the good things the king possesses "breed *hubris* in him, and, sated, he commits many reckless deeds, some from *hubris* and some from envy" (*Hist.* 3.80). While "the tyrannical man ought to be free from envy, possessing as he does all that is good," the opposite is the case. In fact, he meddles with or removes ancestral customs and observances, forces women, and kills men indiscriminately without trial (3.80).

Similarly, Plato contends that the age of Kronos was blissful because "Kronos was aware of the fact that no human being ... is capable of having irresponsible control of all human affairs without becoming filled with *hubris* and injustice" (*Laws* 713c; 1926, 285). In the *Statesman* (301d), he had implied that this was not only Kronos's view but that of humans themselves. Even the younger, less cynical Plato of the *Republic* (417a; cf. 547b) believed that the only way to breed a truly disinterested golden age ruler was to keep him as far away from gold as possible. In fact, gold and silver are taboo for the guardians who will become philosopher-kings: "for them alone ... it is not lawful to handle and to touch gold and silver, nor to go under the same roof with it, nor to hang it from their persons, nor to drink from silver or gold" (1968, 96). Such a king is the exact opposite of a tyrant. The tyrant is "*the* man of desire" (1968, 421), who is himself ruled by the tyrant Eros (ὁ Ἔρως τύραννος; *Rep.* 573b; cf. 571a–579e). ·

Greek warnings about the dangers of satiety (*koros*) and *pleonexia* (injustice, in the sense of wanting more, when that "more" belongs to someone else) are not limited to discussions of rich and powerful kings. For example, Solon asserts that *koros* breeds *hubris* whenever wealth "attends on men whose minds are not well balanced" (5.9–10; Freeman: 209). Good rulers check *koros* and confuse *hubris* (3.35). Later writers like Epicurus continually admonish their readers not to encourage unlimited desire or wealth. In a letter, Epicurus offers this advice: "if you wish to make Pythocles rich, do not give him more money, but diminish his desire" (U 135; 1926, 126–27; cf. Horace, *Odes* 2.16). The danger is insatiability. As Epicurus puts it, "nothing satisfies the man who is not satisfied with a little" (U 473; 1926, 137).

For Greek and Roman authors, it is excessive wealth and satiety that turn golden ages into iron ages. The citizens of Plato's gold-filled Atlantis enjoyed a blissful existence until their human element became dominant and they became "filled with unjust *pleonexia* and power" (*Critias* 120–121b). For Ovid and Lucretius, one trait of the iron age is "the accursed love of possession." Another is the introduction of mining, which uncovers the wealth hidden in the bowels of the earth. This became an "incentive to evil," especially when "noxious iron and gold more noxious were produced" (Ovid, *Metam.* 141–142; cf. Lucretius, 5.1108–1114). Ironically, depictions of "golden ages" do not include gold or stress wealth; in fact, "the discovery and use of gold was a characteristic of the degenerate iron age, and was ... a major factor in the destruction of earlier happiness" (Guthrie 1957, 72). When one views the references to Solomon's awe-inspiring holdings in gold and silver in terms of such texts, one cannot help expecting Solomon's golden age to become "a degenerate iron age" before very long.

Expectable Negative Effects according to the Hebrew Bible

> David: "A king is not supposed to need anything."
> Bathsheba: "Only a fool would suppose that."
> —*David and Bathsheba* (film; 1951)

If Schopenhauer's notion that a wealthy and powerful king will be just and public-minded would lead one to forecast success for Solomon, Deuteronomy suggests quite a different outcome. In contrast to Schopenhauer, who believes that a wealthy king will be just because "*for himself* there is nothing left to desire," Deut 17:16, 17 explicitly prohibits a future king from multiplying horses, wives, and silver and gold "for himself." Deuteronomy 17:14–20 assumes that making a king personally rich makes him insatiable and arrogant, rather than "annihilating" egoism and desire, as Schopenhauer supposes. This idea had already been made explicit in Deut 8, when Moses alerted his audience to the dangers of prosperity in a land filled with a variety of desirable foods and metals such as iron and copper (8:8–9). Moses warns that when they have become sated with food and multiplied their silver, gold, and all their other possessions, they might become arrogant and forget Yahweh their God (8:12–14; cf. 11:15–16 and Hos 13:6). Later Yahweh tells Moses that the people will indeed eat their fill, grow fat (LXX: κορήσουσι), and turn to other gods (Deut 31:20; cf. 32:15).

The fact that Yahweh gives Solomon riches "because … you have not asked for yourself long life; nor have you asked riches for yourself" (1 Kgs 3:11) would seem to accord with the values expressed in Deut 17:16–17. However, if Yahweh is assuming that an older, wealthy King Solomon will not desire more riches for himself because the young Solomon did not do so, Deut 8 and Hos 13 suggest that this assumption is unwarranted. So does Ezekiel's condemnation of the king of Tyre. Ezekiel tells the king, "by your wisdom and your understanding you have amassed wealth for yourself, and have gathered gold and silver into your treasuries" (Ezek 28:4 NRSV). His realm was Eden, the garden of God, filled with precious stones and gold (28:13). In itself, this account of a royal golden age is indistinguishable from the claims of the kings discussed earlier. Zechariah 9:3 increases the typicality of this picture by asserting that Tyre "heaped up silver as the dust and fine gold as the mud in the streets." However, Zechariah's similes carry a negative implication lacking in Sargon's declaration that silver was valued as copper in his city and Aššur-uballiṭ's claim that gold was like dust in Egypt. Viewed together with Ezekiel's condemnation of Tyre, the implication is that, while wisdom brings wealth, wisdom can also be corrupted by wealth.

Similar views are expressed by "Solomon" himself. "Solomon" (that is, Qoheleth) contends that "the appetite is never filled" (Qoh 6:7) and that a toiler's "eye is never sated with wealth" (4:8). And in the Wisdom of

Solomon, "Solomon" says of wisdom, "Neither did I liken to her any price-less gem, because all gold is but a little sand in her sight, and silver will be accounted as clay before her" (7:9 NRSV). While Sargon and the narrator of 1 Kgs 10:27 compare silver to copper and stones in order to communicate its loss of value due to its abundance, "Solomon" likens silver to clay because of its lack of value relative to wisdom. As "Solomon" puts it in Proverbs, wisdom "is more profitable than silver, ... and nothing you desire bears comparison with her" (3:14–15). According to these texts, when a king gathers wealth "for himself" while losing sight of its insignificance relative to wisdom, he risks becoming like the king of Tyre, to whom Ezekiel says "your heart became proud in your wealth.... you corrupted your wisdom for the sake of your splendor" (Ezek 28:4, 17).

Because these legal, prophetic, and wisdom texts all lead one to expect that God's gifts of wealth and honor would have a negative impact on Solomon's regime, one might well ask if any biblical narratives also create this expectation. The best places to look for an answer are the stories of Solomon's predecessors, Saul and David. Saul's appearance is preceded by Samuel's diatribe against monarchy (1 Sam 8:11–17), in which the king is portrayed as a prototypical coveter, taking the property of the people for himself and his servants and ultimately making the people his slaves. If Saul does not conform to Samuel's depiction of a despot, it is not because Samuel's polemical portrait obscures the actual benefits of a centralized administration and taxation to subsidize an army for national defense (see, e.g., McCarthy 1982, 83; Talmon 1986, 22–24, 62–67). One simply cannot know whether wealth, power and security would have led Saul to become insatiable and unjust because he never achieves the necessary degree of wealth, power, or security. Rather than focusing on Saul's desires, the narrative emphasizes the fact that "all the desire of Israel" was "on" Saul (1 Sam 9:20).

While the story of David also describes a king on whom all the desire of Israel is focused, the nature and significance of this desire is totally different from the desire directed toward Saul. As discussed in chapter 5, David is introduced as a figure whom *everyone* desires and "loves." I also noted that when Yahweh condemns David for his actions with Bathsheba and Uriah, he does not consider the possibility that it was the gifts he had given David that led the king to violate his commandments against coveting, adultery, and murder. Given the statements we have examined in Deuteronomy, 1 Samuel, Hosea, Ezekiel, and other texts, it should hardly have been surprising that a man who had been given his master's wives would go on to "take" (2 Sam 12:9–10) more women who belonged to another. Clearly, Yahweh's experience with David furnishes more evidence that gifts of wealth and power only increase the likelihood that a king will become insatiable and unjust.

Actual Negative Effects in 1 Kings 4–11

In light of Plato's contention that a ruler must avoid all contact with gold and silver if he is to avoid becoming infected with *pleonexia,* Solomon's actions in 1 Kgs 4–11 put him on the road to becoming a tyrannical "man of desire" rather than a philosopher-king who has mastered his personal desires. Plato's guardians cannot drink from gold and silver vessels; all of Solomon's drinking vessels are made from gold (1 Kgs 10:21). Plato's future kings cannot go under the same roof with these metals; Solomon "made" all the gold objects for the holy place (זהב appears seven times in 1 Kgs 7:48–51) and all his gold shields (1 Kgs 10:16–17). While it is unlawful for Plato's rulers to touch or handle gold and silver, 636 talents of gold come to Solomon annually (1 Kgs 10:14).

But does Solomon *actually* exhibit the traits of a tyrant in 1 Kgs 4–11? Solomon certainly does achieve satiety, the early warning sign of monarchical *hubris* described with equal precision by Deuteronomy and Solon. Yet, of the tyrannical traits listed by Herodotus's Otanes, Solomon only displays the tendency to "remove ancestral customs and observances," if one takes as "ancestral" the laws against intermarriage and syncretism in Deuteronomy. It is his father David who "forces women and kills men indiscriminately without trial," not Solomon himself. David, who is never said to love a woman, covets and takes the woman who becomes Solomon's mother, while Solomon loves a thousand women (1 Kgs 11:1–2) but covets none. Finally, in spite of the innumerable gifts with which he is continually inundated, Solomon is not shown to be akin to Hesiod's "gift-eating kings" (βασιλῆς . . . δωροφάγοι) who are bribed into making crooked judgments (*Op.* 264; cf. 39, 221).

On the other hand, many readers of 1 Kgs 4–11 (e.g., Clements 1974, 403) believe that it is Solomon, not Saul, who most conforms to Samuel's polemical portrait of a tyrant, that is, a king who exhibits *hubris* and *pleonexia* by taking what belongs to others. According to this reading, Solomon's use of taxation and the corvée increasingly leads to more personal wealth at the expense of the public interest rather than promoting the public interest by annihilating personal desire, as Schopenhauer predicted.

Can We Determine Whether There Was a Solomonic "Golden Age"?

I do not know of any biblicists who have described the account of Solomon's "golden age" as a narcissistic wish-fulfillment fantasy. However, for those scholars who do *not* view Solomon as an Israelite tyrant, the extrabiblical parallels to 1 Kgs 3–11 show that Solomon is in the ancient Near Eastern monarchical mainstream. From their perspective, the narrator (if not the preexilic author) is depicting either an age of enlightenment or a golden age, and the positive account of Solomonic prosperity is either historically plausible or an appropriate and oft-used propaganda device. For example, Meyers justifies Solomon's building activities and accumulation of goods by arguing that they were required in order to communicate an important message: Israel, and its "cosmic center" Jerusalem, has the right to dominate. The "immediate audiences" for this message were the representatives of conquered peoples at the capital and palace officials (1983, 421–24). Solomon's foreign wives played a part by bringing with them more members of the target audience (421). And to the extent that Solomon had to maintain Jerusalem as an empire, his policies on taxation, tribute, and the corvée are also justifiable (424; cf. 427).[7]

In contrast, scholars who are negative about Solomon tend to say little about specific ancient parallels, preferring to characterize the narrative as projecting a false image of a golden age designed to cover up the fact that the empire maintained itself through coercion and exploitation. They do so on behalf of their own vision of the true golden age that ended when Solomon introduced imperial rule. These scholars also tend to assume that the narrative reflects historical reality, although their assumptions about the realities of monarchy differ totally from the views held by commentators who are positive about Solomon. According to Mendenhall (1975, 160), Solomon turned Jerusalem into "a thoroughly paganized Syro-Hittite regime" that "eroded" the "basic principles of the new religious ethic that stems from Moses." Taking his lead from Gottwald, Brueggemann (1992, 5:971) finds Samuel's denunciation of monarchy to be a "discerning" and realistic portrayal of the perils of Solomon's monarchy: "to embrace monarchy is to embrace the very exploitative, rapacious power of a legitimated state from which Moses and Joshua had emancipated Israel." Gottwald later attempted to distance himself from this scenario: "Unlike ... Mendenhall, we do not moralize or absolutize tribal Israel as 'a golden age' and the monarchy as a fall from grace" (1986, 7). While he insists that his view of "communitarian" tribal Israel does "not posit an 'idyllic,' perfectly just society of absolute equals ... [or] a mere nostalgic 'ideal' or religious 'vision'" (1992, 6:83), the terms in which Gottwald continues to describe the aspirations of tribal Israel and the alleged realities of Solomonic Israel still encourage one to view Solomon's regime as a "fall from grace."

---

7 Similarly, Ishida (1992, 110) assumes that the historical Solomon had "good reasons" for building his defense constructions and palace-temple complex; these buildings were all "vital" for governing such a vast kingdom. Malamat (1982, 203) believes that Solomon was "forced" to increase taxation and the corvée for other good reasons, namely, internal unrest and anticipation of external threats, especially from Egypt.

While other ancient texts indicate what one might expect to be the significance of Solomon's wealth and power, they obviously have not led scholars with differing ideologies to agree about the ideology of the text or the ways in which actual ancient audiences may have evaluated the intertextual matrix of 1 Kgs 3–11. Key questions remain: Would the target audience view the account of Solomon's wealth and prosperity as yet another example of a god giving a king the means to make his country prosperous and blissful? Would they take any of these texts as historically accurate or judge them to be blatantly self-serving and propagandistic? Would they expect royal wealth to lead to justice, as described in Ps 72, or would they view Solomon's riches and his policies as signs of the insatiability, arrogance, and injustice described in Deuteronomy and Ezekiel? Do the optimistic views of Dante and Schopenhauer and the pessimistic views of Solon, Plato, and Aristotle represent widespread human attitudes and expectations that might also be shared by ancient Israelite audiences? One way to address a few of these questions is to examine more closely the way Solomon's desires are represented in the narrative.

SOLOMON'S INVISIBLE DESIRES

> the king's heart is inscrutable. For multitude of jealousies, and lack of some predominant desire ... make any man's heart hard to find or sound. Hence it comes likewise that princes many times make themselves desires, and set their hearts upon toys: sometimes upon a building, sometimes upon erecting of an order.
> —Bacon, *Of Empire* (1858c, 419)

When you think about the way in which Solomon's situation is represented in 1 Kgs 3–11, it may seem as though he hardly had any choice *but* to become sated with desirable objects. He's at the center of a monarchical world in which the seminal principle governing the exchange of goods is the mutual satisfaction of desire. Hiram king of Tyre fulfills all Solomon's desires (5:22, 24 MT; 9:11).[8] The Queen of Sheba tells Solomon, "blessed be Yahweh your God who has taken pleasure in you" (10:9) and then gives him an enormous quantity of desirable gifts (10:10). For his part, Solomon (5:23, 25 MT) fulfills the desires of Hiram (at least initially; cf. 9:12–13) and gives the Queen of Sheba all her desire, whatever she asks (10:13; cf. 3:5, 13). In addition, Solomon fulfills all his own desires for his own pleasure (9:1, 19). The narrator not only stresses the fact that Solomon's wealth—

---

[8] Walsh (1996, 97) points out that Hiram's use of the "key phrase ... 'do whatever [the other] wants'" for fulfilling *both* kings' desires (5:22–23 MT) "puts the arrangement officially into the category of a courteous exchange of gifts between friendly kings."

and wisdom—exceed that possessed by anyone else (5:10–11 MT; 10:7, 12, 23–25) but the fact that the very people who are most impressed by his unequaled wealth and wisdom give him even more.

The Queen of Sheba shows that when someone is attracted to Solomon's visible wealth and wisdom, she or he may also assume that others experience the same desire. When she "sees" all of Solomon's wisdom and the various examples of his wealth and power, the sight takes her breath away (10:4–5). With her next words she enthusiastically affirms the truth of the reports she had received about Solomon's "deeds and wisdom" and his "wisdom and prosperity," but now that her eyes have seen it she realizes it far exceeds what she had heard (10:7). She then imagines how blessedly happy (אַשְׁרֵי) his wives (LXX) and servants must be, because they can continually be in his presence, hearing his wisdom (10:8). This rhetorical strategy is an invitation to readers, asking them to join this mutual admiration society. To put it in terms of Girardian "triangularity of desire" (1966, 1–52), readers are being invited to desire what these other desirable people desire. And if they *do* respond in the same way, their response would be in full accord with the many ancient Near Eastern reports of awe-inspiring royal wealth, prosperity, and divine favor.

While the account of royal gift giving in 1 Kgs 10 is in accord with other ancient Near Eastern texts, it goes far beyond them. Solomon is depicted as though he were at the center of a Hegelian heaven. Here is a subject who has gained recognition and fame by requiring others to recognize his desire, that is, by having others desire what he desires (see, e.g., Butler 1987, 57–58, 76–78). At the same time, the description of Solomon's wealth in 1 Kgs 4–10 includes elements that would lead one to expect that Solomon will fall from this heavenly state. By describing Solomon as the object of everyone's desire, the narrator has portrayed a Solomon who is force-fed the ingredients of *hubris* as though he were a royal veal calf. It is therefore remarkable that Solomon never engages in the kind of violence against others that is the hallmark of a true tyrant. Nor does he suffer the alternative fate typical of the tyrant; that is, he never becomes the scapegoat of those who fatten him up (namely, everyone else in the story, from the corvée workers to foreign monarchs to Yahweh). The narrative does not describe a king who fulfills the people's desire for unanimity, whether as their idol or their scapegoat (see Girard 1987a, 10–18; Lasine 1993b, 176–83). The people of Israel are therefore not akin to Aristophanes' Demos ("the People"), who confesses that he likes to feed and maintain one leader at a time so that the fattened political idol can be sacrificed and devoured by the people (*Eq.* 1111–1150).

Among Greek writers the tyrant is traditionally described as being in perpetual fear of enemies and envious of others (e.g., Herodotus, *Hist.* 3.80; Plato, *Rep.* 579b–580a). That the wealth and power of a king also inspires the envy of others is hardly surprising; as Barrakkab puts it, "My brother kings were envious because of all the good fortune of my house" (Gibson 1975, 90). In turn, envy leads to what Girard calls "mimetic rivalry" (e.g., 1987b, 338–47). Taking the envied person as a model the envious person identifies with the model's desires. At that point, the model also becomes an obstacle preventing the acquisition of the desired object—in short, an enemy. Yet, in spite of the fact that Solomon possesses most of what others would want to possess, he is not said to be envied by anyone, let alone hated by anyone. In fact, his regime is characterized by the absence of any adversaries (1 Kgs 5:18 MT), at least until 1 Kgs 11. Soggin is correct to find it "strange" that "our sources report no resistance to the actions of Solomon by traditionally minded circles in Israel" (1977, 369). Yet the strangeness is far greater, for there is no resistance from *any* circle—in fact, there is nothing but assistance from all circles, from the center of Jerusalem to the periphery of the empire. Only at the beginning and the end of the narrative is there mention of any rivals or enemies. And these do not model themselves on Solomon; in fact, Adonijah and Jeroboam are described as potential doubles of David. Only Rehoboam is portrayed as imitating Solomon's desires, explicitly outdoing his father in tyrannical traits such as taxation, forced labor, and coercion, the very traits that are muted in the Solomon narrative itself.

If the narrator of 1 Kgs 4–10 emphasizes the satisfaction of all Solomon's desires, unimpeded by rivals and enemies, the report of Solomon's acquisition of his many wives in 1 Kgs 11 is followed by condemnation and a list of enemies. According to 1 Kgs 11:1–8, Solomon is condemned because he married women from proscribed nations and allowed them to turn away his heart to other gods. While it is tempting to understand the primary function of his foreign wives as aiding his international economic and political policies, the narrator never makes this explicit. In fact, the only foreign woman who is described as being engaged in any kind of economic *Verkehr* with Solomon is the Queen of Sheba, the only woman in 1 Kgs 3–11 who is *not* Solomon's wife, concubine, or daughter.

Instead, 1 Kgs 11:1–2 describes Solomon's wives and concubines in terms that suggest personal desire as much as they do economic exchange. When the narrator states that Solomon "loved many foreign women" (1 Kgs 11:1) and repeats that "Solomon cleaved to these in love," he allows readers to hear a note of personal love beyond the legal nuances of the verbs אהב and דבק (on which, see Moran 1963). While this note is muted in Neh 13:26, which stresses the foreignness of the women, it is amplified in the LXX of 1 Kgs 11:1, which omits the element of foreignness, simply calling Solomon a "lover of women" (φιλογύνης). In Sirach this note is both amplified and extended. Here Solomon is told: "you heaped up gold like so much iron, amassing silver as though it were lead, and you gave to women your loins and gave them dominion over your body" (47:18–19; see Skehan and Di Lella 1987, 528). As noted by Beentjes (1984, 9, 11), this is "a *quite*

personal picture of Solomon," which "underlines the sexual behaviour."
Josephus stresses this aspect of Solomon's behavior even more, claiming
that the king "became madly enamoured of women and indulged in
excesses of passion" (τὴν τῶν ἀφροδισίων ἀκρασίαν) (*Ant.* 8.7.5 §191). Even
Solomon's desire for *foreign* women is motivated by insatiable passion
rather than the desire to make international treaties: "not satisfied [ἠρέσκετο]
with the women of his own country alone, he married many from foreign
nations as well, ... and he began to worship their gods to gratify his wives
and his passion [ἔρωτι] for them" (*Ant.* 8.7.5 §§191–192).

While 1 Kgs 11 suggests that Solomon felt personal desire for his
wives, remarkably little is said about the wives and Solomon's passion for
them in 1 Kgs 3–11. We've already noted the narrator's silence regarding
the king's marriage to Pharaoh's daughter and contrasted that report with
other accounts of diplomatic marriages. However, the aridity of Solomon's
loves is equally striking when it is compared to those of his father. None
of Solomon's many wives is said to love him as David was loved by Michal.
None pursues and flatters Solomon as did David's wife-to-be Abigail. Of
the six wives who are listed as giving birth to David's sons at Hebron in
2 Sam 3:2–5, three are already known to readers—and readers will soon
learn in detail how David came to make Solomon's mother Bathsheba his
wife. In contrast, of Solomon's one thousand wives and concubines only
Pharaoh's daughter receives any attention at all in 1 Kgs 3–11. It is therefore difficult to view the women as objects of desire acquired through the
expenditure of effort and will.[9] And nowhere in 1 Kgs 3–11 is anything
said about sons resulting from any of Solomon's many marriages. All the
prosperous king is said to produce in chapter 11 are "high places" (במות)
for the gods of his foreign wives (11:7–8).

Thus, while most of Solomon's thoughts and feelings remain indeterminate, readers may be given all the data they need to determine the
nature of his unexpressed desires. Even though the king's desires are recognized by all others, his enormous stores of goods and women ultimately
seem to represent the sterility of those desires. As noted by Goodheart,
"when desires are unbound, free to 'imagine' their course irrespective of
obstacles and resistances ... they exhaust themselves ... and terminate in

---

9 As mentioned earlier, the Queen of Sheba is the only woman in 1 Kgs 3–11
whom Solomon is not said to love. It is only in postbiblical traditions that these
two great knowers come to know each other in the biblical sense. In Jewish tradition, their affair is at times traced back to 1 Kgs 10:13, in which Solomon gives
the queen "all that she desired" (see Silberman 1991, 71, 77; for Islamic traditions,
see Watt 1974, 97–99). In Ethiopian tradition, the relationship issues in a royal son,
Menelik I (see n. 3 to ch. 6 above; on the version in the Ethiopic *Kebra Negast,*
see Ullendorff (1974, 108–12).

the experience of nullity" (1991, 139). While Solomon's behavior finally gives birth to adversaries and rivals in chapter 11, they arrive too late to prevent his desire from becoming illimitable and too late to intensify it through rivalry (see, e.g., Girard 1966, 17–26). If the fulfillment of Solomon's desire *does* result in a sterile and empty paradise, Solomon's insatiability is being indicted in chapters 4–10 as well as in chapter 11, even though this indictment lacks the vehemence of Ezekiel's condemnation of the insatiable prince of Tyre. If so, the explicit condemnation in chapter 11 serves to splice together the indictment of insatiability and the indictment of idolatry through intermarriage by emphasizing both the enormous number and the foreignness of Solomon's wives.

If these conclusions sound tentative, it is because so much remains uncertain about the audiences for which 1 Kgs 3–11 was rhetorically designed. One cannot identify the audiences if one cannot date the text, and without knowing the audience one cannot determine the social functions the narrative might have served. If one assumes the narrative was first read or heard in the monarchical period, one might argue that it is an example of preexilic propaganda designed to promote the interests of the monarchy. Even if one dates it as late as the Persian period, one can assign it a similar function, namely, to promote the interests of the "ruling caste" and priestly elite in Yehud (P. R. Davies 1992, 113–20). Alternatively, if one assumes the narrative functioned as theodicy, one can say that it justified the splintering of the united kingdom (if the text is preexilic) or that it instilled hope concerning the restoration of the temple or the advent of a more humble and continent Davidic king (if the text is exilic or postexilic). As long as the date of the narrative remains indeterminate, so will its social function. If the narrative is not addressing an audience that was in the midst of a social crisis, however, it is likely that different members of the audience responded to the account of Solomon's wealth and the representation of his desires in a variety of different ways.

Determining Yahweh's Character and Motives in the Solomon Narrative

It is a well-known fact that in this world pride does not go before a fall—that is: some may fall in their own pits, but hardly ever without somebody else pushing them.... in Isaiah there is one who pushes: Yahweh.
—Jensen, The Fall of the King (1991, 135)

Divine Testing and Divine Justice

As I have already suggested, the many biblical and extrabiblical texts that warn against the negative effects of wealth and satiety raise serious questions about Yahweh's actions in 1 Kgs 3. Should Yahweh have known better than to give Solomon so much wealth? Is it he who bears the primary responsibility for Solomon's eventual sins? One possible answer is suggested by a talmudic simile based on the passages from Deuteronomy and Hosea cited earlier. The issue is Yahweh's role in the sin of the golden calf:

> Thus spoke Moses: … Sovereign …, the silver and gold which Thou didst shower on Israel until they said, Enough, that it was which led to their making the Calf.… R. Hiyya b. Abba said: It is like the case of a man who had a son; he bathed him and anointed him and gave him plenty to eat and drink and hung a purse round his neck and set him down at the door of a bawdy house. How could the boy help sinning? (*b. Ber.* 32a; Epstein 1935a, 195–96)

Given the dangers of excessive wealth and prosperity, readers of 1 Kgs 3–11 might respond to Yahweh's gifts to young Solomon by asking the same question: "How could the boy help sinning?"

Few scholars seem comfortable with the idea that Yahweh might have been irresponsible in exposing Solomon to the dangers of excessive personal wealth. Even fewer entertain the idea that Yahweh might have been tempting Solomon to become insatiable and arrogant and therefore condemnable. Most readers are more happy with the Yahweh who acts according to the principle that "a person is led down the path he chooses to pursue" (*Num. Rab.* 20:12) than with a Yahweh who leads Solomon down a perilous road he had just chosen not to pursue. Eslinger is an exception to this rule. Noting that wealth and honor are "potential traps for human weakness," Eslinger asks why God would "unbalance Solomon with temptation that the latter had avoided" (1989, 136, 137). His answer is that God has "sinister" intentions; in fact, he is setting a "trap" for the king (143; 138; cf. 150). Yahweh "helps him along his road to ruin" in order to "end the unconditional promises that he made to David" (140, 147). Moreover, Eslinger's Solomon seems to be asking for punishment. In spite of the lack of information concerning Solomon's thoughts and feelings in 1 Kgs 3–11, Eslinger has no doubts about his character. Although he claims that "there can be no certainty about Solomon's hubris" in 1 Kgs 3:1–15, Eslinger goes on to sketch a cunning and manipulative character who is driven by "an Eve-like will to power" (135). This "sycophantic" and "unctuous" Solomon plays upon God's sense of covenantal obligation before slipping in his "surreptitious request" to play a "Moses-role" as judge, a request that he couches "in a studied naïveté" under the "guise of innocence" (132–33, 135). Even his judicial wisdom (1 Kgs 3:16–28) is questionable (138–40). Having established Solomon's character in 1 Kgs 3, Eslinger is able to interpret later passages in terms of that character (e.g., "given Solomon's personality" [141]).

One might ask how Eslinger achieves such a determinate reading of Solomon's request, God's bonus gifts, and the king's personality, given the lack of access into Solomon's thoughts and the complex intertextual network of which 1 Kgs 3:1–15 is a part. One reason is that he leaves out of account all the other biblical and extrabiblical examples of gods giving kings whatever they desire, even though educated readers of 1 Kgs 3–11 in the postmonarchical period would be familiar with many of these texts, as well as biblical texts that suggest a less negative assessment of Solomon's marriage with Pharaoh's daughter (see above). Another reason is that Eslinger bases his debunking of the characters Solomon and Yahweh on the assumption that the narrator continually communicates his negative view of Solomon and Yahweh by means of irony. Yet one cannot confirm or disconfirm the presence of irony without taking into account other key factors, such as the authorial audience's knowledge of literary conventions, rhetorical devices and relevant historical events and the different ways in which readers evaluate ethical literature in their roles as members of the authorial and narrative audiences (see Lasine 1989a, 52–58; 1992, 138–39). Eslinger has little to say on these issues, apart from dismissing the usual theories about the "trite" function of the Deuteronomistic History as theodicy (1989, 225–30).

Most scholars would add that the ancient audiences would not be receptive to a critical view of Yahweh, if the response to David Gunn's depiction of God's "dark side" in the Saul narrative is any indication. Gunn does not explicitly state that Yahweh felt rejected by the people's request for a king and therefore chose Saul as king because he knew Saul would fail. However, he does argue that "Saul when 'tested' is bound to fail" (1984, 71), that the ambiguity of Samuel's words to Saul in 1 Sam 10:8 become the "trap" in which Saul is caught (67), that Yahweh is "over-eager to condemn Saul" (124), and that Saul is "kingship's scapegoat" (125). Ackerman's response to Gunn's interpretation of Yahweh is typical: "I can find no warrant for inferring that any of the original readers for whom [the Saul narrative] was intended would be expected to raise the issue of God's justice" (1982, 439). Far from considering that Yahweh might be shown to be cruel or vengeful with Saul, Ackerman's ancient authorial audience would not even *raise the issue* of God's justice.[10]

---

[10] More recently, Noll is not reluctant to describe repeatedly the Yahweh of the David story (and of Job) as "capricious" and "impish" (1999, 33, 34, 36, 37, 38, 49, 50). However, because he assumes that Yahweh's characterization is "a narrative necessity only" (38 n. 20; cf. 37), required "to make the plot work" (34), Noll barely touches on the issue of justice. He contends that it is a mistake to assume that the characterization of Yahweh "mattered"; in fact, "it almost certainly did not" (38). On the issue of Yahweh's "capriciousness," see ch. 11, below.

But can we be so certain that ancient audiences would be expected to swallow their theodicy whole, like a bitter pill that one hurries to swallow before it begins to dissolve in one's mouth? One need not assume that any criticism of Yahweh or his kings need be as virulent and extreme as Eslinger's interpretations suggest. Elsewhere I have suggested that 2 Kgs 3–6 gives readers ample reason to sympathize with King Jehoram in besieged Samaria and to question the justice of Yahweh's (and Elisha's) actions (Lasine 1991a, 40–49). And 2 Kgs 21 leaves open the possibility that even the arch-villain Manasseh can be viewed as a scapegoat (see Lasine 1993b, 173–83). The question is whether the ancient audiences of 1 Sam 8–15; 2 Kgs 3–6; 2 Kgs 21 (or 1 Kgs 3–11) actually *did* challenge Yahweh's justice or recognize the possibility that Yahweh could be fashioning scapegoats when he prepared his kings for office.

Against Ackerman, it can be argued that at least some ancient readers—*and* illiterate hearers—of these texts might have been ready, willing, and able to question Yahweh's justice. Crenshaw finds evidence for the "popular rejection of God's justice" in prophetic quotations; in fact, he finds that the "questioning of God's justice ... [has] more affinity with popular religion than with official Yahwism" (1970, 393–94).[11] Moreover, this phenomenon is attested in other cultures. For example, evidence from ancient Greece suggests that during certain periods people commonly assumed that their gods were capable of bestowing excessive wealth on kings and later tempting them (or deceiving them or driving them mad) in order to destroy them. Thus, in Aeschylus's *Persae* the Chorus and several characters express the view that great success and wealth bring disaster, because of the envy (φθόνος) of the gods. Winnington-Ingram notes that these opinions were "common beliefs of the average Greek" (1973, 214). However, one character has a different view. This is the ghost of Darius, who believes that his son Xerxes was exposed to temptation as punishment for *hubris*. According to Dodds, it is this character who speaks for the author: "Aeschylus himself knows better" (1951, 39) than to attribute Xerxes' misfortune to divinely sent madness or deception (*atē*) or an evil demon. Like Solon and the other Greek thinkers cited earlier, Aeschylus assumes that success produces insatiability (*koros*), which generates *hubris;* it is the *hubris* that prompts divine temptation and punishment. Here a god uses temptation only to punish a person who has already succumbed to the temptations of wealth and prosperity.

Dodds calls this transformation of success into *koros* and *hubris* "a moral link" that is inserted "between the primitive offense of too much

---

[11] Admittedly, such "evidence" is open to challenge. As Berlinerblau points out, the "elitist literati" who produced these texts may have intentionally or unintentionally misrepresented the "*vox populi*" (1993, 13–14).

success and its punishment by a jealous Deity." This "moralization of *phonthos* tends to transform Zeus into an agent of justice" (1951, 31). In other words, the notion that fulfilled desire generates insatiability and *hubris* is an example of theodicy by psychology. It is also an example of ideology that undermines itself. For if the deity is aware that extreme wealth produces *koros* and *hubris* that trigger divine temptation and disaster, the deity is *already* tempting the subject to destroy herself or himself just by granting that person extreme wealth and success. The god *creates* the unquenchable desire for more. If so, the "common belief of the average Greek" that extreme wealth and success bring disaster is right on the mark. The same is true for the belief that it must be the jealousy of the deity that motivates the dangerous gifts of extreme wealth and power.

In *Republic* 380a, Plato quotes a fragment from Aeschylus in which a god is said to implant the cause in mortals when he wants to utterly destroy a house. Plato will not allow such ideas into his republic unless it is added that the mortals needed punishment and benefitted from it, because the gods are just and good. In other words, Plato also knows better than the "average Greek" whose views are reflected in the fragment. Do biblical scholars who deny that ancient readers of the Saul narrative would even raise the issue of God's justice also "know better" than the average Israelite? They certainly know better than to entertain the possibility that Yahweh would tempt or trap Saul—or Solomon. And they know better than to assume that the ancient authors and redactors would be any different from Plato's Socrates; if Plato would not allow such seditious notions in his *Republic,* the literate elite who produced Joshua–Kings would hardly allow them in their History. But what kind of "knowing better" is this? Is this not another example of knowledge in the service of theodicy (i.e., ideology), whether or not such knowledge is presented in scholarly dress?

Yahweh's Testing of Hezekiah and the Tempting of Solomon

In order to answer such questions, we have to consider specific examples of divine testing in biblical texts and determine whether any of the tests are actually traps. If someone attempts to test someone else by giving that person a desirable object, that procedure will turn into a trap if the desired object functions as bait, in other words, when acquiring the object causes destruction rather than the fulfillment of desire. Thus, if extreme wealth is certain to lead to *koros* and *hubris,* then the use of wealth in a test transforms it into a trap. God *does* lay traps (מוֹקֵשׁ; Josh 23:13; Judg 2:3; Isa 8:14), but they do not ordinarily involve trapping humans with unparalleled wealth and power. God usually tests humans with pain, misfortune, or the threat of both (e.g., with Abraham, Job, the wilderness generation [Deut 8:2], and the Israelites in Canaan [Judg 2:22; 3:1, 4]). In the cases of Abraham and Job, testing follows a period in which both were given wealth and success by God, and both are rewarded again after they have completed their ordeals successfully. But are there any instances in which the granting of a reward is *itself* the test? Does God test with wealth and prosperity rather than with the loss of wealth or life?

The only king who is explicitly said to be tested by Yahweh is the Chronicler's Hezekiah. According to 2 Chr 32, Hezekiah's faith and fortitude in the face of Sennacherib's invasion is followed by wealth and honor; many bring him valuable gifts, and he is exalted in the eyes of all nations from that time on (v. 23; cf. Solomon in 2 Chr 9:23–24). We then learn that his heart was lifted up in pride. After being punished for his pride, Hezekiah humbles himself for that pride of heart and is rewarded with "exceedingly great riches and honor" from God (2 Chr 32:25–27, 29; cf. Solomon in 1 Kgs 3:13). Hezekiah makes treasuries for his Solomon-like possessions (silver, gold, shields, 2 Chr 32:27; cf. Solomon in 2 Chr 9:16; 12:9) and, like Solomon, builds towns for himself (2 Chr 32:29). It is at *this* point that the Chronicler makes a fleeting reference to the visit of the Babylonian envoys and adds "God abandoned [עֲזָבוֹ] him to test him [לְנַסּוֹתוֹ] to know all that was in his heart" (v. 31; cf. Deut 8:2). While the text does not state that the king passed the test, the fact that the concluding regnal resume refers to his acts of piety and the honor done him by all the people at his death suggests that he did so.[12]

In the last chapter, I noted the ongoing debate over the question whether the Chronicler expected his audience to have some version of Samuel–Kings in mind when reading passages in Chronicles. When it comes to 2 Chr 32:24–31, it is difficult to disagree with Ackroyd's conclusion that "we should be totally at a loss to understand the matter if we did not have the earlier narrative" (1991, 326; cf. Dillard 1987, 258). Now, readers who *do* fill in the blanks by going back to the fuller account of the Babylonian visit in 2 Kgs 20:12–19 might have difficulty in concluding that Hezekiah passed the test after all. According to this report, Hezekiah displays pride, arrogance, and complacency that belie his self-characterization as wholeheartedly obedient to Yahweh (2 Kgs 20:30; cf. Solomon in 1 Kgs 8:23, 61;

---

[12] Ackroyd (1991, 326) puts it more strongly: "on this occasion Hezekiah shows himself entirely able to deal with the test." Japhet is more cautious. She suggests that "some elements" of 2 Kgs 20:12–19 "may have encouraged the Chronicler in [the] direction" of concluding that Hezekiah passed the test. Specifically, "*if*" the Chronicler interpreted Hezekiah's words in 2 Kgs 20:19 as expressing "absolute resignation to the divine will, … *then* Hezekiah indeed passed the test" (1993, 996; emphasis added). For the view that Hezekiah failed the test, see the scholars cited by Dillard (1987, 260).

11:4, 9). In a scene reminiscent of the Queen of Sheba's visit, foreign dig-nitaries bring a present (מנחה; 2 Kgs 20:12), and the king displays his wealth: his treasuries, silver, gold, armor—everything in his house and in all his dominion (2 Kgs 20:13). In Chronicles the treasuries and towns Hezekiah made "for himself" (2 Chr 32:27, 29) are justified by the conclud-ing explanation: "for God had given him very great riches" (32:29). In Kings, on the other hand, the description of his treasure recalls the prohibition of personal wealth in Deut 17:17. As noted by Hobbs (1985, 294), it is a way of "representing *hubris* on the part of Hezekiah." The punishment for this arrogance is announced by Isaiah: exile for his "sons" and the removal of all his accumulated wealth to Babylon (2 Kgs 20:16–18). Hezekiah's response to this verdict combines submission with complacency (v. 20).

If one reads 2 Kgs 20:12–19 in terms of the Chronicler's claim that God left Hezekiah to test him, this *is* a case in which Yahweh tests a human by giving him wealth and honor. Curtis and Madsen combine portions of 2 Chr 32:30 and 32:31[13] in a way that supports this reading: "And Hezekiah prospered in all his works *and so* God abandoned him ... in the case of the ambassadors" (1910, 492; emphasis added). Now, the Chronicler's Hezekiah is wealthy both before he falls ill (32:23) and after wealth and prestige have gone to his head and triggered Yahweh's wrath (vv. 24–25). At whatever precise moment Hezekiah is "abandoned" by God, the king is abandoned as a wealthy, prestigious king in a palace, not as a newly impoverished sick man on a dung hill, and not as an ostrich egg on the freeway (Job 39:14–15; see ch. 10, below). At the very least, the Chronicler implies that a wealthy king *can* theoretically pass such a test. On the other hand, 2 Kgs 20 shows a king whose personal wealth prompts arrogance sufficient to call forth a prediction of exile to Babylon—just as Solomon's sins begin the long process that results in the Babylonian exile.[14] Anyone who reads Kings and Chronicles together could easily conclude that if God used riches and international prestige to test Hezekiah's heart, he may have used the same means to test Solomon. That is, he may have given Solomon the kingdom and the wisdom to acquire unparalleled riches and honor in order to see how he dealt with the fulfillment of his desires—including the desires awakened by the test itself.

According to Japhet, the brief reference to Hezekiah being tested in 2 Chr 32:31 "indicates that the Chronicler was familiar with the idea that human beings were sometimes tested by God" (1989, 194). The Asa and Jehoshaphat narratives also include "trials [that] test moral fibre" (195). In Chronicles, riches and honor can also be a "hidden test" that "may lead to

---

[13] They also switch the word order of v. 31.

[14] Some rabbinic texts blame the exile on Solomon's marriage to Pharaoh's daughter, citing Jer 32:31 as support. See Faerber 1902, 58.

disaster" (Japhet 1993, 747). Citing Deut 8:11–17 and 32:15 in connection
with Rehoboam, Japhet notes that "material strength and security make the
people confident and tempt them to assert their own powers" (676) and
that "material prosperity has inherent dangers" (747). And commenting on
Uzziah's pride Japhet remarks that "it is the Chronicler's conviction that the
integrity to withstand this fatal *hybris* was a virtue with which *only very
few kings* were blessed" (884; emphasis added). While the Chronicler's
Solomon seems to be one of the very few who is able to resist the temptation of wealth and satiety and pass the test, the Solomon of Kings is
clearly not.

One midrash depicts a Solomon who mistakenly thinks that he is one
of the few exceptions to the rule:

> Said R. Isaac: Why were the reasons of the Torah not revealed? Because
> in two verses where they were revealed they caused the greatest in the
> world to stumble. Thus it is written, "he shall not multiply wives to him-
> self, that his heart not turn away," and King Solomon said, "I shall
> multiply and not turn away." It is written: ". . . when Solomon was old, . . .
> his wives turned away his heart." It is written: "he shall not multiply
> horses for himself, that he cause the people to return to Egypt." King
> Solomon said: "I shall multiply horses and not cause the people to return
> to Egypt." And it is written: "And a chariot went out of Egypt." (*b. Sanh.*
> 21b; Epstein 1935c, 118, slightly modified).

This text seems to operate on the assumption that what the "greatest in the
world" doesn't know won't hurt him. It is not Yahweh but the laws of the
king in Deuteronomy that cause Solomon "to stumble" (especially, it would
seem, the law telling him to read these dangerous laws [Deut 17:19])!
Solomon should have known better than to assume that he could resist the
temptations of wealth, honor, and power—unless he was already suffering
from *hubris*. But what about *Yahweh's* role? Did Yahweh *also* think
"Solomon will multiply and not turn away"? Did Yahweh give Solomon
wealth, honor and wisdom *after* he married the Egyptian king's daughter
because he thought "Solomon will multiply horses and not cause the people to return to Egypt"? While the narrative does not allow a definite
answer to such questions, it does allow one conclusion: if Yahweh *did*
think in this way, he too should have known better. In the next three chapters, we will investigate other cases in which Yahweh tempts, tests, or traps
people. In these cases, the people put under the divine king's microscope
are the neonate courtiers Adam and Eve, and the loyal courtier Job, "the
greatest of all the children of the East" (Job 1:3).

8

GOSSIPING ABOUT GOD: ROYAL INFORMATION MANAGEMENT AND SCAPEGOATING IN THE GARDEN OF EDEN

According to informed sources, there's a king in the garden of Eden. Most reports say it's Adam.[1] He is raised from the dust like a king being enthroned. Like a king, he is made in the image of God and exercises dominion. He lives in the center of the world, as in a royal capital. Adam only loses this royal status when he attempts to acquire the knowledge and wisdom that is the prerogative of a king. He is stripped of the royal robe and becomes a serf (John Chrysostom, quoted in Warner 1976, 52).

James Kennedy thinks it is Yahweh who is the king. It is he who makes the garden, and it is he who maintains control of knowledge (1990, 4–7). Adam and Eve are peasants in revolt. But what kind of knowledge is God controlling? Kennedy takes it to be "humanistic knowledge" (6) and gives examples that sound like departments in a liberal-arts college. Educating the peasants is dangerous because it can increase their "awareness of a world beyond the confines of their immediate environs and open up behavioral options and alternative styles of living" (6). This sounds like Gen 3 is an allegory warning parents of what might happen if they send their kids away to school. Kings might fear peasants rebelling, but they are unlikely to rebel because they just ate a course in analytic philosophy. What about a *science* course? Nietzsche contends that Gen 3 exposes God's "hellish fear of science": "It is all over with priests and gods when man becomes scientific" (*Antichrist,* §48; Nietzsche 1969, 224–25).

Why don't we drop the educational model and ask what kings fear most. What kind of knowledge do *they* most want to control? We know the answers by now; they're the same whether we're talking about Neo-Assyrian kings, King Saul, ancient Greek tyrants, or Louis XIV. It's knowledge about what's going on inside the palace gates and knowledge about what the citizens outside are saying to one another about the king. Actually, it is *information* that needs to be controlled. Kings want to plug

---

[1] E.g., Wyatt 1981, 14–17; Brueggemann 1972, 2–5; Engnell 1969, 110–19; against this idea, see, e.g., Wallace 1985, 161–63; Landy 1983, 355 n. 162.

up news leaks. All information flowing from the center must be shaped before press conferences can be scheduled. On the other hand, kings must prevent uncontrolled speech among the citizenry, whether it be gossip, slander, or seditious talk. They control information from within by presenting a facade that renders them impenetrable to the people—if not invisible and inaudible.

If Yahweh is the king in Gen 3, he would not seem to need the eyes and ears of others to tell him what's going on. Nor would Yahweh seem to need palace (or garden) walls to grant him invisibility, as though he needed to hide some scandalous or deflating secret. After all, we're not talking about the Wizard of Oz—*are we?* If God can see and hear everything while remaining invisible to his subjects, he has all the tools for successful information management. Are information leaks even possible in this setting? And if they are, is it King Yahweh who has cause for fear, or the gossipers? Is the garden story a cautionary tale about the disastrous consequences of gossip, in the sense that, say, Apuleius's *Golden Ass* warns readers about the dangers of unbridled curiosity?

Who then is the dangerous gossiper in Gen 3? Predictably, the majority of commentators have assumed from the start that the villain—or the fool—must be the only female in the story. Here are some typical charges: Eve softened up Adam with her cajoling words and broke him as if he were a plaything (Tertullian, quoted in Warner 1976, 58). The serpent questions Eve "of much idle prattle, as women they delight to talke and tattle" (Peyton 1967, 269). Eve is guilty of unwise speaking and listening.[2] She began as advisor but ends up as an eavesdropper, like the snake; in fact, she is "Adam's snake" (*Gen. Rab.* 20:11). She is a temptress (see, e.g., Higgins 1976). Because of Eve and her imitators, women have "slippery tongues, and are unable to conceal from their fellow-women those things which by evil arts they know" (*Malleus Malificarum,* pt. 1, ques. 6; Krämer and Sprenger 1928, 44). In some of the indictments, Eve's supposedly deadly words are described as liquids—liquid poisons. Thus, Eve "destroyed life's gathered crown," illustrating "the deadly poison that the proud tongue of an evil woman has."[3] The poison may be described as beer or wine. In one text, Eve prepared a brew for Adam (*Guthlac* 980–85; see Evans 1968, 149–50); in another, it is the wine she pressed for humankind that poisons them (Ephrem of Syria, quoted in Warner 1976, 60).[4]

---

[2] Spacks (1986, 41), describing the implications of Christian denunciations of Eve.

[3] From "On Women," a poem from the early Middle Ages, possibly written by St. Columbanus. Quoted in W. Davies 1983, 161.

[4] Eve has also been accused of "vnquiet vanitie" (Ralegh 1971, 142) and depicted as a narcissist (e.g., in Milton's *Paradise Lost* [e.g., 4.460–480]; see Earl 1985).

Let's slow down for a minute. Is there any special reason why Eve would be described not only as a tattler but as a kind of bartender and poisoner? Studies of the social dynamics of gossip do recognize the function served by people like bartenders. They often serve as confidantes for patrons; Robert Paine calls them "knowledge bankers" (1970, 186–87). Gossipers participate in an economic system in which the currency is information. Knowledge bankers (bartenders, clergy, psychologists) accept deposits of information from their clientele; they are trusted to keep it out of circulation and not broker it for profit. Who holds the most power in this system? Those who control the dissemination of the information.

In the economic system of the Hebrew Bible, it is Yahweh who most effectively controls the dissemination of knowledge and regulates its use. In a sense, he is the head of the Federal Reserve or the World Bank. What kind of a banker is Eve? It would be more accurate to call her an apprentice teller, using *teller* in both senses of the term. As everyone knows, she tells too much when responding to the serpent's initial statement (Gen 3:3). We have no record of God telling Adam anything about not touching the tree. So is she handing out counterfeit currency?

One remarkable midrashic tradition has it that Adam never doled out all the true information to Eve in the first place, so that her bank's assets were suspect even before the serpent stepped up to the teller's window: "Adam ... did not wish to speak to Eve the way the Holy One ... had spoken to him" (*'Abot R. Nat.* 1). Instead of giving her God's exact words, he told her just what she reliably reports to the serpent. In other words, it is *Adam* who first planted the seeds of disinformation. In this scenario, Eve receives unreliable information from both male speakers in the garden: Adam and the serpent.

Yet, from another perspective, it is the fruit of the tree that informs Eve. What kind of tree is it that can dispense information so powerful that it must be classified "top secret"? Writing on gossip, Maryann Ayim (1994, 99) provides a clue when she declares, "like that ill-fabled tree in the Garden of Eden, gossip promises us knowledge of good and evil. Like that same tree, it threatens us with expulsion if we are caught." We need go only a step further to identify the tree: *it must be a vine, a grapevine!* Eve heard it through the grapevine.

Here someone might say, "Stop focusing on Eve and the tree; it's the serpent who is the true gossiper." It *is* he who first talks like a gossiper to Eve. I am not simply referring to the view that he "questioned her of much idle prattle." What he says is neither idle nor prattle. The serpent tries to look *behind* God's prohibition, in order to expose his motives for making it. And he does so in order to make a value judgment about God's behavior. We've already discovered that such interest in penetrating facades in order to unmask and evaluate the subject's motives is a defining trait of the gossiper. Gossipers are epistemophiliacs, driven to know precisely what the subject wants to keep hidden; they never take a person at face value. The serpent refuses to take God's prohibition at face value. Instead, he insinuates that God's motive is to keep valuable knowledge of good and evil out of circulation. If the woman assimilates this hoarded knowledge, it will greatly inflate her power. From this perspective, it is hardly surprising that some commentators believe the serpent symbolizes curiosity (see Westermann 1969, 237). To my knowledge, none has claimed that the serpent symbolizes gossip; however, at least one writer has personified Gossip as a serpent, although without reference to Gen 3 (Le Gallienne 1912, 123).

The serpent's *method* of insinuation is also typical of the gossiper. According to Paine, it is part of the gossiper's art to "distribute and circulate *some* information when managing it, . . . to make their definition of the situation prevail" (1967, 283). In order to have *his* definition of the situation prevail, the serpent tells Eve that if they eat from the tree they will become like God, knowing good and evil. The accuracy of this information is confirmed by God himself in verse 22. However, this does not mean that the serpent's information-currency has "In God We Trust" printed on it. As Maimonides acutely observed, "the evil tongue can ruin the world *even if what is said is true*" (*Code De⁽ot* 7; 1937, 56a; emphasis mine). In this sense, the serpent is like Homer's Sirens, who accurately report their panoptic knowledge of the past and present world to their listeners (*Od.* 12.184–191) but do so in such a way that those who drink in their flowing speech end up dead.

While the serpent indeed displays traits shared by all gossipers, he also exemplifies a specific type of gossiper, one to which both the King's Eye and court gossiper belong. This is the informer. God suggests there is an informer in the garden when he asks Adam, "*Who told you* that you were naked?" (3:11). Of course, we know that the tree told them. However, when the serpent informs Eve—"a citizen"— that they would become like God, he becomes a disloyal informer, a *śāṭān*, a *diabolos*. Now, a *śāṭān* or *diabolos* is not *necessarily* a disloyal slanderer; at first these terms denote any informer or accuser, even when the accusation is true (see, e.g., Tur-Sinai 1957, 39–44; Oppenheim 1968, 176–77; LSJ, ad loc.). However, even though the serpent seems to tell Eve the truth, the fact that he is telling her at all shows him to be disloyal. In fact, he becomes precisely the kind of courtier a King's Eye would accuse to a monarch! Eve does eventually accuse the serpent to King Yahweh, but only after the damage has been done.

Like Eve, the serpent has been described as both bartender and poisoner. Francis Bacon accuses the serpent of "infusing venom" (1858d, 20). In the *Apocalypse of Moses*, Eve says the serpent "sprinkled his evil poison on the fruit" before he gave it to her (*Apoc. Mos.* 19:3). Psalm 140:4

mentions those who have sharpened their tongue like a *nāḥāš;* the venom of vipers is under their lips. According to Josephus (*Ant.* 1.1.4 §50), God himself puts poison beneath the tongue of the serpent in the garden, after depriving him of speech. Here poison replaces deadly words. While the serpent is fated to eat dust in Gen 3, only in Josephus is it clear that this punishment shuts him up. In this sense, the dust functions like the medieval torture device called "branks." This iron mask has a spike or pointed wheel that was forced into the mouths of female gossipers (see Emler 1994, 119).

Although I said poison replaces deadly and sharp words in Josephus, I might just as well have said it *represents* them. This is not a unique occurrence. In Genesis, Potiphar's wife uses words in her attempt to seduce Joseph; in the *Testament of Reuben* she uses magicians and *pharmaka* (4:9). Reuben claims that all women use enchantment, poison, and deception to conquer males (5:1–3).

Words, the sharpness of knives, poison—what exactly is the connection? My answer will require a series of sudden segues. Deadly words are often represented by the tongue. In reference to gossip, the tongue may be described as a knife or sword (e.g., Ps 52:4; see ch. 2, above), as poison (e.g., Ps 140:4; Jas 3:8), as sharp (see below, on accused witches), as evil (e.g., Maimonides, *Code Deʿot* 7.2), as proud (St. Columbanus, above), or as slippery (*Malleus Maleficarum,* above). Perhaps the best way to illustrate the identity of knives and words is to quote from *The British Museum Book of Ancient Egypt:* "women did not take part in activities that involved wielding blades, ... presumably because this would threaten male dominance.... Women were also generally excluded from washing clothes, because crocodiles threatened the riverbanks" (Quirke and Spencer 1992, 22). The first time I read this something smelled funny: Why would the same males who are so afraid of armed women suddenly be so solicitous of their welfare when it comes to doing the laundry? While it is true that women are not described or represented wielding blades or doing laundry, no reasons are given in existing sources.[5] However, the two apparent prohibitions fit together perfectly, once one notes that, in at least one other culture, state authorities have attempted to prevent women from gossiping by replacing traditional washing places with mechanized washhouses.[6]

---

[5] Thus, Gay Robins (1993, 120–21) notes the evidence of these peculiarities, but makes no attempt to provide a motivation for either one.

[6] See, e.g., Bergmann 1993, 59–66, and esp. 165 n. 42, citing Michelle Perrot. Cf. Perrot 1990, 193. Perrot is describing situations in Second Empire France (1852–1870). The women boycotted the mechanized laundries, which were then removed.

Their assumption is that men can be just as mortally wounded by malicious gossip as by a knife. And poison? Same thing. It is hardly accidental that in medieval Germany women were forbidden to pursue the pharmaceutical profession. In Luther's day, women who continued to prepare traditional medicines were suspected of witchcraft (see Brauner 1995, 55).

The weapons of poison and gossip have something crucial in common: they are prepared and practiced out of the sight and hearing of males, in the private sphere assigned to women, and then used to unman them. Any man going home from a day in the public realm to eat food prepared by his wife could become a guest at the witch Circe's table, eating and drinking a drugged meal. The effect could be as deadly as a rest stop at Jael's house (Judg 4:17–22), where milk functions like a drug and a tent peg like a knife.

Circe's name ("Kirke") probably comes from *kirkos,* which has a secondary meaning of "circle," like *kuklos.* Let's shift to another *kuklos,* the Ku Klux Klan (yes, that *is* where the name comes from). In mid-America in the 1920s, the women of this self-proclaimed "Invisible Empire" exerted enormous political and economic power through gossip; one leader declared a political victory a "victory of gossip." She proudly proclaimed that their power was attributable to "a poison squad of whispering women," which could spread any gossip over the entire state of Indiana in twelve hours (quoted in Blee 1991, 115). No wonder Memucan feels so threatened in the book of Esther, when he describes for Ahasuerus the lightning speed with which women are spreading throughout the empire the news of Queen Vashti's refusal to obey her husband (1:16–18; see ch. 3, above). What makes the Clanswomen's poison so politically potent is the fact that women's gossip is assumed by men to be apolitical (Blee 1991, 149). Although they were generally relegated to the private realm, these women managed to arrogate to themselves many of the keys to royal power, including invisibility, information management, and the ability to touch all parts of their realm almost instantly.

Invisibility, secrecy, and the ability to speed through the air are also power sources for *witches.* Perhaps we are now in a position to understand how Eve the gossiper, bartender, and poisoner became Eve the ancestress of witches and destroyer of Adam and Christ. Many of the accusations made against Eve are also made against witches. Accused witches had only the power of their language to defend themselves. As Larner puts it, "where men might use knives, women used words" (1984, 86). Hence they are accused of having "sharp tongues" and of being scolds (Brauner 1985, 19). According to Briggs (1989, 60), "masculine fears of the whole world of feminine gossip" led misogynistic stereotypes to become established as witch trials went on. Emler (1994, 119) goes so far as to suggest that witches were burned for gossiping. And in many cases, it was women's gossip that led to accusations of witchcraft against a fellow-woman outside the gossip circle.[7]

So Eve and witches gossip and have sharp, deadly tongues. *But maybe all women do.* Maybe all women are Eve, and all women are witches. Many have said so. In her study of European witch-hunting, Elspeth Whitney found that two equations defined the atmosphere of this culture: "witch = woman" and "every woman is an Eve" (Whitney 1995, 88). Another scholar found Baldung's satires of witches to be aimed at all women: "witchcraft is merely an extreme manifestation of female vice and folly" (Hults 1987, 272). Even earlier (1487), the *Malleus Maleficarum* describes Eve as the first to display universal female traits such as the slippery tongue, credulousness, deceptiveness, carnality and feebleness of mind and body (1.6–7; Krämer and Sprenger 1928, 43–48), all of which predispose women to witchcraft.

However, the Dominican authors of this "hammer of witchcraft" seem unable to eliminate all traces of threatening female power in their indictment of women's feebleness and vice. They must concede that gossiping women are communicating "things which *by evil arts they know.*" The authors also fear woman's voice when it is directed to men: "in her speech she stings while she delights us. Wherefore her voice is like the song of the Sirens" (*Malleus* 1.6; Krämer and Sprenger 1928, 44, 46).

So women are both feeble *and* powerful, stupid *and* in possession of dangerous knowledge, credulous *and* capable of deceiving credulous males. This paradox has not gone unnoticed by students of the European witchhunts (e.g., Hults 1987, 266–67; Whitney 1995, 85–86). Nor has the presence of this paradox in the early church fathers been ignored, what Marina Warner (1976, 59) calls "the contradiction between the accepted passivity of women and their marked evil hegemony." This same paradoxical fear of female power and knowledge, combined with insistence on female triviality, idleness, and feebleness, characterizes male attitudes toward female gossipers from ancient Greece to Western society today (see, e.g., D. Cohen 1991, 146 n. 56, and passim).

What kind of knowledge can generate so much fear that kings attempt to control women's speech, communities engage in witch-hunting, and male authorities even prevent women from doing laundry together? This is the question with which I began: What kind of powerful knowledge is King Yahweh keeping from Eve and her husband? Now, we know it resembles royal knowledge in its secrecy and ability to be transmitted instantly. Even the necromancy practiced by "wise women"[8] and witches

---

7 See, e.g., Briggs 1989, 77–78, 88; Larner 1984, 89; Roper 1994, 207; Whitney 1995, 88.

8 Apart from the "wise women" of the Hebrew Bible (2 Sam 14; 20), women who were thought capable of communicating with the knowledgeable dead were

fits this pattern. Necromancers gossip with the knowledgeable dead (see, e.g., Bottero 1992, 266, 283), eliciting the kind of penetrating and extensive information that is unavailable to the living, the kind offered by Sirens and serpents. King Saul knew what he was doing when he specifically asked his courtiers to locate a *woman* who was a master of ghosts (1 Sam 28:7). One term used for the ghost (or possibly the woman herself), is simply, the "Knower" (ידעני; 28:3, 9; see Schmidt 1996, 147–58, esp. 154).

The kingpins of the business world also benefit from female knowledge and witchcraft. As I mentioned in the first chapter, the greatest German merchant capitalist of the sixteenth century secretly consulted a crystal gazer to help him control his massive trading empire. With the aid of this witch and the knowing spirits trapped in her crystal, he could instantly "see" what his subordinates were doing throughout his international realm, while he remained invisible.

Now Yahweh has panoptic knowledge already, his subjects cannot see his face and live (Exod 33:20), and he keeps "the secret things" to himself (Deut 29:28). *Nevertheless,* given woman's supposed ability to communicate with the dead and with all things bodily and earthly,[9] she might actually present a danger for the already omniscient divine king. Therefore, women must be taught not to tap into the knowledge hidden in that notorious tree, or they might start communicating it to others and transform the tree into a grapevine. Like Ahasuerus, Yahweh has to pass a law making women obey their husbands, so they can't rival Yahweh's monopoly on the flow of information.

That means that Eve must be the fall guy, the scapegoat. Think about it—she's really the only one in the story who is truly open, truly naked. Only *her* motives and intentions are penetrated and exposed to public view, the way gossipers try to penetrate and expose the motives of their targets. The motives of the serpent, Adam, and Yahweh all remain hidden, mysterious—and private. Eve's transparency signals her vulnerability.

Being a woman, Eve is a ready-made scapegoat. Scapegoats resemble gossipers and witches in one important respect: they are a paradox— allegedly feeble, yet powerful. According to students of scapegoating, such as René Girard (e.g., 1986, 17–18), the scapegoat is usually marginal and

---

considered wise as well. Late second-millenium personal letters from Egypt refer to such women as "*rekhet,*" or, "knowing one" (Pinch 1995, 56). The same is true of female spell-casters and accused witches in early modern Europe. In France they were referred to as *penseurs de secrets* and *sages et prudent crones* (Muchembled 1985, 66, 90; cf. Burke 1978, 107–8).

[9] On women's special connection with the bodily and earthly, see, e.g., Muchembled 1985, 66–67.

vulnerable, without a "support system," so that all others can unanimously agree that he or she is the sole cause of chaos. This vulnerability also means the scapegoat will be unable to resist accepting the communities' view of her. Even though the scapegoat is usually vulnerable and weak, she is *also* assumed to wield enormous power—the power to pollute the community with her crimes, and the power to save the community by being expelled or sacrificed.[10]

The many traditions that describe Eve as a feeble and foolish gossiper are describing the vulnerability of a potential scapegoat. The fact that only Eve's motives are exposed by the narrator shows not only her vulnerability but her difference from all the other players. The many traditions that blame Eve for bringing death and sin into the world are acknowledging the destructive power of the scapegoat. Eve herself sometimes agrees, making the verdict unanimous. In one medieval Irish poem she confesses, "it was I who violated Jesus in the past; it was I who robbed my children of heaven; it is I by right who should have been crucified."[11] The ultimate scapegoat is one who is labeled a scapegoater by her victimizers. By claiming that she violated Jesus, Eve identifies herself with the scapegoaters who sacrificed the Savior.

Eve must be sacrificed to keep order in the court, Yahweh's royal court. The power of the king resides in his monopoly on information management. His people must assume that he is in possession of special secret knowledge if he is to keep control—*whether he actually possesses any knowledge worth knowing or not*. It is the secrecy that grants the power, not the content of the knowledge. Eve and Adam had to learn this the hard way. The fruit was empty calories, a Twinkie, not an apple. All they learned from it was their visibility and their inability to hide from a panoptic king. They learned the lesson that a panoptic king *wants* all his subjects to learn, and were promptly expelled from court. From that point on, all humans have been marginal, in the sense that they are excluded from the center of power and knowledge. To be more precise, humans remained marginal until they realized that the garden tool of gossip works just as well outside the center. We've been gossiping about God ever since.

---

[10] In ch. 11, we will be examining the troubling topic of parental child abuse and similar forms of victimization and scapegoating, including the paradoxical fact that children may view their parental abuser as a god. It is therefore worth noting that, at one point, Freud believed that seduction in childhood underlay not only the symptoms of his patients but medieval ideas of possession and of exorcism. In order to study more closely what he sardonically called the "stern therapy of the witches' judges," he purchased a copy of the *Malleus Maleficarum* (Krüll 1986, 45–46).

[11] Anonymous; quoted in Warner (1976, 50).

9

THE DEVIL MADE ME DO IT:
ROYAL UNACCOUNTABILITY IN THE
FRAME NARRATIVE OF JOB

The king's word is authority, and who can say to him, "What are you doing?"
—Qoheleth 8:4

The king can do no wrong.
—Kutler, *The Wars of Watergate* (1990, 473; cf. Black 1979, 782; Kantorowicz 1957, 4)

Royal Inaccessibility and the Question of Accountability

Even the most inaccessible of the kings we have discussed do not eliminate all information traffic between inside and outside, private and public. Instead, they attempt to control the traffic. They may also attempt to be inaccessible to *moral* judgment from the outside. That is, they may claim not to be accountable for their actions. This is what Qoheleth is suggesting when he says that "the king's word is authority [שִׁלְטוֹן], and who can say to him, 'What are you doing?'" (8:4). One should keep the king's command, because of the loyalty oath (שְׁבוּעַת אֱלֹהִים; with Crenshaw 1987, 150; *pace* M. V. Fox 1989, 246). After all, the king is pampered; he does everything that delights him (8:3).

The formula "Who can say to him, 'What are you doing?'" appears (with slight variations) in two other contexts, in both of which the unaccountable "king" is the divine sovereign, Yahweh. One of the passages is Dan 4:32. King Nebuchadnezzar had been at ease in his palace when he had a frightening dream (4:1–2). A year after Daniel has explained the meaning of the dream, Nebuchadnezzar is walking on his palace and applauds himself on the great city he has built with his power, for the sake of his glory (v. 27). At this very moment of narcissistic self-congratulation, the promise of the dream is fulfilled. The king is driven from his throne and made to live and act and look like a wild beast. It is when his reason is returned to him at the end of the appointed time that Nebuchadnezzar acknowledges the Most High as the one who can do as he wants and to whom no one can say, "What are you doing?"

In the book of Daniel it is a human king who recognizes the Most High as unaccountable. The other time this formula is used in reference to God, it is not voiced by a king, but by the regal figure[1] Job (9:12). However, in Job's mouth, it is less an affirmation of loyalty to the idea of the king's unaccountability than a complaint or accusation. In the prologue, Job had indeed behaved like the kind of loyal courtier that kings want to have around them. He accepts unquestioningly whatever the sovereign dishes out. Yet, what Yahweh dishes out here may be as bizarre as the edicts emanating from the fortress of Shushan in the book of Esther, the kind of stupifying monarchical behavior that leaves the citizenry perplexed (Esth 3:15). (We can only imagine what the people of Babylon thought when they realized their feral king was growing his nails as long as those of the inaccessible industrial king, Howard Hughes.) From this perspective, the proposals of the courtier *haśśāṭān* are analogous to the proposal made to Ahasuerus by Haman (who happens to be described as *diabolos* in LXX Esth 7:4, 8:1; see Gammie 1985, 12). Job is never granted access to the information about the divine council meetings that

---

[1] For Job's "royal traits," see, e.g., Caquot 1960; Perdue 1991, 189–93. The argument is often overstated. The best case can be made for ch. 29, although even here it can be argued that Job is a chief or sheikh rather than a king (see, most recently, Dell 1998, 163). Job says that when he took his seat in the broad place, the נערים hid and the aged got up and stood (v. 8). He is treated with the deference shown to King Solomon in Wis 8:12. That is, the princes restrained themselves from talking and the voices of the nobles (נגידים) were "hidden" (Job 29:10). Men kept silent for his counsel (עצתי; v. 21) and waited for him as for the rain (v. 22). In v. 19, Job had spoken of the טל lying on the branch all night. In Prov 19:12, a king's favor is like the טל on the grass/vegetation. Job had carried out some of a king's central duties: protecting the weak and marginal, investigating judicial matters, and enforcing justice (29:12–17). Job's regal self-portrait is complete when he declares that he had sat as head and dwelt like a king among the troops (v. 25; see further in ch. 10, below). Finally, when Job ends his oath of clearance in Job 31, he says he would wear his indictment scroll as a crown (v. 36) and approach God as a prince (כמו־נגיד; v. 37). However, when Job lists crimes of which he is innocent, the offenses he targets are not specifically those a king might commit. For example, when he claims that he did not make gold his hope (v. 24), Job does not specify the misappropriation of royal funds or amassing personal wealth in the manner prohibited by the law of the king (Deut 17:17) and illustrated by Solomon and Hezekiah. Nor is Job's denial of adultery (vv. 9–12) linked to the abuse of royal power illustrated by David's sin with Bathsheba. And the punishment Job would call down on himself if guilty is not the kind with which David was cursed in 2 Sam 12, and it is not national in scope. Finally, when Job mentioned the fates of kings and princes back in 3:14–15, he did not talk as though these were fellow monarchs whose ruin parallels his own. Similarly, when he listed types of leaders manipulated by God in 12:17–21, he did not add himself to the list as yet another king undone by God.

we are privileged to read in chapters 1–2, the transcript of the biblical version of the Nixon "White House tapes." Nevertheless, by chapter 9 Job is no longer content to remain out of the loop. He is no longer content with the idea that God should have full control over the dissemination of information, let alone unaccountability for the actions he has taken against a loyal servant. Job accounts for his actions, and his life, throughout the book, and he finally succeeds in having Yahweh give up his executive privilege and give an account of himself, although Yahweh's account may seem rather perplexing in its own right.

YAHWEH'S ACCOUNTABILITY IN THE FRAME NARRATIVE OF JOB[2]

> *... and he still holdth fast his integrity, although thou movedst me against him to destroy him without cause.* Said R. Johanan: Were it not expressly stated in Scripture, we would not dare to say it: [God is made to appear] like a man who allows himself to be persuaded against his better judgment.
> —*b. Baba Batra* 16a (Epstein 1935b, 78)

René Girard's work on Job (1987a) represents the most sustained attempt to come to terms with the roles of collective violence and scapegoating in the book (see Lasine 1991b). However, even he fails to appreciate the antiscapegoating (or, in his terms, the "anti-mythical") thrust of God's speeches, the prologue and the epilogue. This thrust is discernible only when one interprets these passages as *functionally integrated with* the dialogues rather than as attempts to annul or obscure the message of the dialogues. The prologue serves this function in a surprising fashion: by confronting readers with the possibility that their God may be a *victimizer,* not a protector of victims. In fact, Job 1–2 presents a God who is so blatantly a persecutor that readers are immediately challenged to side with the victim Job against both God and his agent the *śāṭān.* Furthermore, the fact that readers are made aware of the cruel wager and experiment in heaven puts the audience in the position of co-conspirators, a position they must then accept or reject.[3] When the audience with its guilty knowledge

---

[2] This portion of the chapter is based on the second part of a paper I gave at the 1991 meeting of the Colloquium on Violence and Religion at Stanford University, a group devoted to the study and use of Girard's theories. The first part was published as Lasine, 1991b. The presentation raised such a "violent" ruckus that I was too chicken to publish the rest of it until now.

[3] As stressed by literary theorist Shoshana Felman and psychoanalyst Dori Laub (1992, xvi, 72), "witnessing" to the testimony of trauma survivors (such as Holocaust survivors)—*and* to "traumatic narratives"—are activities "fraught with dangers" and "hazards." As Laub puts it, listeners may experience "a range of defensive feelings" designed to protect them "from the intensity of the flood of affect" directed toward

witnesses Job's view of his new situation vis-à-vis God, a view he formulates without the benefit of our superior insight, he may appear to be more vulnerable than ever. In fact, he may appear to be a successful scapegoat, not the "failed scapegoat" Girard believes him to be later (1987a, 35). While Job may passively accept his fate at this point because he believes his rights are defined solely by his status as a creature made by and belonging to God, the scenes in heaven tell the audience that the God who has permitted the tormenting of Job is not a benevolent slaveholder or suzerain but a deity who cannot be relied upon to follow his own better judgment.

Put polemically, one will not go too far afield if one views the prologue as a dramatic representation of the consequences that follow from a specific mistaken notion about God's way of interacting with human beings—a representation the audience is expected to recognize as the depiction of a theological mistake. By projecting the way a rather inane persecutor-God might affect his favorite human's life, the narrator of the prologue shows his readers that it is wrongheaded for humans to evade their personal responsibility for their life circumstances by projecting responsibility for those circumstances onto an absent divine Cause. The prologue imagines a God who cannot be trusted to follow his own rules of conduct (as humans down below choose to understand those rules) to the point of tormenting his favorite servant "without cause" (חנם 2:3; 9:17; cf. 1:9), that is, gratuitously.

The fact that the deity complains that he has been "incited" (ותסיתני; 2:3) by one of his heavenly "sons" to afflict Job without cause (i.e., to no effect, because God already knew that Job would continue to display this kind of piety under pressure) is often ignored, downplayed, or explained away by scholars.[4] But it won't go away. סות is the same verb used to

---

them (Felman and Laub 1992, 72–73). Why? Because "as one comes to know the survivor, one really comes to know oneself.... The survival experience ... is a very condensed version of most of what life is all about: it contains a great many existential questions, that we manage to avoid in our daily living, often through preoccupation with trivia.... The listener can no longer ignore the question of facing death; ... of the limits of one's omnipotence; ... the great question of our ultimate aloneness; our otherness from any other" (72). In Freud's terms (see ch. 1, above), one could say that the Holocaust provided the *final* blow to human narcissism. Witnessing can make listeners *feel* that blow. This includes readers of the book of Job. On ways in which listeners and readers "protect themselves" from accounts of child abuse (both inside and outside the Bible), see chs. 10 and 11, below.

[4] For a recent example, see Clines 1989, 5, 43. A notable exception is Whybray 1996, 106–7; cf. Handy 1993, 117 and the sources cited in Penchansky 1990, 110–11 nn. 63 and 65. Noll, who characterizes the Yahweh of the David "tale" as

describe people who are incited, or enticed, by their family or friends to worship other gods (Deut 13:7). It is also used of Ahab being incited to sin by Jezebel (1 Kgs 21:25) and David being incited to commit a sin by none other than Yahweh himself (2 Sam 24:1; contrast 1 Chr 21:1)! Here, Yahweh claims to be the incited one and blames his courtier: "the not-yet devil made me do it!" This exculpatory maneuver is just about as transparent as that of Adam, when he blamed Yahweh for giving him the fruit-giving woman to be with him ("the woman whom *you* gave to be with me, she gave me" [Gen 3:12]).

At the very least, Job 2:3 shows that the persecution of Job is something that this all-too-humanlike deity did not want to occur or at least did not feel was necessary to make his point. Yet immediately after expressing these opinions God is incited *again* by his Prosecutor's critique of the experimental setup. So God agrees to up the ante and make a wager that is certain to increase the torment inflicted on his favorite servant! Such divine fatuousness renders pointless the ongoing debate about whether the prologue is primarily concerned with piety as the cause of reward, sin as the cause of pain, or the possibility of disinterested piety. For readers of the prologue, any future guesses about the relationship between one's prosperity and one's degree of suffering must include the possibility that the only cause may be God's being bamboozled into making a sucker bet. The prologue reduces to absurdity the enterprise of attempting to figure out the causes of one's happiness or suffering in terms of divinely deliberated agendas.

From the worm's-eye perspective of humans down below, Job's initial response may nevertheless be correct. He refers all that has happened to him to divine causation without speculating on what precipitated these effects. For the Job of the prologue, the only decision to be made is whether to accept what has happened and the God who caused it or to follow his wife's advice to "bless God and die" (2:9), that is, to incite his Creator into committing assisted suicide. This is the vertical dimension of human life and a decision between him and God alone. For readers of the prologue, on the other hand, who can translate the seemingly "natural" calamities suffered by Job into the capricious acts of a violent God, there is no question about who deserves one's allegiance and who should be rejected, in spite of the fact that commentators rarely acknowledge the extent of this God's violence, including the violence he is incited to commit and later regrets. For example, it is rarely pointed out that the victims of Yahweh's probing of Job's character include not only Job's children,

---

"capricious" and "impish" (see ch. 7 n. 9, above), says that the book of Job also presents "a deity very near caricature" (1999, 38). Yahweh's "capriciousness" is discussed further in ch. 11, below.

servants, and his suffering wife but all those for whom Job had provided
sustenance, legal support, and shelter (29:12–17; 31:16–20, 31–32) before
Yahweh took away Job's ability to do so. The prologue dares readers to
reject the actions of this deity.

From Job's earthly and ignorant vantage point, all may have ended
with his passive acceptance of the "acts of God" that, like cancers and car
wrecks and broken necks, can rewrite one's life-story in mid-sentence
without cause or reason—if it were not for the arrival of the friends. Girard
(1987a, 3–4) is certainly correct to stress the fact that the arrival of the
friends eclipses all other causes of sufferings for Job. Girard (49) speculates—with no evidence whatsoever—that Job must be a man who has
worked himself up from the ranks and who has by some unspecified early
success earned the deadly envy of his confreres. However, the prologue
presents a different picture. The friends are attracted by the series of
calamities that befall Job, not by his success.

The behavior of this representative crowd toward Job causes him to
experience the one type of suffering that Yahweh and *haśśāṭān* did not
explicitly plan to inflict upon him. Did they refrain from doing so because
this kind of suffering is sure to follow without divine assistance, given the
nature of human beings in groups? As Freud dryly observes,

> We are threatened with suffering from three directions: from our own
> body, … from the external world, … and finally from our relations to
> other men. The suffering which comes from this last source is perhaps
> more painful to us than any other. We tend to regard it as a kind of gra-
> tuitous addition, although it cannot be any less fatefully inevitable than
> the suffering which comes from elsewhere. (1930, 77)

Ironically, while Job does not dwell on many of the specific disasters that
Yahweh permits *haśśāṭān* to bring down on him, he is quite certain that
it is God who has caused him to be persecuted by his fellows (e.g., 17:4;
19:13). They "pursue him like God" (19:22), imitating God's persecution of
him. Given the consistently pessimistic assessment of uncontrolled human
group behavior in the book, one cannot argue from the silence of the prologue that God did not intend Job to suffer deeply because of his fellows,
only that he had no need to prompt their victimization of Job. They were
certain to follow in his divine footsteps (cf. Girard 1987a, 16).

This complex presentation of divine and human causation of communal behavior is echoed by the lament in Jer 20. While the similarities
between Jer 20:14–20 and Job 3:1–2 are often noted, the way in which
Jeremiah understands his suffering at the hands of Yahweh and his fellows
in 20:7–12 is also similar to the situation in Job. Jeremiah, like Job, feels
"surrounded" (Jer 20:10; cf. Job 16:13; 19:12) by the violence of others
who yearn to denounce him (Jer 20:10; cf. Job 17:5). If Yahweh has

"seduced" and prevailed over him (Jer 20:7), he also quotes his closest friends as saying "Maybe he will be seduced, and we shall prevail against him," as they await his fall (20:1). When Jeremiah cries "Violence and spoil" (20:8; cf. Job 19:7), he does so in response to the pain he is enduring at the hands of God *and* humans. This double source of pain is not merely due to the fact that Yahweh makes Jeremiah deliver oracles that cause him to be attacked by his fellow-citizens. The fact that Jeremiah uses the same words to describe his friends' waiting for him to be seduced *and* Yahweh's seduction suggests that his friends are waiting for Jeremiah to be victimized by God so that they can imitate this violent God and join the deity in attacking the abandoned prophet. In other words, they are waiting to jump on the divine bandwagon. This passage begs for a Girardian interpretation.

The passage also recalls the words of Camus's guilt-obsessed lawyer Clamence, who describes what he believes an individual must do when faced with a group of family or friends who are always hungry for sacrificial violence:

> We are obliged to take the same precautions as the animal tamer. If, before going into the cage, he has the misfortune to cut himself with his razor, what a feast for the wild animals! I realized this all at once the day I had the suspicion that perhaps I wasn't so admirable.... In my eyes my fellows [*semblables*] ceased to be the respectful audience to which I was accustomed. The circle of which I was the center broke and they lined up in a row as on the judge's bench. From the moment I grasped that there was something to judge in me, I understood, in short, that there was in them an irresistible vocation for judgment. (Camus 1956, 77–78)

Although the defining traits of Camus's speaker are *mauvaise foi* and manipulativeness, his perspective on the group's desire to judge a vulnerable friend is illuminating when applied to Job and Jeremiah. The friends of these biblical personages, like the other members of the community, are deeply threatened by the message they are hearing from Job and Jeremiah. The more they perceive the two as suffering at the hands of their vengeful God, the more they are willing to exercise their own "irresistible vocation for judgment." The more the isolated victim accepts the idea that "there is something to judge" in him, the more effective the sacrificial mechanism can be. This point is central for Girard, who correctly describes Job as "a failed" scapegoat—in contradistinction to "successful" scapegoats such as Sophocles' Oedipus—because Job refuses to grant unanimity to the community's judgment that he is guilty (1987a, 35). Instead, Job insists on his integrity and thereby exposes the friends' strategy of victimization.

Clearly, the book of Job describes not only the way the powerful oppress the most marginal individuals in the society but the way the entire community can unite to attack even the very individuals they had venerated most, once those people are viewed as vulnerable and guilty in a way that threatens the community's basic concept of God and justice. Job's attack on the friends focuses on their participation in such victimization and on their comforting assumption that God shares their perception of vengeance and guilt. After God responds to Job's suit by letting him know it is Job's duty to abase the arrogant insofar as he is able (see Lasine 1988, 38–43), he begins by giving Job control over the life and death of these friends. When Yahweh tells the friends that Job must intercede on their behalf to prevent Yahweh himself from doing *nᵉbālâ* (נבלה; usually translated "folly") to them, he is implying that such divine action would be appropriate because the friends have been guilty of doing *nᵉbālâ* (42:8). Yahweh's use of this term associates the friends' actions with communal violence and the sacrificial mechanism, for *nᵉbālâ* consistently appears in passages that describe some sort of sacrificial violence, victimization, or vengeance, usually collective in nature.[5]

In praying for the "foolish" friends at Yahweh's direction, Job is playing the intercessory role of a powerful prophet like Abraham. In his account of his earlier life Job describes himself as being similar to a powerful, just king who protected the disenfranchised in the society and broke the jaws of the unrighteous as he believes God should do. However, once Job becomes the advocate of the silently suffering masses he sees from the dust, who cling to the rock for want of shelter (24:1–12), he no longer speaks as someone whose self-image is that of a powerful force in the center of society (see Lasine 1988, 37). While Job's actions at this point fulfill Aristotle's definition of justice as the only virtue that puts another's good ahead of one's own (*Eth. nic.* 1130a4), they also illustrate Levinas's belief (1974, 203) that "the forgetting of self drives justice." The more Job eludes the friends' attempts to pin him down and to force him to see himself as guilty, the more he forgets himself, shifting his attention to the plight of countless other innocent victims who have not captured the spotlight by their appropriateness as a potential scapegoat.

What first incites the friends against Job is not the rise to power and success postulated by Girard but Job's curse of his birth-day (3:1–3). This imprecation becomes an attack on the cosmos as God has created it when

---

[5] In narrative texts other than the prologue to Job, the noun נבלה appears only in the accounts of the rapes of Dinah and the concubine, both of which lead to extravagantly violent unholy battles (Gen 34:7; Judg 19:23, 24; 20:6, 10); the account of the rape of Tamar, a crime that also initiates a cycle of vengeance and murder (2 Sam 13:12); the story of the possible scapegoat Achan (Josh 7:15); and the story of David's near massacre of the aptly named Nabal and all the males in his employ (1 Sam 25:25). Yahweh's use of נבלה in Job 42:8 also echoes Job's earlier statement to his wife: "You speak like one of the 'foolish women'" (הנבלות; 2:10).

Job proceeds to curse that day by inverting the "Let there be light" of the creation story in Genesis into "Let there be darkness" יְהִי חֹשֶׁךְ; 3:4). God's cosmos allows those who are in constant torment to live on in pain, rather than allowing them to find relief in death, where the oppressed are finally free of their oppressors (3:17–22). As a number of scholars have observed, God's later speeches respond to specific charges uttered by Job in chapter 3, just as 38:12–15 and 40:9–15 respond to 24:1–17 and 29:17, respectively.[6] If the friends' response to Job begins with Eliphaz's first speech, Yahweh's response does not begin until Job's debate with his friends has led him to forget his personal grievance with God. Job gradually becomes an impassioned advocate for the multitude of silent sufferers he perceives from his new vantage point in dust and ashes. Job's increasingly urgent desire to stop those who oppress these victims is accompanied by increasing violence on the part of the friends who are oppressing him. The more Job resists the friends' desire to make him their scapegoat, the more he seeks the abasement of *all* proud oppressors. Because God has incapacitated him, he calls on—and expects—God to "break the jaws of the unrighteous" as he himself had once done, for there is again "no man" to intervene (see Isa 59:15–16 and Lasine 1988, 40–41). In his speeches God allows Job to see for himself that it is only humans, and not God, who can be depended upon to abase the arrogant. It is only after Job has been made privy to this fact that he is restored to his former place of power.

Does this interpretation make the Job of the dialogues into a persecutor? According to Girard, "every persecutor believes he knows the true god of victims: for them he is their persecuting divinity" (1987a, 154). When Job "argues universally" that there is "injustice everywhere," is he truly "lapsing" into the community's notion that the deity is a "mimetic God who demands victims," as Girard contends (134–35)? But isn't he *correctly* acknowledging the ubiquitous victimization that characterizes the human social world as it appears from the worm's-eye view? His one perspectival error is corrected in the divine speeches and the epilogue. That error is his assumption that God should intervene forcefully and swiftly to persecute all persecutors. This error is corrected not by a demonstration that it is unnecessary or evil to prosecute/persecute the persecutors, but that such action is the responsibility of humans like Job, not God. Rather than being a "God who demands victims," he is a God who demands that his human creatures act with urgency to rescue victims, even when this means using the victimizers' methods (see Lasine 1988, 30). Justice, regarded as the virtue that puts another's benefit ahead of one's own, might require one to

---

6 See Lasine 1988, 34–5. The interpretation given in the remainder of this paragraph is fully worked out and defended in that article.

risk becoming a double of the persecutors, impaled on the horns of the means-end dilemma.

This alternative understanding of the book's message concerning victimization is supported not only by the God-speeches but by the epilogue, the one alleged "addition" to the dialogues not yet discussed. However, one might well ask how the epilogue could support this reading of the book when it says absolutely nothing about Job using his increased insight into the plight of the poor to better their situation.[7] It is clear that the restored Job is in a position to restrain escalating cycles of sacrificial vengeance through his doubled wealth, quasi-regal leadership, and the contribution he could make to the judicial system. Yet, far from doing so, he is not even said to do any of the things for others that he claimed to have done before Yahweh tested him! In fact, he seems more "hedged in" by wealth than ever.

This impression is reinforced by the narrative angle of the epilogue. After having heard Job report his ideas and his deepest feelings throughout the dialogues, the audience is suddenly prevented from gaining access to Job's innermost thoughts and emotions. Nor has Job become a "focalizer," through whose eyes we see and judge the others who are present. Readers are forced to observe the family festivities from "outside" in every sense. (We are not even told if Job's health is restored.) One wonders what Job is really feeling as he endures a celebration attended by the very family members and friends who were so conspicuously absent during his ordeal—and whose absence was at the heart of his victimization (see 19:13–19 and above on 19:12). According to Habel (1985, 585),

> there is no reason to dub Job's table companions fair weather friends even though he berated all his relatives and companions for rejecting him as a man accursed (19:13–19). Here their presence marks a celebration of Job's restoration which is appropriate as a closure for the narrative plot.

No reason? This interpretation denies all seriousness to the sacrificial violence Job has endured from his fellows and reduces the reason for the friends' presence here to that of a handy device for attaining narrative closure. Yet it is precisely scenes like this that make it impossible to achieve closure on the important themes of the book.

Although it is incapable of proof, I would like to believe that readers are meant to be astounded by Job's apparent indifference to the presence

---

[7] In stark contrast to the biblical Job, the Job of the *Testament of Job* resumes his "good works for the poor" as soon as he is restored (44:2). He even asks each of his friends and acquaintances to give him "a lamb for the clothing of the poor who are naked" (44:4; Spittler 1983, 863).

of the very people whose previous absence had so deeply wounded him and by his apparent unawareness of the irony inherent in their offering him money precisely when he has no need of it. When these aspects of the epilogue are viewed together with Job's seeming obliviousness to the plight of the myriads of homeless sufferers whose predicament he had so eloquently reported to the friends and God—as well as his obliviousness to the whereabouts of his absent wife—it becomes clear how many bewildering questions are left open by the epilogue. If these features give an air of unreality to the epilogue (at least for audiences who expect the characters to act in a way consistent with their previous behavior in the story, if not with the way readers assume people "really" act), this ambiance is only heightened by the seeming artificiality of the "children" Job gets to replace the children killed as part of Yahweh's testing of their father. Job's original children were "born to" him (1:2); these he "has" (42:13). No mention is made of their having been born, let alone of the identity of their mother. The only children described with any detail are the girls, and they are described as physical possessions rather than as people. What is noteworthy about them is their physical beauty, their names (which refer to physical beauty or aids in beautification), and the fact that Job gave them an inheritance along with their brothers (42:14–15). As presented by the narrator, they are just as superficial and fabricated as the consolation and comfort offered by the newly restored friends and family at the homecoming party (42:11), if that commiseration at all resembles the earlier consolation and comfort provided by Job's three friends (2:11). Significantly, those who are again near (if not dear) to Job console him for "all the evil Yahweh had caused to come upon him" (42:11), not for all the "evil" their own abandonment and victimization had caused Job. Compared to the homecoming of a suffering hero-liminar like Homer's Odysseus, Job's *nostos*[8] is indeed a homecoming in an inverted world.

Because of the epilogue, there is no closure on the issue of social justice in the book of Job—at least not until readers decide for themselves what kind of closure *must* be made. The sense of astonishment fostered by the epilogue may well prompt the audience to make sense of what is going on, even if Job himself seems to have no interest in doing so. Closure *must* be made, not only to solve the riddle presented by the protagonist's possibly condemnable indifference to others, but because the problem of social injustice is too urgent for readers to leave all the questions raised by the epilogue in permanent suspense. The disinterestedness of the divine bird's-eye view is just as inappropriate for readers of the book of Job as it is for the Job of the dialogues.

---

[8] Literally, "homecoming." The Greek term can denote a literary genre devoted to this theme.

Are readers being challenged to repudiate the Job of the epilogue? Are they being led to declare, "If I had experienced what he did, and had his insight into the workings of the universe and the human part in the moral ecology of the social world, I would kick out all those scapegoating hypocrites. Then I'd offer most of my wealth to the poor, keeping just enough to maintain a position of social preeminence that would allow me to accept God's challenge and abase as many powerful oppressors as I could. Even following Jehoram's lead [in 2 Kgs 6:24–33] by tearing my clothing and crying out to God in frustration and anger at a world gone topsy-turvy would be preferable to accepting such a sterile, insulated existence."

While the most bizarre aspects of the epilogue serve to force readers to make a definite judgment about Job and human ethical responsibilities, this is not the first time the book has raised the issue of the ethics of reading and called for readers to make judgments. In fact, this is a major function of the complex juridical metaphor that pervades the book (see Lasine 1990, 188–91). Scholars typically explain legal metaphor in Job as a means of organizing narrative and theological components of the book in a creative and dramatic way (Habel 1985, 54) and, on a deeper level, as a forceful way of communicating "the bankruptcy of conceiving the man-God relationship along the lines of legal justice" (Dick 1979, 50). In contrast, Cox asserts that the legal metaphor serves as "a vehicle for involving the reader in the affair ... [as] the 'judge'" (1987, 21). He argues that the prologue has established the reader in the position of being the only one who stands outside the action, and that in the end the reader is "called on to decide: who is 'in the right'." Why? Because the epilogue is "nothing more than a conventional ending" that "solves nothing" (15). Rather than simply give up on the epilogue in this fashion, I would suggest that it prompts readers to "become involved in the affair" precisely because it is so "*un*conventional" in terms of the denouement the dialogues have led readers to expect. And if readers of Job *are* being put in the role of judge or jurors, it's not merely to involve them in making disinterested decisions about "who is in the right." It's to decide what would be the right thing to do if the narrated events were taking place in their own world (see Lasine 1989b, 56–58).

This is not to deny that the book may offer more than one possible meaning to its readers or even that intellectually it is like "a tangram, one of those puzzles with pieces that fit together in countless ways," as Alan Cooper (1990, 74) puts it. Human beings are constantly forced to make determinate decisions in their daily lives even when the information on which these decisions must be based is vague or ambiguous. Texts that mirror this indeterminacy are like ambiguous figure drawings rather than tangrams. Rather than remaining detached game players, readers are forced to "practice" such ethical choices by revealing their own assumptions and expectations about reality and moral values. The distinction between readers as spectators watching a drama and jurors observing a trial is again relevant here. Kafka captures the essence of this distinction in his diary, when he illustrates moral agency by making an analogy with an audience's response to a whipping scene in a stage play. He notes that if an actor goes beyond the script in his excitement and really whips another actor, "the spectator must become a person and intervene" (1951, 220). Readers of the book of Job are prompted to take a definite stand on the suffering of the innocent and on Yahweh's attitude toward that suffering, in spite of the fact that the book does not tell its audience in dogmatic terms what stand is correct, or even if there is one correct stand, when the issue is viewed solely from a detached theoretical perspective.

According to one midrashic tradition, Job was originally afflicted because he remained silent and did not intervene on behalf of helpless victims (the doomed male Israelite babies) when he was one of Pharaoh's counselors (*b. Soṭah* 11a; *b. Sanh.* 106a). In a late version of this tradition, Job responds to the pharaoh's request for advice by saying "Let the king do as seems good in his eyes" (*Sepher Ha-yashar* 68.43). Considering the apparent indifference of the Job of the epilogue to the plight of the helpless victims he had perceived when he was in dust and ashes, one might wonder whether he is leaving himself open to be afflicted all over again. Nevertheless, readers of the book of Job can retain the lesson of the dialogues, even if the Job of the epilogue seems to act as though he had never learned it. For readers who have learned *this* lesson from the dialogues, the epilogue offers an opportunity to test their abilities to detect and indict indifference to the plight of the victims whose very existence may be discreetly ignored, whether by the narrator, the "restored" Job, or by all who persecute through passivity.

10

ROYAL NARCISSISM: THE KING ON THE COUCH

"Spare me that word 'narcissism,' will you? You use it on me like a club."
"The word is purely descriptive and carries no valuation," said the doctor.
"Oh, is that so? Well, you be on the receiving end and see how little 'valuation' it carries! ... You've got a psychology, too, you know."
—Roth, *My Life As a Man* (1975, 258)

In this chapter and the next, I will be using "that word 'narcissism'" many times. While our previous discussion in chapter 1 focused on Freud's concepts of "primary narcissism" and His Majesty the Baby, here we will also ask whether there are occasions when royal—and divine—narcissism should be viewed as a form of pathology. We will therefore become familiar with what is now dubbed "narcissistic personality disorder." And because human and divine kings also tend to be parents, we will pay special attention to narcissistic parenting practices in royal households. In extreme form, such parental behavior can constitute child abuse, sometimes subtle and sometimes blatant. For this reason, we will ultimately have to wrestle with the question of whether the divine king Yahweh is an abusive parent to his special child Israel.

The epigraph from Roth's novel reminds us that interpreting behavior as narcissistic is a tricky business. As noted in chapter 1, the word *narcissism* has been used in so many ways that one must be careful to define and illustrate the sense in which one uses the term in any specific instance. Peter Tarnopol, the fictional patient ("analysand") in *My Life As a Man,* feels that his analyst has been using the term "like a club," that is, using it judgmentally and reductively whether it applies or not (see, e.g., 217, 246). The analyst, Dr. Spielvogel, assumes that Tarnopol's mother had been a "phallic threatening" figure, especially in contrast to his "ineffectual" father (219–22, 246). Yet Tarnopol insists that his mother had adored and worshiped him, leading him through his childhood years like a "young prince ... toward the throne" (218). In other words, he was His Majesty the Baby, while the doctor sees him as Lucretius's shipwrecked child who had felt helpless, vulnerable, and profoundly anxious and therefore idealized his mother as a defense against the "pain such a mother might so easily inflict" (221). Two totally different stories about the same life, both based on models of infantile experience that, in chapter 1, we found to be intimately connected with the paradoxical situation of the king. Which story is correct? Or is correctness out of the question when interpreting lives, especially lives read as texts?

In the epigraph, the doctor insists that his use of the term *narcissism* is purely descriptive. Tarnopol suggests that if Dr. Spielvogel were on "the receiving end," he'd change his tune. After all, "you've got a psychology, too, you know." Tarnopol could have gone a step further and asked whether the way the doctor has heard his life story might also have been influenced by the doctor's psychology. Although Roth is a veteran in the battles of psychoanalytic interpretation,[1] he does not allow Tarnopol to consider the roles played by transference and countertransference in his debates with Dr. Spielvogel. Although the characteristics and functions of transference are understood differently by different analysts, the term basically refers to feelings and images associated with the analysand's earlier emotional attachments to others (either negative or positive), which are now projected onto the figure of the analyst. The analysand is sometimes described as unconsciously attempting to manipulate the analyst into playing the role of an incorporated other, usually a parent. Countertransference involves the feelings prompted in the analyst by aspects of the analysand's personality and behavior, including feelings and images associated with the analyst's past, which remain psychological "unfinished business" in the present. Depending upon the therapeutic model or individual therapist, the complex processes of transference and countertransference are viewed as either an obstacle or an essential aid to therapy, if not both.[2] In the case of Roth's novel, the analysand knows nothing about his doctor's life outside the consulting room (1975, 224–26). Apparently the doctor has followed the rules dictating neutrality in the analyst, which can mean anything from

---

[1] In fact, his portrait of Dr. Spielvogel is based on the actual psychoanalyst he was seeing at the time; see Berman 1985, 262–69. Freud himself referred to transference as a "battlefield" (letter to Eitingon, quoted in Gay 1989, 301; cf. 690).

[2] Freud's basic statements on transference are contained in a series of papers on technique published between 1912 and 1915 (see, e.g., Freud 1912b; 1915). Discussions of countertransference are rare in Freud's work; most can be found in the 1915 essay (1915, 160–61, 165–66, 169–70). Among analysts who specialize in narcissistic personality disorders, Kohut differentiates between what he calls "idealizing" and "mirror" transference. The former arises from the "therapeutic mobilization of the idealized parent imago," while the latter arises from the mobilization of the patient's "grandiose self" (1971, 28). Some analysts contend that "transference elements enter to a varying degree into *all* relationships," even nonclinical ones, including the element of manipulation (Sandler 1976, 44). For a view of countertransference that incorporates ideas from both classical psychoanalysis and object relations theory, see Winnicott (1958, 194–203; 1965, 158–65). The views of other theorists will be considered below.

maintaining a "professional attitude" (Winnicott 1965, 160–62) to being a "mirror" (Freud 1912a, 118; Sandler 1976, 43), a "blank screen" (Fink 1997, 32), or a "dummy" (*le mort*), as the term is used in the card game of bridge (Lacan 1977, 229–30; see further below).

Nevertheless, Tarnopol has projected several characteristics onto his analyst, all of which are reminiscent of the traits of the king we outlined in chapter 1. To the patient, Spielvogel appears to possess dazzling "immunity to criticism" and "imperviousness." His admirable "armor" and "impregnability" are "a condition to aspire to" (Roth 1975, 265). To Tarnopol, the doctor has a "rhinoceros-thick" hide, while his own is so thin that one could "shine a flashlight" through it (267). In other words, Tarnopol views the doctor in terms of the kind of armored self-sufficiency and invulnerability that we earlier found to be characteristic of narcissistic, royal and Stoic fantasy. Analysts are often viewed by their patients as possessors of "unattainability and self-control"; they are "the abstinent, knowing, impenetrable physician" (Benjamin 1995, 151). In a typical case, one of Kernberg's patients thought that the analyst displayed "olympian untouchability" (Kernberg 1985, 281). The patient Tarnopol continues to view his doctor in this fashion even after he realizes that the analyst does *not* possess another characteristic that patients attribute to their doctors; Spielvogel is not a perfect "God-like ... all-knowing Other" (Fink 1997, 35; Kernberg 1985, 280; Ornstein 1991, 189), an omniscient figure "who can see what is hidden" (Benjamin 1995, 149). Tarnopol is painfully aware that Spielvogel is not "the subject supposed to know" (*le sujet-supposé-savoir*), as Lacan puts it (1977, 111 n. 96; 1981, 232–33). Nevertheless, he does not dismiss the doctor as a "humbug," as Dorothy and her friends call the Great and Terrible Oz after *his* "blank screen" has been tipped over, temporarily disrupting their "idealizing transference" of the Wizard (see Baum 1958, 109 and ch. 6, above).[3] The fact that Tarnopol continues to admire and emulate the doctor's "impregnability" may be more an indication of his own narcissistic ideal than a pose of regal self-sufficiency on the part of the analyst.

The questions raised so far have urgent relevance for the investigation we will be undertaking in these last two chapters, if we accept that there is an analogy between the analytic situation and that of readers of both the Bible and scholarly books about the Bible, like this one. Among psychoanalysts, Roy Schafer has argued most vigorously and extensively on behalf of this analogy, although his central concern is the way that analysts and creative writers both present a kind of "second self."[4] In contrast,

---

3 The similarity between Oz and Lacan's *sujet-supposé-savoir* has also been noted, in passing, by Garber 1998, 21.

4 Schafer believes that the way in which analysts present themselves to patients (their "second self") is similar to the distance between a creative writer and the

psychoanalytic literary critic Jeffrey Berman stresses the "interactional nature" shared by the patient-analyst relationship and reading. The difference is that the therapeutic process involves a "double act of reading: the patient attempts to read the analyst as if he were a text . . . , just as the analyst is seeking to decipher the patient's text" (1985, 21).[5]

---

second self or implied author they present in their works (1983, 44). While his basic analogy is between analyst and author, he also contends that the analyst is in a position analogous to that of an informed reader of literature, one with interpretive competence (49). Finally, as the analysis progresses, the analysand becomes "coanalyst" and "coauthor," as he or she becomes a more daring and reliable narrator (222). The literary critic's position in this analogy has also been considered. Writing from a Lacanian perspective, Jane Gallop suggests that while a psychoanalytic critic may want to identify with the role of "someone who knows," in the "relation of transference [she] is no longer analyst but patient" (1985, 29, 30).

[5] Among biblical scholars, David Jobling has recently employed the concept of transference to analyze 1 Samuel (as well as to explain to himself his "bondage" [1998, 24] to this biblical book). Jobling uses the term *transference* to "trace the ways in which the dynamics in the text are reproduced in the interpretation of the text. . . . the transferential reading has to be a reading of the self" (23). He believes that Josipovici is expressing this concept when he asserts that the Bible "'is actually *about* many of the critical and hermeneutical issues' that arise when we try to read it" (289). The quote from Josipovici suggests that reading the Bible is a process of mirroring; we see in the text a reflection of what we bring to it. Jobling's definition of transference implies that our interpretations also mirror something that is "in" the text and is able to come out and speak through the critic's transferential response. Jobling (249) believes that his transference experience has enabled him "to discern dimensions of meaning in 1 Samuel that I would not otherwise have seen." This view of transference is somewhat akin to what Stephen Moore calls the deconstructive tradition in psychoanalytic literary criticism, the "myth of the prescient text." Here, the critic becomes "enveloped in the folds of the text even while attempting to sew it up" (S. Moore 1992, 28). For a study of the ways in which Hebrew Scripture addresses (and mirrors) individual readers, see Lasine 1984b, 128–31.

Rashkow asserts that "transference [is] an activity quite similar to that of reading" (1993, 35–36). In fact, "the relationship of a reader and a text replicates that of analyst and analysand" (36). Rashkow bases these strong claims on the supposedly shared element of repetition: "transference is a repetition linking the analyst to the analysand. Similarly, reading is a repetition of the text it seeks to analyze" (36). Although Rashkow cites only Lacan in her brief description of "*the* psychoanalytic account of transference" (36; emphasis added), not all psychoanalysts would accept that transference is repetition; in fact, Lacan himself balks at the idea. Although he does not deny that there is an element of repetition in the transference, Lacan contends that "the concept of repetition has nothing to do with the concept of the transference" (1981, 33; cf. 128–29, 143). It should also be noted that Rashkow does not consider the factor of countertransference when she compares analyst and reader.

If we attend to the way that some theorists describe the analytic situation, analyst-analysand interaction might be more complicated than Berman suggests. According to these accounts, the analyst and patient are not alone in the consulting room. Herman (1997, 141) believes that transference with traumatized patients involves a "triad"; the "third image is the victimizer." For Lacan, the analysis consists in distinguishing the person lying on the couch from the person who is speaking; "with the person listening, that makes three persons present." Actually, the "situation is not three-way, but four-way, since the role of the dummy, as in bridge, is always part of the game" (Lacan 1968, 100). This fourth player is the partner of the analysand, "whose hand the analyst, by his tactics, will try to expose" (Lacan 1977, 229). In Kristeva's version, transference love also involves three people, the subject, his real or imaginary love object, and "the Third Party, the stand-in for potential Ideal"; the analyst plays this role of "the Other" (1987, 13). Working with an entirely different approach than Lacan, Schafer (1983, 42–43, 52, 57) also arrives at a total of four, because both analyst and analysand organize and present a "second self" to the other, although these constructed selves are no more fictional than the selves they present outside the analytic situation. Put together, these accounts might well leave one with the impression that *all* therapy is group therapy and that an analytic consulting room is more crowded than Groucho Marx's tiny cabin in the famous "stateroom scene" from *Night at the Opera*. A patient may project a mirror image of a grandiose self onto the analyst, an idealized version of a parental figure, an unsettling image of a victimizer, and/or a fabricated version of himself or herself, designed to attract, fend off, or manipulate the analyst—that is, the analyst as an ordinary person, the analyst as screen onto which the patient is projecting feelings and images, the analyst's "second self" in her or his "analytical attitude," and/or the analyst whose presentation is affected by her or his countertransference feelings.

Clearly, any analogy between the analytical process and the act of reading must acknowledge the kinds of complexity and nuance that make it seem as though there are phantomlike third and fourth parties in the consulting room, even if we leave aside the fact that a reader also plays more than one role when reading.[6] Nevertheless, if we want to analyze royal figures in the Hebrew Bible in terms of narcissism, including King Yahweh, it is particularly important that all these complexities be taken into account, for several reasons. First, narcissistic patients make the problem

---

[6] Narratologists have offered a number of different labels for the various narrative personae. See especially Rabinowitz (1977), whose "typology of audiences" includes the reader's role as member of the authorial audience, the actual audience, the narrative audience, and the ideal narrative audience; cf. Lasine 1989b. Schafer himself (1983, 44, 53) mentions only Booth's notion of the "implied author."

of countertransference even more acute. Such patients tend to ignore or denigrate the therapist and her interventions, demand total attention without any reciprocity, arouse narcissistic anxieties in the analyst, and display cold grandiosity that can arouse a retaliatory anger in the therapist (A. M. Cooper 1986, 131; cf. Saretsky 1980, 85–88; Schafer 1983, 147). And because a narcissistic patient will either derogate or idealize the analyst, rather than there being three or four persons in the consulting room, there are *not even two!* As Modell (1986, 302) puts it, in the opening phase of analysis, there is an "illusion that there is only one person in the consulting room—either the analyst is not there or the patient is not there." Ironically, the same countertransference feelings that make life especially difficult for analysts who deal with narcissistic patients are especially helpful in promoting a cure. According to Kernberg (1985, 247), "because these patients treat the analyst as extensions of themselves, or vice versa, the analyst's emotional experience reflects more closely than usual what the patient is struggling with internally, and thus the use of countertransference reactions is particularly revealing in treatment."

Second, and more important, the analytic models that stress the complexities of countertransference have profound implications when the analogy with reading is taken seriously. As long as we assume that the reader as analyst can easily maintain a detached "professional" attitude when reading literature—even literature that addresses one as personally as does the Hebrew Bible—we will never be able to come to terms with narcissism in Scripture, especially if the most serious example of narcissism in the text turns out to be none other than the God who presents himself to us as our parent as well as our king. If narcissistic patients can make their analysts feel angry, rejected, or inflated with self-importance, how would—or should—a narcissistic divine parent make his children feel when they read about the way he alternately adores and destroys his "special" children, *our* ancestors. After all, we've "got a psychology, too." Should *we* retain our ideal image of this parent, or should we conclude that there is a third party present as we read, a party who is none other than the image of our divine victimizer? And if we are indeed children of a narcissistic parent, what kinds of defenses will we have developed in order to cope with that fact, and how do they affect the way in which we read our family history in the Bible? With which family members will we identify, and whose suffering will we choose to justify or ignore?[7]

Earlier I noted Jobling's emphasis on "transferential reading" as a process of mirroring. Now, if what "you" see in the textual mirror is a

---

[7] On the difficulty and "dangers" of "witnessing to" the testimony of trauma survivors—and of reading "traumatic narratives" like the book of Job—see ch. 9, n. 3, above.

narcissistic, abusive God, then you'd better make up your mind whether what you are seeing is an illusion, a reflection of your self and your past life, or something that is all too real and that demands an urgent ethical response. In order to make that decision, one needs to know something both about oneself and about the text one is reading. When the text at issue is the Bible, which addresses "you," the reader, in an eternally present tense whenever you read it, and which makes strong claims of relevance to "your" life, the urgency is heightened further.[8] Here someone might remind us that we are looking into a mirror that is well over two thousand years old and that was crafted in a culture that is much different from that of most of those who are currently looking into it. Does the mirroring process act as a kind of purifying filter, reflecting elements that reader and text have in common, while blocking out all the rest? Or does the mirroring reduce what is seen to a function of that specific viewer-reader's mind?[9]

These are the kinds of difficult personal and theoretical issues that cannot be avoided if we take seriously the analogy between the analytic situation and the act of reading. In the remainder of this chapter, I will attempt to grapple with these issues by presenting an account of a possibly narcissistic biblical scholar attempting to tell his therapist

---

[8] See Deut 30:11–15, 19; 32:47; and Lasine 1984b, 131, 135 n. 44; 1989b, 56–58.

[9] Regardless of how one answers these questions, the fact remains that the Bible is a collection of ancient texts. Does viewing it through the optic of modern, Western disciplines such as psychoanalysis and literary theory merely increase the extent to which it becomes nothing more than a mirror of the interpreter's self? The analogy between psychoanalysis and reading avoids the charge of anachronism as long as it is restricted to the way in which the text mirrors the reader when he or she is reading "now." What about Jobling's claim that the reader's transference reactions tell us something about what is actually "in" the text? Do readers who apply intellectual models from the modern West *necessarily* produce reductive mirror images of the text? Do they *necessarily* distort or fail to reflect those aspects of the text that are most radically foreign to their ways of thought, expertise, and culture? The answer, I think, is no. Many ancient (and modern) texts transcend the culture that gave them birth and are reborn in different form in the minds of readers whose native language (and DNA language) has nothing in common with that of the original producers of the texts. Nevertheless, scholarly comparative analyses must be made carefully and with adequate familiarity with all the materials involved. Comparative studies of this nature encourage even the most historically minded scholars to look at the ancient material from a fresh perspective and thereby help them to avoid reductiveness in their own interpretations. Psychoanalytic models and concepts (including narcissism) have already been applied to ancient Greek texts by a number of scholars (e.g., Slater 1968; B. Simon 1978; Walcot 1996; see ch. 11, below), with varying degrees of effectiveness and insight.

about problems he is having with his research. This patient bears some resemblance to the author of this book, in the sense that patient, therapist, and author construct a "second self" for specific purposes in Schafer's schema. The fact that this speaker is a "patient," that is, an analysand as well as a textual analyst, raises the question whether his criticisms of Yahweh as a parent should be dismissed as negative transference or as reflecting a dynamic that is actually present "in" the text. In the next (and final) chapter, the difficult and controversial issues raised by this biblicist patient will be taken seriously and investigated from a number of different angles. In this way, the "fictional" case history to which we now turn will become a means to read Yahweh's biblical self-presentation.

I

I am a king by nature,
ruler to whom one does not give.
I conquered as a fledgling,
I lorded in the egg,
I ruled as a youth. . . .
I was nursed to be a conqueror.
—Pharaoh Sesostris I (Lichtheim 1973, 116–17)

an organization which was a slave to the pleasure principle and neglected the reality of the external world could not maintain itself alive for the shortest time, . . . the infant—provided one includes with it the care it receives from its mother—does almost realize a psychical system of this kind. . . . A neat example of a psychical system shut off from the stimuli of the external world, and able to satisfy even its nutritional requirements autistically. . . , is afforded by the bird inside the egg with its food supply enclosed in its shell; for it, the care provided by its mother is limited to the provision of warmth.
—Freud, Formulations on the Two Principles of Mental Functioning (1911, 219–20 n. 4)

I've got to finish this book; it gets more personal the more I work on it. I know you think it's ridiculous, but I still believe that the king's situation isn't altogether different from mine—or yours, for that matter: with you sitting there like Moses in a pope's tomb, I could take a picture and use it for the cover of my book. You know my *Spiel;* there's something quintessentially human about that situation. Haven't you read the sections I e-mailed you? Don't answer; I know. I don't really *want* to talk shop, but these kings are starting to invade my dreams. Last night I dreamt I was an infantile, momma-pampered prince, a kind of Richard II, infused with self and vain conceit, as if this flesh that walls about our life were brass impregnable. Yes, the Shakespeare play.[10] Allowed my little scene, my chance to monarchize, be fear'd and kill with looks. But then King Death arrived, and with a little pin he bore through my castle wall, and farewell king!

I thought I'd exploded, but my body was still there—not the Body corporate, just the Body natural. My physical body remained, stripped of its wall of brass flesh. I was more naked and helpless than the day I was born. I was Lucretius's neonate birthed by the sea as a shipwrecked sailor abandoned on the shore—not Job, who had parental knees and breasts to receive him at birth. Then the Bible took over. I was as naked as Saul, stripped of clothing, and all loyalty he might have expected from son, daughter, courtiers, prophet, Urim, *and* God. And stripped of the solace of dreams that tell him what to do now.

A moment later I was Saul when he was younger, trying and trying to please my father, but Dad wasn't Kish, he was, in turns, Samuel and Yahweh. Whatever I did wasn't enough. It was almost as though they didn't *want* it to be enough. They demanded perfection, without modeling it. I was obsessed with Dad's darling David, who got strokes no matter what *he* did. I wished I was even that big baby Ahab, sulking and wolfing down Prozac until Mom stole that other boy's toy for him. I couldn't even look for the place where Kish parked his she-asses without getting into trouble. I kept asking myself, what do they want from me? Why did they single *me* out in the first place? Me, a *nagid?* I barely say hello to Samuel before he's telling me all Israel's desire is focused on me. Hi, my name's Samuel and you're on *Candid Camera!* God's made you the star of *The Truman Show!* Good Lord! I felt like shrinking into bug-size, but in the dream I was much taller than I really am, too tall even to hide behind the scenery when the show started. And thanks, impresario Samuel, for making the audience feel so damned guilty about having a king, just before bringing me out on stage!

Stage fright woke me up then, but I did manage to fall back to sleep. Right away I started to feel itchy. You know that I never had kids, but suddenly I'd had ten of them stolen from me. No chance to see myself in child-mirrors; no chance to live again, through them. I'd always been a good son and discreet courtier, but somehow it was my own father—the King—who'd stripped away my family, turned me into a homeless person, and given me the itch. All my years of compliance and being a pleaser—for nothing. I'd felt like the center of Dad's world, hedged in so that nothing could hurt me—and now I was hedged in a world of hurt! I was a biblical Lear in the storm. I wanted to shatter Dad's world, shiver his egg,[11] go

---

10 See *Richard II* 3.2.164–70.

11 See *Richard II* 4.1.289; *King Lear* 1.4.148–54; and ch. 1, above.

postal, turn his palace upside down like wiping a dish. I feel omnipotent—
a mighty mouse capable of turning "let there be light" into "that day—let
there be darkness!"

No, it wasn't that. I wasn't dreaming about *my* father; it was *the* father,
Job's divine father. Just like the other dream; I kept asking myself, what
does he want from me? Even if I'd given him a hard time in presentations,
I didn't see him at any biblical conferences. I was just another academic
ʾîšôn[12] in Dad's eye, but in the dream he seemed to think that I was some
kind of nuclear threat. I couldn't possibly be a bugbear to him, but in the
dream I *was* the bug he'd bet on in a race, and he'd bet the farm on me—
bet his self-image on me.

I think I started to wake up at that point, but then I settled back down,
because nothing hurt any more. I'd become the apple of Dad's eye again.
I was king in Jerusalem and had the leisure and the money to test out my
libido on women, wine, and song, all in the name of "scientific research."
I thought: finally some wish-fulfillment! But when I reached for the wine
list, I started to awaken again. I must have still been half asleep, because
I was standing in the bathroom, looking at my mystified face in a hand mirror. A deposed Jewish Richard II no longer believing his parental press
clippings. Then the alarm went off, the flattering glass[13] dropped, shat-
tered, and I really woke up.

II

How did I feel? I felt like it was time to admit out loud that my academic writing has been a way of dealing with things that bug me, deep
down. Take the topic of kings. I must have chosen it for a reason; after all,
it's absorbed an awful lot of my time for years. I'm sure, now, that it has
to do with the king being a bundle of contradictions, powerful and independent—and *also* totally dependent on others, invisible to public
view—and *also* totally visible, the most developed individual and father
figure in the kingdom, and *also* the most infantile.

I know that you have little use for Freud, or all classical psychoanalysis for that matter, but I'm going to use Freud and other analysts to convey
what I'm trying to say. I can see that your cognitive therapy can be useful
in some situations, but not in this one. Yes, I know that it traces its roots
back to Stoicism,[14] especially to Epictetus's line that what disturbs our
minds isn't events but our judgments on events (*Ench.* 5). Yes, distorted

---

[12] That is, a "little man" of his eye, traditionally translated "the apple of his eye";
see Deut 32:10 and below.

[13] See *Richard II* 4.1.265–91.

[14] See R. Montgomery 1993, 7–9, 12–17; cf. Pies 1997, 30–32.

thinking. But to me the stoic attitude is part of the problem, not a real solution. That is, it's an expression of one end of the royal fantasy: the yearning
for independence and inviolability. All your emphasis on "correcting distorted thinking" and acting "realistically"[15] sounds nice as long as we all
agree on what "correct" thinking and "reality" are. Of course I agree that
there is such a thing as illogical thinking that leads to self-defeating and
destructive behavior, whether or not it's the thinking that prompts negative
emotions and behavior, or the other way around. Yes, I've done my share
of it. But there are also unpleasant and illogical realities that really *can*
defeat the self and that humans tend to ignore or deny. Therapy is perfectly
situated to aid the denial process by labeling emotional responses to
socially denied realities as distorted or incorrect. Sometimes you remind me
a little of the psychiatrist in *Invasion of the Body-Snatchers.*

Look, let me keep hogging the microphone today, so I can go through
all this one time, using my own frames of reference. Did you look at the
short e-mail I sent this morning, the one with the two quotes, one from
the Egyptian king Sesostris and the other from Freud? Good. Why those
two? It's the eggs. I wanted to organize my thoughts around something
simple, a pregnant image, so to speak, so I wouldn't lose track of what I
wanted to say. First, there's the king-in-the-egg stage. The king is supposedly self-sufficient and self-contained. Sesostris I makes no bones
about it: "I lorded in the egg." Just like Freud's bird-in-the-egg-like infant.
Maternal care is "limited to the provision of warmth." More or less what
old hypothermic David got from Abishag, who was young enough to be
his granddaughter. Now, Ferenczi alludes to Freud's egg comment and
says that insofar as we have a mental life in the womb we think we're
omnipotent and have nothing left to wish for (1950, 218–19).[16] We don't

---

15 Beck et al. (1979): "the individual's affect and behavior are largely determined
by the way in which he structures the world.... [the therapy is designed to] identify, reality test, and correct distorted conceptualizations and the dysfunctional
beliefs (schemas) underlying these cognitions. The patient learns to master problems
... by ... correcting his thinking [and acting] more realistically" (3–4). For the recent
history and development of cognitive (and "cognitive-behavioral") therapy, see
Kuehlwein 1993, 1–24; Rachman 1997, 12–23. For an attempt to apply cognitive
therapy to the treatment of narcissistic personality disorder, see Peyton and Safran
1998. Although Peyton and Safran do not use the terms *transference* and *countertransference,* the interplay they describe (392–93) between narcissistic patient and
therapist is identical to that denoted by *transference* and *countertransference,* as discussed above. Cognitive therapy has also been translated into the now-ubiquitous
language of information theory; here therapy becomes a matter of corrrecting or
"modifying" "biases in information-processing" (Mathews 1997, 49–54, 61–2).

16 Perhaps the most extreme expression of this psychoanalytic view is
Grünberger's comment that "God is the omnipotent fetus before becoming the

even need to need; we're that self-sufficient (Glatzer and Evans 1977, 89). But that's *also* Schopenhauer's ideal *king*, who's given so much power, wealth, and security that he'll not need to need—that's why he won't need to take *other people's* vineyards and Bathshebas.

But there are also *in*sufficient and very vulnerable egg-kings, the eggs the ostrich mom abandons on the fast lane of the interstate during rush hour, according to Yahweh in Job (39:14–16). No motherly nurturing there! Just like the kings Oedipus and Cyrus, and, with a twist, Moses. Exposure for death, followed by nurturing from foster parents: a nice way to tame the paradox of our double heritage—mother-born *and* earth-born.[17] It also

---

Father (or mother) in the various mystical systems" (1991, 219). His linkage of omnipotence, divinity, and the fetal condition naturally leads to the conclusion that "the human child is a fallen god who has to confront a narcissistic trauma inherent in the human condition just at the moment when the vicarious means of continuing in the prenatal state fail" (220).

According to some feminist scholars, the fetus has recently been described and depicted in American culture in ways that we have found (and will continue to find) in descriptions of gods, kings, *and* narcissists. These scholars refer to a fetal "astronaut floating in space" (2000, Oaks: 87), who is "self-created," "self-willed," and "resting serenely" (Stormer 2000, 128, 130). This "idyllic" image expresses "self-evident sovereignty" and resembles "a self-conceiving body politic" (128, 130, 134). Here the fetus is "utterly alone" and "autonomous," as though the woman in whom it resides, the doctor, the family, and the community had all been "erased" (Stormer 2000, 128, 129; Oaks 2000, 63). Such images embody "entitlement" (Stormer 2000, 129–30), a telltale sign of narcissism (see below, and compare the image of the isolated, narcissistic divine warrior [see ch. 11, below]). Taken together, these descriptions suggest that the idyllic condition of His Majesty the Baby fabricated by parental narcissism has now been projected back into the womb. While the scholars quoted here focus on the rhetorical uses to which these images are put in debates over abortion and the responsibilities of pregnant women toward their fetus, the image of the "*public fetus*" as a godlike "entitled Man alone in command of his environment" (Stormer 2000, 134, 130) may express the narcissistic fantasies of contemporary American culture as a whole, as well as the feelings of "vulnerability" (Oaks 2000, 63–64) that those fantasies are designed to obscure (see ch. 1, above).

[17] This double heritage is mostly painfully expressed in the image of Mount Cithaeron in Sophocles' *Oedipus tyrannus*. When Oedipus learns that he is not the son of the king and queen of Corinth but had been found as an infant on Cithaeron, he declares that Chance (Τύχη) was his mother (*Oed. tyr.* 1026; 1080–1082). The Chorus immediately announces that it will celebrate Cithaeron as Oedipus's "nurse and mother" (τροφὸν καὶ ματέρ'; 1090–1092). However, after Oedipus learns who his biological parents *really* are (and, therefore, that he has committed patricide and incest), he asks why Cithaeron had received him at all and wishes that the mountain had killed him immediately (1391–1392). Shortly thereafter, the now-blind king asks that he be exiled to "this mountain of mine," because his mother and father had intended Cithaeron to be his tomb (1451–1453).

highlights the twin *hazards* that follow birth: the hazard of being exposed by an unfeeling parent *and* the hazard of being treated as a king by Mom and Dad.

The egg-king most in need of therapy is the geriatric chick in the egg. No, King David isn't a good example of what I mean here. Take King Lear. He thinks egglike self-sufficiency is an appropriate retirement plan for a king, allowing him to "unburdened crawl toward death" (1.1.37–40) with Cordelia providing the maternal warmth as his nurse ("I ... thought to set my rest on her kind nursery"; 1.1.123–24). His Majesty the Baby in second childhood. What he ends up doing is to cut his kingdom in the middle and "eat up ... the two crowns of the egg," as the Fool puts it (1.4.151–52).

Then there's the paradoxical egg I can best relate to, the one who's both powerful king *and* breakable baby; the Humpty Dumpty type. Humpty's traditionally assumed to be a king; it's even been suggested that he might be based on Richard III (Shannon 1980, 32–34). In one version, he's a foundling put on the wall by his princess-rescuer (see Shannon 1980, 19–20); in Carl Sandburg's, he's lifted onto the wall by other eggs, who laugh at giving this egg a great fame.[18] In *Through the Looking-Glass,* the high wall is so narrow that Alice "quite wondered how he could keep his balance" (Carroll 1963, 261). The fact that he's also a kid led Winnicott to come up with "the humpty-dumpty stage" of child development. The wall on which he is "precariously perched" is the child's mother, who "has ceased to offer her lap" (Winnicott 1965, 75; cf. 1958, 226). The child Humpty knows he has a skin—a contact boundary with the world—a shell—but he won't learn how breakable it is until he practices falling off the mother-wall.

But my question, Doc, is why the little boy/child-egg is treated like a *king*. You know the old joke? A guy goes to a psychiatrist and says, "Doc, my brother's crazy; he thinks he's a chicken." The doctor says, "Why don't you turn him in?" The guy says, "I would, but we need the eggs."[19] The guy doesn't do anything to end his brother's delusion. On the contrary—he "enables," as you like to say, and perpetuates it. Why? Because *delusions lay real eggs*—they yield real benefits, for others, anyway. Same for the idea that babies are kings and that kings should be treated like omnipotent babies. Queen-mother chickens *don't lay eggs, they lay egos.* And the people need their kids and their kings to have impossibly big egos, or, at least, to *appear* to have them, or to *act as though* they had them. One of your analytically oriented colleagues agrees. He says that narcissists "have a need

---

[18] In his poem, "From Two Commentaries on Humpty Dumpty"; Shannon 1980, 62–63.

[19] This version of the joke is the one told by Woody Allen's character in his 1977 film *Annie Hall.*

for omnipotent others" (Bursten 1986, 381; cf. Kohut 1971, 8–9). A historian agrees too. He thinks that "the function of kings [is] to have people in the world who [don't] have to give up anything" (Sagan 1985, 327).

Do you think the *baby* believes it's a king?—*if* it could think or had a discrete, congealed self to think about. Ferenczi does: "all children live in the happy delusion of omnipotence" (1950, 232). My childhood says the opposite. It's the parents who maintain the "happy delusion" that their special kid is His Majesty the Baby—smarter, cuter, and bigger than everybody else's baby.

What really galls me is that the parents and royal subjects who "adore" the infant-king also place him *precariously* on the wall, inviting a tumble! Do they need to *smash* this egg as well as deify it? We're told that all of Humpty's horses and men couldn't put him together again. I think they *could* have re-membered his Body politic—if they'd *wanted or needed to*. There's always the crazy-glue of sacrificial violence—of mimetic mass madness—to bring people together. The Levite might have dismembered his tumbled concubine, but the sacrificial violence it sparked glued all the kingless tribes of Israel together as "one man" against brother Benjamin. And if a people empower a pampered tyrant to be their omnipotent king, look out! Francis Bacon (1858b, 431–32) says that great self-lovers "waste the public." They won't hesitate to "set a house on fire, just to roast their eggs." That's exactly what happens when the Shechemites make Abimelech their king. Abimelech not only sets their city on fire but roasts them inside it! Headline: "Bramble-king burns down cedars of Lebanon" (see Judg 9:15, 49).

Now, you've heard me talk about Freud's His Majesty the Baby. This kid probably can't imagine being toppled and cracked, given the special kinds of hen-warmth his adoring parents give him. They act as though the child won't be touched by illness, death, or restrictions on his will. He's the center and heart of creation. Freud's really less interested in the infant than in his parents. But he's not simply chewing them out for spoiling their kid. That's *Plato's* thing. Plato thinks it's a fatal mistake for kings like Cyrus to allow their sons to be overpampered and undisciplined from infancy on. Women raised them, "treating them as the special favourites of Heaven, and forbidding anyone to oppose them in anything, and compelling everyone to praise their every word and deed" (*Laws* 694d; 1926, 227). King Lear proves Plato's point. He orders his daughters to compete to decide who can warm his ego the most. Why such folly? Because he'd been pampered, just like Cyrus's sons. Lear says "they flattered me like a dog and told me I had the white hairs in my beard ere the black ones were there. To say 'ay' and 'no' to everything I said 'ay' and 'no' to was no good divinity.... they told me I *was* everything; 'tis a lie, I am not ague-proof" (4.6.96–104). Even Lear needs a flu shot. He repents having been deluded into believing he was His Majesty the Baby; it didn't prepare him for a hostile world whose infantile gods are like wanton boys torturing human flies for sport.[20] Lear's living in an ancient "pagan" world; it's a lot scarier to ask whether our world is governed by infantile divine powers when you've got the biblical God hovering overhead.

III

I've hardly used the word "narcissism" today, but that's really what I've been talking about. For Freud, the heart of *narcissism* is self-sufficiency (which, for him, is associated with inaccessibility, impregnability, and the "blissful isolation" of the womb).[21] All that ends at birth. Parents try to keep the prenatal feeling of inviolability on "life support" by serving as the infant's adoring courtiers. For selfish reasons: to revive and restore their own lost feelings of narcissism in the mirror of their pocket-sized prince. For the baby, the lack of self-sufficiency translates into fear of the loss of love or the loss of the object. Many *never* become sufficiently independent of other people's love and so remain infants forever. Codependent? I suppose—sort of—but there's more to it than that; just bear with me a bit longer.

There's another constant in Freud: the idea that the external world is essentially hostile and alien. We're bombarded by external stimuli so much that developing a shield against stimuli (*Reizschutz*) is an almost more important task than receiving stimuli (1920, 27). We're constantly projecting unpleasure outside, in order to form a pure pleasure-self. Bailing out fouled water from our little ego-boat into the world sea. But we also envy the sea. We want to become one with it again. In fact, the mystical "oceanic feeling" is an effort to restore the primal condition of "limitless narcissism" (1930, 72). For Freud, a *lot* of what we do as adults is an attempt to restore the bliss of the fetal condition and the royal state of His Majesty the Baby, mostly because the external world can be such a bitch, to say nothing of other people or one's own fallible material body (1930, 77). And he says it so dryly and matter-of-factly that it takes the sting out of thinking that he may be right.

In his essay "On Narcissism," Freud also lists examples of perpetual narcissists, self-contained, inaccessible, and indifferent to others. It's quite

---

[20] As Gloucester puts it; *King Lear* 4.1.37.

[21] E.g., sleep conjures up "the picture of the blissful isolation of intra-uterine life," the "primal state of . . . total narcissism," with a "self-sufficing ego" (1917b, 417) and "by being born we have made the step from an absolutely self-sufficient narcissism to the perception of a changing external world" (1921, 146; cf. 121). Freud (1930, 83) also speaks of the "narcissistic man, who inclines to be self-sufficient" (*der eher selbstgenügsame narzisstische*).

a list: women (especially good-looking ones), cats, some large beasts of prey, great criminals in literature, and humorists (1914, 88–89). *Kings* are noticeably absent. Noticeable to me, of course, because I'm writing about them. But without much effort you *can* find kings hiding in his metaphors—for example, when he describes how we forge inner armor against the arrows of the external world. Among other things, he says the royal ego is housed in a citadel guarded by a garrison, to keep out the rabble rapping at the gates for admission.[22]

That's Freud, but it's also Plato—and, yes, Epictetus as well. Plato explicitly describes the wall of our inner citadel as "kingly." And Stoics like Seneca say we *can* make our inner fortress and wall and our skin majestically indifferent to the missiles, siege machines, and hailstones aimed at them from outside. External blows merely graze the skin.[23]

Now, that part *isn't* Freud. Freud's metaphors highlight the monarch's radical dependency and vulnerability. Take his three blows to human narcissism. First Copernicus knocked us out of the center of the cosmos, then Darwin pushed us off our throne above the animals, and now Freud delivers the knockout punch: we aren't even master in our own house. "We"—"*das Ich*"—act "like absolute rulers satisfied with the information given us by our court officials," but we shouldn't be. The reports the ego-king receives from its intelligence department and courtiers are "incomplete and untrustworthy" (1917a, 10–11). Same for historical kings. Evidence is everywhere, from Saul's story to the *topos* of the ignorant king in European satire. In fact, Freud's ego-kings are most at home in Norbert Elias's court society, where the court is a filter mediating *everything* reaching the king.

And the *child*-king can't trust *his* information givers, either. When Mom and Dad snuff out his curiosity with stories about storks and such, kids like Freud's Little Hans receive this unreliable information with deep, often lasting, mistrust. The good news is that his "intellectual independence [dates] from this act of disbelief" (1909a, 79).

So you could say that we've got a *psychē, polis,* and *oikos*[24] isomorphism here: in each case, lone royal knowers must learn to mistrust mediated information, if they are to become independent and truly powerful. If you want to bet on which *kings* will be the winners and losers, just ask which ones control information and which don't. Or, in the Bible,

---

[22] In addition to the passages discussed in ch. 1, above, see Freud (1900, 568; 1932, 221; 1933, 110).

[23] The references for these passages are given in ch. 1, above.

[24] That is, an isomorphism not only between soul and state, as described by Plato (see ch. 1, above), but also between both and the household/home/family (the *oikos;* see, e.g., D. Cohen 1991, 76–77; Arendt 1958, 24; and ch. 5, above).

ask which does father-Yahweh protect by keeping them informed, and which does he expose by keeping them ignorant? David ensconced in his covenant-egg, or Saul's ostrich egg splattered on the freeway? Which does he treat as special?

But to me the deepest paradox is still that kings and egos and pampered babies are *simultaneously* powerful and weak, hedged in and vulnerable. That's why Winnicott can say that the infant's condition is "at one and the same time [one] of absolute independence *and* absolute dependence" (1958, 163). And kings? Take Bill Clinton. During the Lewinsky fiasco a *Newsweek* article already diagnosed him as a "classic . . . narcissist" (Clemetson and Wingert 1998, 46). Now, as president he has the isolation of a fetus, but is it *blissful?* President Taft called the White House "the loneliest place in the world" (Maraniss 1998, A1). Nowadays, the president is hedged in by thirty-five Secret Service agents and a ring of a hundred uniformed agents. He's never alone. This *does* represent the power of the White House, but it's *also* a panopticonesque prison. Clinton himself called the White House "the crown jewel in the American penal system" (Maraniss 1998, A1). Yet Clinton the prisoner has *also* been powerful. If he weren't, how could he have remained perched on his royal wall with so many Rupert Murdochs trying to push him off? And whenever he *did* fall, Humpty-like, his ratings in the polls didn't, and all the king's men *did* manage to put him back together.

Winners and losers: kings like Deiokes are able to surround themselves and their palaces with seven ring walls, while the castle wall of a king like Richard II can also be penetrated by Death with just a pinprick. Maybe we're all Richards in that sense. Epicurus thought so: "when it comes to death all mortals live in a city without walls" (*Vatican* 31; 1926, 110). But it's also true that many of the defensive walls erected by kings and ordinary people *do* function as effectively as a hedgehog's pin-pricking quills or Deiokes's walls. The paradox is just easier to spot with special representative individuals like kings.

In the end, the ego, the baby, and all kings are treated as special, although narcissistic "specialness" is a mixed blessing at best. First of all, narcissists are *made,* not born. Lowen said it: "if a boy thinks himself a prince, it's because he was raised in that belief" (1997, 21). He calls the promise of specialness a "seductive lure" used by parents to "mold the child" into their image of what the kid should be (105). Why is the bait compelling? Because the kid was actually *deprived* of true closeness with the mother in infancy. That's why Kernberg (1985, 235) thinks it's sometimes "the cold hostile mothers' narcissistic use of the child which [makes] him special" and sends him searching for admiration.

To survive in such a manipulative environment, Winnicott says that such children hide their true self and develop a false self that complies with the parents' expectations. They might grow up with the so-called "Nobel prize complex" (Tartakoff 1966)—feeling singled out for special recognition—and brimming with entitlement feelings, but Kohut and Kernberg think that on a *deeper* level they imagine the world "as being devoid of food and love," filled with "dangerous, sadistically frustrating, and revengeful objects," and they imagine *themselves* as "hungry wolves out to kill, eat and survive" (Kernberg 1985, 276, 311; cf. Kohut and Wolf 1986, 187). If they are narcissistically "self-absorbed," it's "because of the fear of falling apart" (Robert Lifton, quoted in Brooks and Woloch [2000, 231])—that is, fear that their self will shatter like Humpty's shell.

So the paradox: pampered chicks-in-the-eggs, *and* baby-kings who feel themselves abandoned and vulnerable in a hostile world, by ostensibly affectionate, but actually cold and untrustworthy, parents. It's the mother, not the father, who's usually blamed by the experts: the unreliable mother, the "not-good-enough" mother.[25] This sounds suspiciously like sexist scapegoating—even if it does give me flashbacks of my own past.

IV

What I do know for sure is that the parent who most fits the literature is *not* a mother—at least not most of the time. It's the paternal God of my fathers, Yahweh.

—How could I say such a thing? Did I forget Deuteronomy 32?— Yahweh found Israel in the wilderness, encompassed the baby, bestowed attention on it, guarded it as the little man in the eye, bore him as an eagle bears her young, suckled him (vv. 10–13), and so on.... True. But read the fine print: when the baby later forgets the God who suffered labor pains with him (חולל, *poʿlel*; v. 18), Yahweh's response is to heap disasters on her flawed son (v. 23).

No, I haven't forgotten the biblical voices who say Yahweh had been a protective fortress, shelter, or tower of strength for them, or who claim to have taken refuge in the covert of his wings (e.g., Isa 25:4; Pss 61:4–5, 62:7–8, 71:3, 6). But I also haven't forgotten the voices who cry that

---

[25] In one recent collection of "essential papers" on narcissism, reference is made to "unreliable mothers" in at least six of the essays; see Morrison 1986, 133, 181–83, 187, 297, 309–10, 325–28, and 396. The phrase "not-good-enough mother" is Winnicott's (e.g., 1965, 145). One classical scholar has actually attempted to trace the "colossal narcissism" of Alexander the Great, as well as the "narcissism" of St. Augustine, back to frustrated and over-protective, if not seductive, mothers. He concludes by affirming the view that Augustine's mother Monica is but "the last of a long line of terrible mothers [!] stretching all the way back to Thetis in Homer's *Iliad*" (Walcot 1996, 129; cf. 122–23, 128). See further in ch. 11, below.

Yahweh has knocked down or breached their protective walls—or walled up their paths to hinder them (e.g., Job 16:14; 19:8; Hos 2:7 MT; Lam 3:5, 7–9[26]).

Yes, Yahweh *does claim* to be reliable and trustworthy, and he does say he'll never abandon his people. Now that you've dropped your therapeutic neutrality, let's take this all the way. You're trained in Bible too. You know Isa 49. It's very dramatic. Zion charges that Yahweh abandoned them, and Yahweh says that even if a woman could forget her nursing child, he himself will *not* forget Israel (vv. 14–15). But go another five chapters, where Yahweh concedes that he *did* abandon his child for a brief moment (Isa 54:7–8). Brief from *whose* point of view?

And yes, the speaker in Ps 27:10 does believe that Yahweh will "gather him in" even if his mother and father abandon him, and Ps 103:13–14 does compare Yahweh's compassion for those who fear him to a father's compassion for his kids. But note that "who fear him" part. Does that mean "those who are compliant"? Those who give the parents what the parents need—compliance with their expectations, including the expectation that their kid be special, or else? What do such parents do when their seemingly obedient and compliant kids turn out to have minds of their own—like Job?

Trust is a *huge* factor in all of this. The speaker in Ps 22:10–11 says Yahweh made him trust when he was on his mother's breasts. He's been "cast upon" Yahweh from the womb. The speaker in Ps 71:6 says he's leaned upon Yahweh from the womb. But *other* psalms stress the speaker's *vulnerability* to evil oppressors, like the enemies who collectively batter the speaker of Ps 62:4 as though he were a leaning wall. With his own wall leaning, he needs to lean upon Yahweh. God is his high tower (vv. 7–8). But *how often* does being "cast upon Yahweh" mean being hedged in and protected like the chick in an egg, and how often does it mean being one of Lucretius's castaway infants, who have to build *their own* walls to protect themselves in a harsh world?

In my world—*and* in the biblical one—the deeper truth is that of exposure, not protective enclosure. I can't get past Ezek 16. Here's that sequence again: first, exposure by natural parents, and then rescue by a nurturing foster parent. This time, Yahweh isn't the natural parent; they're Amorite and Hittite (v. 3). When the infant was abandoned, it wasn't cut, cleaned, salted,

---

[26] According to psychoanalyst Alice Miller (1991a, 123), "what finds unmistakable expression in the Lamentations of Jeremiah—albeit unconsciously and involuntarily—is the reality of a chastised, i.e., mistreated child. This child refuses to believe that the same parents who speak of love and loyalty are capable of a pitiless massacre—that *this* is what the truth is." Miller's views on child abuse are discussed in ch. 11, below.

or swaddled (v. 4). It wasn't cast upon God—it was simply cast out into the face of the field (v. 5), exposed—literally and figuratively. That's when Yahweh the rescuer passes by (v. 6). But he doesn't hang around to do any parenting. When he passes by again it's years later, and the kid is still naked and caked with blood, although she's got potential, being nubile and attractive (vv. 7–8). *Then* Yahweh acts sort of like a bachelor father, but he's really more like an eager groom prepping his teen bride-to-be (vv. 9–12), a kind of Woody Allen without the whining. And when the bride starts messing with the Sun Devils football team in the car Daddy gave her—that's when his narcissistic rage gets clinical (vv. 37–41).

The birth of the hero plot line here is disingenuous, because, ultimately, Yahweh *is* Israel's birth mother and father *as well as* foster-parent. He's good cop *and* bad cop. He protects, and then he's the kind of parent from whom children *need* protection. Same in Hos 2:5–6 (MT): Yahweh furious with wife Israel, threatening to strip her naked and expose her as in the day she was born. Again the rage: he'll kill her with thirst, have no pity on her children. But then *another* switch: he decides to seduce her in the wilderness, so she'll respond as in the days of her youth (vv. 16–17 MT). To me this sounds like the fantasy of an abusive husband whose wife walked out on him. Or a parent trying to re-seduce an alienated child with the lure of intimacy. The ambivalence—the bouncing between extremes—isn't that also a telltale sign of narcissism?

Yahweh is continually giving Israel mixed signals. First he singles them out, says they *are* special, *or* that they can possibly be special, or that they're not special. Take Deut 9: they're *not* being favored or chosen to occupy the promised land because they're so cool; they aren't cool, they're stiff-necked (v. 6). It's because the aboriginals are even worse (vv. 4, 6). *Or* it's because of an oath to their "fathers" who *were* cool (v. 5). *They* were adequate mirrors for me; *they* were His Majesty The Baby, but I won't nurture *you* because you're bad—or, I *did* nurture you but you were bad so I stopped, *or* I *may* stop, *or* I *may* start being nice again, *or* I *might* abandon you where I found you, or. . . . You get the idea. As a result, Israel can't point to its own merit—they're dependent upon Dad's whim for their special status to continue. In fact, pointing to their own merit and achievement is considered *faithlessness* to father (e.g., Deut 8:17–19). All this ensures that Israel will need Dad as their mirror, but one in which they can only reflect *his* image of their ideal compliant selves or their failure to live up to that ideal.

This obsession with Israel being *special* is the most flagrant sign of Yahweh's parental narcissism. Right off the bat, in Exod 19, he brings Israel to him on eagle's wings and says that if the children of Israel really listen to him, they will be his special possession (סגלה; vv. 4–5; cf. Deut 7:6–8; Mal 3:17). One scholar says that the Bible has no real answer as to why

Yahweh singled out Israel in the first place; the special relationship is a mystery (Machinist 1991, 206). The mystery disappears when Yahweh's own narcissistic nature is taken into account.

Why does Yahweh make Israel so special? I can answer that. It's a matter of need. No, not in the way that Heschel understands "God in need of man." Heschel (1951, 215, 241–44) takes pride in the biblical God not being self-sufficient. In fact, "our need of Him is but an echo of His need of us" (248). Sounds like codependence to me, but Heschel thinks it's utterly benign. I agree—Yahweh isn't portrayed as *really* being self-sufficient any more than any other narcissist is *really* self-sufficient—although Job's friends think he is. It's that Yahweh needs humans *as mirrors*. The hermetic tract *Poimandres* isn't too far off. It portrays God creating *anthrōpos* as an equal and adequate mirror image (§§12–15). Here, *theos* is a lover of his own perfection, a self-lover (§12; 14)—what most nonpros mean by "narcissist." He can only be self-sufficient when his human mirror is his equal (ἴσον; §12).[27]

The problem is that humans can't mirror Yahweh as equals, even if he *did* make them in his image and likeness, and a little less than God. And when Yahweh doesn't see the perfect beauty of a Narcissus in his human mirrors, then *he*, like King Richard, smashes his mirror and *we* collectively cry "ouch." He topples Adam and Cain and Noah's neighbors but keeps putting humans back together again. The difference between Yahweh and Richard is that the mirror Richard breaks is a flattering glass,[28] while Yahweh breaks his *un*flattering human mirrors.

V

Here, Doc, is the great irony: the most perfect mirror Yahweh ever produced is also the one he smashes most utterly—*Job*. Why? The book suggests a lot of highfalutin theological answers—I've given some myself —but now I suspect that they're just red herrings and *Holzwege*. The too-obvious answer is the right one: Yahweh is a cold, narcissistic parent and child abuser here.

But, you say, look at how desperately he tries to prove that Job is perfect and unique. But prove *to whom?* Not to himself, surely; he and the

---

[27] Referring to the God of the book of Revelation, Stephen Moore concludes that this God resembles a Roman emperor who "has become his own love object" (1996, 138). He "craves" the "vast audience of idolizers" that "eternally throngs the heavenly temple." Moore attempts to uncover "the extent to which the biblical God in all his incarnations—Yahweh, the Father of Jesus Christ, Jesus himself—is a projection of male narcissism" (139).

[28] *Richard II*, 4.1.288–89. On narcissistic traits in the historical Richard II, see Nigel Saul's recent biography (1997, 459–65).

narrator both seem pretty convinced from the start. To *haśśāṭān?* He isn't
even around at the end for God to say "I told you so." So who is the audience for this messy proving business? Is this unspecified audience a
Lacanian mirror for God? Does Yahweh need to be on TV in order to be
(see Braudy 1997, 603)? Is that why he, like Nixon, allowed incriminating
tapes to be recorded in Job 1 and 2?

Think about those first two chapters. In effect, Yahweh is bragging to
the neighbors—his courtiers—about this perfect specimen of his, perfect
like an English king or His Majesty the Baby. The neighbor says, "of
course, you cast him in the prequel to the movie *The Truman Show*—
you've hedged him in and made his wealth break out in the earth. *Now*
introduce him to life *outside* the womb, outside plush lily-white gated communities. Let him experience the *other* human reality—human birth
without the swaddling illusions of narcissism and omnipotence. Expose
him as you did unswaddled Israel. He'll diss you as much as she did."

Not at *first,* he doesn't. Patient Job still identifies with Dad in spite of
all the abuse and proudly chooses to affirm Dad's property rights and
reduce himself to nothing more than the function of Father's whims. He's
been toppled, smashed, and exposed to pain, but he still thinks of himself
as born from the shelter of a maternal womb.

But *after* his friends' arrival, *im*patient Job no longer says "naked came
I from my mother's womb" (1:21); instead, he talks about *his own* womb
(3:10). Ironically, the tomb now takes the womb's protective function.
Only in the tomb does he envision the peace and blessed isolation of the
bird in the egg and the foetus in the womb. In between birth and death
there is only the exposed existence of Lucretius's shipwrecked sailors and
other examples of "unaccommodated man."[29]

Job is a perfectly loyal courtier in the prologue. But then he starts talking in a way that any king would call seditious. Job no longer accepts the
executive-privilege notion. He becomes a whistle-blower for the silent
majority of sufferers, and he wants to Ken Starr with God. This unflattering mirror is talking back, and doing some illusion-shattering himself.

Job had *also* been a kind of vassal-king before all this hit the fan. He'd
been surrounded by a circle of admirers who kept their traps shut when
he talked, just like the courtiers of the apocryphal Solomon (Job 29:9–10;
Wis. 8:12). He says that he'd sat as the people's head and dwelt as a king
in the middle of his troops (Job 29:25). *Now,* however, instead of being surrounded by his *own* royal troops, *Yahweh's* troops have surrounded *his*
tent (19:12). God has thrown up siege works against him and encircled him
with his archers (19:6; 16:13). Job cries: "He breached me, breach after
breach" (יִפְרְצֵנִי פֶרֶץ עַל־פְּנֵי־פָרֶץ; 16:14). He feels himself to be a *polis*

---

[29] *King Lear,* 3.4.105; see Lasine 1988, 45.

under divine siege, a one-man tent-city, with tent walls that aren't just lean-ing—they're already jerichoed. Like Richard, King Job's impregnable castle wall is punctured with a pinprick. In fact, Richard's words answer the ques-tion Job himself had already asked: "Is my flesh of brass?" (6:12; *Richard II* 3.2.167–68). *Job's* skin can't repel Yahweh's missiles and hail, Stoic-style. It's shriveled with sepsis and crawling with Septuagint worms (LXX Job 2:9; cf. 7:5). Yahweh not only exposed him on the highway like an ostrich egg; he ran him over repeatedly with his Abrams tanks, like Jehu, after Jezebel's blood had splattered onto her palace wall on her way down to the street (2 Kgs 9:33).

Job is living the *topos* of the ignorant king now, and he doesn't like it. He wants to be in the loop, even if it becomes a noose for him. Yahweh finally *seems* to restore Job to the position of the privileged courtier who gets to see the great king's face; at least that's what Job experienced. But look what Yahweh *says* when he finally talks to his disaffected son and courtier. His words are proudly *un*parental and *un*caring. The conven-tional reading is that he's dealing a cosmological blow to Job's alleged anthropocentrism (see Lasine 1988, 29–33). But look again. Yahweh, the exposer, is not doubling in the role of the foster-parent rescuer. He's not returning in order to swaddle, salt, or pamper exposed Job. No, he comes to remind Job who's the *real* narcissist in the family and to rub salt in his wounds by talking about swaddling baby *Yam,* who, like Job, is also "hedged in" by God (וָאָסֹךְ; 38:8). Job thinks that it's *Yam* who deserves all this negative attention, not he. He's no sea or sea monster (7:12)—or even baby Oedipus. He's no threat. Yahweh doesn't need one of those fancy nursery monitors that allow parents to see and hear what's going on in the baby's room twenty-four hours a day!

Yet, after all this talk of cosmos and sea, in the *end* Job's universe is no bigger than the living room where his coming-home party is held. A materialistic microcosm, full of Hollywood hugs from phony fair-weather friends and relatives who didn't know him when he was down and out—a place where the women are called *qeren happûk* (42:14)[30]—"Revlon Eye Makeup Kit." We're locked out of Job's emotions, viewing all the glitz from outside his window. We'll never know whether he's now all image and no substance. If *I* were Job, with posttraumatic stress syndrome ooz-ing out of every pore, I'd go postal living in all that plastic and silicone. This isn't the *nostos* of a rich hero-king like Odysseus, with a Penelope-like wife waiting patiently by a marriage bed fashioned out of an olive-tree stump (Homer, *Od.* 23.177–204—finally, a royal bed that symbolizes sta-bility and trust, not assassination and betrayal!). No, this poor biblical

---

[30] Literally, the phrase means something like "horn of eye makeup." See the commentaries on Job 42:14.

bastard went through Lucretius's shipwreck, Lear's storm, and Oedipus's foot surgery only to end up in the home version of a narcissist's theme park, a mini-Disney World.

Me? Right now I feel like it's better to stay outside in the storm and nonstoically take my lumps from the hailstones, rather than to be in the shoes of these ideal scapegoat-kings. The weather is worse inside the palace. Girard called the king and his court "marginal insiders" who are often like "the eye of a hurricane" (1986, 18; see ch. 1, above). I don't want to be sitting on the throne when the once-adoring crowd decides to turn on *me*. Just leave me out of the whole thing. Our time's up anyway, isn't it? This is a good place to stop.

11

DIVINE NARCISSISM AND YAHWEH
AS PARENT AND KING

I

Israel is the *familia* (suite or bodyguard) of the King (God), whence it is incumbent upon them to imitate the King.
—Rabbinic sage Abba Saul (*Tôrat Kohanîm* 86c; Schechter 1961, 200)

God, as agent in our sacred texts, does indeed act abusively.... God, as described in the Bible, acts like an abusing male: husband, father and lord.
—Blumenthal, Who Is Battering Whom? (1993b, 79)

Frank Sinatra, Jr: the very name is enough to strike terror into the hearts of men and boys with famous fathers.... In a world full of men no one would want to be, Frank Sinatra, Jr. must rate in the top ten.
—Selgin, The Right Song, the Wrong Face (1995, 1–2)

In the nine sections of this final chapter, I will examine the charges just made by the biblicist patient from a variety of perspectives. Whatever his monologue might say about him, what does it say about the biblical Yahweh and what Jobling (1998, 23) called the "dynamics *in* the text"? The patient claimed that we—the readers of the Hebrew Bible—are put into the position of children, children whose father is narcissistic in nature. At this point, it is clear that when we think of narcissism we should not merely think of someone looking admiringly at his reflection in a pool of water. We should also think of a parent looking adoringly at "the little man in the eye" (Deut 32:10), the mirror supplied by the child His Majesty the Baby. Several rabbinic passages claim that when Yahweh spoke mouth to mouth with his adult servant Moses, it was מַרְאָה, "(as) in a mirror" (Num 12:8).[1]

---

[1] And not מַרְאֶה, "clearly." See *Lev. Rab.* 1:14 and *b. Yebam.* 49b, Milgrom (1990:96, 310), Strack and Billerbeck (1926, 3:452–54), and Allison (1993, 227). On divine mirror-narcissism in the hermetic tract *Poimandres,* see ch. 10, above. The metaphor of "mirroring" is used in many ways by various psychological theorists. See further Stern (1985, 144–45) and the studies cited in nn. 3 and 5 of Lasine 2001. Note 4 of that article also describes the manner in

Nevertheless, the predominant mode of divine narcissism in the Hebrew Bible involves Yahweh the parent using his *child* as a mirror.[2] And, as the biblicist patient proclaimed, such mirrors can end up cracked or smashed to bits. So the question becomes: Do we—*must* we—relate to the biblical God as children relate to a parent who might at any moment pamper, abandon, or annihilate them? And if so, what should we do with that knowledge?

Readers of the Hebrew Bible are introduced to a royal God[3] and, to that extent, are also invited to relate to him in the way that a king's subjects relate to their sovereign. The metaphors of king and father work together to identify us as members of "the *royal* family,"[4] descendants of Yahweh's special patriarchs and his special kings. And *that* means that we might be treated with all the ambivalence, suspicion, rivalry, and strings-attached love that characterize the attitude of a king when he views members of the royal family as competing to succeed—or overthrow—him. Depending on the nature of the king and the "family dynamic," it may also mean that the father will *simultaneously* want his privileged children to be better than he

---

which the metaphor of the "little man [or woman] in the eye" is used by Plato and Ovid.

[2] As I argue below, there is a fine line between a parent being there for the child, enabling it to experience "the fiction of omnipotence," and pampering the child in a way that really expresses and reflects the mother's anxiety and her own dread of being helpless, an attitude that the child will then see and incorporate into herself or himself. Even young babies can tell the difference between true mirroring—seeing their budding selves in a mother's face looking at them—and seeing their mother's face that is really looking inward to *her*self, thereby depriving the baby of being able to use the mother as a necessary mirror in which to "grow" his or her own self. This is what Winnicott is getting at with his use of the Humpty Dumpty story.

[3] Mettinger believes that "the designation of YHWH as 'king' expresses one of the central Israelite notions of God" (1986, 148). In fact, it may even be "the center of the Old Testament understanding of God" (1988, 92).

[4] Bottero (1992, 27–29) applies the metaphor of family to our relationship with our Mesopotamian cultural ancestors. However, in the Hebrew Bible the metaphor is, in part, a rhetorical strategy that functions to define how readers should relate to (and judge) their ancient family members in the text. See Lasine 1989b and ch. 10, above. Attempts to describe the dynamics within actual ancient Near Eastern families (Mesopotamian, Egyptian, Palestinian, and Greek) suggest that there is too little direct, unequivocal evidence for any definite conclusions to be drawn about children's actual experiences with their parents. See, e.g., Duby 1996, 317; Glassner 1996, 117–19; Forgeau 1996, 152–54; Postman 1994, 5–6. Hagedorn's recent sketch of the ancient Israelite model of "parenting styles" (2000, 112) is based on generalizations about honor, shame, and loyalty in "Mediterranean culture," supplemented by quotations from Greek literary sources, biblical and Egyptian instructional literature, and biblical and Platonic law (111–16, 120).

and need them to fail at reaching that goal. He may support *and* undermine them, even if in some cases the double attitude manifests itself in "splitting," in this case, splitting between supported son-kings like David, who function as his narcissistic mirrors, and undermined ones like Saul, the flawed mirrors whom he eventually humiliates or smashes.

According to Abba Saul in the epigraph, "Israel is the *familia* (suite or bodyguard) of the King (God), whence it is incumbent upon them to imitate the King." Does that include imitating abusiveness? David Blumenthal's biblical God acts like an abusing male (1993b, 79).[5] Blumenthal assumes that the way we envision God is necessarily shaped by the way we have viewed our parents and experienced childhood (1993a, 13). Once one accepts the premise that the Hebrew Bible's target audiences are to view themselves as children of a parental God, readers must face—or evade— the possibility that their royal biblical father can be an abusive narcissist, who may seek the loyalty and submission he needs from his children by breaking their spirit, by burdening them with feelings of guilt and inadequacy, or by keeping them cravenly dependent upon him.

If any of this is true, should we then "tame" this biblical God, whom even scholars like Brueggemann (2000, 28) describe as having a "wild dimension"? Perhaps not, if one wants to argue that the biblical Yahweh *does* truly reflect the spectrum of *human* behavior in the world. From this perspective, an all-good and merciful God is a child's fantasy of an ideal perfect parent, like the parental god imagined by abused children as a coping device. Paradoxically, even though Dad or Mom is abusive, the children may view their parental abuser as a god. This is how one psychiatrist (Herman 1997, 92) describes the double perspective of the victim:[6]

> The repeated experience of terror and reprieve ... may result in a feeling of intense, *almost worshipful dependence upon an all-powerful, godlike authority*. The victim may live in terror of his wrath, but she may also view him as *the source of strength, guidance, and life itself*. The relationship may take on an extraordinary quality of *specialness*. Some ... voluntarily [suppress] their own doubts as a proof of *loyalty and submission*. (emphasis added)

This description sounds suspiciously similar to Yahweh's relationship with the children whom he repeatedly tests in the wilderness, the very children

---

[5] Blumenthal's focus is on the God of the Hebrew Bible. However, Christian feminist theologians have also pointed to parental abuse in the New Testament. As Brown and Parker put it (1989, 26), "the predominant image or theology of the culture is of 'divine child abuse'—God the Father demanding and carrying out the suffering and death of his own son."

[6] Herman is speaking here about battered women's perceptions of their batterer.

whom he had earlier singled out specifically to be his "special possession" (Exod 19:4–5; Deut 7:6–8; Mal 3:17; see above). Yahweh's efforts to "discipline" Israel "the way a man disciplines his son" (Deut 8:5) are perfectly suited to make his children view him in this manner: as the source of strength and life to whom they must submit and remain loyal and whom they must worship.

In spite of the many blatant examples of divine abusiveness listed by the biblicist on the couch, this aspect of Yahweh's behavior usually remains unnoticed by many readers, as though it were hidden in plain sight like Poe's purloined letter. How is this possible? Jennifer Freyd not only thinks it's possible; she thinks it is often necessary and inevitable, especially for abused children. Childhood sexual abuse is "the core betrayal trauma" (1996, 3). Because children need to trust their parents and caregivers, they "must block awareness of the betrayal, forget it, in order to ensure that [they] behave in ways that maintain the relationship on which [they] are dependent" (74). In the short run, at least, "such knowledge isolation may be necessary for survival" (69). As a result, "we can simultaneously not know and know about a betrayal." In short, "to know is to put oneself in danger. To not know is to align with the caregiver and ensure survival" (165).

Freyd's description of children coping with abuse should be familiar to us, because it is based on the relationship between information management, trust, and betrayal, issues that we have found to be crucial to the way in which kings attempt to ensure loyalty and maintain dominance and power. Freyd would certainly not dispute that abusing parents are also masters of information management.[7] The ways in which parents, and the communities in which they live, "cover up" abuse through a conspiracy of silence, disseminating disinformation or blaming the victim, have been carefully studied. Judith Herman notes that it is very tempting to take the side of the perpetrator. "All the perpetrator asks is that the bystander do nothing.[8] ... The

---

[7] In fact, she has experienced this firsthand, from her own parents; see Haaken (1998, 21–31, 34).

[8] King David's silence and inaction after Amnon rapes Tamar becomes even more significant when viewed in this light (2 Sam 13:21). The very brevity and terseness of this verse underscore the fact that Tamar is further victimized and betrayed by her silent "bystander" father. The LXX breaks the silence by adding: "and he did not grieve [ἐλύπησε] the spirit of Amnon his son, for he loved him, since he was his firstborn." The addition seems to be based on the later mention of David's pampering of (and/or lack of concern for) Adonijah: "and his father never at any time rebuked [ἐπετίμησεν; for MT עֲצָב֛וֹ, 'grieved/pained'] him" (1 Kgs 1:6, LXX L; LXX B has ἀπεκώλυσεν, apparently representing Hebrew עצר ("restrain") rather than עצב]). On the pampering and abandonment of royal sons by their fathers, see chs. 6 and 10, above.

victim ... asks the bystander to share the burden of pain. The victim demands action." Thus, there is a "conflict of interest between victim and bystander ....the community wants to forget ...and move on" (1997, 8).[9] Herman could easily be describing the conflict between Job and *his* community, as Kimberly Chastain has pointed out (1997, 170–73). Herman (1997, 101) emphasizes that the victim herself may attempt to absolve the parent of responsibility, like a Girardian scapegoat accepting the identity given unanimously by the accusing community. In this instance, what Freyd calls "knowledge isolation" is achieved by the victim accepting the guilt pinned on her by her victimizers.[10] In the book of Job, this often daunting task of denial is performed by Job's friends; Job himself refuses to participate.

Even the youthful perpetrators of the Columbine slaughter went out of their way to exonerate their parents (*Denver Post* online). In a video tape made prior to the shooting, one of them quotes Shakespeare's *The Tempest:* "good wombs give birth to bad seed" (1.2.119).[11] Alice Miller asserts that killers and other criminals who were once abused typically insist that their mothers were loving, and if their fathers had beaten them, it was because they "had been bad and deserved it" (1991b, 25). Miller would take it for granted that the Columbine killers had been somehow abused. She insists that "*all destructive behavior has its roots in the repressed traumas of childhood*" and that "a full one hundred percent" of inmates in American prisons had been abused as children (1991b, 25, 138).[12] Shakespeare's reference to "bad seed" might also put one in mind of father Yahweh's reference to his people as "a seed of evil-doers" (זרע מרעים) in Isa 1:4 (on the phrase, see G. B. Gray 1912, 15). Who first

---

[9] Recent mass killings at American schools, including Columbine High School in Colorado and Westside Middle School in Arkansas, provide further examples. Parents of the victims who have continued to speak out about these traumatic events or used them as a reason to argue for tighter gun control have been criticized harshly and even threatened for their failure to "move on" (Callahan 1999, 1). On the "second injury" to victims that results from the perceived lack of concern or assistance on the part of the community, see Chastain (1997, 162).

[10] Alice Miller makes a related point using the Bible as her example: "Sparing the parents is our supreme law; under its sway the Abrahams of this world sacrifice their Isaacs over and over again, unless God, touched by His sons' obedience, should take pity on them" (1998, 209–10).

[11] Plato's Socrates agrees that parents cannot pass along their virtues to their son—not even famous parents like Pericles (*Men.* 93a–b; *Prot.* 319d–320a; *Alc. 1* 118d–119a)—no matter how diligently they seek to teach them (cf. *Men.* 95e–96a; *Prot.* 319d–e). For Socrates' own sons, see Xenophon, *Mem.* 2.2.

[12] For a balanced assessment of Miller's controversial views, see Haaken (1998, 78–79). Miller's ideas are applied to the religious abuse of children by Capps (1995, 3–20, 78–95 and passim).

planted this biblical seed? Yahweh didn't create his world, or people, by spilling his seed[13] or his tears, like the Egyptian Re or Atum. But he *did* go through labor pains in delivering both her son Israel and the world as a whole (Deut 32:18; Ps 90:1–2). Can bad seed issue from Yahweh's womb? How good a parental role model and teacher *is* Yahweh?

It's difficult being the son of a powerful, famous father like Yahweh. Call it the "Frank Sinatra Jr. Complex." As Selgin puts it in our epigraph, "the very name [of Frank Sinatra Jr.] is enough to strike terror into the hearts of men and boys with famous fathers." No father in the Hebrew Bible is as famous (or as concerned with his fame) as is Yahweh. Yahweh's special kids, whom he picks to take over the family business of domination and kingship (Gen 1:26–28; Ps 8) are like all such children who are expected to step into their father's shoes. They have to listen over and over—when they get up and when they go to bed, when they're on a walk, and when they're having supper (cf. Deut 6:6–7)—to the tale of how Dad built up the business with his own two hands, alone, from scratch, from *tohus* and *bohus*. Or, in the heroic war-story versions, by winning it through combat with primordial monsters (e.g., Ps 74:12–17). And to make it worse, these kids "look like" Dad; they represent him. That is, they are created "in his image." Whatever else that might mean, in family terms this kind of mirroring means that if Dad is narcissistic, he will view their bad behavior as reflecting on himself.

There are two basic metaphoric clusters surrounding the figure of the child who follows in Yahweh's royal footsteps, one positive and one very negative. The first is the king as judge, battle leader, and trampler of rival gods. That's Yahweh's "legitimate" business that the son is to take over. The second is the king as arbitrary tyrant and insatiable narcissist. When the sons start showing this flip side of the king's position, it reflects badly on their royal father. In fact, it might suggest that maybe the kid also got *this* side from Dad; maybe he's mirroring something in the family gene pool.

Perhaps most unsettling for a child is the abusive parent's disturbing doubleness. In Chastain's words, "the father who terrorizes the night is the playful, affectionate father of the morning.... The mother who comforts the terrified child is also the one who responds, 'Oh honey, you must have been dreaming,' causing the child to doubt her perception of reality" (1996, 164). Freyd speaks of abused people who describe themselves as having been split between a normal "day child" and an abused "night child" (160; cf. 76). The biblical Job would find this form of doubleness to be very familiar. His indictment of Yahweh highlights the fact that God

---

[13] E.g.: "I [Re] was the one who copulated with my fist, I masturbated with my hand" ("Repulsing of the Dragon and the Creation," *ANET* 6); "Amun-Re, King of the Gods, ... who formed the land with his semen" ("Khonsu Cosmogony"; Lesko 1991, 105).

has created night-walking criminals to break his laws, while his good, compliant children obey these laws during the daylight business hours. Yahweh's response to this accusation does not deny this basic split in the temporal fabric of his realm (see Job 24:13–17; 38:12–15 and Lasine 1988, 34–35). Moses also experienced the night-and-day difference between a diurnal deity who singles out and nurtures a special emissary[14] and the nocturnal divine attacker who seeks to kill this same special child (Exod 4:24–26; cf. v. 19). As for the hypothetical mother's "You must have been dreaming," Job would hear in this a clear echo of Zophar's appeal to the unreality of dreams as a way of dismissing Job's victimization by God (Job 20:8; cf. Ps 73:20). While abused children often view their parents with adoring eyes, through the adult eyes of the biblical narrators Yahweh appears as *both* the heroic king *and* the unreliable parent whom Jeremiah calls a "deceitful brook" (15:18).

II

Do not hate your brother in your heart.
—Leviticus 19:17

I loved Jacob, and Esau I hated.
—Malachi 1:2–3

According to Blumenthal (1993a, 19), one of Yahweh's "personalist attributes" is that he is "partisan." If "God has personality, of course God has preferences." Moreover, "to be partisan is to be loyal and to demand loyalty." As his example, Blumenthal cites "the election of the Jews." Their "special-ness" has caused some Jews to rejoice and others to be embarrassed. Blumenthal adds that "there is no real reason for one's preferences."[15] Like the readers who dismiss David's crimes with "he's only human," as though all humans murder and commit the other crimes of which David is guilty, Blumenthal's argument has the effect of "naturalizing" and thereby excusing Yahweh's preferential treatment of some of his children with a simple, "he's only human—at least, as he's depicted in the Bible."

In Mal 1:2–3, Yahweh declares "I loved Jacob, and Esau I hated." He says "hate" (שנא), and he *means* hate.[16] Although Yahweh had earlier told

---

[14] Even here, the nurturing father's message concerns his intention to slaughter other children if his demands are not met by his royal rival Pharaoh.

[15] In this respect, Blumenthal echoes Peter Machinist's view of Israel's special-ness, which we challenged in ch. 1.

[16] See Redditt (2000) for a review of commentators' attempts to soften the mean-ing of "hate" in this context and reasons for taking the word literally. Redditt (175)

his children, "Do not hate your brother in your heart" (Lev 19:17), his parental hatred toward one of his children is apparently another matter. Blumenthal does not cite this example of divine partiality. However, he does quote a survivor of abuse who contends that "any [family therapist] would recognize immediately the pattern of pathology that God established in His family.... He showed extreme, irrational preferences and provoked the child-Cain to a rage" (Blumenthal, 1993a, 199). Although the survivor's other examples are also taken from Genesis, she might have noted that Yahweh shows preference for the Levites precisely because of their willingness *not* to "acknowledge" their human fathers, mothers, and children in order to follow their divine father's dictates (Deut 33:9; cf. Luke 14:26), even when this meant slaughtering their sons and brothers (Exod 32:25, 29; see Lasine 1994, 212–14). Such an extreme demand on the part of a human being would be taken as evidence of a severe personality disorder. If theologians like Blumenthal are going to be so accepting of Yahweh as a "personality,"[17] with all that may imply, they have to consider that this personality can also be "disordered" or "pathological." Blumenthal's ultimate diagnosis is that "God is abusive, but not always"—merely "from time to time" (1993a, 247). Is Yahweh then capricious as well as abusive?

Abusers *do* cultivate capriciousness as a tool to impose domination. As Herman puts it, "in the abusive family environment, the exercise of parental power is arbitrary, capricious, and absolute" (1977, 98; cf. 77–78, 100). Brueggemann and others have come right out and said that Yahweh is "capricious" (2000, 21, 26, 30).[18] At the same time, Brueggemann continues

---

believes that שׂנא primarily designates revulsion. Marshall (1978, 592) contends that שׂנא "has the sense 'to leave aside, abandon'" and that this sense may also be present in Luke 14:26: "If anyone comes to me and does not hate his father and his mother, ... he cannot be a disciple of mine." We have already discovered that "hateful" abusive parenting leaves the child feeling abandoned (see further below). More typically, Nolland (1993, 762) believes that Jesus' use of "hate" in Luke 14:26 is simply a case of "typical Semitic hyperbole." However, even he admits that "the language of hate is intended with all seriousness in such Old Testament verses as Ps 139:21–22." See below for discussion of Yahweh hating Israel in Deut 1:27; 9:28 and Jer 12:7–8; 22:5 (in connection with Jesus' allusions to Jeremiah when he expresses his Yahweh-like ambivalence toward Jerusalem in his role as "mother bird" [Matt 23:37–39; Luke 13:34–35]).

[17] Muffs would certainly agree with Blumenthal on this point. He asserts that Yahweh is "probably the most [highly] articulated personality ... of all Near Eastern deities" (1992, 63).

[18] Cf. Noll (ch. 9 n. 4, above) and contrast Balentine (1983, 147): "It is not a question of divine caprice but rather of human disobedience." The adjective "capricious" is usually applied by scholars to the behavior of Mesopotamian and other so-called "pagan" gods (see, e.g., Finkelstein 1958, 439).

to offer hope that Yahweh might act with less "brutality" (40) in the future, precisely because his character is not only "unsettling" (27, 30, 35) but "unsettled" (28). By this he means that Yahweh's darker traits "are live and present in the past of this God" (40). These "'past texts' are enduringly painful memories still available to the character of Yahweh, mostly not operative, but continuing to work even in the present" (38).

Although Brueggemann does not mention Jean-Paul Sartre, he seems to have made peace with Yahweh by employing a distinction similar to Sartre's description of human existence in terms of "facticity" and "transcendence" (1943, 91–106). We cannot evade the facts of our past, but we can never be identical to the sum of our past actions. As long as we are still alive, we also reach out into the future, in terms of our plans and intentions. When we play off one aspect of our temporal identity against another, or attempt to deny one dimension altogether, we are committing *mauvaise foi* or bad faith. Is Yahweh saying, "I'm not really an abusive God; the real me is what's coming in the future"? Or, are *we* trying to make him say that, practicing *mauvaise foi* on his behalf, like Job's friends?

This concept of bad faith—playing off one aspect of one's temporal identity against another—is something that abusive parents are uniquely positioned to put into practice. The "daytime" father can disown or deny the "nighttime" father. Blumenthal (1993, 240) cites Ellwood's description of the biblical God as the "nurturing betrayer" or the "betraying nurturer." When the two terms are welded together in a powerful parental figure, this double identity cannot help but confuse the children who are totally dependent upon such a god or parent. Bad faith helps abusers to escape accountability for the "night side" of their double character. Abusers also cultivate capriciousness as a tool to impose domination. As Herman (1977, 77) points out, those who practice psychological domination increase fear "by inconsistent and unpredictable outbursts of violence and by capricious enforcement of petty rules."

As long as the child views her parent's "daytime" self as perfect and all-powerful, she will be unable to "hate" the bad-faith parent properly. Benjamin (1988:214) argues that the notion of the all-giving and perfect mother "expresses the mentality of omnipotence, the inability to experience the mother as an independently existing subject."[19] This idealization

---

[19] Benjamin highlights the role of omnipotence in narcissism. When the child becomes aware of her helplessness in relation to parents' power (which Benjamin dubs "the great fall from grace"), it is a shocking "blow to the child's narcissism," which the child seeks to repair through identification with the person who embodies the power (Benjamin 1988, 101). Such identification is a circuitous way for the child to prolong the experience of omnipotence in relation to the father, even after

"testifies to the failure of destruction; hate has not been able to come forth and make the experience of love less idealized and more authentic." Confusion is inevitable: "since the child has not been able to engage in successful destruction, he is less able to distinguish the real person from the fantasy." Benjamin is not speaking about abusive parents or abused children, but parenting in general. Her understanding of the productive purpose of hate builds on Winnicott's work. Winnicott once declared that "the mother hates her infant from the word go." And the human child "needs this hate to hate" (1958, 201, 202).

From this perspective, Yahweh's demand for total love (Deut 6:5) is an example of enforced idealization that precludes his children from experiencing the kind of hate needed to make love authentic. Although Yahweh promises swift destruction to those who hate him (Deut 7:10)—and who therefore "destroy" him in Winnicott's sense—biblical narrators also show him acting hatefully toward his children.[20] Yahweh is a father who describes *himself* not only as compassionate and merciful but as jealous and wrathful. No wonder he might seem to be confusingly ambivalent to his children,[21] including the readers of the

---

mother has ceased providing the fiction of omnipotence. While a human mother can (and should) fail at providing unbreaking womblike protection and presence (and thereby surrender omnipotence), omnipotent Yahweh refuses to give up omnipotence. Given his commitment to his idealized perfect image, he must blame his children for his lapses in protection and attention, by charging them with having rejected him.

[20] Job, for one, believes that God actively hates and persecutes him (16:9; for the meaning of שָׂטַם here, see, e.g., Driver and Gray 1921, 2:105). It is rarely pointed out that Yahweh is never said to love Job. In fact, the root for "love" (אהב) appears only once in the entire book, when Job himself laments that those whom *he* had loved have turned on him (19:19).

[21] Job illustrates the plight of such children when he imagines God hiding him in Sheol until his rage turns back, at which point God would remember and yearn (כסף) for him. God would then call, and Job would answer (14:13–15). While Clines is correct in assuming that the adult Job knows this to be a "hopeless ... impossible dream" (1989, 330–31), children might need to hope that an abusive parent could be caring *even while* raging against them. Job's wish for the angry Yahweh to shelter him from his own anger recalls Yahweh's reluctance to go up among the children of Israel after the golden calf incident: "if I go up among you for one moment, I shall consume you" (Exod 33:5; cf. v. 3). Yahweh has to steer clear of his children because they "push his buttons"; they might make him lose his temper and destroy them even though he doesn't want to do so. The same logic can be found in 1 Sam 18:10–15, if one is willing to assess Saul's motivation generously. Under the influence of an evil spirit from God, Saul attempts to kill David. He is afraid of David because Yahweh is with him and has "departed" (סור, *qal*) from Saul. Does Saul attempt to kill David again? On the contrary, he makes David

biblical family album who are belated witnesses to his behavior as a single parent.

The child who has been allowed to hate and destroy his parents makes a crucial discovery: "that he has destroyed everyone and everything, and yet the people around him remain calm and unhurt" (Benjamin 1988, 212). This is *not* the experience that Homer's childish Achilleus is seeking when he wishes for the destruction of his own people, as we shall see in section VII below. If human parents can allow their children to have this experience, is the same possible for a god like Yahweh, who *is* omnipotent? Is this what the flood was all about? When infanticidal fathers express their hate for their kids, the children can *really* die, as when the "nighttime" father Yahweh visits destruction on the Egyptian children in the so-called "night of watching [ליל שמרים] unto Yahweh" (Exod 12:42). Oedipus's father Laius is far less successful at infanticide, although he tries hard enough. Now, Benjamin (1988, 142) defines the oedipal father as the one who cannot give up omnipotence. This would make all-powerful father-gods like Yahweh oedipal by definition. Benjamin describes "the oedipal son" as the one "who cannot bear his wish to unseat his father, because its fulfillment would deprive him of the authority who protects him." This puts the "oedipal son" in the position of Freyd's abused children, if not Yahweh's special child Israel, needing to remain dependent on the father whom they might otherwise have wanted to hate or "unseat."

III

His elder son was in one of the fields; and when he came and approached the house, he heard music and dancing. He called one of the slave boys [παίδων] and inquired what this might be. He said to him, "Your brother has come, and your father has killed the fatted calf, because he received him back in good health." He was angry and refused to go in. His father came out and pleaded with him. But he answered his father, "Look, for all these years I have slaved [δουλεύω] for you, and I never disobeyed your command; yet you never gave me even a goat so that I might make merry with my friends. But when this son of yours came back, who has devoured your livelihood [βίον] with prostitutes, you killed the fatted calf for him." He said to him, "Child, you are always with me, and all that is mine is yours. But it was necessary to make merry and rejoice, because this brother of yours was dead and has come to life, lost and has been found."
—Luke 15:25–32

"depart" (סור, *hip'il*) from him, thereby protecting David from his fits of rage, and also increasing David's opportunity for success and independent action by making him commander over a thousand (on Saul's character, see ch. 2, above).

It may be easier to grasp the nature of parental partiality, divine hatred, and Yahweh's double identity as "betraying nurturer" by reading the so-called prodigal son parable against the grain. A man has two sons. The younger demands his portion of the estate from the father, leaves home for a distant land, and squanders his property in dissolute living. His resources spent, a famine forces him to work as a hired hand feeding pigs. The younger son eventually realizes that his father's hired hands have plenty to eat and decides to go home. He rehearses the speech he intends to make to his father, in which he will declare that he has sinned and no longer deserves to be called his son, asking only to be treated as one of the hired hands. When he returns, his father runs out to meet him and calls for the best robe to be put on the son, as well as a ring and sandals. The son stops his speech before mentioning the request to be a hired hand. The father orders the fatted calf slaughtered for a celebratory feast. It is at this point that the elder brother returns and the conversation given in the epigraph takes place. He is angry and feels slighted. His anger is directed to the father, not to his brother. Like Cain, this elder brother focuses on the fact that his father is treating him unfairly. He feels that his constant obedience has been taken for granted, while his prodigal younger brother is being treated as "special."

What kind of parenting are we witnessing here on the part of the father, who is often likened to God (e.g., Fitzmyer 1985, 1085; Culpepper 1995, 9:302) and who is said to be associated with "kingly motifs" (Marshall 1978, 606)?[22] The parable brackets out all hint of how the family felt about one another, including the emotional background that led to the younger son's desire to receive his patrimony and leave. In fact, the only stated reason for the younger son wanting to return is economic. He plans to tell his father that he has sinned, and does tell him (v. 21), but we are given no information that indicates whether or not this was a ploy designed to ensure that his father would take him back. The fact that he never completes his speech is usually taken to mean that his father interrupted him; however, he could also have realized that his father was offering him a much better deal, so it would be wiser to keep his mouth shut (*pace* Nolland 1993, 785; Fitzmyer 1985, 1089; Marshall 1978, 610). Other information about the family dynamic is also lacking. Is there a mother around somewhere? What's her opinion on all this? Are the two boys even sons of the same mother? How come no one informed the elder son that there was a welcome-home party going on? Is he out of the loop among his own

---

[22] However, Marshall disagrees with Rengstorf's view of an original "'kingly' element in the parable that has been edited away" (1978, 606). The father's giving of the best robe to the younger son (v. 22) has been compared with similar acts by two biblical kings: the pharaoh of the Joseph story (Gen 41:42; Drury 1985, 144) and Xerxes in the book of Esther (Esth 6:6–11; Nolland 1993, 785).

family and servants? In spite of these unanswered questions, the story implies a family drama worthy of King David's court. While many commentators take the point of view of the father, and Alice Miller takes the prodigal's return home as a tragic surrender to the father,[23] the obedient elder son's plight has gone relatively unlamented.[24]

In fact, the elder brother is usually made into the villain. He is often said to exemplify the "murmuring" and "blind self-complacency of the Pharisee" and to represent "the Jews" (Plummer 1990, 371, 377–78). He "represents all of us who think we can make it on our own" (Culpepper 1995, 9:305). His charge that he has been treated unfairly merely shows his "childish selfishness and jealousy" (Tolbert 1979, 104). Though some concede that the elder brother "has been a model son" (Nolland 1993, 790), his compliant behavior is usually discounted by readers and commentators, just as it seems to be discounted by the father. Commentators like to speculate on what the elder son's duties and rights would have been in a typical Jewish household during this period and then find him remiss for not preventing his younger brother's earlier departure. They see him as petty and greedy. Deuteronomy 21:16 is cited as an indication that firstborns would expect to get a double portion of the father's estate. Yet the elder brother isn't concerned with property or wealth. He misses the recognition he has never received from his father,[25] as well as the lack of support for his own growth and autonomy. He isn't complaining that he was never pampered like His Majesty the Baby with royal clothes and fatted-calf menus; he laments that his father has not recognized his years of loyal service with even a modest party that he could have enjoyed *with his own friends,* something that might express that he had a life of his own, with companions of his own choosing.[26]

---

[23] Miller (1998, 201–2) cites therapist Helm Stierlin's interpretation of the parable as an example. She faults him for identifying with the father's interests and for failing to notice that it is only through obedience that the son finds his way back to his father: "Stierlin does not realize that a restoration of harmony is being celebrated here only at the price of the son's acquiescence in his father's definition of everything that separated his son from him as 'death'." Miller herself fails to notice the predicament of the ever-obedient *elder* son.

[24] Except, perhaps, in entertainments designed to placate the obedient elder sons of this world, like Frank Capra's film, *It's a Wonderful Life.*

[25] See Benjamin (1995, 123) on the importance for a child's development of "the father as a symbol of recognition."

[26] If this is the (unstated) basis for Culpepper's claim that the elder brother "represents all of us who think we can make it on our own," it is clearly inadequate. Culpepper finds such a drive for autonomy to be condemnable, but what, in terms of family relations, is the alternative? Craven dependence on one's parents? (It also seems odd to characterize the *elder* brother for wanting to "make it on his own," when it is the *younger* brother's desire to do precisely this that begins the story.)

This tale can be read as a parable about controlling parents who appreciate sons who "hate" them, leave home, display autonomy, through whom they can rekindle their own narcissism by proxy, as opposed to the slavishly obedient, compliant, too-easily controlled son. In this sense, Saul is an elder son of Yahweh. On the other hand, Yahweh affirms the "correctness" of the feisty Job who had accused God of abandoning him. Yet Job never left God in order to go his own way, as did the prodigal. He was totally obedient until Yahweh sent him packing (so to speak). Far from being a wastrel, Job and his property are "wasted" by God, not by himself. In fact, they are made to waste away precisely because he was the most obedient, stay-at-home son of all, rather than the most prodigal. By crushing his obedient servant whom he himself has prodigalized, Yahweh ends up affirming and rewarding this unhealthy[27] prodigal in the same way as the father did in the parable.

The spurned elder son in Luke resembles the elder brother Esau in Genesis, who has also been maligned, not just by ancient commentators, but by modern ones who malign Esau and the elder brother in the parable at the same time: "our elder brother is just as jealous as Esau" (Derrett 1970,120). Yet Genesis makes it clear that Esau cares as little about wealth and property as does the elder brother in the parable (see Gen 33:9; cf. 25:32–34). He too strives to be obedient to his parents' wishes (Gen 27:3–5; 28:7–8). And in Gen 33, Esau actually plays the additional role of the father in the parable, for it is he who welcomes back the "prodigal" Jacob, although this time the prodigal is anything but destitute.

The heart of the Jacob-Esau story is the stealing of the blessing in Gen 27. Here, the mother Rebekah is the agent of father Yahweh's prior preference for the younger son (25:23). Her machinations express and enact *Yahweh's* "hatred" of Esau, in what is very much a zero-sum game. Interestingly, while we are told that Rebekah loved Jacob, we are not told that she hates Esau (even though Jacob himself is later said to "hate" one of his wives [29:31, 33]). Nevertheless, Rebekah treats Esau in a hateful way, the way in which Yahweh led her to treat him by means of his oracle. Admittedly, Rebekah enacts Yahweh's preference using skills with which her family seems uniquely endowed: deception and information management.[28] While Yahweh too possesses these skills, the rabbis make

---

[27] While the servant in the parable makes a point of the prodigal returning "healthy" (v. 27), we are never explicitly told that father Yahweh restored Job's health.

[28] She overhears Isaac's directions to Esau and is later informed of the words that Esau uttered *to himself* (27:5, 41–42). And in both cases, when she repeats what she has heard to Jacob, she adds to or changes the information, leaving open the possibility that she does so in order to manipulate Jacob into doing what she wants him to do (27:7, 42–43).

special note that this is one of the four areas in which we should *not* imitate God (see Schechter 1961, 204–5).[29]

IV

For one thousand years he [the great god Zurvan] offered sacrifice in order that he might perhaps have a son who would be called Ormazd.... Then he pondered in his heart and said: "... do I strive in vain?" And even while he reflected in this manner, Ormazd and Ahriman were conceived in the womb: Ormazd through the offered sacrifice, Ahriman through the doubt. When he became aware of this, Zurvan said, "Lo, two sons are in the womb. Whichever ... appears swiftly before me, him I shall make king." Ormazd, being aware of their father's purposes, revealed them to Ahriman ... [who] pierced the womb ... and presented himself to his father. Zurvan ... knew not who he might be, and asked "Who are you?" And he said: "I am your son." Zurvan answered him: "my son is fragrant and bright, and you, you are dark and stinking."
—Eznik of Kolb (Boyce 1984, 97–98)

In analysis, the small and lonely child that is hidden behind [the] achievements [of the narcissistically disturbed patient] wakes up and asks: "What would have happened if I had appeared before you, bad, ugly, angry, jealous, lazy, dirty, smelly? Where would your love have been then? And I was all these things as well. Does this mean that it was not really me whom you loved, but only what I pretended to be? The well-behaved, reliable, empathic, understanding, and convenient child, who in fact was never a child at all? What become of my childhood? Have I not been cheated out of it? ... From the beginning I have been a little adult. My abilities—were they simply misused?"
—Alice Miller, *Prisoners of Childhood* (1981, 15)

I began the preface to this book with a different story about a father who had a rejected elder son and a favored younger son. In this story, the Persian god Zurvan is a father who intends to make a king of his soon-to-be-born son. The son who presents himself fresh from the womb is not His Majesty the Baby, as Dad had expected. Zurvan would have trouble resuscitating his lost narcissism on this kid. The dark, stinking Ahriman is a

---

29 Rebekah's maneuvering is also reminiscent of court intrigue during a succession crisis. We have already analyzed similar situations in 1 Kgs 1 and in Saint-Simon's account of Louis XIV's last days (see ch. 5, above). In 1 Kgs 1, David may not be as infirm and passive as it seems at first glance. In this instance, there is no mention of an explicit divine preference between David's remaining sons (unless we go back to the name Jedidiah ["beloved of Yahweh"] in 2 Sam 12:25). In 1 Kgs 1 Yahweh is not playing the role of the true controlling father, and Yahweh's agent Nathan does not need to prompt Bathsheba to play Rebekah's role.

grotesque mirror, made through splitting within the image of god, splitting said to be caused by divine father's doubt. The son whom Zurvan desired is a fragrant and bright mirror, and compliant and obedient as well, no doubt.

I have no idea whether Alice Miller ever heard of Zurvan and his twins, these Zoroastrian cousins of the twins Jacob and Esau. In either case, the complaint she puts in the mouth of her "well-behaved" and "reliable" modern child in the epigraph highlights the narcissistic disturbances in this Persian cosmic family. In effect, Miller's modern model child asks his dad: "What if I had appeared before you as Ahriman, not Ormazd? Would you have loved me then? Because I *am* Ahriman *as well as* Ormazd. I've formed myself according to the idealized image you had of me when you sacrificed to make my birth possible, just as a divine potter might form his self-portrait from the clay of the ⁱᵃdāmâ. But 'I,' the self you need to see in me, isn't real. The real me is less Ormazd than Ahriman, the true firstborn whom you rejected." At least the human father Isaac accepted *his* Ahriman. It took a conspiracy between Ahriman-Esau's mother and their patriarchal god to remove him, in favor of the gifted, special Ormazd-Jacob. And this biblical Ormazd was later tutored in the master arts of information management and deception by his mother's family, not the family of the father Isaac, who as a child had himself been put into a traumatic situation on the altar by his father Abraham.[30]

In terms of compliance, the younger son Ormazd is analogous to the *elder* son in Luke's parable, while he is analogous to the *younger* son in terms of paternal preference. Could it be that the father in the parable strove to produce Ormazd-like sons, but nevertheless identified with, and ends up excusing, Ahriman-like behavior? In other words, while it might seem logical for fathers to prefer compliant child-mirrors (a message the Zurvanian story seems to reinforce), the Lukan parable suggests that this is not the case. Even the well-behaved narcissistic child-mirror described by Miller does not feel that he is loved by the father for *himself.* One cannot build an autonomous life for oneself if one is nothing more than a mirror for a parent's split self-image. A father who desires *this* for his child is not only a narcissist, but a tyrannical ruler.

V

The selfishness of parents—the true parental feeling—knows no boundaries at all.... These are the two parental means of upbringing, both born out of selfishness: tyranny and slavery in all of their gradations, whereby the tyranny can express itself very tenderly ... and the slavery very

---

[30] For a provocative, but uneven, treatment of Isaac as abused child, see Delaney 1998).

proudly ("You are my son, therefore I will make you into my savior"), but they are two horrible means of education, two anti-educational means, designed to stomp the child back into the ground out of which it came.
—Kafka, *Briefe 1902–1924* (1958, 344–45)

[In the rapprochment stage, the infant] will tyrannically enforce his demands if he can.... To the child, it now appears that his freedom consists in absolute control over his mother.... [If the mother cannot set limits and recognize the child's will], omnipotence continues, attributed either to the mother or the self; ... she is likely to appear not as a person but as an all-powerful figure, either omnipotently controlling or engulfingly weak.... The point here is not to dismiss fantasy, play, or the narcissism of Her or His Majesty, the baby, but to acknowledge the necessity of struggle.
—Benjamin, *The Bonds of Love* and *Like Subjects, Love Objects* (1988, 34; 1995, 38, 90)

Writing in reply to his sister Elli's questions concerning the education of children, Kafka sketched a picture of the parent-child relationship that is based entirely on royal power relations between a dominating tyrant and his slavish subjects. His depiction stresses the reversibility of these relations—either party can play the role of tyrant or slave. It also shows that narcissistic mirroring is at the root of this power struggle. Kafka gives the example of the father who finds in the child things that he loves in himself or for which he yearns. In this case, everything else about the child is a matter of indifference to him. He clings to the beloved element, ultimately lowering himself to the status of his slave (*er erniedrigt sich zu seinem Sklaven;* 1958, 345–46).

That Kafka would use a metaphor of kingship to express family relations is understandable, considering that he describes his own father as possessing many of the royal (and divine) traits we've discussed. In his famous "Letter to his Father," Kafka describes his father Hermann as a "tyrant" (1953, 169, 186) who "ruled the world" from his easy chair (169). To the child Franz, everything he shouted was a "command from heaven" (172). He was inscrutable (*rätselhaft;* 169, 177), inaccessible (*unangreifbar;* 177), and unaccountable (169, 173, 210). He possessed the mistrust that is an "emblem of the ruler" (196). Through his "regime," he made his son feel like a completely defenseless "slave" (172, 173), like "a nothing" (165, 167), like a worm (202), like hunted prey (182), like filth (212). In other words, his son was totally subjugated and humiliated. In addition to all this, Kafka (186–88) describes his father's way of dealing with his employees as that of a verbally abusive narcissistic tyrant with a lust for domination (*Herrschsucht*) and an annihilatory desire as strong as that of Homer's Achilleus, who wants no one else left alive when Troy is taken except for himself and his alter ego Patroclus (see section VII, below). At home, Hermann Kafka would revile all the "nations" (the Czechs, the Germans, and the Jews, that is, all the groups with whom he might have contact), so that "ultimately no one else was left except for himself" (169).

One might dismiss Kafka's remarks as products of a time and place where kingship was still the prevailing form of government in his patriarchal society.[31] Freud, who formulated his ideas in the same cultural milieu, went so far as to equate the characteristics of the father, the great man, and the leader. In fact, the father *is* the great man (*der grosse Mann*) in childhood. Their traits are identical, in particular their independence (*Selbstständigkeit*), autonomy (*Unabhängigkeit*), and their "divine unconcern [*göttliche Unbekümmertheit*] which may grow into ruthlessness." One must admire the great man–father, one may trust him, but "one cannot avoid being afraid of him too" (Freud 1939, 217). In an earlier work, Freud had described the leader in identical terms, with one significant addition: "the leader himself need love no one else, he may be of a masterful nature [*von Herrennatur sein*], absolutely narcissistic, but self-confident and independent [*aber selbstsicher und selbstständig*]" (1921, 138).

The leader is absolutely narcissistic, "*but* self-confident and independent." Interestingly, Strachey's translation omits the intriguing "but." Is Freud acknowledging the fact that narcissists are not really self-confident and independent and implying that leaders only appear to be? Is Freud in agreement with Tolstoy, who believes that "a king is the slave of history" (1957, 718) and that Napoleon's role as leader is to "*appear* to be in supreme control" (933; emphasis added).[32] That is how Adorno seems to understand Freud's statement: "in order to allow narcissistic identification, the leader *has to appear* himself as absolutely narcissistic" (1951, 289; emphasis added). And while Freud had said that the leader "*need* love no one else," Adorno asserts that "the leader can be loved *only* if he himself does not love" (289). This would seem to invalidate Freud's composite portrait of the father-leader. What becomes of the modern idea of the family if father and children cannot love one another reciprocally?

Of course, one might ask whether there is room for reciprocal love in Kafka's description of family life as a tug-of-war between tyranny and slavery. Jessica Benjamin uses language very similar to Kafka's when she describes parent-child relations, although she, like Freud, invokes the concept of narcissism in her analysis. Benjamin is also heavily influenced

---

[31] Alternatively, one might want to write them off as the impressions of an abused child with an overfertile imagination. On Kafka as an abused child, see especially A. Miller 1998, 240–97.

[32] For the role of "appearance" in a leader's exercise of power, see chs. 1 and 6, above.

by Hegel's chapter on master/slave (*Herr/Knecht*) relations in his *Phenomenologie*. The child who is going through a "rapproachment crisis" is "ready to be the master in Hegel's sense" (34). For the mother, this crisis involves a "blow to her own narcissism," because she cannot make a perfect world for her child. If she responds to this failure by "self-obliteration" and permissiveness, the child will experience her behavior as abandonment. In this case, the parent is no longer acting as an "other" who sets a boundary to the child's will. Only the child exists; the "other" is effaced. Alternatively, the parent may be unable to tolerate the child's independence, let alone surrender to it. When this occurs, the child will either feel that the price of freedom is aloneness or that freedom is not possible. If the child does not want to do without approval, she must give up her will (35–36; cf. 39, 70–71). When either the child or the parent exercises "omnipotent" control, "the state of omnipotence, with its absence of tension, gives birth to domination. . . . the underlying wish to interact with an equivalent center of desire, does not emerge" (73). In this "negative cycle of recognition," aloneness is only possible "by obliterating the intrusive other," and attunement is only possible by surrendering to the other (28).

Kafka, who also associates freedom with aloneness,[33] makes it quite clear that as a child he felt like an obliterated slave in his relationship with his father, the royal *Herr*. And the adult Kafka certainly felt as though he had been "obliterated" and abandoned by his tyrantlike father. According to Lowen (1997, 75–77), narcissistic parents typically use force and humiliation to control their children, in order to maintain their child's inflated view of them and, thereby, their inflated view of themselves. Using humiliation also allows such parents to punish the children who fail to provide the kind of flattering mirrors they need. The use of humiliation is appropriate for narcissistic parents, because it is a feeling with which they themselves are very familiar (see A. Miller 1981, 64–76). As Kohut puts it, "the ego may wallow in a state of humiliation when it fails to live up to its ideals" (1986, 68). Bursten (1986, 396) cites the craving personality and connects it to the helplessness of the baby and the humiliation of being weak. Finally, A. M. Cooper (1986, 140) notes that the narcissist derives satisfaction from mastery of his own humiliation.

---

[33] And, at times, both together with a combination of narcissism and hopelessness, as in this scene from *The Castle,* involving the novel's main character (and focalizer), the land surveyor K.: "It seemed to K. as if people had now broken off all connection with him, and as if he were now certainly freer than ever, . . . as if he had fought for this freedom for himself, as no other person could have, and no one could touch him or drive him away, or even speak to him; but—and this conviction was at least just as strong—as if at the same time there was nothing more senseless, nothing more desperate than this freedom, this waiting, this invulnerability" (1946, 157).

Now, Yahweh *does* use humiliation as a punishment tool; a number of passages in Isaiah and other books make that clear.[34] Is it for the same reasons? In a letter, Kafka once envisioned a situation where God would have called the "wrong" Abraham to sacrifice his son, in order to teach a lesson through humiliation:

> It is as if the best student were solemnly to receive a prize at the end of the year and in the expectant silence, the worst student, because of a mistake in hearing, comes forward from his dirty back bench and the whole class cracks up. And perhaps it is no mistake in hearing, his name was really spoken, the teacher's intention is that the reward of the best should at the same time be a punishment of the worst. (1958, 334)

One could argue that this is precisely what Yahweh did by calling "the worst student" Saul before the "best" student David in his royal zero-sum game. Kafka himself actually describes the humiliation of a Balaam-like character. In *The Trial,* he describes the lawyer Huld's grotesque humiliation of the merchant Block in terms that precisely echo Yahweh's treatment of Balaam in Num 22 (see Lasine 1985).

These retellings raise a troubling question: How often *is* Yahweh's alleged "humbling," disciplining, and chastising of his sons really a matter of humiliating them to support a habit of narcissism? Considering that narcissistic leaders from ancient kings to modern totalitarian dictators like Stalin have relished humiliating their adversaries,[35] the possibility that this technique would be in Yahweh's royal repertoire does not seem unlikely. Whom does Yahweh "obliterate," and with which of his children does he actually play the *slave* role? The first question is easy to answer; Job certainly felt obliterated and humiliated (e.g., Job 19:5–6 [חרפה[36]; 30:1–15),

---

[34] שפל: Isa 2:9, 11, 17; 5:15; 25:11; Job 40:11; Prov 29:23; ענה: Deut 8:2, 3, 16; 1 Kgs 11:39; כנע: Job 40:12; קלל: Job 40:4 (compare and contrast 3:1). On חרפה (Job 19:5), see n. 36 below.

[35] For ancient kings, see, e.g., the inscriptions of Aššurnaṣirpal II (which include the familiar motif of "the strong male, who treads upon the necks of his foes" [Grayson 1991, 221; cf. Josh 10:24]) and, in the Bible, Adoni-Bezek (Judg 1:6–7) and the Ammonite kings Nahash and Hanun (1 Sam 11:2 [see n. 36, below]; 2 Sam 10:4–5). On Stalin, see especially Fromm (1975, 317–22). Khruschev described Stalin's character as "capricious and despotic" (Conquest 1973, 117). Stalin's manner of humiliating his friends and subordinates illustrates both traits; see Conquest 1973, 117–22. On Yahweh's capriciousness, see section II, above.

[36] חרפה is used by Tamar (2 Sam 13:13) to describe the disgrace she anticipates suffering if Amnon rapes her; as it turns out, she is sexually abused and then further humiliated (13:14–19). The God-abandoned speaker of Ps 22:7 (MT) uses חרפה to convey the disgrace he suffers being a "worm and no man." חרפה is also

and there are many examples of humans obliterated by the thousands through the wrath of Yahweh the divine warrior-king (see below). At first glance, the second question seems outrageous and certainly more difficult. However, like the father in Luke's parable, we've found that Yahweh does seem to appreciate feisty child-mirrors like Moses and the "impatient" Job more than obedient "good little boys" like Esau (see Gen 27:1–5; 28:8–9), Saul, and Balaam, who so mechanically do what Yahweh wants, and are so eager to please Dad, that Dad gets as little satisfaction out of it as Hegel's *Herr* gets from his *Knecht*. With *disobedient* sons like David and Solomon, on the other hand, Yahweh's behavior approaches that of the permissive, "slavish" parent more than it does the tyrannical one (see chs. 5–6, above).

VI

> Sunk deep in the night. In the way one sometimes sinks one's head in order to reflect, to be that utterly sunk in the night. All around people are asleep. A little bit of playacting, an innocent self-deception, that they are sleeping in houses, in solid beds, under a solid roof, stretched out or curled up on mattresses, in sheets, under the covers; in reality they have encountered one another as they once did back then, and again later, in a desolate region, a camp in the open [*im Freien*], a countless number of people, an army, a nation [*Volk*], under cold sky on cold earth, thrown down where they had earlier stood, forehead pressed on an arm, face toward the ground, quietly breathing. And you are awake watching [*du wachst*], are one of the watchmen [*Wächter*], you find the next one by brandishing a piece of burning wood from the brushwood pile beside you. Why are you watching? Someone must remain wakeful [*einer muss wachen*], it is said. Someone must be there.
> —Kafka, "At Night" ("Nachts"; 1970, 309)

> Behold, he who watches over [שׁוֹמֵר] Israel
> will neither slumber nor sleep.
> . . .
> Unless Yahweh watches over [יִשְׁמָר] a city
> the watchman [שׁוֹמֵר] remains wakeful[37] [שָׁקַד] in vain.
> (Luther: *wacht der Wächter umsonst*)
> —Psalms 121:4; 127:1

Earlier, the biblicist in therapy mentioned that narcissistic patients often view the outside world as cold, empty, and hostile. One could explain this

---

employed by Nahash the Ammonite to describe the disgrace he intends to inflict on the men of Jabash-Gilead by gouging out all their right eyes (1 Sam 11:2).

[37] Both Hebrew שָׁקַד and German *wachen* can mean "be awake" and "watch, guard."

as the result of childhood feelings of being abandoned by the mother who does not set boundaries to the child's tyrannical will, as Benjamin puts it. At first glance, this makes His Majesty the Spoiled Baby akin to people who have suffered severe trauma. They too feel "utterly abandoned" and "utterly alone." Robbed of their "sense of basic trust," they feel "cast out of the human and divine systems of care and protection that sustain life" (Herman 1997, 52).[38] However, this might not be the only kind of upbringing that could result in such a vision of the external world and their own placement in it. Alice Miller cites child-rearing manuals that implore parents to instill Stoicism in their little children (1983, 29). In chapter 1, I noted that the Stoic ideal of self-sufficiency is based on an experience of the external world that is very similar to that described by the narcissistic patients described by psychoanalysts such as Kernberg and Kohut. When parents heed the advice of experts who tell them to make little Stoa out of their children, they are creating for their kids an unpredictable, hostile outside world in which they feel abandoned and isolated, rather than a parental refuge and protection from an objectively hostile outside. In this instance, Lucretius's shipwrecked infant, whom we discussed in chapter 1, is dumped on a "shore" that is actually located in the center of the family unit. Such children live in a state of "internal exile." When they view the outside world as cold and abusive, are they merely perceiving a projection of their abusive family situation? Or does marginalization and victimization within the family offer them an unwelcome window into the true bitterness of the world outside, a bitter truth that families may be designed to block out?

The first epigraph to this section was used in a different context at the beginning of this book, but it can help us to answer this last question. In chapter 1, I compared Kafka's unsleeping watchman with Liverani's wakeful and vigilant pharaoh and Lévi-Strauss's watchful anthropologist-hero. In the present context, Kafka's piece illustrates a different aspect of the complex network of ideas we have been tracing throughout the book. The narrator describes a world of play-acting, innocently self-deceived,

---

[38] While Herman does not mention biblical examples, her comments sound like a description of the traumatized Job. This is also true of her contention that survivors of trauma seek from witnesses "the willingness to share the guilty knowledge of what happens to people in extremity" (1997, 69). A major function of the prologue to Job is to make readers deal with their "guilty knowledge" of what has transpired in the invisible divine halls of government (see ch. 9, above). As readers of the Hebrew Bible as a whole, we must also ask how much "guilty knowledge" we are given about God's abused and abandoned children throughout the biblical corpus. What kind of witness or "bystander" *we* become depends upon how—and whether—we handle this guilty knowledge.

sleepers. What is their innocent illusion? That they are like Freud's chick, safe in its egg. They are curled up or stretched out on mattresses within their eggs, on solid beds, under the covers and under solid roofs. A solid world of enclosures, a determinate world with walls. What is the "reality," according to the narrator? That they are exposed in a desolate region in the open, thrown down on cold earth under a cold sky, face down. A world with no womblike warmth, no walls, no inside.

In this indeterminate world there also seems to be a temporal indeterminacy. It is a world with a history, albeit a vague one. This is not the first time that the people camped in this desolation have encountered one another in this way. When? Who? What nation? What army? We are left in the dark. At this point the narrator addresses a familiar "you," who is awake watching. A "you" within the world of the story, presumably, if not "you, the reader," who is awake reading his words (and mine). Which nocturnal world is the *Wächter* watching? Does he see a world of sleepers enclosed in their solid dwellings or a world of countless people exposed to the cold out in the open? Or both? Does this watchman know what the narrator knows? That those asleep in their houses are *really* lying out in the cold? The watchman is not alone. He locates the next one by brandishing burning brushwood. This is the only act of communication between people in the story. The narrator asks the watchman why he is watching. He does not ask him what he is watching *for*—or what threat he is watching against. The only answer seems to be a traditional one: "it is said" that someone must watch, someone must be there. A tradition requires history, but, as is usual with Kafka, it remains unclear whether the watchman—or anyone else—still knows the reason for the tradition, knows *why* someone must watch, knows *why* someone must be there, wherever "there" is.

One might well ask how this nebulous bedtime story might relate to the problems being discussed here. Sure, kings stay awake and watch over their sleeping followers; we already discussed Shakespeare's Henry V doing that in the first chapter. Is that all there is to it? Not quite. In the first chapter, and again in chapter 10, we explored an opposition between the insulated world of Freud's His Majesty the Baby and Lucretius's picture of the "shipwrecked" baby exposed on the shore. Kafka's narrator is setting up a similar opposition. The narrator sees human reality as quite Lucretian; the people aren't tossed out of the sea onto the shore, but they are thrown down on the cold earth. The humans whom Lucretius describes lack the natural protections and insulation of other animals. Unless they fabricate clothing and walls to protect themselves, like Kafka's sleepers, they are exposed to the elements. Freud's affectionate parents, who treat their child as His Majesty the Baby in order to prolong its "chick-in-the-egg" stage (and to resuscitate their own lost narcissism through the child's performance), are, in Kafka's words, engaging in play-acting and an innocent self-deception. But is it an "innocent" one? In this chapter and the last one, we have learned that in many cases it is not at all innocent.

What about the limiting case, when the parent is divine? Yahweh continually talks about being a nurturing parent who encloses and protects his human child like the little man in his eye. Is that an innocent self-deception? Are Yahweh's expectations for his human children realistic ones? And what about the expectations he sets up in his children? We are led to expect consistent, reliable, "good enough" parenting. Admittedly, we *are* warned that we will be punished when we disappoint our divine father's expectations. But what about Job, who fulfilled Dad's expectations better than anyone? Could there be a better example of the insulated chick in the egg than the Job whom Yahweh hedged in with prosperity? On the other hand, could there be a better example of Lucretius's exposed humans than Job out on the ashheap? Of course, in Kafka's terms Job goes from being a sleeper in a solid house to being thrown down on the cold earth after a solid house caved in on his children. In the book of Job, worlds collide: the world of safe sleepers and the world of cold refugees from who knows where. Job is forced into the role of the *Wächter,* once he becomes aware of the many other exposed, abused, and victimized people out there in the open. Job's friends, on the other hand, are still asleep and are bound and determined to pull Job back into their stage-play world of walls and platitudes. As self-deceptions go, their brand may be the least "innocent" of all.

The epigraphs from Psalms remind us that Yahweh too plays the role of unsleeping *Wächter,* for Israel at least. Kafka's story ends on the note that "someone must remain wakeful [*einer muss wachen*]"; Ps 127:1 declares that if Yahweh is not watching over a city, "the watchman remains wakeful [Luther: *wacht der Wächter*] in vain." Indeed. We have already discussed a number of occasions when, far from watching over his special child Israel, Yahweh abandons him. On the other hand, Yahweh the watchman can also be an oppressive force when he is on duty. After Job has been exposed, he asks God if he is the sea, or a sea monster, that God has set a guard (Luther: *Wache*) over him (7:12; cf. 7:20). In the next section, we will examine Third Isaiah's startling depiction of Yahweh as a bloody warrior challenged by a watchman as he comes from Edom (Isa 63:1–2), perhaps one of the *Wächter* whom King Yahweh had commissioned to act as "remembrancer," to prevent him from resting until he established Jerusalem (62:6–7). Earlier, Second Isaiah had imagined Yahweh as a king returning victoriously to Zion, with the *Wächter* singing for joy (52:7–10; see Mettinger 1986, 153–56). Given our examination of Yahweh's royal parenting style, however, we must ask whether his watching children should be quite so joyful when they see Dad coming home from work covered in the blood of the peoples he has just trampled.

Is this what his children expected when they longed for the return of Yahweh to Zion (40:10; cf. Sawyer 1993, 75)? It is from Edom that the warrior Yahweh returns, as he had done in the past (Judg 5:4). Edom—home of the elder son Esau and of the fall guy Doeg (see ch. 2, above). And look what happened to Job, that traditional Edomite king (LXX Job 42:17d; see Dhorme 1984, xvii–xx)! According to Job, warrior Yahweh has obliterated his psychic city, destroying his defenses breach after breach (see Job 16:14; 19:10–12). Now, while Yahweh set a watch on Job, Job himself has been on the watch for the appearance of the divine father who has abandoned him. When Yahweh finally comes, he does so in precisely the stormy[39] fashion that Job had feared (9:17; 38:1; 40:6); he certainly knows his old man. Nevertheless, Yahweh's verbal assault on his son is enough to flatten Job's *psychē* in a more subtle way. It reduces Job to acting like a humiliated and obedient child who is forced to admit once again that he has no knowledge or rights in relation to his omnipotent and abusive father.

VII

For as to her unwinged young ones the mother bird brings back
morsels, wherever she can find them, but as for herself it is suffering,
such was I, as I lay through all the many nights unsleeping,
such as I wore through the bloody days of the fighting,
striving with warriors for the sake of . . . [booty] women. . . .
Father Zeus, Athene and Apollo, if only
not one of all the Trojans could escape destruction, not one
of the Argives, but you [Patroclus] and I could emerge from the slaughter
so that we two alone could break Troy's hallowed coronal.
—Homer, *Iliad* 9.323–327; 16.97–100 (1951, 206–7, 332–33)

"What is this, father Amun?
Has a father ever neglected his son? . . .
I am among a host of strangers;
All countries are arrayed against me,
I am alone, by myself, no other with me!
My numerous troops have abandoned me. . . .
Behold, Amun gave me his strength. . . .
He caused every distant land to see
My victory through my strong arm. . . .
I attacked millions of foreigners, while I was alone [*iw.i wᶜ.kwi*]."

---

[39] Retaining the MT for 9:17, rather than revocalizing שַׂעֲרָה ("tempest/whirlwind") in order to produce the meaning "hair," even though the other appearances of this term for "tempest" in Job (38:1; 40:6) use the more common spelling סְעָרָה, not שְׂעָרָה. For commentators who favor revocalization here, see Clines (1989, 218).

[The Hittites said] "No deeds of man are these his doings,
They are of one who is unique [*wᶜ wᶜty*]. ...
I killed among them ... they ... lying flung down in their blood in one
     place."
—Ramesses II Qadesh inscriptions[40]

"Who is this who comes from Edom [אֱדוֹם]?"
"I who speak in righteousness, mighty to save, ..."
"Why is there red [אָדֹם] on your clothing,
and your garments like his who treads in the winepress?"
"I have trodden the trough of the winepress alone,
And from the peoples[41] there was no man with me,
And I trod them in my anger, ...
And their juice is spattered against my garments, ...
And I looked, and there was none to help, ...
Therefore my own arm brought salvation to me." ...
"Where are your jealous zeal and your might,
the moaning of your inner parts and your womblike[42] compassion? ...
For you are our father ... you, Yahweh, are our father."
—Isaiah 63:1–3, 5, 15–16

Three divine (or at least semidivine) warriors. Each fighting alone
against a mass of others, violently causing their victims' blood to flow. Each
feeling abandoned, disappointed, disgraced, or betrayed by others. Each
identified by their membership in a family, whether as son, father, or
mother. Each seemingly open to the charge of being a narcissist. And each
is a king. One is the returning warrior Yahweh, of whom we were just
speaking. The others are Homer's Achilleus and the Egyptian king
Ramesses II. These three figures are significantly similar in some ways and
even more significantly different in others. By examining them as family
members, kings, and narcissists, we will be better able to locate warrior
Yahweh's distinguishing traits in all these roles.

The epigraph from Homer's *Iliad* quotes the warrior Achilleus.
Achilleus has withdrawn from the battle against Troy because Agamemnon
has "degraded" or "disgraced" (ἀσύφηλον) him, treating him as though he

---

[40] Poem, lines 92–93, 111–114, 196–197, 266, 158–159, 291–294; Lichtheim 1976,
65–70; Morschauser 1985, 141, 146, 190; Gardiner 1960, 13. On *wᶜ wᶜty*, see
Gardiner (1960, 21). Morschauser (1985, 153) renders the phrase "a truly Unique
One." On the translation of line 93 (*is pȝ.n it ḥm ḥr sȝ.f*), see Morschauser (1985,
146) and Gardiner (1960, 19–20).

[41] 1QIsaᵃ: "from my people" (מֵעַמִּי).

[42] See Gruber (1992, 5–6) on Trible's assumption that ancient Hebrew speakers
"were fully conscious of the etymological relationship of the verb *riḥam* 'be compassionate' and the noun *reḥem* 'womb'" (5 n. 5).

were a dishonorable refugee (*Il.* 9.647–648; 16.59). In the first part of the epigraph, Achilleus is in the process of refusing the overtures of the embassy sent to persuade him to return to his army. The second part is taken from a later scene. Achilleus has agreed to the request made by his best friend and alter-ego Patroclus, namely, that Patroclus be allowed to dress in Achilleus's armor and go into the fighting, so that the Trojans will think it is Achilleus (16.40–43; cf. 11.795–800). Just as the enemy is supposed to imagine that it is Achilleus himself who is fighting, Achilleus himself imagines that all members of *both* armies—the Trojans and his own Argive army—might be destroyed, so that "we two alone," that is, he and his mirror image Patroclus, might "breach the strong battlements [κρήδεμνα] of Troy" (Nagler 1974, 53).[43] As Janko (1992, 329) puts it, "as far as Achilleus is concerned, the enemy, and the Greeks who allowed his humiliation, can both go to the devil."

Because Achilleus is imagining himself *and* his "buddy" fighting together, it might seem as though this situation is not really analogous to those of Ramesses II and Yahweh. The analogy would be weak even if Patroclus were nothing more than a representation of Achilleus's "humane side," as is sometimes suggested (e.g., Whitman 1965, 199–200). However, this is not what Patroclus signifies in Achilleus's fantasy. Achilleus is not dressing up Patroclus to act out Achilleus's own kinder, gentler side. Rather, he is making Patroclus into a projection of his own fierce martial self. And this is precisely how Patroclus behaves in battle. In effect, when Achilleus imagines "we two alone" in battle destroying everyone else who is left to be killed, he really has in mind two versions of himself.

When Achilleus likens himself to a bird in the first part of the epigraph, he is recalling his past fighting, not imagining a future scene of annihilating all others by himself. At first, it might seem odd to hear this iron-hearted warrior-king describing himself as a mother bird feeding her chicks.[44] It might seem even stranger when we realize that Jesus also

---

[43] As Nagler points out, because κρήδεμνα also denotes "veil" and sometimes signifies "chastity," Achilleus is envisioning a rape of the city (Nagler 1974, 53; cf. Pucci 1998, 17).

[44] The image of kings as parental birds caring for their young can also be found in Aeschylus's *Agamemnon:* "crying ... like eagles in pathless places [ἐκπατίοις], circling in pain for their children [παίδων], very high above their bed [λεχέων] ... their toilsome watch over their young ruined and in vain [ὀλέσαντες]" (49–54; cf. Homer, *Od.* 16.216–218). Here the image of parental grief is combined with the traditional Greek use of the eagle (or vulture) as an emblem of the king's loneliness and remoteness (e.g., Horapollo, *Hieroglyphica* 2.56; see Headlam 1902, 436; on the loneliness and isolation of kings and their burdensome task of watchful vigilance, see chs. 1 and 10, above). The precise meaning of this Aeschylean passage is debated; see Aeschylus 1962, 29–34; 1968, 71–73.

described himself as a mother bird wanting to nurture chicks (see below). The "morsels" in Achilleus's case, however, are "warrior food," that is, captured women, representative of the booty that Achilleus's prowess has made it possible for his people to gain. Far from increasing his similarity to Yahweh and Jesus as mothers, the image of Achilleus as a mother bringing back women for his men recalls a very different "maternal image," the one envisioned by Sisera's mother and her ladies in Deborah's song, with the soldiers dividing up "one womb, two wombs, for the head of every warrior" (Judg 5:30). Yet mother Achilleus does suffer for her children, fighting all day and enduring sleepless nights.[45] Achilleus later returns to the idea of himself as mother, just before Patroclus asks Achilleus for permission to impersonate him. Patroclus is weeping because of all the comrades who have been wounded or killed thanks to Achilleus's refusal to fight. Achilleus mocks him by likening him to "some poor little girl ... who runs after her mother and begs to be picked up and carried, and clings to her dress" (Homer, *Il.* 16.7–9; 1951, 330). One can only wonder what kind of a mother Achilleus would have really made.

This raises the question: What kind of mother did Achilleus have? After all, it is difficult *not* to apply the term *narcissistic* to his grandiose destructive fantasy, as has been recognized by Slater and MacCary.[46] If so, what role—if any—might his parents have played in the development of his apparent narcissism? In the *Iliad,* Achilleus's goddess-mother Thetis comforts her son (e.g., 1.360–363) and watches after him (as his grandfather Zeus puts it, "always his mother is near him night and day"; 24.72–73). She also acts as his informer, cluing him in on Zeus's intentions (17.408–409). Thetis herself refers repeatedly to how she had nurtured [θρέψασα] Achilleus (18.57, 437). In one of these passages, she tells the god Hephaistos the history of her marriage. Zeus has caused her "many grim sorrows" because "he gave me to a mortal, ... and I had to endure

---

[45] Achilleus does not say whether he stays awake in order to remain vigilant or to protect himself, like the kings we discussed in ch. 1.

[46] Slater (1968, 36): "perhaps the most dramatic demonstration of Homeric [*sic*] narcissism is Achilles' willingness to sacrifice his comrades to his own glory." MacCary (1982, 87) views Achilleus as a literary embodiment of Kernberg's portrait of the narcissist, especially in the "strange contradiction between apparent strength and actual dependence on others." Rather than focusing on the parents attempting to recover their lost narcissism through their child, MacCary works with the assumption that the narcissistic child is attempting to regain what Freud described as the "chick-in-the-egg" existence and that the mother serves primarily as the child's mirror. For MacCary, Thetis functions as Achilleus's "all-powerful" and "all-bountiful" mother "to whom he constantly turns for reassurance of his own existence." While she is constantly available, the father is aged, weak, and absent (22, 166).

mortal marriage though much against my will. And now he, broken by mournful old age, lies away in his halls.... For since he has given me a son to bear and raise up [τραφέμεν] ... I nurtured him (18.430–438; 1951, 386–87). According to her own testimony, then, Thetis was primarily responsible for raising her son, while the husband she hadn't wanted became increasingly decrepit and immobile.

This is indeed a marriage made in heaven—particularly for Philip Slater, considering his well-known theories concerning ancient Greek mothers and their sons. Slater contends that "stories that reflected an entirely narcissistic attitude of the mother toward the child appealed to the Greek mind (1968, 33). He describes ancient Greek women as imprisoned and isolated by "indifferent and largely absented" husbands. This caused some of the mother's sexual longing to be turned upon her son. Therefore, "along with, and in direct contradiction to, her need to belittle and discourage his masculine striving, she attempted to build him up into an idealized replacement of her husband" (31). Due to this "deeply narcissistic ambivalence," the mother "does not respond to the child as a separate person, but as both an expression of and a cure for her narcissistic wounds" (33). While Slater does cite the myth of Thetis and Achilleus as an example of "maternal ambition for the son" (31), he does not examine any of the versions of their story. And while Walcot pays more attention to information about Thetis in the *Iliad*, he concludes only that Thetis is "ambitious for her son" and "obviously ... over-protective" (1996, 119).

These commentators are suggesting a mother-son relationship in which Achilleus is in the position of His Majesty the Baby. Surprisingly, later tradition turns this picture totally upside down, so that Achilleus is more like one of Lucretius's shipwrecked infants than Freud's pampered child, even though Thetis is portrayed as being equally narcissistic in these seemingly contradictory examples of mothering. According to Apollodorus, Peleus had married Thetis after he seized her and managed to hold on in spite of her shape-shifting. After Thetis has a baby, she wishes to make it immortal. She secretly attempts to use fire to destroy the mortal element he had inherited from his father and anoints him with ambrosia during the day. Peleus sees the child writhing on the fire and cries out. Thetis, "thus prevented from accomplishing her purpose, abandoned [ἀπολείπω] her infant son and departed to the Nereids." Peleus then brings the child to Chiron, who feeds him on lion innards, wild swine, and the marrow of bears, and names him Achilles, "because he had not put his lips to the breast" (*Library* 3.13.5–6; 1956, 67–71; cf. 1997, 129). Apollonius Rhodius's version of the story makes Thetis even more abusive. She angrily snatches up the baby, throws him screaming to the ground, and angrily leaps into the sea, never to return again (*Argon.* 4.867–879; 1961, 352–55).

In these stories, when Thetis realizes that she will not be able to make her son her immortal mirror-image, she simply abandons him and returns to her immortal relatives. Far from being an example of maternal compassion and love, Thetis now recalls the mother described by Kernberg, whose cold hostile narcissistic use of the child sends him out seeking admiration. Although the verb for abandonment (ἀπολείπω) used by Apollodorus sometimes refers to wives deserting husbands rather than to exposing a child, in these stories it sounds more like Thetis is deserting her "little man," in Slater's sense, more than she is leaving Peleus. In the end, however, baby Achilleus is abandoned by *both* parents, for Peleus leaves him with Chiron after his wife leaves the family.

These are hardly Freud's "affectionate parents" trying to recover their lost narcissism through their baby. For that, we need a king like the Sumerian Šulgi, whom the goddess Ninsuna took as a child to her divine throne, fondled at her breast, and told of his specialness: "Shulgi, you sacred seed ... on my holy lap I raised you, ... you are the best that fell to my portion" (Jacobsen 1976, 158–59). Apollodorus's Achilleus is at the other end of the spectrum. He gets his name—his *identity*—from the fact that he *never* had the chance to put his lips to a maternal breast. Nevertheless, the most telling point is that in both the Homeric His Majesty the Baby version and the post-Homeric "Lucretian" versions, the future warrior-king is depicted as the son of a narcissistic mother, thereby highlighting once again the ambivalence and paradox characteristic of narcissism.[47]

At first glance, the speaker in the next epigraph seems to have done what Achilleus could only dream of doing: slaughtering a whole army totally by himself. This warrior is the Nineteenth Dynasty Egyptian king Ramesses II. The quotations are taken from his Qadesh inscriptions, which describe the crucial battle between the Egyptians and the Hittites during the fifth year of Ramesses' reign, roughly 1285 B.C.E. Ramesses had this event recorded in three different forms: a pictorial record, and the so-called "Bulletin" and "Poem," each of which differs from the others in the precise information it offers or does not offer. Ramesses had most or all of these records displayed on ten public buildings, in a total of five temples,[48] so that it was, in Goedicke's words, "without question the most

---

[47] In this light, we might reconsider Homer's image of Achilleus as Patroclus's "mother" and his companion as his "little girl." Taken literally, mother Achilleus is dressing up her child in her own clothes, so that she can go out to fight and die while impersonating the "parent." Although we are already well beyond the limits of reasonable speculation on the psychological dimensions of fiction, I cannot help but suggest the possibility that Achilleus may, in fantasy, be reenacting his experience of childhood by playing the role of his own mother, with Patroclus as his child-self.

[48] Karnak, Luxor, Abydos, the Ramesseum, and Abu Simbel; see Grimal 1992, 253.

extensively advertised event of ancient Near Eastern history" (1985, 111; cf. Grimal 1992, 253). Thus, the grand feats of military prowess described in our epigraph were disseminated in equally grand fashion. No wonder that Ramesses has been described as exhibiting a "craze for self-advertisement" and "self-glorification" (Gardiner 1961, 256, 261), "megalomania" (Lesko 1991, 111), and "excessive self-regard" (E. Otto, quoted in Goedicke 1985, 77–78 n. 3).

One big problem: the battle did *not* result in an Egyptian victory.[49] Moreover, Ramesses' inscriptions include the information that he personally had been fooled by false informers, spies for the Hittites posing as deserters. In other words, he was a victim of disinformation and deceit,[50] like Joshua when he was tricked by Gibeonite emissaries (Josh 9:3–27).[51] However, I doubt that Joshua followed Ramesses' lead, renting billboard space throughout Canaan broadcasting the fact that he too was unable to prevent others from manipulating the information he was fed. Moreover, the inscriptions make it clear that Ramesses made a serious tactical error in stringing out his army so much that a force of Hittite chariots could rout one of the four contingents. In addition, Ramesses highlights the fact that his troops have abandoned him and that even his personal deity, his "father" Amun, had been neglecting him (see Morschauser 1985, 143). Throughout our investigation, we have encountered ample evidence to show that the lapses acknowledged by Ramesses involve many of the most important duties of the king: skillful information management, military skill, ability to maintain the loyalty of his followers, and consistent support

---

[49] Nevertheless, scholars continue to make wildly divergent assessments of the outcome. For some (esp. specialists on the Hittites), there is "no question": it was "a decisive victory for the Hittites" and their king Muwatallis II (Gurney 1990, 28; cf. MacQueen 1986, 49, 57) and "a disaster for the Egyptians" (Pitard 1998, 63). Others contend that it was "probably a draw militarily" (Ahlström 1993, 273) or that we simply do not know whether either side was victorious (Drews 1993, 133). As for Ramesses's own account, it became "a kind of archetype of Egyptian victory over foreign countries" (Grimal 1992, 253). This variety of opinion is itself testimony to the indeterminacy created by the fact that the battle is reported in three different forms that include differing information and that collectively put together competing views of the king that would rarely be found together in any one text or series of drawings.

[50] Liverani (1990, 178) believes that the spies' deception was ineffective and the entire episode is "irrelevant." Modern critics have "partly been taken in by Ramesses's propagandistic account" of the Hittite ambush: "the Egyptians could not seriously believe to reach Aleppo without meeting any resistance! ... of course, each of the two armies knew where the other was."

[51] On King David's use of Hushai as a double agent to deceive Absalom, see ch. 4, above. For accounts of fake deserters and fugitives in ancient Greek sources, see, now, Russell (1999, 122–27, 221–23).

from his god. Thus, it would be hard to overstress the seriousness of these admissions; in this light, the fact that they are included in the inscriptions is even more surprising. Thus, for whatever reason, the inscriptions record the king's most humiliating moments as well as his most grandiose acts of valor and strength.

What might this reason be? Scholars have suggested many answers, some more plausible than others. Wilson (1958, 245–47) assumes that "the ecstatic celebration of [Ramesses'] superhuman courage and prowess" and the "blatant advertising" were designed to "drown out" and "cover up" the fact that Ramesses walked into a trap and "was a stupid and culpably inefficient general." While the "sheer physical weight of his insistence distorts a setback into a stunning triumph," it also shows that Ramesses "protests too much." This last phrase is reminiscent of all the scholars who said the same thing about the narrator of 2 Sam 3, who insists that David had no knowledge that Joab was going to assassinate Abner (see ch. 5, above). Wilson's approach avoids a simple question: Why didn't Ramesses simply omit all mention of the negative aspects of the event? When similar questions are asked about the Davidic Court History, the usual answer is that an apologetic was necessary because the events were too well known to the contemporary audience to be ignored. Goedicke (1985, 78), for one, doubts that the Qadesh inscriptions were "intended in an apologetic vein." Due to mass illiteracy, those who might have been influenced by an apology were "extremely limited in number." And by the time the campaign was advertised, the campaign of Year 8 has been successfully completed, so that "there would not have been any reason to remind anyone of a less glorious affair" (79–80 n. 9). Goedicke speculates that there must have been unrest in the military establishment, especially in the Theban region. This prompted Ramesses to advertise his severe punishment of his troops at Qadesh, particularly around Thebes, as a warning to other potentially disloyal followers (109–15).

While Goedicke's proposal is problematic and no other completely convincing hypothesis has been offered,[52] we can provide a fresh perspective by continuing with our comparison between Ramesses, Achilleus,

---

[52] Morschauser is very cautious about offering *any* conclusions. He believes that Ramesses' speeches, at best, offer a "slim clue" as to the identity of the "wide public" to which the inscriptions were directed (1985, 206 n. 578). Ramesses' allusions to disparaging talk and the references to Thebes and Amun "*might* suggest that there *may* have been *some* criticism of the king among *certain* Theban circles" (emphasis added). The tentativeness and vagueness of Morschauser's statement (and the fact that it is relegated to a footnote) are notable. He makes no mention of Goedicke's proposal, even though his study appears in the same volume as Goedicke's and Goedicke had made comments and suggestions to him as he was writing his paper (123 n. 1).

and Yahweh, focusing on those parts of the inscriptions that further the comparison. While Achilleus depends upon his divine mother Thetis for information and support, Ramesses depends on his "father" Amun. Morschauser (1985, 145) believes that the king is primarily concerned with the legal ramifications of the terms "father" (*it*) and "son" (*s*?), rather than their familial implications. The king's "exercise of this role as son of Amun ... provides a model of the ideal 'servant' ... [and] a prototype of loyalty" (197). By showing himself in this light, he "carefully stress[es] his subordinate role to Amun" and thereby "de-emphasizes" his own responsibility regarding the Qadesh campaign (145). To that extent, the text is apologetic, because it shifts responsibility from the king to his divine father. And because Ramesses had fulfilled his duties toward Amun, he had the right to expect the god to reciprocate.[53]

Morschauser's perspective reminds us that Ramesses is not simply trumpeting his military might—or his blunders—in the inscriptions. By showing himself to be the ideal servant of his god, he is showcasing his piety. Morschauser believes that Ramesses' self-presentation is "characteristic of an attitude of 'personal piety' during the Ramesside period" (145; cf. 197 n. 543). Baines agrees that this was a period of "public elite piety" and suggests that this "royal dramatization of pious relations, personal loss, suffering, and divine succor ... could have been intended in part to show that the king, like his subjects, must experience suffering" (1991, 192–93). From this point of view, one of the king's intentions with the inscriptions may have been "to channel through himself the increasing tendencies toward piety in the wider society" (193) and thereby take control of a cultural trend. In other words, it was in the king's political interest to show himself as being vulnerable and abandoned.

The way in which Ramesses describes the ingratitude of his troops is similar to his grievance with Amun. He goes over his "personal history" (Morschauser 1985, 175) with his troops (and possibly vassals[54]), showing

---

[53] Ramesses exhibits the same attitude when he puts himself in the role of father in another inscription: "I speak to you, all you men, you mighty ones of the earth, and all my soldiers: ... For you I do fine deeds, as would a father" (Morenz 1973, 41). For an example of a pharaoh being addressed as "father" by his vassal Rib-Hadda, see n. 64, below.

[54] The identity of these troops is debated. Morschauser believes that Ramesses' rebuke is primarily addressed to the chiefs (*wr.w*) of one of his four army divisions, the P're (1985, 170–71; on *wr.w*, also see Gardiner 1960, 33). He argues that these "chiefs" are Semitic Palestinian allies (*Ḫ?rw.w*) who formed an auxiliary unit within P're (172–75, 194, 197, 200). Their "lack of bravery" showed their "ingratitude and faithlessness"; it was "dangerously symptomatic of their overall lack of trust in Ramesses as their suzerain" (197). In contrast, Goedicke believes that Ramesses is engaging in a "wholesale condemnation of his troops," who displayed cowardice

how he had placed himself under obligation to them and treated them loyally (Lichtheim 1976, 67–68), so that he had the right to expect them to reciprocate, just as he had the right to expect Amun to do. While Morschauser emphasizes the legal dimension of these relationships, this does not exclude the personal, familial side, any more than the political use of the word *love* in the David and Solomon stories excludes the personal meanings of the word (see chs. 5 and 7, above). When Ramesses feels that he has been let down by his personal god and by the troops whom he personally treated so well, he *does* take it personally. As we saw when discussing ancient Near Eastern loyalty oaths and Saul's disloyal courtiers in chapters 2 and 3, this kind of betrayal hurts most when it comes from those you have reason to trust most, and in many cases, including Saul's son Jonathan and Yahweh's son/wife Israel, this means the family.

This picture of Ramesses as a victim of parental neglect and betrayal by his army is closer to Lucretius's image of the shipwrecked infant than it is to being an example of His Majesty the Baby, such as Šulgi on the goddess Ninsuna's lap. Of course, Ramesses also had occasion to show himself in the latter role as well. In the Abydos inscriptions, Ramesses claims that his father "magnified" him while he was a child: "he gave me the land while I was in the egg. . . . then when my father appeared in glory before the people, I being a babe in his lap, he said concerning me: 'Crown him as king that I may see his beauty while I am alive'" (Gardiner 1961, 257; cf. *ARE* 3:109). Whether or not Ramesses served as coregent with his father Seti I (as is still debated), nothing of Seti's parenting style is known apart from this example of royal propaganda.

Thus, if we are going to decide whether Ramesses is being portrayed in his inscriptions as a narcissist, as is Achilleus, we will have to do so without the benefit of the kind of information we heard from Achilleus's mother Thetis. Are the inscriptions primarily designed to show Ramesses' "specialness" and uniqueness? In a sense, yes. He is the model of a loyal leader of his troops and loyal son to his personal deity. When Amun

---

in battle (1985, 93–94, 98). As for the "high chiefs" who come to congratulate Ramesses after he has driven off the Hittites, they were probably not those who panicked in battle, even though Ramesses excoriates them (99). Goedicke then makes a radical proposal: when Ramesses goes into battle the next day, he is not fighting Hittites, but his own soldiers. His "massacre" of some of those who had exhibited cowardice "constitutes the earliest attested case" of *decimatio*, "i.e. the killing of every tenth solder as punishment for dastardliness in the face of the enemy" (100–2; cf. 114). While bold and rather ingenious, Goedicke's theory is incapable of proof and has not won wide support. See, e. g., Liverani's critiques of Goedicke's basic approach to the inscriptions and his conclusions (1990, 177 n. 21, 178–79 nn. 25–26).

responds to Ramesses' complaint that he has neglected his son by giving him the strength to attack "millions of foreigners" alone, the god is validating the king's loyalty and allowing his uniqueness to be visible to all, including the Hittites who refer to this unstoppable warrior as "one who is unique." However, we cannot go further. The fact that Ramesses does enact what for Achilleus is a narcissistic fantasy does not make Ramesses a narcissist.[55]

On the other hand, the complex portrayal of Ramesses at Qadesh *is* a perfect representation of royal paradox. The king possesses godlike power *and* all-too-human weakness and vulnerability. He is *both* a courageous warrior with superhuman prowess at killing myriads of enemy soldiers singlehandedly *and* an obtuse general gulled by enemy double agents, who left his army strung out and vulnerable to enemy ambush. He boasts of having power granted to him by the god Amun *and* accuses Amun of having ignored him and left him alone. He is *both* an effective leader *and* a king who accuses his soldiers of having abandoned him, leaving him all alone to face the surrounding foe. The fact that there are three different versions of the battle itself enhances the impression of the king's paradoxical nature and elusiveness. This is not to say that Ramesses perceived it to be in his interest to portray himself as an Egyptian analogue to the later European notion of the king's two bodies.[56] Nevertheless, the fact that he is depicted in this fashion could very well have served his interest, by allowing those who knew the inscriptions to "mediate" the seemingly contradictory aspects of their monarch.

Does Third Isaiah's warrior Yahweh also show himself to be a mass of royal contradictions? Does his account of Yahweh's lone victory resemble that of Achilleus, in terms of indicating the warrior's narcissism? One thing stands out immediately: *this* warrior king is not a son, as are the others.

---

[55] However, the uniqueness of the deadly warrior Ramesses does recall Canetti's portrait of the lone "survivor," a figure who displays several of the narcissistic traits we have discussed: "the essence of the situation is that he feels *unique*. He sees himself standing there alone and exults in it.... The dead lie helpless; he stands upright amongst them, and it is as though the battle had been fought in order for him to survive it.... It is a feeling of being chosen.... He is the favoured of the gods" (1981, 227–28). The heroic survivor feels more secure with each enemy killed; his "invulnerability armours him more and more completely" (229).

[56] Speaking about Egyptian kingship in general, Morenz (1973, 37–40) employs the phrase "the king's two bodies" to describe the "astonishingly consistent distinction [that] was drawn terminologically between the divine character of the royal office and the human nature of the person holding it" (37; on the terminology, see Silverman 1991, 67–68). However, Morenz does not refer to the doctrine of "the king's two bodies" in later European tradition (see ch. 1, above, for an account of that doctrine).

And while Yahweh can be a mother and a bird caring for chicks, as Achilleus describes himself, the last part of our epigraph shows that, in this instance, Yahweh is definitely a father and a king. In fact, Tomasino (1993, 85) points out that with the exception of Isa 45:9–11 the references to Yahweh as father in Isa 63–64 constitute the only uses of the father-son metaphor in all of Isaiah since 1:2, 4, where Yahweh refers to his sons as "a seed of evil-doers" (see above).[57] And while the root מלך for king does not appear in Isa 56–66, "several passages are saturated with royal divine imagery" (Brettler 1998, 106). Brettler's example is Yahweh's statement that "heaven is my throne" in 66:1; he does not mention[58] that when Yahweh had set watchmen on the walls of Jerusalem, he had done so in order for them to be his "remembrancers" (המזכרים), a term used for one of the king's officials (Isa 62:6; see, e.g., 2 Sam 8:16; 1 Kgs 4:3; 2 Kgs 18:18). And as we noted in the previous section, the royal figure for whom the watchmen are waiting in Isa 52:7–10 turns out to be the divine king and father of chapter 63, who returns in blood-splattered clothing.

In Achilleus's case, the narcissistic fantasy required his victory to be accomplished by himself, with only himself and his mirror Patroclus left alive at the end. Ramesses, on the other hand, wanted and expected help from his troops and vassals. Ramesses' attitude is shared by Yahweh in Isa 63. After announcing that "there was no man with me" when he conducted the slaughter alone, he adds, "I looked, and there was none to help." He wanted human help, but it wasn't there. This shocks and appals him (אשתומם; v. 5). Sawyer (1993, 78–79) renders the word "panic-stricken" and "horrified," and sees it as an indication of "emotional devastation." Rather than viewing Yahweh as horrified at "the enormity of the task to be done" (79), our investigation of loyalty in the royal setting suggests that King Yahweh, like Ramesses, is shocked at the monumental ingratitude of the people whose loyalty he had expected and earned. From whom, then, had he expected this help? As we've seen, Yahweh often feels that his special

---

[57] Some commentators seem unwilling to grant that Yahweh is presented as a "father" in anything other than one narrowly defined sense, although they do not agree on what that sense might be. For example, Westermann asserts that "man is not God's child, but his creature.... what makes him Israel's father is the fact that men may call upon him, and that he can turn in grace towards his chosen people (1969, 393). Similarly, Mettinger claims that "when God is denoted as 'father' in such passages as Jer 3:19 or 31:7–9, the metaphor does not seem to be oriented towards the issue of divine gender.... When God liberates his people from bondage and allots them their inheritances, he is acting like a father" (1988:206). In contrast, we have found that Yahweh's behavior as parent is complex and of critical importance in several senses.

[58] Either in the cited article or in his 1989 book *God Is King*.

children of Israel have let him down. In this case, he says that there was no one "from the peoples" with him. Some commentators think that Yahweh is referring to foreign nations (e.g., Whybray 1975, 253–54; cf. Gosse 1990, 109). Westermann (1969, 384) believes that the reference is to "a single entity, the eschatological 'foe'." Others look within Judah and seek a figure who might have helped in the way that Cyrus had earlier; Hanson (1995, 234) points at Sheshbazzar and Zerubbabel, even though there is no biblical evidence of massive disappointment with these governors. We should note that 1QIsa^a reads "from *my* people" in verse 3, not "from the peoples." While some scholars believe that this reading is "hardly appropriate" (Whybray 1975, 254), it cannot be excluded. Achtemeier (1982, 107) is wise to allow for both possibilities: "he had no helper … from foreign nations (cf. 'peoples,' v 3b) or from Judah to rely on."

This should lead us to the next question: Whose blood has he been shedding so copiously? In verse 6 he declares, "I trampled down peoples in my anger." "Peoples"—same word as in verse 3 (עמים). No one from "the peoples/his people" helped him, and it is "peoples" whom he trampled. This vagueness might seem puzzling if Yahweh hadn't already spent a lot of time in earlier books crushing both other nations *and* his own people. As mentioned above (n. 54), Goedicke believes that the slaughter Ramesses conducted on the second day of the fighting was against his own troops. While Goedicke's hypothesis lacks support, it brings to mind the Levite slaughter in Exod 32:25–29. Here Yahweh rewards the slaughterers because they disregarded their own fathers, mothers, and children in favor of him (Deut 33:9). Even assuming that all the blood on Yahweh's clothing is from his non-Israelite children, how confident can his special children be that Daddy won't bring his work home with him and turn on his own "people" again, when they fail to meet his expectations? In the worst-case scenario, Yahweh would annihilate *all* his people, from whatever nation, and be the only one left standing. In other words, only he is capable of enacting the half-divine Achilleus's fantasy. In fact, Isaiah envisions a situation with which Achilleus could readily identify: "the loftiness of the human being [הָאָדָם] will be bowed down, and the haughtiness [רוּם] of men shall be brought low [or: humiliated], and *Yahweh alone* will be exalted on that day" (2:17, emphasis added; cf. Isa 5:15–16).

Such images of rampant divine violence might seem contradictory to the accounts of Yahweh as a nurturing parent. In chapter 10, the biblicist patient found the dissonance between these two basic images to be very troubling. Yet even Achilleus has no problem combining fantasies of total destructiveness and portraits of himself as a mother. In fact, Achilleus's comparison of himself to a mother bird nurturing her wingless chicks invites us to examine one last example of divine parenting in the Bible, an example that takes us beyond the borders of the Hebrew Bible and then quickly returns us to it. These are the passages where Jesus describes himself as a mother bird who had often wanted (ἠθέλησα) to gather Jerusalem's "children" together as a bird gathers her brood under her wings, but they didn't want (οὐκ ἠθελήσατε) it. As a result, their "house" is abandoned and forlorn (Matt 23:37–39; Luke 13:34–35).

The image of Jesus as a mothering bird became a powerful emblem of his compassion in the writings of some medieval monks and nuns (see Bynum 1982, 110–35, 189–90). However, when the cited passages are looked at in their entirety, Jesus begins to resemble his father not merely in being a nurturing bird (Deut 32:11) but in being the kind of parent who abandons·or destroys children who don't act according to her wishes, who don't want what she wants. Jesus' statement that "your house is abandoned and desolate" is an allusion to Yahweh's words in Jeremiah: "I have abandoned [עזב] my house, ... given the beloved of my soul into the palm of her enemies.... She has raised her voice against me: that is why I hate her" (12:7–8; see Holladay 1986, 383). The children refused to comply with parental wishes, by abandoning (עזב) the covenant that codifies those wishes (Jer 22:5–9), so their nation is destroyed and rendered desolate. Because the child "raised her voice against" her parent, she becomes an object of hatred instead of the beloved child of the parent's soul.

Earlier, the biblicist patient pointed to such rapid switches from love to hate as an indicator of narcissism. When Yahweh believes that his ungrateful, disloyal children have abandoned him (e.g., Deut 31:16; Jer 1:16 [MT]), he does the same to them (e.g., Deut 31:17; Isa 54:7).[59] Deuteronomy, which concludes shortly after Moses' image of Yahweh as a bird spreading out its wings to protect its young (32:11), begins with Moses' statement that the Israelites accused God of bringing them out of Egypt because he hated them (1:27). Could there be some basis for the people's scandalous allegation? After all, Moses later tells Yahweh that the Egyptians would conclude *the very same thing:* that Yahweh hated the Israelites and therefore brought them out to put them to death in the wilderness (Deut 9:28).

Given Yahweh's ambivalence, it should not be surprising that Isa 63, which begins with the return of the bloody royal father, goes on to praise

---

[59] As noted above, when Apollodorus describes Thetis abandoning her son Achilleus, he used the verb ἀπολείπω, which is also used for wives deserting husbands. When the LXX describes husband Yahweh deserting wife Israel in Isa 54:5–7; 62:4, the verb is καταλείπω (translating עזב). However, in Isa 49:14–15, where Zion speaks as Yahweh's child, and in Isa 60:15, the verb is ἐγκαταλείπω (Hebrew also עזב), the same verb used in Ps 22:1 LXX/Matt 27:46, which are perhaps the most famous biblical examples of a child feeling abandoned by Yahweh as a father.

Yahweh for his womblike compassion and fidelity (63:7–9) and then immediately proceeds to recount that the children's "rebellion" turned him into an enemy who fought against them (v. 10). It is only then that the children speak, uttering the words that conclude our epigraph: "Where are your jealous zeal and your might, the moaning of your inner parts and your womblike compassion? ... for you are our father ... you, Yahweh, are our father" (vv. 15–16). The question put by Ramesses, "Has a father even neglected his son?" is answered by the Hebrew Bible with a resounding yes.[60]

VIII

The relationship of father to sons has the form of kingship, since the father's care is for his children. And that is why Homer calls Zeus "father," for paternal rule is the ideal of kingship.

. . .

It would be eccentric [ἄτοπον] for anyone to claim that he loved [φιλεῖν] Zeus.
—Aristotle, *Ethica nicomachea* 1160a25–28; *Magna moralia* 1208b31–32[61]

Zeus [is the "father of gods and men"] in that he wields the power associated with the headship of a family; they are not his children in the sense that he regards them with a father's love.... Zeus has no special partiality for men. Hesiod and other early writers don't reproach him for this.... they wouldn't have thought it reasonable to expect Zeus to have their interests at heart in preference to his own.
—Lloyd-Jones, *The Justice of Zeus* (1983, 32–33)

[In a monotheistic religion] the possibility of a *real* rival is beyond conception.... this deity is in no way limited by any external forces which could restrict the full expression of his own personality.... This god may then be conceived of as being motivated in his decisions by the highest ideals and never by the baser or selfish impulses which inhibit the realization of these ideals by man and polytheistic deities alike. He is therefore completely free to give his complete and unselfish attention to all that goes on in the universe. By the same token he is in a position ... to guarantee man's well-being if his will is complied with.
—Finkelstein, Bible and Babel (1958, 439)

---

[60] In the Mesopotamian context, Jacobsen (1976, 160) cites an Old Babylonian letter aimed at the writer's personal god: "To the god, my father, speak! ... Why have you neglected me (so)?"

[61] For texts and translations, see 1934, 492–95; 1962, 650; Dodds 1951, 35. While attributed to Aristotle, the *Magna moralia* is usually assumed to have been "compiled by a Peripatetic of the next generation" (Rackham in Aristotle 1934, xviii).

[In personal religion] the aspect that first strikes one is the self-abasement of the penitent.... [It] would be pointless were it not for an underlying conviction ... that God still cares deeply and personally about him.... The penitent becomes so centrally important in the universe that he can monopolize God's attention, ... and before this onslaught of unlimited ego, ... God ... dwindles to "the God of *my* salvation." As in love that is *only* need-love, the beloved ceases to be a person in his own right and is seen only as a means of gratifying desires in the lover, so here God is in danger of becoming a mere instrument for relieving personal needs in one individual.
—Jacobsen, *The Treasures of Darkness* (1976, 150)

Clearly, the speakers in Isa 63:15–16 expect their divine father to feel compassion and to act on those feelings by rescuing them. They are not basing their expectations on the *do ut des* principle that seems to govern Ramesses' relationship with Amun (Morschauser 1985, 175). But are such expectations reasonable when one is dealing with a father who is also a god? In the first epigraph, Aristotle assumes that fathers relate to their sons as kings do to their subjects (cf. *Eth. nic.* 1161a11–20), and that paternal rule includes caring (μέλει) for the children (*Eth. nic.* 1160b26). Yet, according to the *Magna moralia,* it would be eccentric for anyone to claim that he loved Zeus.[62] In the next epigraph, Lloyd-Jones adds that Zeus does not regard humans with a father's love; in fact, Zeus "has no special partiality for men." His role as father is based on the power that comes with heading a family, not on love or compassion. Zeus is not a *philos,* an intimate friend or affectionate relative of humans, in the way that a human father is related to his son or even in the way that a human king is related to his human subjects (Aristotle, *Pol.* 1259b11–17; on *philos,* see Vernant 1990b, 100–2 and D. Cohen 1991, 84–85). For these reasons, the early Greek writers "wouldn't have thought it reasonable to expect Zeus to have their interests at heart in preference to his own."

One might object that God Yahweh *does* have our interests at heart, precisely because his rule is disinterested. The epigraph from Finkelstein argues that such disinterestedness stems from the nature of monotheism. Because a single God has no rivals and nothing preventing him from "the full expression of his personality," he is not hampered by the "baser" and "selfish" impulses that characterize humans and polytheistic deities. His attention to the universe is "complete and unselfish." And he is also in a position to "guarantee man's well-being." In chapter 7 I discussed

---

[62] While Dodds (1951, 35) cites this statement as representative, Lloyd-Jones asserts that it actually represents only "a sophisticated city-dweller of the late fourth century." He believes that "ordinary people felt affection for the gods whose cults were familiar to them, and particularly for their own tutelary deities" (1983, 193).

Schopenhauer's notion that a king is given so much power and security that he can be a totally disinterested judge. Finkelstein's view of a monotheistic God is equally naive, especially because the God he has in mind is Yahweh. Finkelstein is not taking account of Yahweh the father, who expresses himself through his children, his special human mirrors. His children often inspire him with jealousy and hate—hardly "unselfish" emotions—and they can also evade his parental demands by following rival "no gods." Even Finkelstein's statement that Yahweh is in a position to guarantee the well-being of his children has a catch to it: "*if* his will is complied with" (emphasis added). That's a big "if," as we've already seen. When Yahweh's expectations for his children are not met, Yahweh's "full expression of his own personality" is hardly disinterested.

Our third epigraph provides another perspective on the roles of caring, love, and selfishness in relations between divine parents and their human children. Jacobsen's subject is the "polytheistic" gods of Mesopotamia, but here he is focusing on the metaphors that characterize personal religion.[63] While the human penitent might practice self-abasement before his personal god, he nevertheless assumes that the god "cares deeply and personally" about him. Jacobsen views the penitent's attitude as being hypocritical, selfish, and manipulative. The ostensibly humiliated penitent assumes that he is "so centrally important in the universe" that he monopolizes his god's attention. The god "dwindles" before "this onslaught of unlimited ego." Jacobsen likens this attitude to "need-love," where the beloved is merely an object used by the lover. His penitent sounds suspiciously like a narcissist. He is incapable of loving others; he merely uses and exploits them. He displays "unlimited ego." Versnel (1981, 17–21) invokes the concept of *Gebetsegoismus* ("prayer-egoism") when speaking of ancient Greek and Roman prayers; the term is an even more appropriate description of the attitude sketched by Jacobsen. The penitent seems to have followed the advice given by the slave to his master in the Babylonian "pessimistic dialogue": "You may teach a god to trot after you like a dog" (*ANET* 438, 601; cf. Bottero 1992, 251–67).

However, Jacobsen's penitent is not merely a narcissist but the narcissistic child of a divine *parent*. Jacobsen (1976, 158) notes that in Mesopotamia the image of the god as divine parent is unique to personal religion. While this image seems best suited to the relationship between human kings and the god, and most cases *do* involve royal sons, there are exceptions (158–60; cf. Saggs 1978, 170–72). We have already had occasion

---

[63] As noted by Muffs (1992, 63), a personal god "may be either (a) a god who is concerned with my person or (b) a god with a clearly articulated person(ality). Jacobsen clearly opts for the first meaning ... a personality-less 'personal' god." Muffs goes on to point out that Yahweh is a personal god in *both* senses.

to trace narcissistic behavior in children back to their parents—could that
be the case here as well? The penitent makes the god "dwindle," like the
parents described by Benjamin, who "obliterate" themselves rather than
counter their "tyrannical" child's will. The penitent assumes that he is "centrally important in the universe." In the case of Freud's His Majesty the
Baby, it was not the child but his affectionate parents who attempt to make
him "the centre and core of creation" (1914, 91; see ch. 1). They do so in
order to recover their lost narcissism through their child. As the biblicist
patient pointed out, "if a boy thinks himself a prince, it's because he was
raised in that belief" (Lowen 1997, 21). If human children have "unreason-
able" expectations of love and caring from their divine parent, we must ask
where they got those expectations from in the first place.

Jacobsen's penitents do not merely act like spoiled, egotistical princes;
they *also* feel humiliation and practice self-abasement, just like the abused
children we discussed earlier. The penitent believes that his god still cares
deeply for him even though he feels abased and humiliated.[64] Is it possible
that the divine parent cares *because* the child has abased himself, not in
spite of it? In other words, the parent-god can afford to be generous and
caring now that the child has surrendered his will (see above on Benjamin).
Admittedly, Jacobsen's penitent uses his god; Jacobsen does not describe
the god needing and using the abased penitent. In the Mesopotamian context, that involves a different metaphor, that of the master and slave.
Humans were created as slaves, to provide the gods with sustenance and
to support their temples. Of course, this too has a flip side: "if men had to
labour to support the gods, … the gods were dependent upon men. In the
last resort, man was lord of all" (Saggs 1978, 170). In the case of Yahweh,
however, we have found that the needs that humans serve are much more
"personal." Here the human children are needed as mirrors for the deity.

---

[64] Avruch (2000, 257 n. 21) finds the same combination of self-abasement and
belief in paternal caring in the very different context of the Amarna letters (EA 73;
82). Rib-Hadda writes to Pharaoh, referring to himself as "your son," and says "I
fall at the feet of my father" (EA 82:1–4; Moran 1992, 152). At the same time, he
warns Pharaoh that the "violence done to me is your responsibility, if you neglect
me" (EA 82:31–33). Avruch believes that Rib-Hadda is combining "kinship with
self-abasement"; he is "deeply hurt" because he "genuinely expects more paternal
succor from the lord to whom he has given such filial fealty." I would suggest that
Rib-Hadda's use of the "root metaphor" of the family should not be taken so literally. Rib-Hadda displays a complex personality in his many letters. While some
scholars compare his self-presentation to the figure of the "righteous sufferer" and
the loyal vassal victimized by his disloyal peers (see Moran 1985), others suggest
that he may simply be "a tiresome fellow" (James 2000, 121), a rather neurotic
complainer who pesters the king instead of following normal diplomatic procedures (e.g., R. Cohen 2000, 96; Na'aman 2000, 132–33).

Jacobsen (1976, 161) explains the "paradoxical character of personal religion"—its combination of "conspicuous humility" and inflated self-importance—in terms of relations among human parents and their children. Within human experience, "even the highest, greatest, and most terrifying personages in society have a mild, human, and approachable side in their relations to their children. Children, in their ... certainty of being loved, can overcome ... the terror and awe of power and status." This allows the parental metaphor of personal religion to serve as a "psychologically possible bridge" to the terrifying cosmic powers: "the possibility that even the cosmic powers could ... have an unfrightening, loving, ever-forgiving side toward their little human children, is psychologically conceivable." Jacobsen then points to human child development in order to contrast divine and human parenting.[65] He notes that "there is a stage in childhood when parents are all-powerful and divine to the child," but the child eventually adjusts to the "disturbing realization" that parents are after all human, with human limitations (1976, 161). Divine parents, on the other hand, must remain divine. Therefore, "experience could not but drive its cruel wedge ever more deeply between the dispassionate, terrifying, cosmic aspect of the divine that governs *the way things really are and really happen,* and the personal, concerned, angry, forgiving, loving aspect in which I, the individual, matter so profoundly" (161–62, emphasis added).

Jacobsen's sketch of parent-child relations begins with the assumption that even the "most terrifying" people have a mild side in their relations to their children and that children can be certain of being loved. Would that were the case! When he comes to divine parenting, Jacobsen associates the way things "really" happen with the terrifying aspect of the divine, not with the loving, caring aspect. He does not seem to consider the possibility that *human* parents can be just as terrifying, indifferent, or abusive to their children as any cosmos governed by a god. The developmental process alluded to by Jacobsen, during which the child adjusts to the "disturbing realization" that parents are limited humans and not gods, is itself fraught with danger when the child's parents are narcissistic. Admittedly, what Kohut calls the "idealized parent imago" is a normal and necessary part of child development (Kohut 1986, 64–66). If parents have provided their child with a strong sense of self, the child can tolerate "inevitable disillusion" (Kohut and Wolf 1986, 182) and the mother playing her role as "the one who disillusions the

---

[65] Like Jacobsen, Dodds appeals to aspects of child development in order to explain the paradoxical combination of traits attributed to a paternal god, in this case, Zeus *pater:* "It was natural to project onto the heavenly Father those curious mixed feelings about the human one which the child dared not acknowledge even to himself" (1951, 47).

infant" (Winnicott 1992, 145).[66] However, if narcissistic parents refuse to permit the child to gradually discover their shortcomings, the result will be traumatic, because "the ultimate confrontation with the parent's weakness cannot be avoided" (Kohut 1986, 66 n. 6). Jacobsen describes the normal process of development as being impossible when the parents are divine, because gods will never have human limitations and weaknesses. They *cannot* give up the illusion of omnipotence, because it's not an illusion with them. Their "reality," according to Jacobsen, *is* to be cosmically terrifying and unconcerned with humans. With divine parents the illusion is not omnipotence and perfection; the illusion is that they are personal, caring, and loving. In Jacobsen's cosmos, His Majesty the Baby may suddenly realize that he is Lucretius's shipwrecked sailor.[67]

Jacobsen's depiction of Mesopotamian divine parents does not coincide with the biblical portraits of Yahweh as parent. Yahweh never ceases to insist that he loves and cares for his special children. He continues to give his children the expectation that if they are obedient they will enjoy the security of the chick in the egg. Yet, at the same time, he manifests a number of "human" weaknesses and limitations, including narcissism. And like Kohut's narcissistic parents, he will not permit his children to gradually discover and acknowledge his less-than-ideal qualities.

Ironically, it is the children of abusive parents who may idealize their parents the most and for the longest time (see Herman 1997, 106, and above). In such cases, idealization functions as denial, allowing the abused child to endure in the abusive situation. Benjamin (1988, 136) believes that paternal idealizing generally functions to mask fear of the father's power.[68] She is influenced here by Freud's account of the Oedipal stage of development, in which the son's ambivalence toward the father is a result of having identified with him. This includes identifying with the father's desire for the mother, which turns the father into a very dangerous rival. As noted in section IV above, Freud describes the traits of the father, the "great man," and the leader in almost identical terms, terms that characterize the narcissist. His portrait of the father/great man included a passing reference to this figure's "divine unconcern" growing into "ruthlessness." One must admire him, but "one cannot avoid being afraid of him too" (1939, 217). Freud proceeds to note the presence of such a "mighty prototype of a

---

[66] Such "de-adaptation" is "the second part of the maternal function, the first being the giving of opportunity to the infant for an *experience of omnipotence.* Normally, the mother's adaptation leads on to graduated adaptive failure" (Winnicott 1992, 145; cf. 1958, 240; 1965, 87).

[67] For Jacobsen, this discordance is what leads to the problem of the so-called "righteous sufferer" (1976, 162).

[68] She adds that the fear is displaced onto the now-dangerous mother.

father" in Moses as well as in Moses' God, a "wrathful temper" (*Zorn-mütigkeit*) being among their shared paternal traits. Ruthlessness and wrathful temper, combined with total power over the child, would be enough to make any child feel ambivalent toward the father/god and attempt to deny the terrifying aspects of his personality by idealizing him.

IX

> He had no mother, ... he had no father who had begotten him, and who might have said: "This is I!" Building his own egg, ... the divine god ... came into being by himself.
> —Leiden Hymn to Amun, Stanza 100 (iv 9–11, *ANET* 368)

> Eternal One, Mighty One, Holy El, God autocrat
> ... unbegotten, self-perfected, self-devised,
> without mother, without father, ungenerated
> —*Apocalypse of Abraham* 17:8–10 (Rubinkiewicz 1983, 697)

> the Father of All, the Creator of All, has neither father nor mother nor beginning of days, or end of life (for this is agreed to by everyone).
> —Epiphanius, *Panarion* 55.9.11–12 (Horton 1976, 106)

One thing that King Yahweh's children never learn about their father is his family history. Genesis 1 and Second Isaiah are insistent about Yahweh being alone at the start of things. The God of Israel is "self-originate," "without mother, [and] without father," as the *Apocalypse of Abraham* (first to second century C.E.) puts it. Around three hundred years later, Epiphanius assumes that "this is agreed to by everyone."[69] Nor does the God of Israel have a wife, as does the Babylonian Anu[70] (unless we believe the tabloids from Kuntillet ʿAjrûd[71]). Like the depictions of Yahweh as a lone father who uses his children as mirrors and as a king who commissions portraits of himself as a glorious lone warrior, this aspect of Yahweh's aloneness suggests the narcissistic desire to make the self absolute and omnipotent.

---

[69] Epiphanius is refuting the heretical view that the priest Melchizedek is described in Heb 7:3 in terms that fit the "Father of All." According to this verse, Melchizedek is "without father, without mother, without genealogy, having neither beginning of days nor end of life." See Horton 1976, 105–13; Attridge 1989, 190–95.

[70] Anu's wife is named Antu[m]; see, e.g., *Gilgamesh* 6.82 and the ritual text translated in *ANET* 338–39. Saggs (1968, 329) refers to Anu as "often a rather shadowy figure" and to Antum as his "even more shadowy consort."

[71] On the controversy concerning the meaning and significance of the inscription "to the Yahweh of Samaria and his asherah," and its relationship to the drawings that accompany it, see, e.g., McCarter 1987; and Dever 1990, 144–49.

Jessica Benjamin gives this desire a voice: "I want to affect you, but I want nothing you do to affect me; I am who I am" (1995, 36; 1988, 32). According to Benjamin, narcissistic omnipotence is exhibited by the insistence on being one ("everyone is identical to me") and all alone ("there's nothing outside of me that I don't control"; 1995, 36). The claim that there is nothing outside beyond my control is typical of Egyptian royal ideology (e.g., Liverani 1990, 59–65). But it is also typical of Yahweh. In fact, Benjamin's entire description sounds like a paraphrase of Exodus, Deuteronomy, and Second Isaiah: "I am who I am" (Exod 3:14); "Yahweh our God is one Yahweh" (Deut 6:4);[72] "there is none else, beside me [זולתי] there is no God" (Isa 45:5; cf. Deut 4:35, 39);[73] "I, I [אנכי אנכי] am Yahweh, and besides me [מבלעדי] there is no savior" (Isa 43:11); "Yahweh, the king of Israel … I am the first, and I am the last" (Isa 44:6); "I make peace and create evil, I, Yahweh do all these things" (Isa 45:7).

As the epigraph from the Leiden papyrus illustrates, Yahweh is not the only deity in the ancient Near East who lacks parents. Like Yahweh, the Amun of Ramesses II[74] was not forced to become a mirror for a narcissistic divine father who looked at him and declared "This is I!"[75] Unlike Amun, however, Yahweh offers no *alternate* explanation of his origin, not even to Moses, the human mirror with whom he is on the most intimate terms. Nothing about building his own egg. Nothing, in fact, about his coming into being in *any* fashion.[76] All we get is "I am that I am" (Exod 3:14).

---

[72] Scholars like Driver (1902, 90) and Weinfeld (1991, 337) believe that when Moses declares "Yahweh our God is one Yahweh" in Deut 6:4, "one" (אחד) implies not only unity but aloneness and uniqueness.

[73] Also Isa 45:6, 18, 21, 22; 46:9.

[74] The Leiden papyrus I 350 dates from the reign of Ramesses II (*ANET* 8). On the growth of Amun-Re into a powerful universal deity and "King of the Gods" during the Eighteenth and Nineteenth Dynasties, see, e.g., Lesko 1991, 104–6; Wilson 1958, 170–71. On Amun/Amun-Re as the "vizier of the poor" and champion of the distressed, see Lichtheim 1976, 111; *ANET* 380; Morenz 1973, 104–6. At his magnificent (if not narcissistically grandiose) temple at Abu Simbel, Ramesses II put a statue of himself seated to the left of Amun-Re in the inner sanctuary. In light of our discussions of Freud's views on narcissism, kings (including himself), and "the great man," it is worth noting that Freud had a Twenty-Sixth Dynasty statue of Amun-Re on his desk (now in the Freud Museum, London) and a large picture of the Abu Simbel temple on the wall of the study in which the desk was located (Gay 1989, 171).

[75] Assmann believes that this declaration means that "the father recognizes himself in his child and knows the child as his child" (1998, 263 n. 88; cf. Erman 1966, 299), in other words, exactly the opposite of what occurred when Zurvan looked at Ahriman and declared, in effect, "This is *not* I!!" (see above).

[76] In other words, Yahweh has neither "parentage" (Whybray 1975, 37) *nor* "nativity" (Levenson 1988, 5).

And while Amun-Re is called "King of the Gods" (e.g., *ANET* 25, 376), King Yahweh's brand of divine royalty and self-sufficiency denies even the existence of gods over whom he might rule.

At the same time, we have found that narcissists are *never* self-sufficient, no matter how much they might claim to be. Whenever we viewed Yahweh as a narcissist, it highlighted his need for others, even when he trumpets that he alone is God and there is no other. And it is precisely in his behavior as father that Yahweh most clearly displays this neediness—a kind of need that is hardly what Heschel had in mind when he spoke of "God's need of man."[77] Yahweh is not a narcissist because he is absolute and self-sufficient; he is a narcissist precisely because he is *not* self-sufficient. Narcissists cannot declare "I am that I am" in good faith. Yahweh, who possesses "personality," cannot evade his "being for others"—or *mauvaise foi*—any more than Sartre's incomplete humans can. In fact, for Sartre human reality is expressed in the opposite formula: "I am *not* what I am" (1943, 92; emphasis added).[78]

The quintessential narcissistic fantasy does not feature the uniqueness or aloneness of a king, not even a king who alone "rules over the gods," as one Ugaritic text puts it (Weinfeld 1991, 338; cf. Ps 82)—unless that king is also a father. As we discussed in chapter 1, kings inevitably become enmeshed in a net of interdependence. Only in the closed world of the patriarchal *family* is this fantasy potentially realizable.[79] This kind of family is a reduced world where the ultimate authority of one person is imaginable. The world of the Hebrew Bible is such a family world, totally controlled by one father-king. At the same time, the text undermines this fantasy from start to finish. Genesis is particularly adept at exposing the

---

[77] See the biblicist patient's remarks on Heschel in ch. 10, above. Heschel (1951, 241) believes that "God is in need of man for the attainment of His ends, … because [God] freely made him a partner in His enterprise." He quotes R. Simeon ben Lakish's view (*Gen. Rab.* 30) that God needs our honor (243). If we understand God's "enterprise" as involving his use of us to mirror his "honor," Heschel's account is compatible with that given here.

[78] Humans can never be self-identical because human being has the "double property … of being a *facticity* and a *transcendence*" (1943, 91). On these two dimensions, and the ways in which bad faith (*mauvaise foi*) attempts to avoid acknowledging and synthesizing them, see above.

[79] Levenson (1993, 37) contends that the God of Israel is "in no way enmeshed in familial relationships…. he has no wife and no children, but exercises his universal dominion in solitary majesty." While I agree that Yahweh is generally depicted as exercising his power in "solitary majesty," without being enmeshed in the kind of interdependence that characterizes the relationship between kings and their courtiers, his relationship with his *human* children *does* involve a complex network of emotional, and narcissistic, interdependencies.

folly of the "father is in control"/"father knows best" fantasy. It's as though the family history is not being told solely from Dad's point of view, but from Mom's, the kids', the servants', and the ethnic neighbors' who live on the wrong side of the tracks or on Father's favorite fishing spot.

Nevertheless, biblical monotheism could still be considered the supreme expression of divine narcissism in the sense that the divine head of the family has no family background himself. Yahweh remains self-sufficient in the sense that he owes nothing to incorporated images of his parents, no genetic debt to his forebears, no siblings in comparison with whom he might look bad. (And he's impervious to psychoanalytical probing into his past, because we're given no information about his childhood—*if* he had one. There's no "Infancy Gospel of Thomas" for Yahweh.)

Yet, even though he claims to be the only God who exists or ever existed, Yahweh is contrasted with a divine Other, the *Elohim* who are shown stripped of power and humiliated. And even when their existence is denied, the gods of the nations and their idols remain Yahweh's rivals. In spite of all the gifts that Yahweh gives to his special human children, they still run away from home in order to cling to these foster parent/false gods—these pieces of wood and stone whom they call "my father" (Jer 2:27)—even though these unreal parental mirrors[80] are powerless to nurture and protect them. For that reason alone, Yahweh can never rest supremely secure, indifferent to his children and his unreal rivals.

In terms of narcissistic divine parenting, it would seem that monotheism and polytheism have entirely contrasting "family values." According to Jan Assmann, in ancient polytheisms "nobody contested the reality of foreign gods and the legitimacy of foreign forms of worship" (1998, 2–3; cf. 44–47), an attitude that is diametrically opposed to that found in Mosaic "counter-religion."[81] Not even the "oneness/singleness/uniqueness" of Amun-Re excludes the existence of other gods (193–94). Whatever one thinks of Assmann's wide-sweeping formulations, our discussion of the use of royal and parental metaphors in biblical and ancient Near Eastern texts reveals a similarly stark contrast. Only Yahweh is a parent to his

---

[80] If humans are made in Yahweh's image, when they worship idols they start to mirror the detestable objects of their affection (Hos 9:10; Ps 115:8; cf. Jer 2:5; 2 Kgs 17:15).

[81] Assmann contends that "we are still far from a full understanding of polytheism" (1998, 217), because Judaism and Christianity have replaced any authentic traditions of polytheism with "a polemical counter-construction" of paganism and abomination (216–17; cf. 2–4). He believes that ancient polytheisms "functioned as a means of intercultural translatability," producing "a coherent ecumene of interconnected nations." Mosaic religion, on the other hand, repudiated everything outside itself as paganism and, in so doing, "functioned as a means of intercultural estrangement" (3).

human children in the sense that he needs them as his narcissistic mirrors. One might object that it is better to be created in the image of a single, royal divine father than to be created in order to bear the burdens of a royal court[82] comprised of many gods, as in Mesopotamian tradition.[83] Perhaps, but polytheism also removes a burden—the burden of being used as human mirrors for the one and only biblical God, the jealous and demanding father and king.[84] And since we can't choose our parents, we who are Yahweh's children must bear this burden—or catch the first boat bound for Tarshish.

---

[82] As Bottero (1992, 224) puts it, here "human life has no other sense, raison d'être, or goal than service to the gods—just as the subjects in a state have no other goal than service to the ruler and his household."

[83] E.g., *Atrahasis* 1.189–243 OB; *Enuma Elish* 6.1–36. See Foster 1993, 165–66, 384–85.

[84] In his essay, "In Praise of Polytheism," philosopher Odo Marquard offers a very different contrast between monotheism and polytheism, expressed through political, but not family, metaphors. He contends that monotheism dominates individuals by negating other gods and "liquidating" their "many stories/histories" (*Geschichten*) in favor of the only story that is needful: the *Heilsgeschichte* (1979, 48; cf. 46). In contrast to this "monopolistic myth" (47), "the great humane principle of polytheism" effects a "separation of powers in the absolute," and offers a "plurality of *Geschichten*" (50; cf. 46, 53–54). As long as many gods were powerful, the individual had room to maneuver, because he could always be excused in relation to each god through the service he owed another and thus be moderately inaccessible (54–55). Monotheism, on the other hand, demands total service and obedience to the sole God. Here one can only establish individuality through inwardness, countering omnipotence with "ineffability" (55). In chs. 1 and 6, we discovered that inaccessibility and silence are both ways in which kings also exercise power. In the present context, however, the key point is that Marquard's contrast between biblical monotheism and polytheism is weakened by the fact that it does not take into account the biblical God's individual personality and his complex familial ties with his human children/courtiers/servants.

WORKS CITED

Achtemeier, Elizabeth Rice. 1982. *The Community and Message of Isaiah 56–66: A Theological Commentary*. Minneapolis: Augsburg.

Ackerman, James S. 1982. Review of David M. Gunn, *The Fate of King Saul: An Interpretation of a Biblical Story. JBL* 101:438–39.

———. 1990. Knowing Good and Evil: A Literary Analysis of the Court History in 2 Samuel 9–20 and 1 Kings 1–2. *JBL* 109:41–60.

Ackroyd, Peter R. 1991. *The Chronicler in His Age*. JSOTSup 101. Sheffield: Sheffield Academic Press.

Adorno, Theodore W. 1951. Freudian Theory and the Pattern of Fascist Propaganda. Pages 279–300 in vol. 3 of *Psychoanalysis and the Social Sciences*. Edited by Géza Róheim. New York: International Universities Press.

Aeschines. *Speeches*. 1948. Translated by Charles D. Adams. LCL. Cambridge, Mass.: Harvard University Press.

Aeschylus. 1962. *Agamemnon*. Vol. 2. Edited by Eduard Fraenkel. Oxford: Clarendon.

———. 1968. *Agamemnon*. Edited by John Dewar Denniston and Denys Page. Oxford: Clarendon.

Ahlström, Gösta W. 1993. *The History of Ancient Palestine*. Edited by Diana Edelman. Minneapolis: Fortress.

Allison, Dale C., Jr. 1993. *The New Moses: A Matthean Typology*. Minneapolis: Fortress.

Alter, Jonathan. 1994. Black and White and Read All Over. *Newsweek* 1 August, 19–21.

Alter, Robert. 1981. *The Art of Biblical Narrative*. New York: Basic Books.

Altmann, Alexander. 1969. *Studies in Religious Philosophy and Mysticism.* New York: Cornell University Press.

Apollodorus. 1956. *Library.* Vol. 2. Translated by Sir James George Frazer. LCL. Cambridge, Mass.: Harvard University Press.

———. 1997. *The Library of Greek Mythology.* Translated by Robin Hard. Oxford: Oxford University Press.

Apollonius Rhodius. 1961. *The Argonautica.* Translated by R. C. Seaton. LCL. Cambridge, Mass.: Harvard University Press.

Apuleius. 1962. *The Golden Ass.* Translated by Jack Lindsay. Bloomington: Indiana University Press.

Archer, John Michael. 1993. *Sovereignty and Intelligence: Spying and Court Culture in the English Renaissance.* Stanford: Stanford University Press.

Arendt, Hannah. 1958. *The Human Condition.* Chicago: University of Chicago Press.

Ariès, Philippe. 1979. The Family and the City in the Old World and the New. Pages 29–41 in *Changing Images of the Family.* Edited by Virginia Tufte and Barbara Myerhoff. New Haven, Conn.: Yale University Press.

———. 1989. Introduction. Pages 1–11 in *Passions of the Renaissance.* Vol. 3 of *A History of Private Life.* Edited by Roger Chartier. Translated by Arthur Goldhammer. Cambridge, Mass.: Harvard University Press.

Aristotle. 1934. *The Nicomachean Ethics.* Translated by H. Rackham. LCL. Cambridge, Mass.: Harvard University Press.

———. 1955. *On Sophistical Refutations, On Coming-to-Be and Passing-Away, On the Cosmos.* Translated by E. S. Forster and D. J. Furley. LCL. Cambridge, Mass.: Harvard University Press.

———. 1959. *Politics.* Translated by H. Rackham. LCL. Cambridge, Mass.: Harvard University Press.

———. 1962. *Oeconomica and Magna Moralia.* Translated by G. Cyril Armstrong. LCL. Cambridge, Mass.: Harvard University Press.

———. 1986. *Aristotle's Politics.* Translated by Hippocrates G. Apostle and L. P. Gerson, with commentaries and glossary. Grinnell, Iowa: Peripatetic.

Assmann, Jan. 1998. *Moses the Egyptian: The Memory of Egypt in Western Monotheism*. Cambridge, Mass.: Harvard University Press.

Attridge, Harold W. 1989. *The Epistle to the Hebrews*. Hermeneia. Philadelphia: Fortress Press.

Avruch, Kevin. 2000. Reciprocity, Equality, and Status-Anxiety in the Amarna Letters. Pages 154–64, 256–58 in *Amarna Diplomacy: The Beginnings of International Relations*. Edited by Raymond Cohen and Raymond Westbrook. Baltimore: Johns Hopkins University Press.

Axskjöld, Carl-Johan. 1998. *Aram As the Enemy Friend: The Ideological Role of Aram in the Composition of Genesis–2 Kings*. ConBOT 45. Stockholm: Almqvist & Wiksell.

Axton, Marie. 1977. *The Queen's Two Bodies: Drama and the Elizabethan Succession*. London: Royal Historical Society.

Ayim, Maryann. 1994. Knowledge through the Grapevine: Gossip As Inquiry. Pages 85–99 in *Good Gossip*. Edited by Robert F. Goodman and Aaron Ben-Ze'ev. Lawrence: University Press of Kansas.

Bacon, Francis. 1857. New Atlantis. Pages 129–66 in vol. 3 of *The Works of Francis Bacon*. Edited by James Spedding, Robert Leslie Ellis, and Douglas Denon Heath. London: Longman.

———. 1858a. Of the Wisdom of the Ancients. Pages 701–64 in vol. 4 of *The Works of Francis Bacon*. Edited by James Spedding, Robert Leslie Ellis, and Douglas Denon Heath. London: Longman.

———. 1858b. Of Wisdom for a Man's Self. Pages 431–33 in vol. 6 of *The Works of Francis Bacon*. Edited by James Spedding, Robert Leslie Ellis, and Douglas Denon Heath. London: Longman.

———. 1858c. Of Empire. Pages 419–23 in vol. 6 of *The Works of Francis Bacon*. Edited by James Spedding, Robert Leslie Ellis, and Douglas Denon Heath. London: Longman.

———. 1858d. The Great Instauration. Pages 7–33 in vol. 6 of *The Works of Francis Bacon*. Edited by James Spedding, Robert Leslie Ellis, and Douglas Denon Heath. London: Longman.

Bailey, Randall C. 1990. *David in Love and War: The Pursuit of Power in 2 Samuel 10–12*. JSOTSup 75. Sheffield: JSOT Press.

Baines, John. 1991. Society, Morality, and Religious Practice. Pages 123–200 in *Religion in Ancient Egypt: Gods, Myths, and Personal Practice*. Edited by Byron E. Shafer. Ithaca, N.Y.: Cornell University Press.

Baker, Keith Michael. 1994. A Foucauldian French Revolution? Pages 187–205 in *Foucault and the Writing of History*. Edited by Jan Goldstein. Oxford: Blackwell.

Balentine, Samuel E. 1983. *The Hidden God: The Hiding of the Face of God in the Old Testament*. Oxford: Oxford University Press.

Balzac, Honoré de. 1972. *A Murky Business (Une Ténébreuse Affaire)*. Translated by Herbert J. Hunt. London: Penguin.

Baranger, Willy. 1991. Narcissism in Freud. Pages 108–30 in *Freud's "On Narcissism: An Introduction."* Edited by Joseph Sandler, Ethel Spector Person, and Peter Fonagy. New Haven, Conn.: Yale University Press.

Bartlett, John R. 1995. *You Shall Not Abhor an Edomite For He Is Your Brother: Edom and Seir in History and Tradition*. Archaeology and Biblical Studies 3. Edited by Diana Vikander Edelman. Atlanta: Scholars Press.

Baudelaire, Charles. 1961. *Œuvres Complètes*. Bibliothèque de la Pléiade. Edited by Y.-G. Dantec and Claude Pichois. Paris: Gallimard.

————. 1972. *Selected Writings on Art and Artists*. Edited and translated by P. E. Charvet. Baltimore: Penguin.

Baudrillard, Jean. 1993. *Symbolic Exchange and Death*. Translated by Iain Hamilton Grant. London: Sage.

Baum, L. Frank. 1958. *The Wizard of Oz*. Apple Classics. New York: Scholastic Books.

Bechtel, Lyn M. 1991. Shame As a Sanction of Social Control in Biblical Israel: Judicial, Political, and Social Shaming. *JSOT* 49:47–76.

Beck, Aaron T., A. John Rush, Brian F. Shaw, and Gary Emery. 1979. *Cognitive Therapy of Depression*. The Guilford Clinical Psychology and Psychotherapy Series. New York: Guilford.

Beentjes, P. C. 1984. "The Countries Marvelled at You": King Solomon in Ben Sira 47:12–22. *Bijdr* 45:6–14.

Benardete, Seth. 1964. Sophocles' *Oedipus Tyrannus*. Pages 1–15 in *Ancients and Moderns: Essays on the Tradition of Political Philosophy in Honor of Leo Strauss*. Edited by Joseph Cropsey. New York: Basic Books.

Bendix, Reinhard. 1978. *Kings or People: Power and the Mandate to Rule*. Berkeley and Los Angeles: University of California Press.

Benjamin, Jessica. 1988. *The Bonds of Love: Psychoanalysis, Feminism, and the Problem of Domination*. New York: Pantheon.

———. 1995. *Like Subjects, Love Objects: Essays on Recognition and Sexual Difference*. New York: Yale University Press.

Bennett, Michael. 1999. *Richard II and the Revolution of 1399*. Stroud: Sutton.

Berger, Peter L., and Thomas Luckmann. 1967. *The Social Construction of Reality: A Treatise in the Sociology of Knowledge*. New York: Anchor.

Bergmann, Jörg R. 1993. *Discreet Indiscretions: The Social Organization of Gossip*. Translated by John Bednarz Jr. New York: Aldine de Gruyter.

Berlinerblau, J. 1993. The "Popular Religion" Paradigm in Old Testament Research: A Sociological Critique. *JSOT* 60:3–26.

Berman, Jeffrey. 1985. *The Talking Cure: Literary Representations of Psychoanalysis*. New York: New York University Press.

Bettelheim, Bruno. 1967. *The Empty Fortress: Infantile Autism and the Birth of the Self*. New York: Free Press.

Black, Henry Campbell. 1979. *Black's Law Dictionary*. 5th ed. St. Paul: West.

Blee, Kathleen M. 1991. *Women of the Klan: Racism and Gender in the 1920s*. Berkeley and Los Angeles: University of California Press.

Blumenthal, David R. 1993a. *Facing the Abusing God: A Theology of Protest*. Louisville: Westminster John Knox.

———. 1993b. Who Is Battering Whom? *CJ* 45:72–89.

Bogard, William. 1996. *The Simulation of Surveillance: Hypercontrol in Telematic Societies*. Cambridge: Cambridge University Press.

Bok, Sissela. 1984. *Secrets: On the Ethics of Concealment and Revelation.* New York: Vintage.

Borger, Riekele. 1956. *Die Inschriften Asarhaddons Königs von Assyrien.* AfO 9. Graz: Ernst Weidner.

Bottero, Jean. 1973. Le pouvoir royal et ses limitations d'apres les textes divinatoires. Pages 119–65 in *La voix de l'opposition en Mesopotamie.* Edited by Andre Finet. Brussels: Institut des Hautes Etudes de Belgique.

———. 1992. *Mesopotamia: Writing, Reasoning, and the Gods.* Chicago: University of Chicago Press.

Boyce, Mary, ed. 1984. *Textual Sources for the Study of Zoroastrianism.* Totowa, N.J.: Barnes & Noble.

Brand, Dana. 1985. Reconstructing the "Flâneur": Poe's Invention of the Detective Story. *Genre* 18:36–56.

Braudy, Leo. 1997. *The Frenzy of Renown: Fame and Its History.* New York: Vintage.

Braun, Roddy. 1973. Solomonic Apologetic in Chronicles. *JBL* 92:503–16.

Brauner, Sigrid. 1995. *Fearless Wives and Frightened Shrews: The Construction of the Witch in Early Modern Germany.* Amherst: University of Massachusetts Press.

Brenner, Athalya. 1997. *The Intercourse of Knowledge: On Gendering Desire and "Sexuality" in the Hebrew Bible.* Leiden: Brill.

Brettler, Marc Zvi. 1989. *God Is King: Understanding an Israelite Metaphor.* JSOTSup 76. Sheffield: JSOT Press.

———. 1991. The Structure of 1 Kings 1–11. *JSOT* 49:87–97.

———. 1998. Incompatible Metaphors for YHWH in Isaiah 40–66. *JSOT* 78:97–120.

Briggs, Robin. 1989. *Communities of Belief: Cultural and Social Tension in Early Modern France.* Oxford: Clarendon.

Brooks, Peter. 1993. *Body Work: Objects of Desire in Modern Narrative.* Cambridge, Mass.: Harvard University Press.

Brooks, Peter, and Alex Woloch, eds. 2000. *Whose Freud? The Place of Psychoanalysis in Contemporary Culture*. New Haven, Conn.: Yale University Press.

Brown, Joanne Carlson, and Rebecca Parker. 1989. For God So Loved the World? Pages 1–30 in *Christianity, Patriarchy, and Abuse: A Feminist Critique*. Edited by Joanne Carlson Brown and Carole R. Bohn. Cleveland: Pilgrim.

Brueggemann, Walter. 1972. From Dust to Kingship. *ZAW* 84:1–18.

———. 1990. *First and Second Samuel*. IBC. Louisville: John Knox.

———. 1992. Samuel, Book of 1–2: Narrative and Theology. *ABD* 5:965–73.

———. 2000. Texts That Linger, Not Yet Overcome. Pages 21–41 in *Shall Not the Judge of All the Earth Do What Is Right?* Edited by David Penchansky and Paul L. Redditt. Winona Lake, Ind.: Eisenbrauns.

Buccellati, Giorgio. 1996. The Role of Socio-Political Factors in the Emergence of "Public" and "Private" Domains in Early Mesopotamia. Pages 129–51 in *Privatization in the Ancient Near East and Classical World*. Edited by Michael Hudson and Baruch A. Levine. Peabody Museum Bulletin 5. Cambridge, Mass.: Peabody Museum of Archaeology and Ethnology.

Buck, A de. 1937. The Judicial Papyrus of Turin. *JEA* 23:152–64.

Burke, Peter. 1978. *Popular Culture in Early Modern Europe*. New York: New York University Press.

———. 1993. *History and Social Theory*. New York: Cornell University Press.

Bursten, Ben. 1986. Some Narcissistic Personality Types. Pages 377–402 in *Essential Papers on Narcissism*. Edited by Andrew P. Morrison. New York: New York University Press.

Butler, Judith P. 1987. *Subjects of Desire: Hegelian Reflections in Twentieth-Century France*. New York: Columbia University Press.

Bynum, Caroline Walker. 1982. *Jesus As Mother: Studies in the Spirituality of the High Middle Ages*. Berkeley and Los Angeles: University of California Press.

Callahan, Patricia. 1999. Divided by Tragedy. *Denver Post* 11 July. Denver Post Online 1 December 1999.

Camus, Albert. 1956. *The Fall.* Translated by Justin O'Brien. New York: Vintage.

Canetti, Elias. 1981. *Crowds and Power.* Translated by Carol Stewart. New York: Continuum.

Capps, Donald. 1995. *The Child's Song: The Religious Abuse of Children.* Louisville: Westminster John Knox.

Caquot, A. 1960. Traits royaux dans le personnage de Job. Pages 32–45 in *Maqqēl shâqédh. La branche d'amandier: Hommage à Wilhelm Vischer.* Montpellier: Causse, Graille & Castelnau.

Carlson, R. A. 1964. *David, the Chosen King: A Traditio-Historical Approach to the Second Book of Samuel.* Stockholm: Almqvist & Wiksell.

Carroll, Lewis. 1963. *The Annotated Alice: Alice's Adventures in Wonderland and Through the Looking Glass.* Cleveland: World.

Castan, Nicole. 1989. The Public and the Private. Pages 403–45 in *Passions of the Renaissance.* Vol. 3 of *A History of Private Life.* Edited by Roger Chartier. Translated by Arthur Goldhammer. Cambridge, Mass.: Harvard University Press.

Cawelti, John G. 1976. *Adventure, Mystery, and Romance: Formula Stories As Art and Popular Culture.* Chicago: University of Chicago Press.

Chadwick, H. Munro, and N. Kershaw Chadwick. 1936. *The Growth of Literature.* Vol. 2. Cambridge: Cambridge University Press.

Chastain, Kimberly Parsons. 1997. The Dying Art of Demon-Recognition: Victims, Systems, and the Book of Job. Pages 161–78 in *Power, Powerlessness, and the Divine: New Inquiries in Bible and Theology.* Edited by Cynthia L. Rigby. Atlanta: Scholars Press.

Childs, Brevard S. 1979. *Introduction to the Old Testament As Scripture.* Philadelphia: Fortress.

Civil, Miguel. 1992. Education (Mesopotamia). *ABD* 2:304–5.

Clements, Ronald E. 1974. The Deuteronomistic Interpretation of the Founding of the Monarchy in I Sam. VIII. *VT* 24:398–410.

Clemetson, Lynette, and Pat Wingert. 1998. Clinton on the Couch. *Newsweek* 28 September, 46.

Clines, David J. A. 1989. *Job 1–20*. WBC 17. Dallas: Word.

Coats, George W. 1988. *Moses: Heroic Man, Man of God*. JSOTSup 57. Sheffield: JSOT Press.

Cogan, M., and H. Tadmor. 1988. *II Kings*. AB 11. Garden City, N.Y.: Doubleday.

Cohen, David. 1991. *Law, Sexuality, and Society: The Enforcement of Morals in Classical Athens*. Cambridge: Cambridge University Press.

Cohen, Raymond. 2000. Intelligence in the Amarna Letters. Pages 85–98 in *Amarna Diplomacy: The Beginnings of International Relations*. Edited by Raymond Cohen and Raymond Westbrook. Baltimore: Johns Hopkins University Press.

Cohen, Shaye J. D. 1984–1985. Solomon and the Daughter of Pharaoh: Intermarriage, Conversion, and the Impurity of Women. *JANESCU* 16–17:23–37.

Collins, Louise. 1994. Gossip: A Feminist Defense. Pages 106–14 in *Good Gossip*. Edited by Robert F. Goodman and Aaron Ben-Ze'ev. Lawrence: University Press of Kansas.

Conquest, Robert. 1973. *The Great Terror*. Rev. ed. New York: MacMillan.

Conrad, Joseph. 1983. *The Secret Agent: A Simple Tale*. World's Classics. Oxford: Oxford University Press.

Cooper, Alan. 1990. Reading and Misreading the Prologue to Job. *JSOT* 46:67–79.

Cooper, Arnold M. 1986. Narcissism. Pages 112–43 in *Essential Papers on Narcissism*. Edited by A. P. Morrison. New York: New York University Press.

Corbin, Alain. 1990. The Secret of the Individual. Pages 457–547 in *From the Fires of Revolution to the Great War*. Vol. 4 in *A History of Private Life*. Edited by Michelle Perrot. Translated by Arthur Goldhammer. Cambridge, Mass.: Harvard University Press.

Cox, Dermot. 1987. The Book of Job as Bi-Polar Mašal: Structure and Interpretation. *Anton* 62:12–25.

Crenshaw, James L. 1970. Popular Questioning of the Justice of God in Ancient Israel. *ZAW* 82:380–95.

———. 1981. *Old Testament Wisdom: An Introduction*. Atlanta: John Knox.

———. 1987. *Ecclesiastes: A Commentary*. OTL. Philadelphia: Westminster.

Culpepper, Alan. 1995. *The Gospel of Luke: Introduction, Commentary, and Reflections*. Pages 3–490 in vol. 9 of *NIB*.

Curtis, E. L., and A. A. Madsen. 1910. *A Critical and Exegetical Commentary on the Books of Chronicles*. ICC. Edinburgh: T&T Clark.

Daniel, Robert. 1967. Poe's Detective God. Pages 103–10 in *Poe: A Collection of Critical Essays*. Edited by R. Regan. Englewood Cliffs, N.J.: Prentice-Hall.

Dante Alighieri. 1957. *On World-Government*. 2d ed. Translated by Herbert W. Schneider. Indianapolis: Bobbs-Merrill.

Davies, Norman de Garis. 1973. *The Tomb of Rekh-mi-reʿ at Thebes*. Vol 1. The Metropolitan Museum of Art Egyptian Expedition. New York: Arno.

Davies, Philip R. 1992. *In Search of "Ancient Israel."* JSOTSup 148. Sheffield: Sheffield Academic Press.

Davies, Wendy. 1983. Celtic Women in the Early Middle Ages. Pages 145–66 in *Images of Women in Antiquity*. Edited by Averil Cameron and Amélie Kuhrt. Detroit: Wayne State University Press.

Delaney, Carol. 1998. *Abraham on Trial: The Social Legacy of a Biblical Myth*. Princeton, N.J.: Princeton University Press.

Dell, Katherine J. 1998. The King in the Wisdom Literature. Pages 163–86 in *King and Messiah in Israel and the Ancient Near East*. Edited by John Day. JSOTSup 270. Sheffield: Sheffield Academic Press.

Derrett, John Duncan Martin. 1970. *Law in the New Testament*. London: Darton, Longman & Todd.

Dever, William G. 1990. *Recent Archaeological Discoveries and Biblical Research*. Seattle: University of Washington Press.

DeVries, Simon J. 1985. *1 Kings*. WBC 12. Waco, Tex.: Word.

————. 1989. *1 and 2 Chronicles.* FOTL 11. Grand Rapids: Eerdmans.

Dhorme, Edouard. 1984. *A Commentary on the Book of Job.* Translated by Harold Knight. Nashville: Nelson.

Dick, Michael Brennan. 1979. The Legal Metaphor in Job 31. *CBQ* 41:37–50.

Dillard, Raymond B. 1987. *2 Chronicles.* WBC. Waco, Tex.: Word.

Dodds, Eric Robertson. 1951. *The Greeks and the Irrational.* Berkeley and Los Angeles: University of California Press.

Donner, Herbert. 1982. The Interdependence of Internal Affairs and Foreign Policy during the Davidic-Solomonic Period (with Special Regard to the Phoenician Coast). Pages 205–14 in *Studies in the Period of David and Solomon and Other Essays.* Edited by Tomoo Ishida. Winona Lake, Ind.: Eisenbrauns.

Draper, Theodore. 1992. *A Very Thin Line: The Iran-Contra Affairs.* New York: Touchstone.

Drews, Robert. 1972. The First Tyrants in Greece. *Historia* 21:129–44.

————. 1973. *The Greek Accounts of Eastern History.* Washington, D.C.: Center for Hellenic Studies.

————. 1993. *The End of the Bronze Age: Changes in Warfare and the Catastrophe ca. 1200 B.C.* Princeton, N.J.: Princeton University Press.

Driver, Samuel Rolles. 1902. *A Critical and Exegetical Commentary on Deuteronomy.* 3d ed. ICC. Edinburgh: T&T Clark.

Driver, Samuel Rolles, and George Buchanan Gray. 1921. *A Critical and Exegetical Commentary on the Book of Job Together with a New Translation.* Parts 1 and 2. ICC. Edinburgh: T&T Clark.

Drury, John. 1985. *The Parables in the Gospels: History and Allegory.* New York: Crossroad.

Duby, Georges. 1996. Introduction. Pages 313–17 in *Distant Worlds, Ancient Worlds.* Vol. 1 of *A History of the Family.* Edited by André Burguière, Christiane Klapisch-Zuber, Martine Segalen, and Françoise Zonabend. Translated by Sarah Hanbury Tenison, Rosemary Morris, and Andrew Wilson. Cambridge, Mass.: Harvard University Press.

Dyer, Robert Rutherfurd. 1989. Vergil's Fama: A New Interpretation of *Aeneid* 4.173ff. *Greece & Rome* 36:28–32.

Earl, James W. 1985. Eve's Narcissism. *Milton Quarterly* 19:13–16.

Edelman, Diana Vikander. 1991. *King Saul in the Historiography of Judah.* JSOTSup 121. Sheffield: JSOT Press.

———. 1995. Solomon's Adversaries Hadad, Rezon and Jeroboam: A Trio of "Bad-Guy" Characters Illustrating the Theology of Immediate Retribution. Pages 166–91 in *The Pitcher Is Broken: Memorial Essays for Gösta W. Ahlström.* Edited by Lowell K. Handy and S. W. Holloway. JSOTSup 190. Sheffield: JSOT Press.

Edmonds, J. M., trans. 1961. *Elegy and Iambus with the Anacreontea.* Vol. 2. LCL. Cambridge, Mass.: Harvard University Press.

Edwards, Catharine. 1993. *The Politics of Immorality in Ancient Rome.* Cambridge: Cambridge University Press.

Ehrlich, Victor. 1981. *Russian Formalism: History-Doctrine.* 3d ed. New Haven, Conn.: Yale University Press.

Elias, Norbert. 1983. *The Court Society.* Translated by Edmund Jephcott. New York: Pantheon.

———. 1994. *The Civilizing Process.* Translated by Edmund Jephcott. Oxford: Blackwell.

Embree, Dan. 1985. "The King's Ignorance": A Topos for Evil Times. *Medium Ævum* 54:121–26.

Emler, Nicholas. 1994. Gossip, Reputation, and Social Adaptation. Pages 117–38 in *Good Gossip.* Edited by Robert F. Goodman and Aaron Ben-Ze'ev. Lawrence: University Press of Kansas.

Engnell, Ivan. 1969. "Knowledge" and "Life" in the Creation Story. Pages 103–19 in *Wisdom in Israel and the Ancient Near East: Presented to Professor Harold Henry Rowley.* Edited by M. Noth and D. Winton Thomas. VTSup 3. Leiden: Brill.

Epicurus. 1926. *Epicurus: The Extant Remains.* Translated by Cyril Bailey. Oxford: Clarendon.

Epstein, Isidore. 1935a. *The Babylonian Talmud: Seder Zeraᶜim*. London: Soncino.

———. 1935b. *The Babylonian Talmud: Seder Nezikin*. Vol. 2. London: Soncino.

———. 1935c. *The Babylonian Talmud: Seder Nezikin*. Vol. 3. London: Soncino.

Erman, Adolf. 1966. *The Ancient Egyptians: A Sourcebook of their Writings*. Translated by Aylward M. Blackman. New York: Harper Torchbooks.

Eslinger, Lyle. 1989. *Into the Hands of the Living God*. BLS 24. Sheffield: Almond.

Evans, J. M. 1968. *Paradise Lost and the Genesis Tradition*. Oxford: Clarendon.

Exum, J. Cheryl. 1992. *Tragedy and Biblical Narrative: Arrows of the Almighty*. Cambridge: Cambridge University Press.

Faerber, R. 1902. *König Salomon in der Tradition: Ein historisch-kritischer Beitrag zur Geschichte der Haggada, der Tannaiten und Amoräer*. Vienna: Schlesinger.

Farge, Arlette. 1989. "The Honor and Secrecy of Families." Pages 571–607 in *Passions of the Renaissance*. Vol. 3 of *A History of Private Life*. Edited by Roger Chartier. Translated by Arthur Goldhammer. Cambridge, Mass.: Harvard University Press.

Felman, Shoshana, and Dori Laub. 1992. *Testimony: Crises of Witnessing in Literature, Psychoanalysis, and History*. New York and London: Routledge.

Ferenczi, Sandor. 1950. Stages in the Development of the Sense of Reality. Pages 213–39 in *Sex in Psychoanalysis: The Collected Papers of Sandor Ferenczi, M. D*. Vol. 1. Translated by Ernest Jones. New York: Basic Books.

Ferguson, Priscilla Parkhurst. 1994. The *Flâneur* on and off the Streets of Paris. Pages 22–42 in *The Flâneur*. Edited by Keith Tester. London: Routledge.

Fink, Bruce. 1997. *A Clinical Introduction to Lacanian Psychoanalysis*. Cambridge, Mass.: Harvard University Press.

Finkelstein, Jacob J. 1958. Bible and Babel: A Comparative Study of the Hebrew and Babylonian Religious Spirit. *Commentary* 26:431–44.

Fish, Stanley. 1994. *There's No Such Thing As Free Speech and It's a Good Thing, Too.* New York: Oxford University Press.

Fishbane, Michael. 1985. *Biblical Interpretation in Ancient Israel.* Oxford: Clarendon.

Fitzmyer, Joseph A. 1985. *The Gospel According to Luke (X–XXIV).* AB 28A. Garden City, N.Y.: Doubleday.

Forgeau, Annie. 1996. The Survival of the Family Name and the Pharaonic Order. Pages 128–54 in *Distant Worlds, Ancient Worlds.* Vol. 1 of *A History of the Family.* Edited by André Burguière, Christiane Klapisch-Zuber, Martine Segalen, and Françoise Zonabend. Translated by Sarah Hanbury Tenison, Rosemary Morris, and Andrew Wilson. Cambridge, Mass.: Harvard University Press.

Foster, Benjamin R. 1993. *Before the Muses: An Anthology of Akkadian Literature.* 2 vols. Bethesda, Md.: CDL.

Foucault, Michel. 1978. *An Introduction.* Vol. 1 of *The History of Sexuality.* Translated by Robert Hurley. New York: Pantheon.

———. 1979. *Discipline and Punish: The Birth of the Prison.* Translated by Alan Sheridan. New York: Vintage Books.

———. 1980. *Power/Knowledge: Selected Interviews and Other Writings, 1972–1977.* Edited by Colin Gordon. New York: Pantheon.

Fox, Adam. 1997. Rumour, News and Popular Political Opinion in Elizabethan and Early Stuart England. *The Historical Journal* 40:597–620.

Fox, Michael V. 1989. *Qohelet and His Contradictions.* JSOTSup 71. BLS 18. Sheffield: Almond.

Frankena, R. 1965. The Vassal-Treaties of Esarhaddon and the Dating of Deuteronomy. *OtSt* 14:122–54.

Frankfort, Henri. 1978. *Kingship and the Gods: A Study of Ancient Near Eastern Religion As the Integration of Society and Nature.* Chicago: University of Chicago Phoenix Edition.

Fraser, Russell A. 1962. *Shakespeare's Poetics in Relation to King Lear.* London: Routledge & Kegan Paul.

Frazer, Sir James George. 1994. *The Golden Bough: A Study in Magic and Religion.* Abridged from the 2d and 3d eds. Edited by Robert Fraser. The World's Classics. London: Oxford University Press.

Freeman, Judi, Alain Robbe-Grillet, and Mark Tansey. 1993. *Mark Tansey.* Los Angeles and San Francisco: Los Angeles County Museum of Art and Chronicle Books.

Freeman, Kathleen. 1976. *The Work and Life of Solon.* New York: Arno.

Freud, Sigmund. 1900. The Interpretation of Dreams. Vols. 4–5 of *The Standard Edition of the Complete Psychological Works of Sigmund Freud.* Edited and translated by James Strachey. London: Hogarth. [Hereafter *Standard Edition*]

———. 1905. Three Essays on the Theory of Sexuality. Pages 130–243 in vol. 7 of *Standard Edition.*

———. 1909a. Analysis of a Phobia in a Five-Year-Old Boy. Pages 5–149 in vol. 10 of *Standard Edition.*

———. 1909b. Notes upon a Case of Obsessional Neurosis. Pages 155–318 in vol. 10 of *Standard Edition.*

———. 1910. Leonardo da Vinci and a Memory of his Childhood. Pages 63–137 in vol. 11 of *Standard Edition.*

———. 1911. Formulations on the Two Principles of Mental Functioning. Pages 218–26 in vol. 12 of *Standard Edition.*

———. 1912a. Recommendations to Physicians Practicing Psycho-Analysis. Pages 111–20 in vol. 12 of *Standard Edition.*

———. 1912b. The Dynamics of Transference. Pages 99–108 in vol. 12 of *Standard Edition.*

———. 1913. *Totem and Taboo.* Pages 1–162 in vol. 13 of *Standard Edition.*

———. 1914. On Narcissism: An Introduction. Pages 73–102 in vol. 14 of *Standard Edition.*

———. 1915. Observations on Transference-Love. Pages 159–71 in vol. 12 of *Standard Edition*.

———. 1917a. Eine Schwierigkeit der Psychoanalyse. Pages 3–12 in vol. 12 of *Gesammelte Werke*. London: Imago, 1947. [A translation appears on pages 135–44 in vol. 17 of *Standard Edition*.]

———. 1917b. *Introductory Lectures on Psycho-Analysis, Part III*. Pages 243–463 in vol. 16 of *Standard Edition*.

———. 1920. *Beyond the Pleasure Principle*. Pages 7–64 in vol. 18 of *Standard Edition*.

———. 1921. *Massenpsychologie und Ich-Analyse*. Pages 73–161 in vol. 13 of *Gesammelte Werke*. Edited by Anna Freud. London: Imago, 1940. [A translation appears on pages 69–143 in vol. 18 of *Standard Edition*.]

———. 1923. *The Ego and the Id*. Pages 12–66 in vol. 19 of *Standard Edition*.

———. 1925a. The Resistances to Psychoanalysis. Pages 213–22 in vol. 19 of *Standard Edition*.

———. 1925b. Die Verneinung. Pages 11–15 in vol. 14 of *Gesammelte Werke*. Edited by Anna Freud. London: Imago, 1948. [A translation appears on pages 235–39 in vol. 19 of *Standard Edition*.]

———. 1927. Humour. Pages 159–66 in vol. 21 of *Standard Edition*.

———. 1930. *Civilization and Its Discontents*. Pages 64–145 in vol. 21 of *Standard Edition*.

———. 1931. Libidinal Types. Pages 217–20 in vol. 21 of *Standard Edition*.

———. 1932. My Contact with Josef Popper-Lynkeus. Pages 219–24 in vol. 22 of *Standard Edition*.

———. 1933. *New Introductory Lectures on Psychoanalysis*. Pages 5–182 in vol. 22 of *Standard Edition*.

———. 1939. *Der Mann Moses und die monotheistische Religion*. Pages 103–246 in vol. 16 of *Gesammelte Werke*. Edited by Anna Freud. London: Imago, 1950. [A translation appears on pages 7–137 in vol. 23 of *Standard Edition*.]

Freyd, Jennifer J. 1996. *Betrayal Trauma: The Logic of Forgetting Childhood Abuse.* Cambridge, Mass.: Harvard University Press.

Frisby, David. 1994. The *Flâneur* in Social Theory. Pages 81–110 in *The Flâneur.* Edited by Keith Tester. London: Routledge.

Fromm, Erich. 1975. *The Anatomy of Human Destructiveness.* Greenwich, Conn.: Fawcett.

Gallop, Jane. 1985. *Reading Lacan.* Ithaca, N.Y.: Cornell University Press.

Gammie, John G. 1985. The Angelology and Demonology in the Septuagint of the Book of Job. *HUCA* 56:1–19.

Garber, Marjorie B. 1998. *Symptoms of Culture.* New York: Routledge.

Garber, Marjorie B., Rebecca L. Walkowitz, and Paul B. Franklin. 1996. Introduction: Field Work. Pages 1–7 in *Field Work: Sites in Literary and Cultural Studies.* Edited by Marjorie Garber, Rebecca L. Walkowitz, and Paul B. Franklin. New York: Routledge.

Garbini, Giovanni. 1988. *History and Ideology in Ancient Israel.* New York: Crossroad.

Gardiner, Sir Alan. 1960. *The Kadesh Inscriptions of Ramesses II.* Oxford: Griffith Institute, Ashmolean Museum.

———. 1961. *Egypt of the Pharaohs: An Introduction.* London: Oxford University Press.

Garelli, Paul. 1973. Les sujets du roi d'Assyrie. Pages 189–213 in *La voix de l'opposition en Mesopotamie.* Edited by Andre Finet. Brussels: Institut des Hautes Etudes de Belgique.

Gay, Peter. 1989. *Freud: A Life for Our Time.* New York: Doubleday Anchor.

Geertz, Clifford. 1973. *The Interpretation of Cultures: Selected Essays.* New York: Basic Books.

———. 1983. *Local Knowledge: Further Essays in Interpretive Anthropology.* New York: Basic Books.

———. 1988. *Works and Lives: The Anthropologist As Author.* Stanford: Stanford University Press.

Gibson, John C. L. 1975. *Aramaic Inscriptions*. Vol. 2 of *Textbook of Syrian Semitic Inscriptions*. Oxford: Clarendon.

———. 1978. *Canaanite Myths and Legends*. Edinburgh: T&T Clark.

———. 1982. *Phoenician Inscriptions*. Vol. 3 of *Textbook of Syrian Semitic Inscriptions*. Oxford: Clarendon.

Ginzberg, Louis. 1969. *The Legends of the Jews*. Vol. 2. Translated by Henrietta Szold. Philadelphia: Jewish Publication Society of America.

Ginzburg, Carlo. 1989. *Clues, Myths, and the Historical Method*. Translated by John and Anne C. Tedeschi. Baltimore: Johns Hopkins University Press.

Girard, René. 1966. *Deceit, Desire, and the Novel: Self and Other in Literary Structure*. Translated by Yvonne Freccero. Baltimore: Johns Hopkins University Press.

———. 1977. *Violence and the Sacred*. Translated by Patrick Gregory. Baltimore: Johns Hopkins University Press.

———. 1986. *The Scapegoat*. Translated by Yvonne Freccero. Baltimore: Johns Hopkins University Press.

———. 1987a. *Job: The Victim of His People*. Translated by Yvonne Freccero. Stanford: Stanford University Press.

———. 1987b. *Things Hidden Since the Foundation of the World*. Translated by Stephen Bann and Michael Metteer. Stanford: Stanford University Press.

Glassner, Jean-Jacques. 1996. From Sumer to Babylon: Families As Landowners and Families As Rulers. Pages 92–127 in *Distant Worlds, Ancient Worlds*. Vol. 1 of *A History of the Family*. Edited by André Burguière, Christiane Klapisch-Zuber, Martine Segalen, and Françoise Zonabend. Translated by Sarah Hanbury Tenison, Rosemary Morris, and Andrew Wilson. Cambridge, Mass.: Harvard University Press.

Glatzer, Henriette T., and William N. Evans. 1977. On Guntrip's Analysis with Fairbairn and Winnicott. *International Journal of Psychoanalytic Psychotherapy* 6:81–98.

Goedicke, Hans. 1963. Was Magic Used in the Harem Conspiracy against Ramesses III? *JEA* 49:71–92.

————. 1985. The "Battle of Kadesh": A Reassessment. Pages 77–121 in *Perspectives on the Battle of Kadesh*. Edited by Hans Goedicke. Baltimore: Halgo.

Goffman, Erving. 1959. *The Presentation of Self in Everyday Life*. Garden City, N.Y.: Doubleday Anchor.

————. 1974. *Frame Analysis: An Essay on the Organization of Experience*. New York: Harper & Row.

Goldberg, Jonathan. 1983. *James I and the Politics of Literature: Jonson, Shakespeare, Donne, and Their Contemporaries*. Baltimore: Johns Hopkins University Press.

Goldstein, Jan. 1984. Foucault among the Sociologists: The "Disciplines" and the History of the Professions. *History and Theory* 23:170–92.

————. 1994. Introduction. Pages 1–15 in *Foucault and the Writing of History*. Edited by Jan Goldstein. Cambridge, Mass.: Blackwell.

Gombrich, E. H. 1969. *Art and Illusion: A Study in the Psychology of Pictorial Representation*. Princeton, N.J.: Princeton/Bollingen.

Goodfriend, Elaine A. 1992. Adultery. *ABD* 1:82–86.

Goodheart, Eugene. 1991. *Desire and Its Discontents*. New York: Columbia University Press.

Gosse, Bernard. 1990. Detournement de la vengeance du Seigneur contre Edom et les nations en Isa 63,1–6. *ZAW* 102:105–10.

Gottwald, Norman K. 1985. *The Hebrew Bible: A Socio-Literary Introduction*. Philadelphia: Fortress.

————. 1986 Introduction. *Semeia* 37:1–8.

————. 1992. Sociology (Ancient Israel). *ABD* 6:79–89.

Gray, George Buchanan. 1912. *A Critical and Exegetical Commentary on the Book of Isaiah I–XXXIX*. ICC. New York: Scribner's.

Gray, John. 1970. *I and II Kings: A Commentary*. 2d ed. OTL. Philadelphia: Westminster.

Grayson, A. Kirk. 1987. Akkadian Treaties of the Seventh Century B.C. *JCS* 39:127–60.

———. 1991. *Assyrian Rulers of the Early First Millennium BC I (1114–859 BC)*. The Royal Inscriptions of Mesopotamia, Assyrian Periods 2. Toronto: University of Toronto Press.

Greenfield, Jonas C. 1965. Stylistic Aspects of the Sefire Treaty Inscriptions. *AcOr* 29:1–18.

Greenstein, Edward L. 1988. On the Genesis of Biblical Prose Narrative. *Proof* 8:347–54.

Grimal, Nicholas. 1992. *A History of Ancient Egypt*. Translated by Ian Shaw. Oxford: Blackwell.

Gros Louis, Kenneth. 1977. The Difficulty of Ruling Well: King David of Israel. *Semeia* 8:15–33.

Gruber, Mayer I. 1992. *The Motherhood of God and Other Studies*. South Florida Studies in the History of Judaism 57. Atlanta: Scholars Press.

Grünberger, Béla. 1991. Narcissism and the Analytic Situation. Pages 216–27 in *Freud's "On Narcissism: An Introduction."* Edited by Joseph Sandler, Ethel Spector Person, and Peter Fonagy. New Haven, Conn.: Yale University Press.

Grzimek, Bernhard. 1990. *Grzimek's Encyclopedia of Mammals*. Vol. 1. New York: McGraw-Hill.

Gunn, David M. 1978. *The Story of King David: Genre and Interpretation*. JSOTSup 6. Sheffield: JSOT Press.

———. 1984. *The Fate of King Saul: An Interpretation of a Biblical Story*. JSOTSup 14. Sheffield: JSOT Press.

Gurney, Oliver Robert. 1990. *The Hittites*. London: Penguin.

Guthrie, W. K. C. 1957. *In the Beginning: Some Greek Views on the Origins of Life and the Early State of Man*. Ithaca, N.Y.: Cornell University Press.

Haaken, Janice. 1998. *Pillar of Salt: Gender, Memory, and the Perils of Looking Back*. New Brunswick, N.J.: Rutgers University Press.

Habel, Norman C. 1985. *The Book of Job: A Commentary*. OTL. Philadelphia: Westminster.

Hagedorn, Anselm C. 2000. Guarding the Parents' Honour—Deuteronomy 21.18–21. *JSOT* 88:101–21.

Handy, Lowell K. 1993. The Authorization of Divine Power and the Guilt of God in the Book of Job: Useful Ugaritic Parallels. *JSOT* 60:107–18.

Hanson, Paul D. 1995. *Isaiah 40–66*. IBC. Louisville: John Knox.

Hatton, Ragnhild. 1977. Louis XIV: At the Court of the Sun King. Pages 233–61 in *The Courts of Europe: Politics, Patronage and Royalty, 1400–1800*. Edited by A. G. Dickens. New York: McGraw-Hill.

Hauser, A. J., and R. Gregory. 1990. *From Carmel to Horeb: Elijah in Crisis*. JSOTSup 85. Sheffield: Almond.

Hayes, William C. 1990. *The Scepter of Egypt, Part I: From the Earliest Times to the End of the Middle Kingdom*. 5th ed. New York: Abrams.

Headlam, Walter George. 1902. Metaphor, with a Note on Transference of Epithets. *Classical Review* 16:434–42.

Heaton, E. W. 1974. *Solomon's New Men: The Emergence of Ancient Israel As a National State*. New York: Pica.

Heller, Joseph. 1985. *God Knows*. New York: Dell.

Herman, Judith Lewis. 1997. *Trauma and Recovery*. New York: Basic Books.

Herodotus. 1981. *Herodotus*. Vol. 1. Translated by A. D. Godley. LCL. Cambridge, Mass.: Harvard University Press.

Hertsgaard, Mark. 1988. *On Bended Knee: The Press and the Reagan Presidency*. New York: Farrar Straus Giroux.

Hertzberg, Hans Wilhelm. 1964. *I and II Samuel: A Commentary*. OTL. Philadelphia: Westminster.

Heschel, Abraham Joshua. 1951. *Man Is Not Alone: A Philosophy of Religion*. New York: Farrar, Straus & Young.

Heym, Stefan. 1973. *The King David Report: A Novel*. London: Hodder & Stoughton.

Higgins, Jean M. 1976. The Myth of Eve the Temptress. *JAAR* 44:639–47.

Hobbs, T. R. 1985. *2 Kings*. WBC 13. Waco, Tex.: Word.

Hoffmann, Kathryn A. 1997. *Society of Pleasures: Interdisciplinary Readings in Pleasure and Power during the Reign of Louis XIV*. New York: St. Martin's.

Holladay, William L. 1986. *Jeremiah 1: A Commentary on the Book of the Prophet Jeremiah Chapters 1–25*. Hermeneia. Philadelphia: Fortress.

Homer. 1951. *Iliad*. Translated by Richmond Lattimore. Chicago: University of Chicago Press.

Hoppe, Leslie J. 1992. Israel, History of (Monarchic Period). *ABD* 3:558–67.

Horton, Fred L., Jr. 1976. *The Melchizedekian Tradition: A Critical Examination of the Sources to the Fifth Century A.D. and in the Epistle to the Hebrews*. Cambridge: Cambridge University Press.

Hudson, Michael. 1996. Privatization: A Survey of the Unresolved Controversies. Pages 1–32 in *Privatization in the Ancient Near East and Classical World*. Edited by Michael Hudson and Baruch A. Levine. Peabody Museum Bulletin 5. Cambridge, Mass.: Peabody Museum of Archaeology and Ethnology.

Hults, Linda C. 1987. Baldung and the Witches of Freiburg: The Evidence of Images. *Journal of Interdisciplinary History* 18:249–76.

Hurowitz, Victor (Avigdor). 1992. *I Have Built You an Exalted House: Temple Building in the Bible in Light of Mesopotamian and Northwest Semitic Writings*. JSOTSup 115. Sheffield: JSOT Press.

Hurston, Zora Neale. 1984. *Moses: Man of the Mountain*. Urbana: University of Illinois Press.

Ishida, Tomoso. 1992. Solomon. *ABD* 6:105–13.

Isocrates. 1961. *Isocrates*. Vol. 1. Translated by George Norlin. LCL. Cambridge, Mass.: Harvard University Press.

Jacobsen, Thorkild. 1976. *The Treasures of Darkness: A History of Mesopotamian Religion*. New Haven, Conn.: Yale University Press.

———. 1987. *The Harps That Once ... Sumerian Poetry in Translation*. New Haven, Conn.: Yale University Press.

James, Alan. 2000. Egypt and Her Vassals: The Geopolitical Dimension. Pages 112–24 in *Amarna Diplomacy: The Beginnings of International Relations*. Edited by Raymond Cohen and Raymond Westbrook. Baltimore: Johns Hopkins University Press.

Janeway, Michael. 1993. The Press and Privacy: Rights and Rules. Pages 107–53 in *The Morality of the Mass Media*. Edited by W. Lawson Taitte. Dallas: University of Texas Press.

Janko, Richard. 1992. *The Iliad: A Commentary. Volume IV: Books 13–16*. Cambridge: Cambridge University Press.

Japhet, Sara. 1989. *The Ideology of the Book of Chronicles and Its Place in Biblical Thought*. Translated by Anna Barber. BEATAJ 9. Frankfurt: Peter Lang.

———. 1993. *I and II Chronicles: A Commentary*. OTL. Louisville: Westminster John Knox.

Jensen, Hans J. L. 1991. The Fall of the King. *SJOT* 1:121–47.

Jobling, David. 1986. *The Sense of Biblical Narrative: Structural Analyses in the Hebrew Bible, I*. 2d ed. JSOTSup 7. Sheffield: JSOT Press.

———. 1991. "Forced Labor": Solomon's Golden Age and the Question of Literary Representation. *Semeia* 54:57–76.

———. 1992. Deconstruction and the Political Analysis of Biblical Texts: A Jamesonian Reading of Psalm 72. *Semeia* 59:95–127.

———. 1998. *1 Samuel*. Berit Olam. Collegeville, Minn.: Liturgical Press.

Jones, Ernest. 1955. *The Life and Work of Sigmund Freud*. Vol. 2. New York: Basic Books.

———. 1957. *The Life and Work of Sigmund Freud*. Vol. 3. New York: Basic Books.

Jones, Gwilym H. 1984. *1 and 2 Kings*. Vol. 2. NCB. Grand Rapids: Eerdmans.

————. 1990. *The Nathan Narratives*. JSOTSup 80. Sheffield: JSOT Press.

Josephus. 1930. *Jewish Antiquities, Books I–IV*. Translated by H. St. J. Thackeray. LCL. Cambridge, Mass.: Harvard University Press.

Kafka, Franz. 1946. *Das Schloss*. New York: Schocken.

————. 1951. *Tagebücher, 1910–1923*. Frankfurt a.M.: Fischer.

————. 1953. *Hochzeitsvorbereitungen auf dem Lande und andere Prosa aus dem Nachlass*. Frankfurt a.M.: Fischer.

————. 1958. *Briefe 1902–1924*. Frankfurt a.M.: Fischer.

————. 1970. *Sämtliche Erzählungen*. Edited by Paul Raabe. Frankfurt a.M.: Fischer.

Kantorowicz, Ernst H. 1957. *The King's Two Bodies: A Study in Medieval Political Theology*. Princeton, N.J.: Princeton University Press.

Kennedy, James M. 1990. Peasants in Revolt: Political Allegory in Genesis 2–3. *JSOT* 47:3–14.

Kernberg, Otto F. 1985. *Borderline Conditions and Pathological Narcissism*. Northvale, N.J.: Aronson.

Kitchen, Kenneth A. 1973. *The Third Intermediate Period in Egypt*. Warminster, England: Aris & Phillips.

Klein, Julie Thompson. 1996. *Crossing Boundaries: Knowledge, Disciplinarities, and Interdisciplinarities*. Charlottesville: University Press of Virginia.

Knoppers, Gary N. 1993. *Two Nations under God: The Deuteronomistic History of Solomon and the Dual Monarchies*. Vol. 1. HSM 52. Atlanta: Scholars Press.

Knox, Bernard M. W. 1971. *Oedipus at Thebes: Sophocles' Tragic Hero and His Time*. New York: Norton.

Knudtzon, J. A., Otto Weber, and Erich Ebeling. 1964. *Die El-Amarna-Tafeln*. Vol. 1. Aalen: Otto Zeller. First published 1915.

Kofman, Sarah. 1985. *The Enigma of Woman: Woman in Freud's Writings.* Translated by Catherine Porter. Ithaca, N.Y.: Cornell University Press.

Kohut, Heinz. 1971. *The Analysis of the Self: A Systematic Approach to the Psychoanalytic Treatment of Narcissistic Personality Disorders.* New York: International Universities.

———. 1977. *The Restoration of the Self.* New York: International Universities.

———. 1986. Forms and Transformations of Narcissism. Pages 61–87 in *Essential Papers on Narcissism.* Edited by Andrew P. Morrison. New York: New York University Press.

Kohut, Heinz, and Ernest S. Wolf. 1986. The Disorders of the Self and Their Treatment: An Outline. Pages 175–96 in *Essential Papers on Narcissism.* Edited by Andrew P. Morrison. New York: New York University Press.

König, Friedrich Wilhelm. 1972. *Die Persika des Ktesias von Knidos.* Graz: Ernst Weidner.

Krämer, Heinrich, and Jakob Sprenger. 1928. *Malleus Malificarum.* Translated by Montague Summers. New York: Benjamin Blom.

Kramer, Samuel Noah. 1991. Solomon and Šulgi: A Comparative Portrait. Pages 189–95 in *Ah, Assyria...: Studies in Assyrian History and Ancient Near Eastern Historiography Presented to Hayim Tadmor.* Edited by Mordechai Cogan and Israel Eph'al. ScrHier 33. Jerusalem: Magnes.

Kristeva, Julia. 1987. *Tales of Love.* Translated by Leon S. Roudiez. New York: Columbia University Press.

Krüll, Marianne. 1986. *Freud and His Father.* Translated by Arnold J. Pomerans. New York: Norton.

Kuehlwein, Kevin T. 1993. A Survey and Update of Cognitive Therapy Systems. Pages 1–32 in *Cognitive Therapies in Action: Evolving Innovative Practice.* San Francisco: Jossey-Bass.

Kuhn, Thomas. 1976. *The Structure of Scientific Revolutions.* 3d ed. Chicago: University of Chicago Press.

Kutler, Stanley I. 1990. *The Wars of Watergate: The Last Crisis of Richard Nixon*. New York: Knopf.

La Bruyère, Jean de. 1963. *Characters*. Translated by Henri Van Laun. London: Oxford University Press.

Lacan, Jacques. 1968. *The Language of the Self: The Function of Language in Psychoanalysis*. Translated with notes and commentary by Anthony Wilden. New York: Delta.

———. 1977. *Écrits: A Selection*. Translated by Alan Sheridan. New York: Norton.

———. 1981. *The Seminar of Jacques Lacan: Book XI, The Four Fundamental Concepts of Psychoanalysis*. Translated by Alan Sheridan. New York: Norton.

Landy, Francis. 1983. *Paradoxes of Paradise: Identity and Difference in the Song of Songs*. BLS 7. Sheffield: Almond.

Lapham, Lewis H. 1986. Gossiping about Gossip. *Harper's* January, 37–50.

Larner, Christina. 1984. *Witchcraft and Religion: The Politics of Popular Belief*. Oxford: Blackwell.

Lasch, Christopher. 1991. *The Culture of Narcissism: American Life in an Age of Diminishing Expectations*. New York: Norton.

Lasine, Stuart. 1977. Sight, Body, and Motion in Plato and Kafka: A Study of Projective and Topological Experience. Ph.D. diss. University of Wisconsin-Madison; University Microfilms International, Ann Arbor, Mich.

———. 1984a. Melodrama As Parable: The Story of the Poor Man's Ewe-Lamb and the Unmasking of David's Topsy-Turvy Emotions. *HAR* 8:101–24.

———. 1984b. Kafka's "Sacred Texts" and the Hebrew Bible. *Papers in Comparative Studies* 3:121–35.

———. 1985. Kafka's *The Trial*. *The Explicator* 43:34–36.

———. 1986. Indeterminacy and the Bible: A Review of Literary and Anthropological Theories and Their Application to Biblical Texts. *HS* 27:48–80.

———. 1987. Solomon, Daniel and the Detective Story: The Social Functions of a Literary Genre. *HAR* 11:247–66.

———. 1988. Bird's-Eye and Worm's-Eye Views of Justice in the Book of Job. *JSOT* 42:29–53.

———. 1989a. The Riddle of Solomon's Judgment and the Riddle of Human Nature in the Hebrew Bible. *JSOT* 45:61–86.

———. 1989b. Judicial Narratives and the Ethics of Reading: The Reader As Judge of the Dispute between Mephibosheth and Ziba. *HS* 30:49–69.

———. 1990. The Trials of Job and Kafka's Josef K. *The German Quarterly* 63:187–98.

———. 1991a. Jehoram and the Cannibal Mothers (2 Kings 6.24–33): Solomon's Judgment in an Inverted World. *JSOT* 50:27–53.

———. 1991b. Review of René Girard, *Job: The Victim of His People. HS* 32:92–104.

———. 1992. Reading Jeroboam's Intentions: Intertextuality, Rhetoric and History in 1 Kings 12. Pages 133–52 in *Reading between Texts: Intertextuality and the Hebrew Bible*. Edited by Danna Nolan Fewell. Louisville: Westminster John Knox.

———. 1993a. The Ups and Downs of Monarchical Justice: Solomon and Jehoram in an Intertextual World. *JSOT* 59:37–53.

———. 1993b. Manasseh As Villain and Scapegoat. Pages 163–83 in *The New Literary Criticism and the Hebrew Bible*. Edited by J. Cheryl Exum and David J. A. Clines. JSOTSup 143. Sheffield: Sheffield Academic Press.

———. 1994. Levite Violence, Fratricide, and Sacrifice in the Bible and Later Revolutionary Rhetoric. Pages 204–29 in *Curing Violence*. Edited by Mark I. Wallace and Theophus H. Smith. Sonoma, Calif.: Polebridge Press.

———. 2001. Divine Narcissism and Yahweh's Parenting Style. *BibInt.* Forthcoming.

Le Bon, Gustave. 1977. *The Crowd*. Harmondsworth: Penguin.

Le Gallienne, Richard. 1912. The Psychology of Gossip. *Munsey's Magazine* 48:123–27.

Le Goff, Jacques. 1989. Head or Heart? The Political Use of Body Metaphors in the Middle Ages. Pages 13–27 in *Fragments for a History of the Human Body, Part Three*. Edited by Michel Feher. New York: Zone.

Lemaire, André. 1995. Wisdom in Solomonic Historiography. Pages 106–18 in *Wisdom in Ancient Israel: Essays in Honour of J. A. Emerton*. Edited by John Day, Robert P. Gordon, and H. G. M. Williamson. Cambridge: Cambridge University Press.

Lesko, Leonard H. 1991. Ancient Egyptian Comogonies and Cosmology. Pages 88–122 in *Religion in Ancient Egypt: Gods, Myths, and Personal Practice*. Edited by Byron E. Shafer. Ithaca, N.Y.: Cornell University Press.

Levenson, Jon D. 1988. *Creation and the Persistence of Evil: The Jewish Drama of Divine Omnipotence*. San Francisco: Harper & Row.

———. 1993. *The Death and Resurrection of the Beloved Son: The Transformation of Child Sacrifice in Judaism and Christianity*. New Haven, Conn.: Yale University Press.

Levinas, Emmanuel. 1974. *Autrement qu'être ou au-delá de l'essence*. The Hague: Nijhoff.

Lévi-Strauss, Claude. 1966. *The Savage Mind*. Chicago: University of Chicago Press.

———. 1983. *Structural Anthropology*. Vol. 2. Translated by Monique Layton. Chicago: University of Chicago Press.

———. 1992. *Tristes Tropiques*. Translated by John and Doreen Weightman. New York: Penguin.

Lichtheim, Miriam. 1973. *The Old and Middle Kingdoms*. Vol. 1. of *Ancient Egyptian Literature: A Book of Readings*. Berkeley and Los Angeles: University of California Press.

———. 1976. *The New Kingdom*. Vol. 2 of *Ancient Egyptian Literature: A Book of Readings*. Berkeley and Los Angeles: University of California Press.

Lie, A. G. 1929. *The Inscriptions of Sargon II King of Assyria*. Part I: *The Annals*. Paris: Paul Geuthner.

Liverani, Mario. 1990. *Prestige and Interest: International Relations in the Near East ca. 1600–1100 B.C.* History of the Ancient Near East Studies 1. Padova: sargon srl.

Lloyd-Jones, Hugh. 1983. *The Justice of Zeus.* 2d ed. Berkeley and Los Angeles: University of California Press.

Lockwood, Richard D. 1987. The "I" of History in the Memoires of Louis XIV. *Papers on French Seventeenth Century Literature* 14:551–64.

Long, Burke O. 1984. *1 Kings, with an Introduction to Historical Literature.* FOTL 9. Grand Rapids: Eerdmans.

———. 1987. On Finding the Hidden Premises. *JSOT* 39:10–14.

Louis XIV. 1970. *Memoires for the Instruction of the Dauphin.* Translated by Paul Sonnino.New York: Free Press.

Lovejoy, Arthur O. 1964. *The Great Chain of Being: A Study of the History of an Idea.* Cambridge, Mass.: Harvard University Press.

Lowen, Alexander. 1997. *Narcissism: Denial of the True Self.* New York: Touchstone.

Luce, T. J. 1989. Ancient Views on the Causes of Bias in Historical Writing. *CP* 84:16–31.

Lucian. 1953. *Lucian.* Vol. 1. Translated by A. M. Harmon. LCL. Cambridge, Mass.: Harvard University Press.

Lucretius Carus, Titus. 1947. *De Rerum Natura.* Vol. 1. Edited and translated by Cyril Bailey. Oxford: Clarendon.

MacCary, W. Thomas. 1982. *Childlike Achilles: Ontogeny and Phylogeny in the* Iliad. New York: Columbia University Press.

Machinist, Peter. 1991. The Question of Distinctiveness in Ancient Israel: An Essay. Pages 196–212 in *Ah, Assyria...: Studies in Assyrian History and Ancient Near Eastern Historiography Presented to Hayim Tadmor.* Edited by Mordechai Cogan and Israel Eph'al. ScrHier 33. Jerusalem: Magnes.

Machlup, Fritz. 1983. Semantic Quirks in Studies of Information. Pages 641–71 in *The Study of Information: Interdisciplinary Messages.* Edited by Fritz Machlup and Una Mansfield. New York: Wiley.

MacQueen, J. G. 1986. *The Hittites and Their Contemporaries in Asia Minor*. Rev. ed. London: Thames & Hudson.

Maimonides. 1937. *The Mishneh Torah*. Book 1. Edited by Moses Hyamson. New York: n.p.

Malamat, Abraham. 1982. A Political Look at the Kingdom of David and Solomon and Its Relations with Egypt. Pages 189–204 in *Studies in the Period of David and Solomon and Other Essays*. Edited by Tomoo Ishida. Winona Lake, Ind.: Eisenbrauns.

Maraniss, David. 1998. It's Lonelier Than Usual for Clinton. *Washington Post* 16 February, A1+.

Marquard, Odo. 1979. Lob des Polytheismus: Über Monomythie und Polymythie. Pages 40–58 in *Philosophie und Mythos: Ein Kolloquium*. Edited by Hans Poser. Berlin: Walter de Gruyter.

Marshall, I. Howard. 1978. *The Gospel of Luke: A Commentary on the Greek Text*. Grand Rapids: Eerdmans.

Mathews, Andrew. 1997. Information-Processing Biases in Emotional Disorders. Pages 47–66 in *Science and Practice of Cognitive Behaviour Therapy*. Edited by David M. Clark and Christopher G. Fairburn. Oxford: Oxford Unversity Press.

McCarter, P. Kyle, Jr. 1980. *I Samuel*. AB 8. Garden City, N.Y.: Doubleday.

———. 1984. *II Samuel*. AB 9. Garden City, N.Y.: Doubleday.

———. 1987. Aspects of the Religion of the Israelite Monarchy: Biblical and Epigraphic Data. Pages 137–55 in *Ancient Israelite Religion: Essays in Honor of Frank Moore Cross*. Edited by Patrick D. Miller Jr., Paul D. Hanson, and S. Dean McBride. Philadelphia: Fortress.

McCarthy, Dennis J. 1981. *Treaty and Covenant: A Study in Form in the Ancient Oriental Documents and in the Old Testament*. New ed. Rome: Biblical Pontifical Press.

———. 1982. Compact and Kingship: Stimuli for Hebrew Covenant Thinking. Pages 75–92 in *Studies in the Period of David and Solomon and Other Essays*. Edited by Tomoo Ishida. Winona Lake, Ind.: Eisenbrauns.

McConville, J. G. 1984. *I and II Chronicles*. Philadelphia: Westminster.

McGlew, James F. 1993. *Tyranny and Political Culture in Ancient Greece*. Ithaca, N.Y.: Cornell University Press.

McKane, William. 1970. *Proverbs: A New Approach*. OTL. Philadelphia: Westminster.

Meier, Samuel A. 2000. Diplomacy and International Marriages. Pages 165–73 in *Amarna Diplomacy: The Beginnings of International Relations*. Edited by Raymond Cohen and Raymond Westbrook. Baltimore: Johns Hopkins University Press.

Mellencamp, Patricia. 1992. *High Anxiety: Catastrophe, Scandal, Age, and Comedy*. Bloomington: Indiana University Press.

Mendenhall, George E. 1975. The Monarchy. *Int* 29:155–70.

Merleau-Ponty, Maurice. 1968. *The Visible and the Invisible*. Evanston: Northwestern University Press.

Mettinger, Tryggve N. D. 1986. In Search of the Hidden Structure: YHWH as King in Isaiah 40–55. *SEÅ* 51–52:148–57.

———. 1988. *In Search of God: The Meaning and Message of the Everlasting Names*. Translated by Frederick H. Cryer. Philadelphia: Fortress Press.

Meyers, Carol. 1983. The Israelite Empire: In Defense of King Solomon. *Michigan Quarterly Review* 22:412–28.

Milgrom, Jacob. 1982. Religious Conversion and the Revolt Model for the Formation of Israel. *JBL* 101:169–76.

———. 1990. *Numbers*. JPS Torah Commentary. Philadelphia: Jewish Publication Society.

Miller, Alice. 1981. *Prisoners of Childhood: The Drama of the Gifted Child and the Search for the True Self*. Translated by Ruth Ward. New York: Basic Books.

———. 1983. *For Your Own Good: Hidden Cruelty in Child-Rearing and the Roots of Violence*. Translated by Hildegarde and Hunter Hannum. New York: Farrar, Straus & Giroux.

————. 1991a. *Breaking Down the Wall of Silence: The Liberating Experience of Facing Painful Truth.* Translated by Simon Worrall. New York: Dutton.

————. 1991b. *Banished Knowledge: Facing Childhood Injuries.* Translated by Leila Vennewitz. Rev. ed. New York: Anchor Books.

————. 1998. *Thou Shalt Not Be Aware: Society's Betrayal of the Child.* Translated by Hildegarde and Hunter Hannum. New York: Noonday Press.

Miller, J. Maxwell. 1987. In Defense of Writing a History of Israel. *JSOT* 39:53–57.

Miscall, Peter D. 1986. *1 Samuel: A Literary Reading.* Bloomington: Indiana University Press.

Modell, Arnold H. 1986. A Narcissistic Defence against Affects and the Illusion of Self-Sufficiency. Pages 293–307 in *Essential Papers on Narcissism.* Edited by Andrew P. Morrison. New York: New York University Press.

Monod, Paul Kléber. 1999. *The Power of Kings: Monarchy and Religion in Europe, 1589–1715.* New Haven, Conn.: Yale University Press.

Montaigne, Michel de. 1958. *The Complete Essays of Montaigne.* Translated by Donald M. Frame. Stanford: Stanford University Press.

Montgomery, James A., and Henry Synder Gehman. 1951. *A Critical and Exegetical Commentary on the Books of Kings.* ICC. Edinburgh: T&T Clark.

Montgomery, Robert W. 1993. The Ancient Origins of Cognitive Therapy: The Reemergence of Stoicism. *Journal of Cognitive Psychotherapy* 7:5–19.

Moore, Barrington, Jr. 1984. *Privacy: Studies in Social and Cultural History.* Armonk, N.Y.: M. E. Sharpe.

Moore, Stephen D. 1992. *Mark and Luke in Poststructuralist Perspectives: Jesus Begins to Write.* New Haven, Conn.: Yale University Press.

————. 1996. *God's Gym: Divine Male Bodies of the Bible.* New York: Routledge.

Moran, William L. 1963. The Ancient Near Eastern Background of the Love of God in Deuteronomy. *CBQ* 25:77–87.

————. 1985. Rib-Hadda: Job at Byblos? Pages 173–81 in *Biblical and Related Studies Presented to Samuel Iwry*. Edited by Ann Kort and Scott Morschauser. Winona Lake, Ind.: Eisenbrauns.

————., ed. 1992. *The Amarna Letters*. Translated by William L. Moran. Baltimore: Johns Hopkins University Press.

Morenz, Siegfried. 1973. *Egyptian Religion*. Translated by Ann E. Keep. Ithaca, N.Y.: Cornell University Press.

Morrison, Andrew P., ed. 1986. *Essential Papers on Narcissism*. New York: New York University Press.

Morschauser, Scott. 1985. Observations on the Speeches of Ramesses II in the Literary Record of the Battle of Kadesh. Pages 123–206 in *Perspectives on the Battle of Kadesh*. Edited by Hans Goedicke. Baltimore: Halgo.

Muchembled, Robert. 1985. *Popular Culture and Elite Culture in France, 1400–1750*. Baton Rouge: LSU Press.

Muffs, Yochanan. 1992. *Love and Joy: Law, Language and Religion in Ancient Israel*. New York and Jerusalem: Jewish Theological Seminary of America.

Na'aman, Nadav. 2000. The Egyptian-Canaanite Correspondence. Pages 125–38 in *Amarna Diplomacy: The Beginnings of International Relations*. Edited by Raymond Cohen and Raymond Westbrook. Baltimore: Johns Hopkins University Press.

Nagler, Michael N. 1974. *Spontaneity and Tradition: A Study in the Oral Art of Homer*. Berkeley and Los Angeles: University of California Press.

Nelson, Richard D. 1987. *First and Second Kings*. IBC. Atlanta: John Knox.

Nietzsche, Friedrich. 1968. Zur Genealogie der Moral. Pages 259–430 in Abteilung 6, Band 2 of *Nietzsche Werke: Kritische Gesamtausgabe*. Edited by Giorgio Colli and Mazzino Montinari. Berlin: Walter de Gruyter.

————. 1969. Der Antichrist. Pages 165–251 in Abteilung 6, Band 3 of *Nietzsche Werke: Kritische Gesamtausgabe*. Edited by Giorgio Colli and Mazzino Montinari. Berlin: Walter de Gruyter.

———. 1973. Die fröhliche Wissenschaft. Pages 13–335 in Abteilung 5, Band 2 of *Nietzsche Werke: Kritische Gesamtausgabe*. Edited by Giorgio Colli and Mazzino Montinari. Berlin and New York: Walter de Gruyter.

———. 1998. *On the Genealogy of Morality*. Translated by Maudemarie Clark and Alan J. Swensen. Indianapolis: Hackett.

Noll, K. L. 1999. Is There a Text in This Tradition? Readers' Response and the Taming of Samuel's God. *JSOT* 83:31–51.

Nolland, John. 1993. *Luke 9:21–18:34*. WBC 35B. Dallas: Word.

Noth, Martin. 1960. *The History of Israel*. Translated by Stanley Godman. Revised by Peter R. Ackroyd. 2d ed. New York: Harper & Row.

———. 1991. *The Deuteronomistic History*. Translated by Jane Doull. Revised by John Barton and Michael D. Rutter. 2d ed. JSOTSup 15. Sheffield: Sheffield Academic Press.

Nussbaum, Martha C. 1994. *The Therapy of Desire: Theory and Practice in Hellenistic Ethics*. Princeton, N.J.: Princeton University Press.

Oaks, Laury. 2000. Smoke-Filled Wombs and Fragile Fetuses: The Social Politics of Fetal Representation. *Signs: Journal of Women in Culture and Society* 26:63–108.

Ockinga, Boyo G. 1980. An Example of Egyptian Royal Phraseology in Psalm 132. *BN* 11:38–42.

O'Day, Gail R. 1995. The Gospel of John: Introduction, Commentary, and Reflections. Pages 493–865 in vol. 9 of *NIB*.

Oppenheim, A. Leo. 1967. *Letters from Mesopotamia: Official, Business, and Private Letters on Clay Tablets from Two Millennia*. Chicago: University of Chicago Press.

———. 1968. The Eyes of the Lord. *JAOS* 88:173–80.

Ornstein, Paul H. 1991. From Narcissism to Ego Psychology to Self Psychology. Pages 175–94 in *Freud's "On Narcissism: An Introduction."* Edited by Joseph Sandler, Ethel Spector Person, and Peter Fonagy. New Haven, Conn.: Yale University Press.

Orwell, George. 1983. *1984*. New York: Plume.

Ostwald, Martin. 1986. *From Popular Sovereignty to the Sovereignty of Law: Law, Society, and Politics in Fifth-Century Athens*. Berkeley and Los Angeles: University of California Press.

Paine, Robert. 1967. What Is Gossip About? An Alternative Hypothesis. *Man* NS 2:278–85.

———. 1970. Informal Communication and Information-Management. *Canadian Review of Sociology and Anthropology* 7:172–88.

Parker, Kim Ian. 1992. Solomon As Philosopher King? The Nexus of Law and Wisdom in 1 Kings 1–11. *JSOT* 53:75–91.

Parkinson, Richard. 1999. *Cracking Codes: The Rosetta Stone and Decipherment*. Berkeley and Los Angeles: University of California Press.

Parpola, Simo. 1972. A Letter from Šamaš-šumu-ukin to Esarhaddon. *Iraq* 34:21–34.

Parpola, Simo, and Kazuko Watanabe. 1988. *Neo-Assyrian Treaties and Loyalty Oaths*. SAAS 2. Helsinki: Helsinki University Press.

Penchansky, David. 1990. *The Betrayal of God: Ideological Conflict in Job*. Literary Currents in Biblical Interpretation. Louisville: Westminster John Knox.

Perdue, Leo G. 1991. *Wisdom in Revolt: Metaphorical Theology in the Book of Job*. JSOTSup 112. BLS 29. Sheffield: Almond.

Perloff, Marjorie. 1995. "Literature" in the Expanded Field. Pages 175–86 in *Comparative Literature in the Age of Multiculturalism*. Edited by Charles Bernheimer. Baltimore: Johns Hopkins University Press.

Perrot, Michelle. 1990. Roles and Characters. Pages 167–259 in *From the Fires of Revolution to the Great War*. Vol. 4 of *A History of Private Life*. Edited by Michelle Perrot. Translated by Arthur Goldhammer. Cambridge, Mass.: Harvard University Press.

Peyton, Thomas. 1967. *The Glasse of Time* (1620, 1623). Pages 267–72 in *The Celestial Cycle: The Theme of* Paradise Lost *in World Literature with Translations of the Major Analogues*. Edited by Watson Kirkconnell. New York: Gordian.

Peyton, Elizabeth, and Jeremy D. Safran. 1998. Interpersonal Process in the Treatment of Narcissistic Personality Disorders. Pages 379–95 in *Cognitive Psychotherapy of Psychotic and Personality Disorders: Handbook of Theory and Practice*. Edited by Carlo Perris and Patrick D. McGorry. Chichester, England: John Wiley & Sons.

Pfeiffer, Robert H. 1935. *State Letters of Assyria*. AOS 6. New Haven, Conn.: American Oriental Society.

Pies, Ronald W. 1997. Maimonides and the Origins of Cognitive-Behavioral Therapy. *Journal of Cognitive Psychotherapy* 11:21–36.

Pinch, Geraldine. 1995. *Magic in Ancient Egypt*. Austin: University of Texas.

Pitard, Wayne T. 1998. Before Israel: Syria-Palestine in the Bronze Age. Pages 33–77 in *The Oxford History of the Biblical World*. Edited by Michael D. Coogan. New York: Oxford University Press.

Plato. 1926. *Laws I*. Translated by R. G. Bury. LCL. Cambridge, Mass.: Harvard University Press.

———. 1968. *Republic*. Translated by Allan Bloom. New York: Basic Books.

Plummer, Alfred. 1900. *A Critical and Exegetical Commentary on the Gospel according to St. Luke*. 3d ed. ICC. New York: Charles Scribner's Sons.

Plutarch. 1957. *Moralia*. Vol. 6. Translated by W. C. Helmbold. LCL. Cambridge, Mass.: Harvard University Press.

———. 1958. *Lives*. Vol. 3. Translated by Bernadotte Perrin. LCL. Cambridge, Mass.: Harvard University Press.

———. *Moralia*. Vol. 10. 1960. Translated by Harold N. Fowler. LCL. Cambridge, Mass.: Harvard University Press.

Polzin, Robert. 1993. *David and the Deuteronomist: A Literary Study of the Deuteronomistic History, Part Three: 2 Samuel*. Bloomington: Indiana University Press.

Pope, Alexander. 1942. *The Rape of the Lock and Other Poems*. Edited by Geoffrey Tillotson. New York: Oxford University Press.

Porter, Barbara Nevling. 1993. *Image, Power, and Politics: Figurative Aspects of Esarhaddon's Babylonian Policy.* Philadelphia: American Philosophical Society.

Porter, Dennis. 1981. *The Pursuit of Crime: Art and Ideology in Detective Fiction.* New Haven, Conn.: Yale University Press.

Posner, Richard A. 1992. *Sex and Reason.* Cambridge, Mass.: Harvard University Press.

Postgate, J. N. 1974. *Taxation and Conscription in the Assyrian Empire.* Studia Pohl: Series Maior 3. Rome: Biblical Institute.

Postman, Neil. 1994. *The Disappearance of Childhood.* New York: Vintage.

Prescott, Anne Lake. 1991. Evil Tongues at the Court of Saul: The Renaissance David As a Slandered Courtier. *Journal of Medieval and Renaissance Studies* 21:163–86.

Pucci, Pietro. 1998. *The Song of the Sirens: Essays on Homer.* Lanham, Md.: Rowman & Littlefield.

Pyper, Hugh S. 1996. *David As Reader: 2 Samuel 12:1–15 and the Poetics of Fatherhood.* Biblical Interpretation Series 23. Leiden: Brill.

Quirke, Stephen. 1992. Religion. Pages 58–85 in *The British Museum Book of Ancient Egypt.* Edited by Stephen Quirke and Jeffrey Spencer. New York: Thames & Hudson.

Quirke, Stephen, and Jeffrey Spencer, eds. 1992. *The British Museum Book of Ancient Egypt.* New York: Thames & Hudson.

Rabinowitz, Peter J. 1977. Truth in Fiction: A Reexamination of Audiences. *Critical Inquiry* 4:121–41.

Rachman, Stanley. 1997. The Evolution of Cognitive Behaviour Therapy. Pages 3–26 in *Science and Practice of Cognitive Behaviour Therapy.* Edited by David M. Clark and Christopher G. Fairburn. Oxford: Oxford Unversity Press.

Ralegh, Sir Walter. 1971. *The History of the World.* Edited by C. A. Patrides. London: Macmillan.

Rank, Otto. 1964. *The Myth of the Birth of the Hero and Other Writings*. Edited by Philip Freund. New York: Vintage.

———. 1993. *The Trauma of Birth*. New York: Dover. Repr. of 1929 edition.

Rashkow, Ilona N. 1993. *The Phallacy of Genesis: A Feminist-Psychoanalytic Approach*. Literary Currents in Biblical Interpretation. Louisville: Westminster John Knox.

Redditt, Paul L. 2000. The God Who Loves and Hates. Pages 175–90 in *Shall Not the Judge of All the Earth Do What Is Right?* Edited by David Penchansky and Paul L. Redditt. Winona Lake, Ind.: Eisenbrauns.

Redford, Donald B. 1992. *Egypt, Canaan, and Israel in Ancient Times*. Princeton, N.J.: Princeton University Press.

Reis, Pamela Tamarkin. 1994. Collusion at Nob: A New Reading of 1 Samuel 21–22. *JSOT* 61:59–73.

Roazen, Paul. 1976. *Freud and His Followers*. New York: Meridian.

Roberts, Jimmy Jack McBee. 1987. In Defense of the Monarchy: The Contribution of Israelite Kingship to Biblical Theology. Pages 377–96 in *Ancient Israelite Religion: Essays in Honor of Frank Moore Cross*. Edited by Patrick D. Miller Jr., Paul D. Hanson, and S. Dean McBride. Philadelphia: Fortress.

Robertson, Ritchie. 1985. *Kafka: Judaism, Politics, and Literature*. Oxford: Clarendon.

Robins, Gay. 1993. *Women in Ancient Egypt*. Cambridge, Mass.: Harvard University Press.

Römer, W. H. Ph. 1965. *Sumerische "Königshymnen" der Isin-Zeit*. Leiden: Brill.

Roper, Lyndal. 1994. *Oedipus and the Devil: Witchcraft, Sexuality, and Religion in Early Modern Europe*. London: Routledge.

Rosenberg, Joel. 1986. *King and Kin: Political Allegory in the Hebrew Bible*. Bloomington: Indiana University Press.

———. 1987. 1 and 2 Samuel. Pages 122–45 in *The Literary Guide to the Bible*. Edited by Robert Alter and Frank Kermode. Cambridge, Mass.: Harvard University Press.

Rosenmeyer, Thomas G. 1989. *Senecan Drama and Stoic Cosmology*. Berkeley and Los Angeles: University of California Press.

Rost, Leonhard. 1982. *The Succession to the Throne of David*. Translated by Michael D. Rutter and David M. Gunn. Sheffield: Almond.

Roszak, Theodore. 1994. *The Cult of Information*. 2d ed. Berkeley and Los Angeles: University of California Press.

Roth, Philip. 1975. *My Life As a Man*. New York: Bantam.

Rubinkiewicz, R. 1983. Apocalypse of Abraham. Pages 681–705 in *Apocalyptic Literature and Testaments*. Vol. 1 of *The Old Testament Pseudepigrapha*. Edited by James H. Charlesworth. Garden City, N.Y.: Doubleday.

Rudd, Niall. 1990. Dido's *Culpa*. Pages 145–66 in *Oxford Readings in Vergil's Aeneid*. Edited by S. J. Harrison. Oxford: Oxford University Press.

Russell, Frank Santi. 1999. *Information Gathering in Classical Greece*. Ann Arbor: University of Michigan Press.

Rysman, Alexander. 1977. How the "Gossip" Became a Woman. *Journal of Communication* 27:176–80.

Sagan, Eli. 1985. *At the Dawn of Tyranny: The Origins of Individualism, Political Oppression, and the State*. New York: Knopf.

Saggs, H. W. F. 1968. *The Greatness That Was Babylon: A Sketch of the Ancient Civilization of the Tigris-Euphrates Valley*. New York: Mentor.

———. 1978. *The Encounter with the Divine in Mesopotamia and Israel*. London: Athlone Press.

Saint-Simon, Louis, Duc de. 1966. *Versailles, The Court and Louis XIV*. Translated by Lucy Norton. New York: Harper & Row.

———. 1967. *Historical Memoirs of the Duc de Saint-Simon: A Shortened Version*. Vol. 1: *1691–1709*. Translated by Lucy Norton. New York: McGraw-Hill.

———. 1968. *Historical Memoirs of the Duc de Saint-Simon: A Shortened Version*. Vol. II: *1710–1715*. Translated by Lucy Norton. New York: McGraw-Hill.

Sancisi-Weerdenburg, Heleen. 1983. Exit Atossa: Images of Women in Greek Historiography on Persia. Pages 20–33 in *Images of Women in Antiquity*. Edited by Averil Cameron and Amelie Kuhrt. Detroit: Wayne State University Press.

―――. 1987. Decadence in the Empire or Decadence in the Sources? From Source to Synthesis: Ctesias. Pages 33–45 in *Achaemenid History, I: Sources, Structures and Synthesis*. Edited by Heleen Sancisi-Weerdenburg. Leiden: Nederlands Instituut voor het Nabije Oosten.

Sandler, Joseph. 1976. Countertransference and Role-Responsiveness. *International Review of Psychoanalysis* 3:43–47.

Saretsky, Ted. 1980. The Analyst's Narcissistic Vulnerability: Its Effect on the Treatment Situation. *Contemporary Psychoanalysis* 16:82–89.

Sartre, Jean-Paul. 1940. *L'imaginaire: Psychologie phénoménologique de l'imaginaire*. Paris: Gallimard.

―――. 1943. *L'être et le néant: Essai d'ontologie phénoménologique*. Paris: Gallimard.

Sarup, Madan. 1989. *An Introductory Guide to Post-structuralism and Post-modernism*. Athens: University of Georgia Press.

Saul, John Ralston. 1992. *Voltaire's Bastards: The Dictatorship of Reason in the West*. Toronto: Penguin.

Saul, Nigel. 1997. *Richard II*. New Haven, Conn.: Yale University Press.

Sawyer, John F. A. 1993. Radical Images of Yahweh in Isaiah 63. Pages 72–82 in *Among the Prophets: Language, Image and Structure in the Prophetic Writings*. Edited by Philip R. Davies and David J. A. Clines. JSOTSup 144. Sheffield: JSOT Press.

Schafer, Roy. 1983. *The Analytic Attitude*. New York: Basic Books.

Schechter, Solomon. 1961. *Aspects of Rabbinic Theology: Major Concepts of the Talmud*. New York: Schocken.

Schmidt, Brian B. 1996. *Israel's Beneficent Dead: Ancestor Cult and Necromancy in Ancient Israelite Religion and Tradition*. Winona Lake, Ind.: Eisenbrauns.

Schopenhauer, Arthur. 1966. *The World As Will and Representation*. Vol. 1. Translated by E. F. J. Payne. New York: Dover.

Schulman, Alan R. 1979. Diplomatic Marriage in the Egyptian New Kingdom. *JNES* 38:177–93.

———. 1986. The Curious Case of Hadad the Edomite. Pages 122–35 in *Egyptological Studies in Honor of Richard A. Parker*. Edited by Leonard H. Lesko. Hanover: University Press of New England.

Schwartz, Peter Hammond. 1989. "His Majesty the Baby": Narcissism and Royal Authority. *Political Theory* 17:266–90.

Schwartz, Regina M. 1989. The Histories of David: Biblical Scholarship and Biblical Stories. Pages 192–210 in *"Not in Heaven": Coherence and Complexity in Biblical Narrative*. Edited by Jason P. Rosenblatt and Joseph C. Sitterson Jr. Bloomington: Indiana University Press.

———. 1991 Adultery in the House of David: The Metanarrative of Biblical Scholarship and the Narratives of the Bible. *Semeia* 54:35–55.

Schwartz, Richard B. 1988. Research and Liberal Learning. Pages 17–22 in *A Clashing of Symbols*. Edited by Phyllis O'Callaghan. Washington, D.C.: Georgetown University Press.

Scott-Kilvert, Ian. 1960. *The Rise and Fall of Athens: Nine Greek Lives by Plutarch*. Baltimore: Penguin.

Seager, Robin. 1967. Alcibiades and the Charge of Aiming at Tyranny. *Historia* 16:6–18.

Selgin, Peter. 1995. The Right Song, the Wrong Face. *Urban Desires: An Interactive Magazine of Metropolitan Passions* 1/5:1–3. Online, 8 January, 2000.

Seneca. 1953. *Tragedies*. Vol. 2. Translated by Frank Justus Miller. LCL. Cambridge, Mass.: Harvard University Press.

Sennett, Richard. 1977. *The Fall of Public Man*. New York: Alfred A. Knopf.

Seow, C. L. 1984. The Syro-Palestinian Context of Solomon's Dream. *HTR* 77:141–52.

———. 1989. *Myth, Drama, and the Politics of David's Dance*. HSM 44. Atlanta: Scholars Press.

———. 1997. *Ecclesiastes: A New Translation with Introduction and Commentary*. AB 18C. New York: Doubleday.

Shakespeare, William. 1961. *King Richard II*. Edited by Peter Ure. The Arden Shakespeare. London: Routledge.

Shannon, George W. B. 1980. *Humpty Dumpty: A Pictorial History*. La Jolla, Calif.: Green Tiger.

Shields, Rob. 1994. Fancy Footwork: Walter Benjamin's Notes on *Flânerie*. Pages 61–80 in *The Flâneur*. Edited by Keith Tester. London: Routledge.

Siebers, Tobin. 1983. *The Mirror of Medusa*. Berkeley and Los Angeles: University of California Press.

Silberman, Lou H. 1974. The Queen of Sheba in Judaic Tradition. Pages 65–84 in *Solomon and Sheba*. Edited by James B. Pritchard. London: Phaidon.

Silverman, David P. 1991. Divinity and Deities in Ancient Egypt. Pages 7–87 in *Religion in Ancient Egypt: Gods, Myths, and Personal Practice*. Edited by Byron E. Shafer. Ithaca, N.Y.: Cornell University Press.

Simon, Bennett. 1978. *Mind and Madness in Ancient Greece: The Classical Roots of Modern Psychiatry*. Ithaca, N.Y.: Cornell University Press.

Simon, Uriel. 1990. Minor Characters in Biblical Narrative. *JSOT* 46:11–19.

Skehan, Patrick W., and Alexander A. Di Lella. 1987. *The Wisdom of Ben Sira*. AB 39. New York: Doubleday.

Slater, Philip E. 1968. *The Glory of Hera: Greek Mythology and the Greek Family*. Boston: Beacon.

Smith, David L. 1992. *Louis XIV*. Cambridge Topics in History. Cambridge: Cambridge University Press.

Smith, W. Stevenson. 1981. *The Art and Architecture of Ancient Egypt*. 2d ed. Revised by William Kelly Simpson. New Haven, Conn.: Yale University Press.

Soggin, J. Alberto. 1977. The Davidic-Solomonic Kingdom. Pages 332–80 in *Israelite and Judean History.* Edited by John H. Hayes and J. Maxwell Miller. OTL. Philadelphia: Westminster.

———. 1985. *A History of Ancient Israel.* Philadelphia: Westminster.

Sontag, Susan. 1966. *Against Interpretation.* New York: Farrar, Straus & Giroux.

Spacks, Patricia Meyer. 1986. *Gossip.* Chicago: University of Chicago Press.

Spence, Donald P. 1987. *The Freudian Metaphor: Toward Paradigm Change in Psychoanalysis.* New York: Norton.

Spittler, R. P. 1983. Testament of Job: A New Translation and Introduction. Pages 829–68 in *Apocalyptic Literature and Testaments.* Vol. 1 of *The Old Testament Pseudepigrapha.* Edited by James H. Charlesworth. Garden City, N.Y.: Doubleday.

Stansell, Gary. 1994. Honor and Shame in the David Narratives. *Semeia* 68:55–79.

Starr, Ivan. 1990. *Queries to the Sungod: Divination and Politics in Sargonid Assyria.* SAAS 4. Helsinki: Helsinki University Press.

Stern, Daniel N. 1985. *The Interpersonal World of the Infant: A View from Psychoanalysis and Developmental Psychology.* New York: Basic Books.

Sternberg, Ernest. 1995. The Economy of Icons. Pages 82–85 in *The Truth about the Truth: De-confusing and Re-constructing the Postmodern World.* Edited by Walter T. Anderson. New York: Jeremy P. Tarcher/ Putnam.

Sternberg, Meir. 1985. *The Poetics of Biblical Narrative: Ideological Literature and the Drama of Reading.* Bloomington: Indiana University Press.

Stormer, Nathan. 2000. Prenatal Space. *Signs: Journal of Women in Culture and Society* 26:109–44.

Strack, Hermann L., and Paul Billerbeck. 1926. *Die Briefe des Neuen Testaments und die Offenbarung Johannis erläutert aus Talmud und Midrasch.* Munich: Oskar Beck.

Sugimoto, Tomotoshi. 1992. Chronicles As Independent Literature. *JSOT* 55:61–74.

Talmon, Shemaryahu. 1986. *King, Cult and Calendar in Ancient Israel: Collected Studies.* Leiden: Brill.

Tarr, Herbert. 1987. Chronicles. Pages 497–511 in *Congregation: Contemporary Jewish Writers Read the Jewish Bible.* Edited by D. Rosenberg. San Diego: Harcourt Brace Jovanovich.

Tartakoff, Helen H. 1966. The Normal Personality in Our Culture and the Nobel Prize Complex. Pages 222–52 in *Psychoanalysis—A General Psychology: Essays in Honor of Heinz Hartmann.* Edited by Rudolph M. Loewenstein, Lottie M. Newman, Max Schur, and Albert J. Solnit. New York: International Universities.

Taylor, A. E. 1928. *A Commentary on Plato's* Timaeus. Oxford: Clarendon.

Tester, Keith. 1994. Introduction. Pages 1–21 in *The Flâneur.* Edited by Keith Tester. London: Routledge.

Thompson, J. A. 1974. The Significance of the Verb Love in the David-Jonathan Narratives in 1 Samuel. *VT* 24:334–38.

Thucydides. 1966. *History of the Peloponnesian War: Books V and VI.* Translated by Charles Forster Smith. LCL. Cambridge, Mass.: Harvard University Press.

Tolbert, Mary Ann. 1979. *Perspectives on the Parables: An Approach to Multiple Interpretations.* Philadelphia: Fortress Press.

Tolstoy, Leo N. 1957. *War and Peace.* Vol. 2. Translated by Rosemary Edmonds. Harmondsworth: Penguin.

Tomasino, Anthony J. 1993. Isaiah 1.1–2.4 and 63–66, and the Composition of the Isaianic Corpus. *JSOT* 57:81–98.

Tur-Sinai, Naphtali Herz (H. Torczyner). 1957. *The Book of Job: A New Commentary.* Jerusalem: Kiryath Sepher.

Ullendorff, Edward. 1974. The Queen of Sheba in Ethiopian Tradition. Pages 104–14 in *Solomon and Sheba.* Edited by James B. Pritchard. London: Phaidon.

VanderKam, James C. 1980. Davidic Complicity in the Deaths of Abner and Eshbaal. *JBL* 99:521–39.

Vernant, Jean-Pierre. 1990a. The Lame Tyrant: From Oedipus to Periander. Pages 207–36, 466–72 in *Myth and Tragedy in Ancient Greece*. By Jean-Pierre Vernant and Pierre Vidal-Naquet. Translated by Janet Lloyd. New York: Zone.

———. 1990b. Oedipus without the Complex. Pages 85-111 and 427 in *Myth and Tragedy in Ancient Greece*. By Jean-Pierre Vernant and Pierre Vidal-Naquet. Translated by Janet Lloyd. New York: Zone.

Versnel, H. S. 1981. Religious Mentality in Ancient Prayer. Pages 1–64 in *Faith, Hope and Worship: Aspects of Religious Mentality in the Ancient World*. Edited by H. S. Versnel. Studies in Greek and Roman Religion 2. Leiden: Brill.

Veyne, Paul. 1988. *Did the Greeks Believe in Their Myths? An Essay on the Constitutive Imagination*. Translated by Paula Wissing. Chicago: University of Chicago Press.

Vidal-Naquet, Pierre. 1990. Oedipus in Athens. Pages 301–27, 483–84 in *Myth and Tragedy in Ancient Greece*. By Jean-Pierre Vernant and Pierre Vidal-Naquet. Translated by Janet Lloyd. New York: Zone.

Virgil. 1965. *The Aeneid*. Translated by Frank O. Copley. Indianapolis: Bobbs-Merrill.

———. 1972. *The Aeneid of Virgil, Books 1–6*. Edited by R. D. Williams. London: Macmillan.

Vlastos, Gregory. 1971. Justice and Happiness in the *Republic*. Pages 66–95 in vol. 2 of *Plato: A Collection of Critical Essays*. Edited by Gregory Vlastos. Garden City, N.Y.: Doubleday.

Walcot, Peter. 1996. Plato's Mother and Other Terrible Women. Pages 114–33 in *Women in Antiquity: Greece and Rome Studies*. Edited by Ian McAuslan and Peter Walcot. Oxford: Oxford University Press.

Wallace, Howard N. 1985. *The Eden Narrative*. HSM 32. Atlanta: Scholars Press.

Walsh, Jerome T. 1996. *1 Kings*. Berit Olam. Collegeville, Minn.: Liturgical Press.

Warner, Marina. 1976. *Alone of All Her Sex*. New York: Knopf.

Watt, W. Montgomery. 1974. The Queen of Sheba in Islamic Tradition. Pages 85–103 in *Solomon and Sheba*. Edited by James B. Pritchard. London: Phaidon.

Weinfeld, Moshe. 1972. *Deuteronomy and the Deuteronomic School*. Oxford: Clarendon.

———. 1976. The Loyalty Oath in the Ancient Near East. *UF* 8:379–414.

———. 1991. *Deuteronomy 1–11: A New Translation with Introduction and Commentary*. AB 5. New York: Doubleday.

Weingreen, J. 1969. The Rebellion of Absalom. *VT* 19:263–66.

Weintraub, Jeff. 1997. The Theory and Politics of the Public/Private Distinction. Pages 1–42 in *Public and Private in Thought and Practice: Perspectives on a Grand Dichotomy*. Edited by Jeff Weintraub and Krishan Kumar. Chicago: University of Chicago Press.

Weintraub, Jeff, and Krishan Kumar, eds. 1997. *Public and Private in Thought and Practice: Perspectives on a Grand Dichotomy*. Chicago: University of Chicago Press.

Weisberg, David B. 1967. *Guild Structure and Political Allegiance in Early Achaemenid Mesopotamia*. New Haven, Conn.: Yale University Press.

Westermann, Claus. 1969. *Isaiah 40–66: A Commentary*. OTL. Philadelphia: Westminster.

———. 1994. *Genesis 1–11: A Continental Commentary*. Minneapolis: Fortress.

Whitelam, Keith W. 1984. The Defense of David. *JSOT* 29:61–87.

———. 1989. Israelite Kingship: The Royal Ideology and Its Opponents. Pages 119–39 in *The World of Ancient Israel: Sociological, Anthropological, and Political Perspectives*. Edited by Ronald E. Clements. Cambridge: Cambridge University Press.

———. 1992. King and Kingship. *ABD* 4:40–48.

Whitman, Cedric H. 1965. *Homer and the Heroic Tradition*. New York: Norton.

Whitney, Elspeth. 1995. International Trends: The Witch "She"/The Historian "He": Gender and the Historiography of the European Witch-Hunts. *Journal of Women's History* 7:77–101.

Whybray, Roger N. 1968. *The Succession Narrative: A Study of II Samuel 9–20; I Kings 1 and 2.* SBT 2.9. London: SCM.

———. 1975. *Isaiah 40–66.* NCB. Grand Rapids: Eerdmans.

———. 1996. The Immorality of God: Reflections on Some Passages in Genesis, Job, Exodus and Numbers. *JSOT* 72:89–120.

Wilde, Oscar. 1930. *Comedies.* New York: Literary Guild of America.

Willi, Thomas. 1972. *Die Chronik als Auslegung: Untersuchungen zur literarischen Gestaltung der historischen Überlieferung Israels.* Göttingen: Vandenhoeck & Ruprecht.

Williams, Raymond. 1983. *Keywords: A Vocabulary of Culture and Society.* Rev. ed. New York: Oxford University Press.

Wilson, John A. 1958. *The Culture of Ancient Egypt.* Phoenix Edition. Chicago: University of Chicago Press.

Winks, Robin W. 1968. Introduction. Pages xiii–xxiv in *The Historian As Detective.* Edited by Robin W. Winks. New York: Harper & Row.

Winnicott, Donald W. 1958. *Collected Papers: Through Paediatrics to Psycho-Analysis.* New York: Basic.

———. 1965. *The Maturational Processes and the Facilitating Environment: Studies in the Theory of Emotional Development.* Madison, Conn.: International Universities.

———. 1992. *Psycho-analytic Explorations.* Edited by Clare Winnicott, Ray Shepherd, and Madeleine Davis. Cambridge, Mass.: Harvard University Press.

Winnington-Ingram, R. P. 1973. Zeus in the Persae. *JHS* 93:210–19.

Wittfogel, Karl A. 1957. *Oriental Despotism: A Comparative Study of Total Power.* New Haven, Conn.: Yale University Press.

Wright, John W. 1993. The Innocence of David in 1 Chronicles 21. *JSOT* 60:87–105.

Wyatt, Nicolas. 1981. Interpreting the Creation and Fall Story in Genesis 2–3. *ZAW* 93:10–21.

Xenophon. 1953. *Cyropaedia*. Vol. 2. Translated by Walter Miller. LCL. Cambridge, Mass.: Harvard University Press.

Zaccagnini, Carlo. 2000. The Interdependence of the Great Powers. Pages 141–53 in *Amarna Diplomacy: The Beginnings of International Relations*. Edited by Raymond Cohen and Raymond Westbrook. Baltimore: Johns Hopkins University Press.

INDEX OF MODERN AUTHORS

INDEX OF ANCIENT SOURCES

HEBREW BIBLE

ANCIENT NEAR EASTERN TEXTS

INDEX OF SUBJECTS